Mastering Business Analysis with Crystal Reports® 9

Chris Tull

Wordware Publishing, Inc.

Library of Congress Cataloging-in-Publication Data

Tull, Chris.
Mastering business analysis with Crystal Reports 9 / by Chris Tull.
p. cm.
ISBN 1-55622-293-9 (paperback)
1. Seagate Crystal reports. 2. Business report writing--Computer programs. I. Title.
HF5719.T85 2003
651.7'8'028557585--dc21 2003014062
CIP

2320 Los Rios Boulevard
Plano, Texas 75074

Printed in the United States of America

ISBN 1-55622-293-9

10 9 8 7 6 5 4 3 2 1
0307

All inquiries for volume purchases of this book should be addressed to Wordware Publishing, Inc., at the above address. Telephone inquiries may be made by calling:

(972) 423-0090

For Niki, who's always a reminder that there's more to life than work.

Contents

Acknowledgments

It's never until you're halfway through a book that you realize you've bitten off more than you can chew — and that you're going to need a lot of help and support to get you through it! Please take a moment to read this page. Without the help of the people listed here, this book would have never been.

I want to thank Niki, my wife. She provides an unlimited supply of enthusiasm for everything I do. I also want to thank my parents, Tom and Carole Tull. Their support and inspiration underlie everything in my life. Acknowledgments must also go out to my grandfather and brother, who offered their sympathies whenever I complained. Finally, I cannot forget the Theriot family. They have taken me in like one of their own.

I'm greatly indebted to Becky Deluna, my technical editor. She offered invaluable opinions, advice, and ideas, and her involvement has improved this book tremendously. The book is better than anything I had imagined because of her.

Thanks must also be given to the team at Wordware, especially Jim Hill, Wes Beckwith, Beth Kohler, Heather Hill, Alan McCuller, Tim McEvoy, and Martha McCuller. Their knowledge and hard work have made this book a reality. Also, thank you to all those at Wordware working behind the scenes. Please forgive me for not mentioning your names, but know that I am greatly appreciative.

Finally, thanks to Spots, Stripes, Max, Dexter, Buddy, Emmy, Mr. Jingles, Bear, and Daisy for keeping me grounded.

Introduction

It seems like database management systems are everywhere these days.

You can find database management systems within Fortune 500 companies, as well as smaller "mom and pop" outfits. Maybe you've heard of ERP (*enterprise resource planning*) packages, such as PeopleSoft, Oracle, and SAP. Such packages are all the rage today — they're essentially database management systems that handle data across various departments (such as accounting, inventory, and billing).

The reason behind this wide popularity of database systems is simple. Databases allow businesses to organize and manage their business operations effectively, handling millions of pieces of data for a company. These systems usually allow you to add, maintain, and delete data through the use of some *user interface*, such as a menu-driven screen that contains windows, icons, and buttons.

Unfortunately, all database systems seem to have one major flaw. That flaw is that it's usually difficult to view data from these systems, especially if one is attempting to view data in some specified format (i.e., a report). Database management systems do contain various query and analysis tools, along with some "canned reports," but these tools are often difficult to use and often do not contain the capabilities you need for your specialized data.

That's where Crystal Reports enters the picture.

Crystal Reports is a BI (*business intelligence*) tool that allows you to extract and format data from a database. Crystal Reports is a software package that works with over 150 leading database packages, allowing you to create custom reports with your data.

If you use a database system in some fashion within your workplace, chances are you can use Crystal Reports to make informed business decisions using your corporate data.

Features and Functionality of Crystal Reports

Crystal Reports contains a number of flexible and innovative features unrivaled in other reporting programs. The ease and quality of these features may explain why Crystal Reports has sold more than 5 million copies worldwide.

The following summarizes some of the more innovative tools that you'll find in Crystal Reports.

Reporting Templates

Crystal Reports comes stocked with a number of reporting templates (shown in Figure I-1), which you may use to create standardized formatting quickly across multiple reports. Crystal Reports allows you to create your own templates or use any of the samples provided within the software or available free from their web site at www.crystaldecisions.com.

We learn more about reporting templates in Chapter 4, "Writing Reports with the Report Wizards."

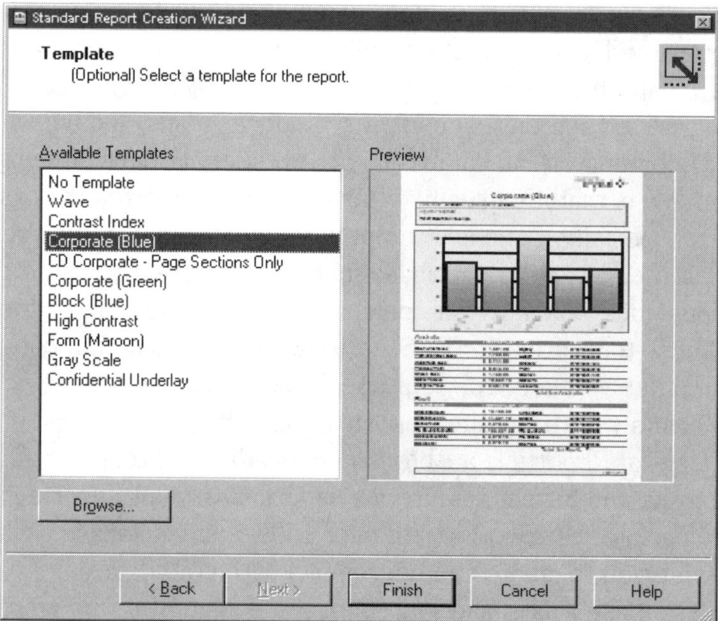

Figure I-1. Crystal Reports' report templates

Exporting Ability to Other Applications

Crystal Reports provides a number of exporting options (shown in Figure I-2), making it easy to transfer data to common software applications, such as Microsoft Excel or Word. With Crystal Reports, you can export only a report's data or the fully formatted report with any included images, graphs, or charts. Crystal Reports allows you to export into a number of different file formats, including PDF, HTML, and XML.

We learn more about Crystal Reports' exporting ability in Chapter 14, "Distributing Reports."

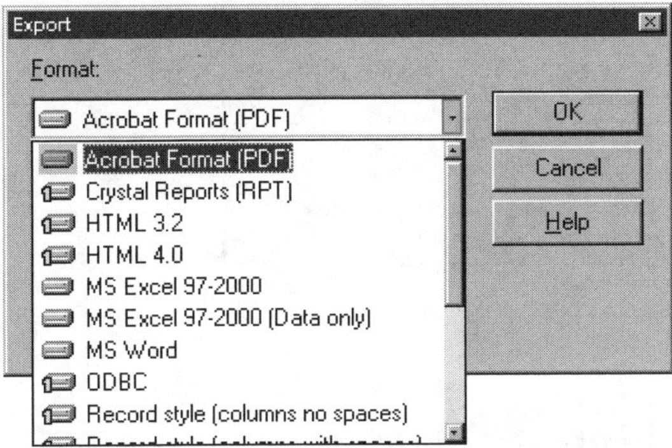

Figure I-2. Crystal Reports' exporting functionality

The Report Wizard

The Report Wizard (shown in Figure I-3 on the following page) is an intuitive interface that walks you through the process of report design. The Report Wizard allows you to quickly create reports, simplifying common reporting tasks such as selecting and grouping data.

We learn more about the Report Creation Wizard in Chapter 4, "Writing Reports with the Report Wizards."

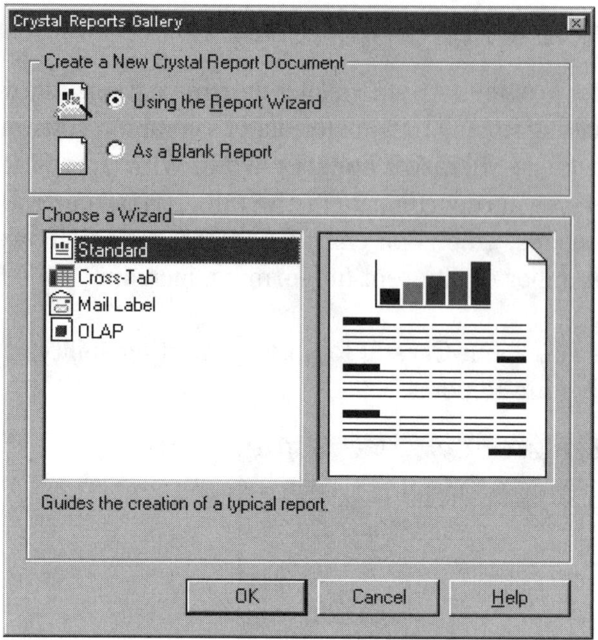

Figure I-3. Crystal Reports' Report Wizards

Crystal Reports' Formula Workshop

Crystal Reports' Formula Workshop (shown in Figure I-4) provides a central place to develop, edit, and customize formulas used in reports. The Formula Workshop contains a number of useful tools for the report writer, including enhanced error tracking and an auto-complete feature for easier formula creation.

Report formulas and the Formula Workshop are discussed in Chapter 10, "Understanding Formulas."

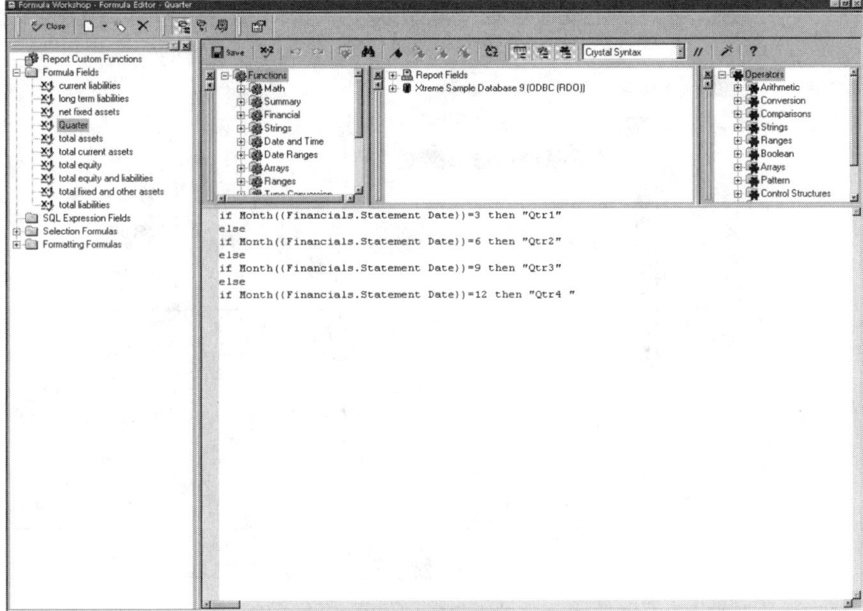

Figure I-4. Crystal Reports' Formula Workshop

Data Charting Tools

Whoever said "A picture is worth a thousand words" must have been a report writer. Presenting data in a graphical format is often the most effective way to present information quickly — a fact the crew at Crystal Decisions understands. As a result, you'll find a number of data charting tools within the Crystal Reports software, including support for a number of different charts and graphical formats (shown in Figure I-5).

We learn more about Crystal Reports' charting capabilities in Chapter 12, "Visualizations with Charts and Maps."

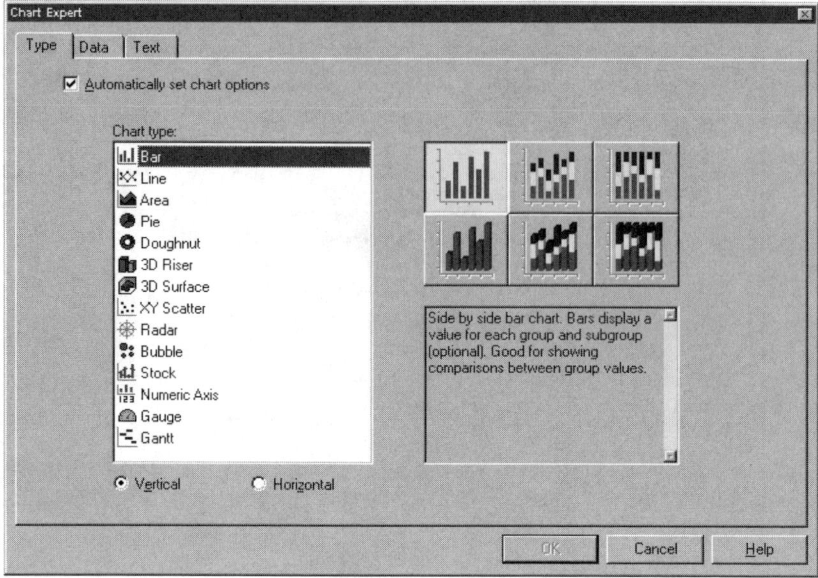

Figure I-5. Charting capabilities in Crystal Reports

Why This Book Was Written

Glance through the shelves of your favorite bookstore, and you'll undoubtedly see a fair share of books about Crystal Reports. "So, why another book?" you might ask. "Aren't there already enough books out there about the subject?"

True, there are several excellent books about Crystal Reports. The difference is that these existing books are aimed at techies or raw novices. What is missing is a Crystal Reports book that provides a context and reference useful to mainstream business users.

In this book, we discuss how to use the features and functionality of Crystal Reports, along with the necessary database concepts to apply Crystal Reports to your specialized database environment. We learn about Crystal Reports by working through detailed, reporting exercises. By the end of this book, you'll have developed a number of real-world reports, suitable for those in accounting, sales, marketing, and a number of related fields.

How This Book Is Organized

This book is divided into four parts, with each part consisting of concepts and functionality necessary to understand Crystal Reports and report writing. We build on these concepts from chapter to chapter, learning as early as the second chapter how to design our own reports.

Part I: Getting Started with Crystal Reports

This portion of the book is designed to get you into the driver's seat quickly. In this part, you learn what report writing is and how Crystal Reports works. You learn about Crystal Reports' user interface, how to work in this interface, and how to define settings to tailor Crystal Reports to your preference.

In Part I, you also begin building reports applicable to the real world, all the while familiarizing yourself with a number of Crystal Reports' report building tools. You learn to design reports within the Report Wizards, as well as develop reports from scratch.

Part II: Working with Records

The hardest part about building reports is selecting (and linking) the specific records you need. In Part II, you learn not only how to define selection criteria but also how to group and sort your records. You also learn the techniques of adding calculations to your reports (a necessity, especially in the realm of financial reporting).

Part III: Advanced Report Writing

In Part III, we explore some of the more advanced reporting functionality that Crystal Reports has to offer, including adding formulas, incorporating subreports, and creating and importing objects (such as graphics, charts, and maps).

Part III concludes with useful information regarding tools and other features that may aid you in your report writing. Here, you learn about using SQL in Crystal Reports and exporting your reports into other software applications, such as Microsoft Excel or Microsoft Word.

Part IV: Reference

This material provides information to aid you in learning Crystal Reports. Here, you'll find a data dictionary for the sample database used within this book, some useful functions that you may utilize within your reports, and further resources to aid in your Crystal Reports endeavors.

In Appendix D, you'll also find a list of several third-party software vendors, whose software may assist you in your report development. This section provides information on how to obtain trial and full versions of their software online.

Additional Resources

All report files and exercises presented in this book are accessible online at www.wordware.com/files/crystal.

Conventions Used in This Book

In this book, you'll find several text conventions designed to help you better understand information and concepts. These conventions provide additional information about a topic within the book and are as follows:

Note

Sometimes, you may thirst for a little more information about a topic. Notes present additional detailed information. You can skip over these if you like without missing out on any of the core concepts.

Tip

Tips present helpful tips or suggestions to help you find your way through potentially tricky concepts.

Caution

Cautions help you avoid reporting pitfalls. These identify potential trouble areas associated with a particular topic.

Sidebar

Sidebars provide additional information related to the chapter discussion.

System Requirements

The following are the necessary hardware and software requirements for installing Crystal Reports onto a local computer. For information regarding a network install, please refer to the Crystal Reports install documentation provided with your software. The information given is for Crystal Reports 9 or higher.

Software Requirements

- Microsoft Windows 95, 98, NT 4.0 (or higher), ME, 2000, XP
- Internet Explorer 4.0 minimum (5.5 or higher recommended), Netscape Navigator 4.08 minimum (4.75 or higher recommended). Netscape 6.0 is not recommended.

Hardware Requirements

- 32MB RAM minimum (64MB for Windows NT)
- 300MB hard disk space available

Installing Crystal Reports

To install Crystal Reports onto your local computer, perform the following steps:

1. **Insert the Crystal Reports CD into your computer.**

   If the CD does not start automatically, browse the CD-ROM drive. Double-click Setup.exe.

2. **Read and accept the License Agreement to continue with the installation.**

3. **Type your name, organization, and Product Key Code into the User Information dialog box.**

   You can find the Product Key Code on the back of the Crystal Reports CD envelope.

4. **Press Next.**

   Once you press this button, the Select Installation Type dialog box displays.

5. **Choose the Typical installation option.**

   The Typical option installs the most common features to your computer. Select the Custom option should you wish to further define the features that you want installed.

6. **Press Next.**

   Once you press this button, the Start Installation dialog box displays. The Crystal Reports software is installed to the default directory location C:\Program Files\Crystal Decisions\Crystal Reports 9\. Should you wish to change this location, press the Browse button before pressing Next.

7. **Press Next (on the Start Installation dialog box) to begin the installation to your computer.**

Tell Me What You Think!

As the reader of this book, *you* are my most important critic and commentator. I value your opinion and welcome your comments. Let me know what you did or didn't like about the book — or maybe just share some words of wisdom you're willing to pass on to me.

When you write, please include your name as well as this book's title in the subject line. I promise to carefully review your comments and respond as quickly as possible.

Send e-mail to feedback@wordware.com.

By the way — thanks for reading!

About the Author

Chris Tull is a web applications developer and Internet technologist based out of the Dallas/Fort Worth area. Besides immersing himself in the design and development of leading-edge Internet applications, Chris has also been involved in the authoring and editing of various other books and magazine articles. Chris is an active member of the Dallas/Fort Worth Crystal Decisions Users Group (DFWCUG) and the Society for Technical Communication (STC).

Part I

Getting Started with Crystal Reports

Chapter 1

The World of Crystal Reports

In the course of a decade, Crystal Reports has become the leading data analysis tool utilized in businesses today. No other program allows users to design presentation-quality reports from essentially any data source on the planet. Crystal Reports is simply the most powerful report-writing program available today. That may sound dramatic, but it's true.

But what are report-writing programs? Essentially, they're programs designed to grab data from a source file and then present that information in an organized and meaningful presentation. In most businesses today, the type of source that you're pulling data from is more than likely a relational database.

Since most business report writing deals with databases, this chapter focuses on how databases and database management systems work, allowing for better understanding of the different features (and possibilities) of Crystal Reports. *Databases* are collections of information, organized so that one can quickly select desired pieces of data.

Exploring Database Management Systems (DBMSs)

Most databases utilize a *database management system (DBMS)*, which is software that allows users controlled access to the data. DBMSs range from small systems that run on personal computers to huge systems that run on mainframe computers. Computerized library systems, flight reservation systems, and any of the ERP packages mentioned in the introduction are all examples of DBMSs.

Users most often communicate with a DBMS by first logging into the system using an appropriate username and password. After successful logon, the user can then store, modify, or extract data from a database, usually through a graphical user interface (GUI).

A *graphical user interface* is a visual computer environment and consists of components such as a pointing device (like a cursor), icons, a display screen, and menus. Graphical user interfaces allow users to easily work with their database systems. Without a GUI, database users would have to use a command language (such as SQL) to work with their database information.

Figure 1-1 summarizes the workings of a database management system.

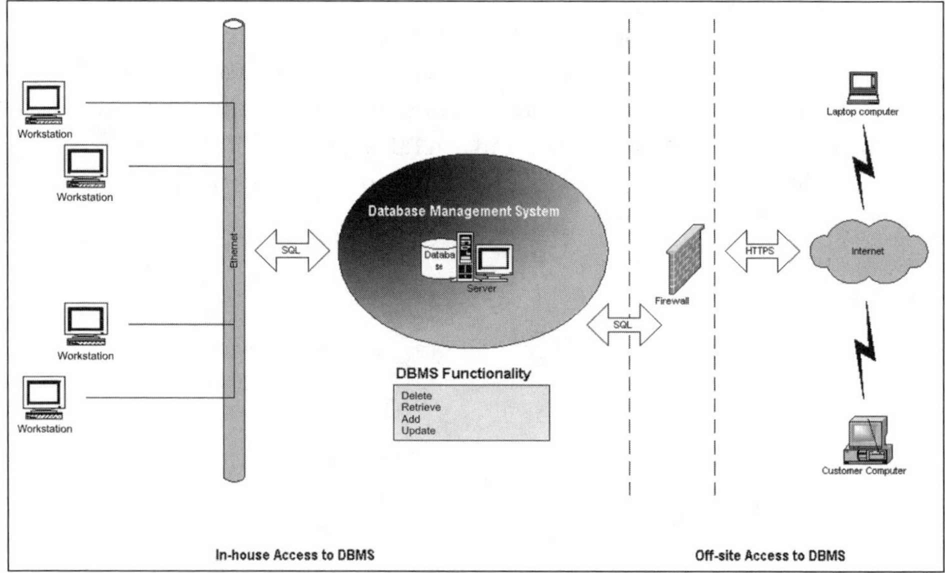

Figure 1-1. A model of a database management system (DBMS)

The Workings of a Relational Database

As mentioned previously, most DBMSs today utilize relational databases. Thus, relational databases are the type of data source that you'll most likely encounter in your report development.

In relational databases, all information is contained within two-dimensional data structures commonly referred to as a *tables*. The function of a table is similar to that of a folder within a filing cabinet.

Relational tables consist of columns (fields) and rows (records). We learn more about columns and rows in a moment.

Note

Fields are sometimes referred to as *tuplets*, and records are sometimes referred to as *attributes*. The terms are used interchangeably. This book sticks to "fields" and "records."

There are two main restrictions to consider with relational tables, which are as follows:

- A single table cannot contain duplicate column names. Each column name within a single table must be unique. There is no restriction involving two columns in two different tables having identical names.
- Tables may contain no rows (an empty table) but must contain at least one column.

Most database manufacturers also impose some maximum limit on the number of columns that a relational table may have, but usually not on the number of rows.

Note

These restrictions are part of the relational database standards created by the International Organization for Standardization (ISO) and the American National Standards Institute (ANSI).

In a relational database, tables are linked together through keys. *Keys* are database fields that provide the basic mechanism for matching records that reside in two or more tables. We learn more about keys in Chapter 6, "Linking Tables."

Database Records

A table's rows (better known as *records*) are a complete set of information and composed of multiple pieces of information (fields). Using the filing cabinet analogy, if a table is similar to a folder, then a record is one of the paper forms within that folder.

Figure 1-2 displays an example of a database record.

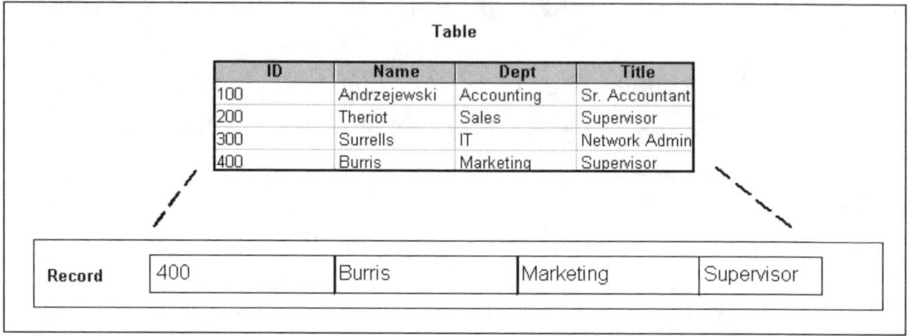

ID	Name	Dept	Title
100	Andrzejewski	Accounting	Sr. Accountant
200	Theriot	Sales	Supervisor
300	Surrells	IT	Network Admin
400	Burris	Marketing	Supervisor

Figure 1-2. A database record

Tip

A record is similar to a row in a spreadsheet.

In Figure 1-2, the fourth record contains information about employee Burris (i.e., the employee's ID, name, department, and title). All these pieces of information together make up a record.

Database Fields

A table's columns (better known as *fields*) contain one unit of information for a particular record. For example, an employee record might contain information such as the employee's name, department, and title. Each of these pieces of information is considered a field.

Figure 1-3 displays examples of fields within a table.

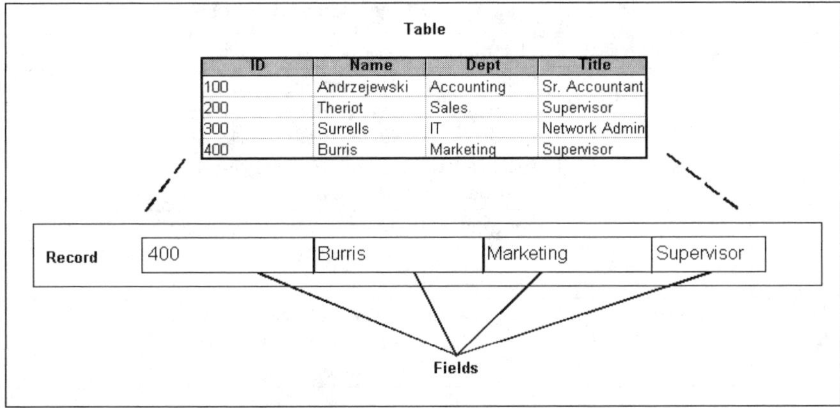

ID	Name	Dept	Title
100	Andrzejewski	Accounting	Sr. Accountant
200	Theriot	Sales	Supervisor
300	Surrells	IT	Network Admin
400	Burris	Marketing	Supervisor

Figure 1-3. Examples of fields within a table

Most database fields have certain attributes associated with them that define the type of data that is allowed within the field. Some fields might contain only numeric information, while other fields may contain only textual information.

For example, a database might contain customer billing amount data, which exists as a currency data type. Customer name information might also reside within a database; however, this data might exist as a text data type.

Tip

The implementation of data types often differs from database vendor to vendor. For example, Oracle, Microsoft, and Paradox all tweak the characteristics of their data types so that their product is unique in comparison to a competitor's product.

Check out the appropriate reference material provided with your database to verify the characteristics of your database's data types.

Data type comes into play when designing reports. For example, you can create summaries and totals from data that uses calculable numbers only (fields that consist of either a currency or number data type). Table 1-1 summarizes some of the basic data types recognized by Microsoft Access, the database you utilize in this book.

Table 1-1. Data types recognized by Microsoft Access

Data Type	Definition	Example
Text	Text and/or combinations of text and numbers, such as addresses. Any numbers that are a text data type do not require calculations (such as phone numbers or zip codes).	1600 Millhouse Drive
Memo	Lengthy text and numbers of virtually any length (often used for notes or descriptions).	Call only after 6 P.M.
Number	Numeric data used for mathematical calculations, except calculations involving money (see Currency type).	123
Date/Time	Displays both date and time information.	12/25/1997 02:31:00
Currency	Displays currency (monetary) values. This data type prevents the rounding off of values during calculations.	$5000.32
AutoNumber	Displays the unique sequential (incrementing by 1) number automatically inserted when a record is added.	6
Logical data (sometimes referred to as Boolean data)	Contains only one of two values, such as Yes/No, True/False, or On/Off.	Yes

We deal more with data types when working with summaries and formulas in Chapters 9 and 10.

How Crystal Reports Works

Users of a DBMS typically perform the following four actions:

- Delete
- Retrieve
- Add
- Update

A day in the life of a DBMS user might consist of deleting records no longer in use, retrieving data to view, adding records to a system, and perhaps editing some incorrect data.

Crystal Reports allows users only one of these four functionality options: the ability to retrieve data. In no way whatsoever can you or your report users add, update, or delete database information using Crystal Reports. This concept is so important, it deserves to be repeated:

In no way can one alter their data with Crystal Reports.

This is a good thing. It means that you can make all the mistakes you want with Crystal Reports and not worry about blowing up any of your company's data.

Crystal Reports allows you to retrieve information from your database without having to write SQL statements (a command language) in order to view and format your database information. Not only does Crystal Reports make retrieving data easier, but it also enables users to format output data in a pleasing and meaningful manner.

How Crystal Reports works with a database is illustrated in Figure 1-4.

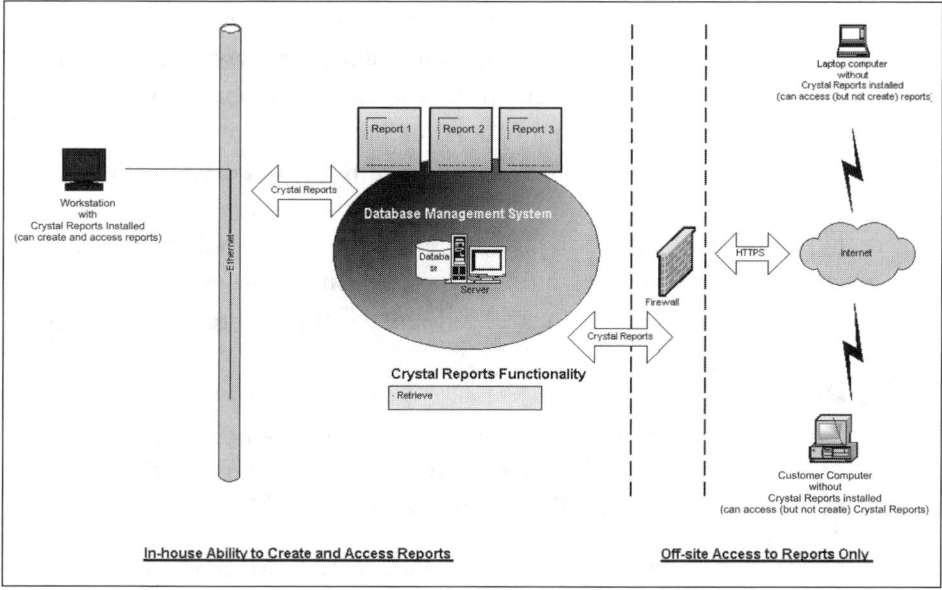

Figure 1-4. How Crystal Reports works with a database

Note

A request to retrieve information from a database is commonly known as a *query*. The set of rules for constructing queries is known as a *query language*.

Different DBMSs support different query languages; however, nearly all DBMSs support a semi-standard query language known as SQL (Structured Query Language) in some fashion. We learn more about the SQL language in Chapter 15, "Exploring Crystal Reports' SQL Commands."

The Report Processing Model

So how does Crystal Reports work?

First, a report writer designs a report prototype, including a connection to the database and the tables and fields to be used within the report. The report writer then works at formatting the report, controlling how the data should display. Once ready, the user previews the report.

When a report is previewed, Crystal Reports begins to retrieve the data in the fashion defined by the report writer. Crystal Reports' retrieval process is known as the *Report Processing Model* and consists of one to three passes against a database. A *pass* is a process that occurs when data is read or manipulated.

The number of passes that Crystal Reports performs depends on the complexity of the report or formulas used. A simple report needs to make only one pass, whereas a report filled with several complex calculations would perform all three passes.

Figure 1-5 displays Crystal Reports' Report Processing Model.

Note

Passes occur on the server where the database resides. This activity performed at the server is better known as *server-side* processing. Servers typically provide a much quicker response time than a client.

Crystal Reports utilizes server-side processing, which results in the faster generation of your reports.

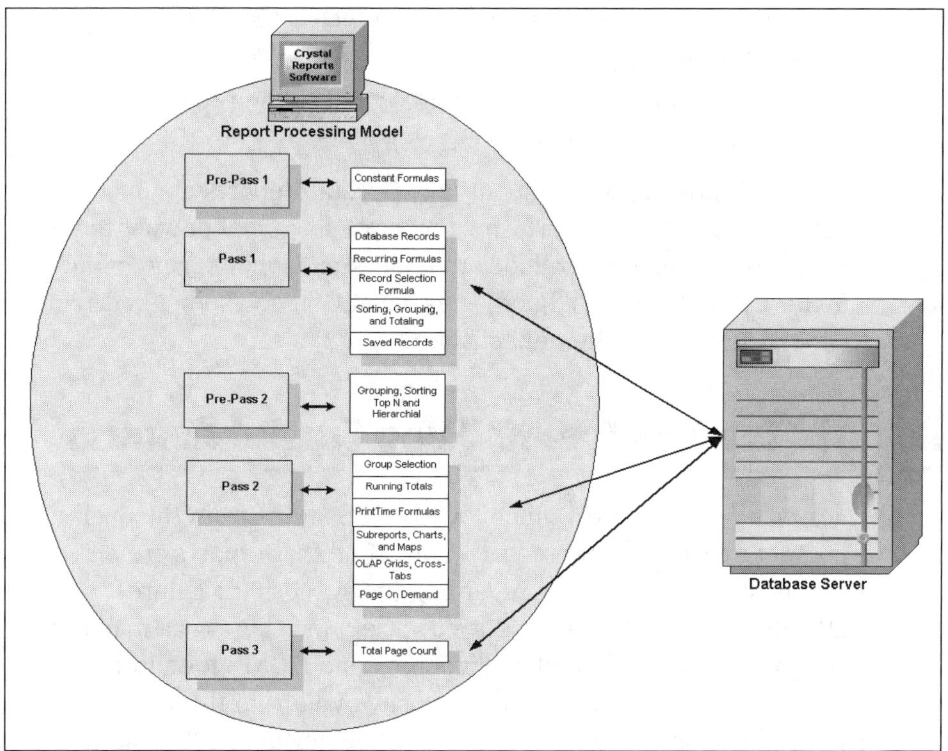

Figure 1-5. The Report Processing Model

The following summarizes the different passes of the Report Processing Model:

- **Pre-Pass 1:** Before your report even passes to the database, Crystal Reports evaluates formulas that do not require data (such as arithmetic statements). The Pre-Pass 1 pass is also referred to as *BeforeReadingRecords*.
- **Pass 1:** After the formulas from Pre-Pass 1 have been evaluated, Crystal Reports begins accessing the database. This process is also referred to as *WhileReadingRecords.*
- **Pre-Pass 2**: For simpler reports, only Pre-Pass 1 and Pass 1 are required. However, for more complex reports, Crystal Reports now begins performing more involved groupings of data.
- **Pass 2:** With this pass, Crystal Reports performs a second pass at the database, evaluating data to meet more formatting

information. This process is also referred to as *WhilePrintingRecords.*

- **Pass 3:** In Pass 3, the total page count of the report is determined.

You won't need to worry about how Crystal Reports obtains its data; Crystal Reports performs these passes unbeknownst to you. However, it's never a bad idea to understand what's happening under Crystal Reports' hood — especially since you begin driving Crystal Reports in the next chapter.

Reports You Can Create Using Crystal Reports

For many people, the value of any DBMS stems from the quality of presentable and usable reports. You'll find that reports are one of the most important areas regarding the success (or failure) of a DBMS. The inability to produce a variety of reports is a major reason many companies end up scrapping one DBMS for another.

Hopefully, Crystal Reports will save you from this outcome. Crystal Reports contains a plethora of powerful and flexible tools, enabling you to create nearly any report imaginable. With Crystal Reports, some of the reports you can create are:

- Form letter reports
- Mailing letter reports
- Cross-tab reports
- Financial reports
- Marketing reports
- Sales reports

Figures 1-6, 1-7, and 1-8 display just a few of the reporting possibilities of Crystal Reports. By the end of this book, you'll have an understanding of how to create these types of reports and more.

Note

You can find these and other sample reports provided in your installed version of Crystal Reports. The Crystal Decisions web site also contains other sample reports for free download at www.crystaldecisions.com.

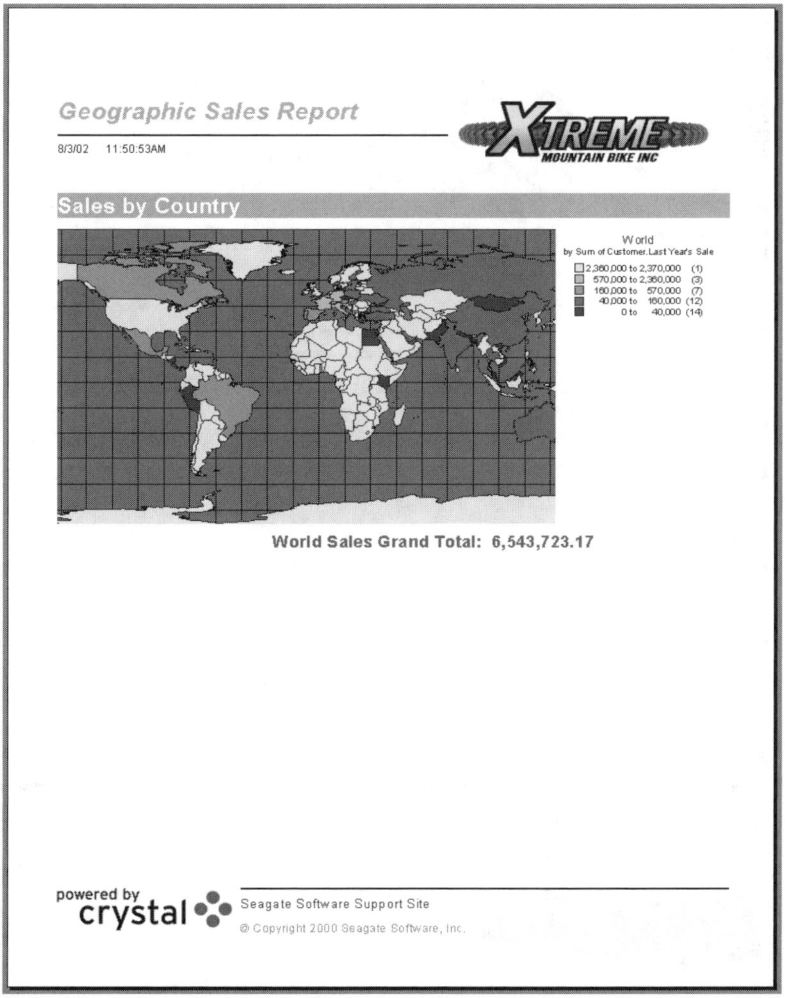

Geographic Sales Report

8/3/02 11:50:53AM

XTREME MOUNTAIN BIKE INC

Sales by Country

World
by Sum of Customer.Last Year's Sale
2,360,000 to 2,370,000 (1)
570,000 to 2,360,000 (3)
160,000 to 570,000 (7)
40,000 to 160,000 (12)
0 to 40,000 (14)

World Sales Grand Total: 6,543,723.17

powered by crystal

Seagate Software Support Site

© Copyright 2000 Seagate Software, Inc.

Figure 1-6. A geographic sales report

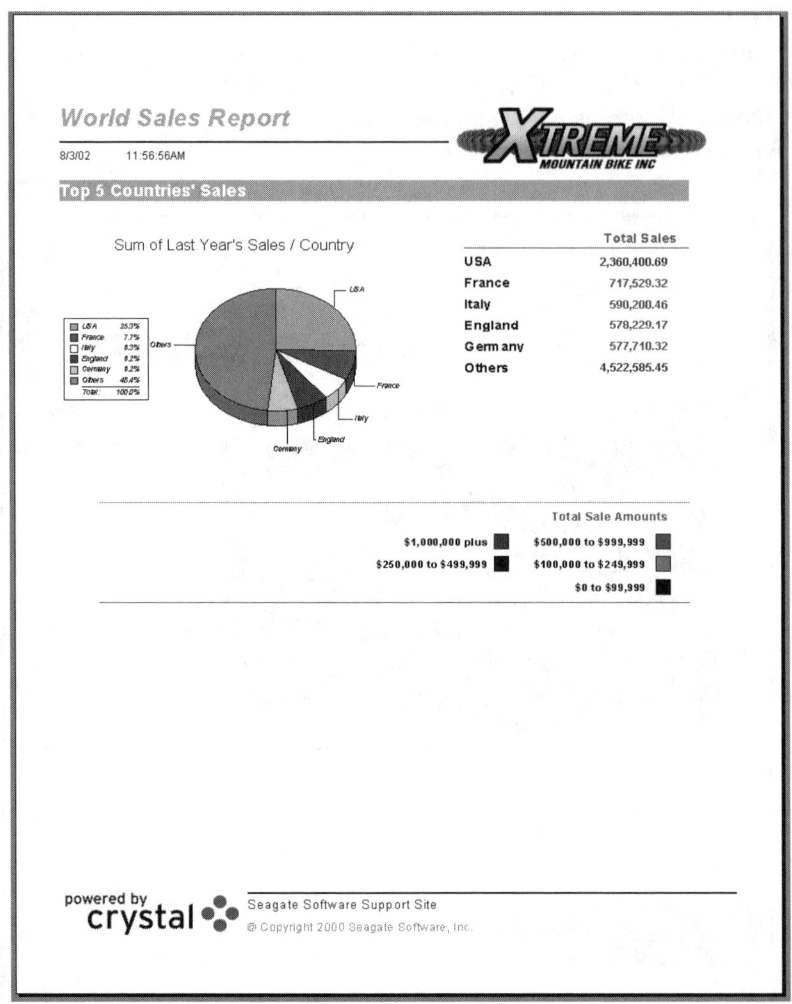
World Sales Report

8/3/02 11:56:56AM

XTREME MOUNTAIN BIKE INC

Top 5 Countries' Sales

Sum of Last Year's Sales / Country

	Total Sales
USA	2,360,400.69
France	717,529.32
Italy	590,200.46
England	578,229.17
Germany	577,710.32
Others	4,522,585.45

Total Sale Amounts

$1,000,000 plus

$500,000 to $999,999

$250,000 to $499,999

$100,000 to $249,999

$0 to $99,999

powered by crystal

Seagate Software Support Site

© Copyright 2000 Seagate Software, Inc.

Figure 1-7. A world sales report

Figure 1-8. A product catalog report

What's Next?

In this chapter, you've learned a lot about databases, database management systems, and how Crystal Reports generates reports against such data sources.

Armed with this new-found knowledge, you're now ready to begin poking and prodding with Crystal Reports. In the next chapter, you'll find yourself working with Crystal Reports hands-on, familiarizing yourself with the tools of the trade!

Chapter 2

The Crystal Reports Environment

Ready for some good news? If you've used word processing programs in the past (such as Microsoft Word), you'll find yourself already familiar with most of the Crystal Reports working environment.

In this chapter, we explore the mysteries of Crystal Reports by poking around the software. You'll familiarize yourself with the program's most common features, as well as plunge into the Crystal Reports design environment — getting a feel for how it all works.

This chapter works as a primer on Crystal Reports. If you're new to the software or your skills need a little refreshing, this chapter is for you. If, on the other hand, you're familiar with Crystal Reports, you might skim through the material within this chapter, perhaps making note where necessary of any new or unfamiliar material.

Starting Crystal Reports

To start Crystal Reports, select Start, Programs, Crystal Reports *x* (where *x* is your version of Crystal Reports). When you perform these steps, a Crystal Reports screen displays (complete with some familiar user interface elements such as toolbars and menu bars). Users are also greeted with a Welcome dialog box.

Figure 2-1 displays the Crystal Reports Welcome dialog box.

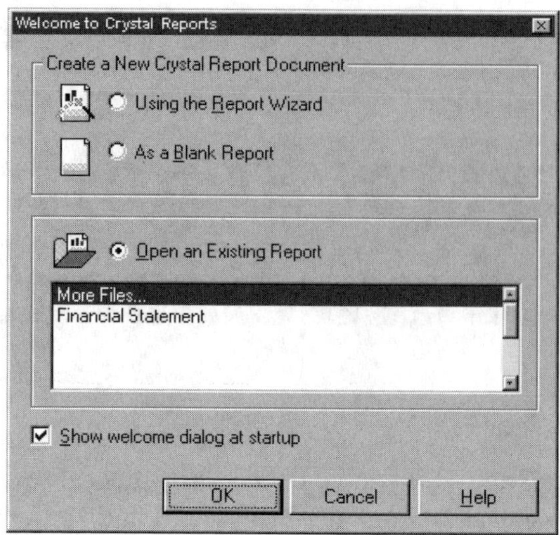

Figure 2-1. The Crystal Reports Welcome dialog box

You can use the Welcome dialog box to perform three main types of functionality:

- Create a new report with the Report Wizards
- Create new reports from scratch
- Open an existing report

Tip

If you want this dialog box to display every time you start Crystal Reports, check the Show welcome dialog at startup check box.

Crystal Reports provides two ways to build new reports. You can create a report from scratch, starting with nothing more than a blank page. You can also use one of the Report Wizards (covered in Chapter 4), which walk you step-by-step through the process of report design.

For now, let's just start a blank report so you can familiarize yourself with the tools of the trade. Select the As a Blank Report option button, and press the OK button. A Report Designer screen displays, followed by the Database Expert dialog box.

Working with the Database Expert

Crystal Reports' Database Expert allows you to select the location of the data and the database tables that you use within your reports. Figure 2-2 displays the Database Expert.

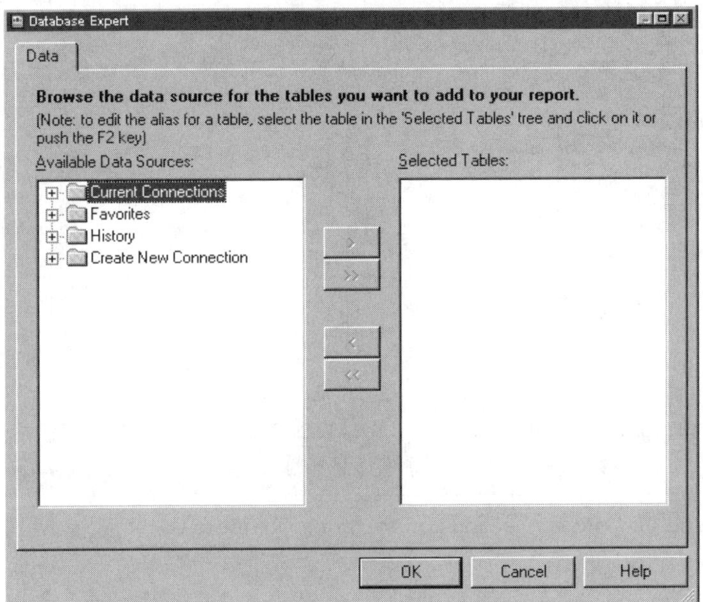

Figure 2-2. The Database Expert dialog box

The Database Expert allows you to select a variety of data sources supported by Crystal Reports. These data sources are categorized into different folder nodes, with collapsible plus signs next to the folders. The folders represent the following database categories:

- **Current Connections:** This folder contains a list of already-existing data source connections. You won't find any connections the first time you expand this node.
- **Favorites:** This folder contains a list of data sources that you commonly use and have added to your Favorites list.
- **History:** This folder contains a list of the last five data sources that you've used.
- **Create New Connection:** This folder contains a list of subfolders, representing the different data sources to which you

can connect. These subfolders (as shown in Figure 2-3) are summarized in Table 2-1.

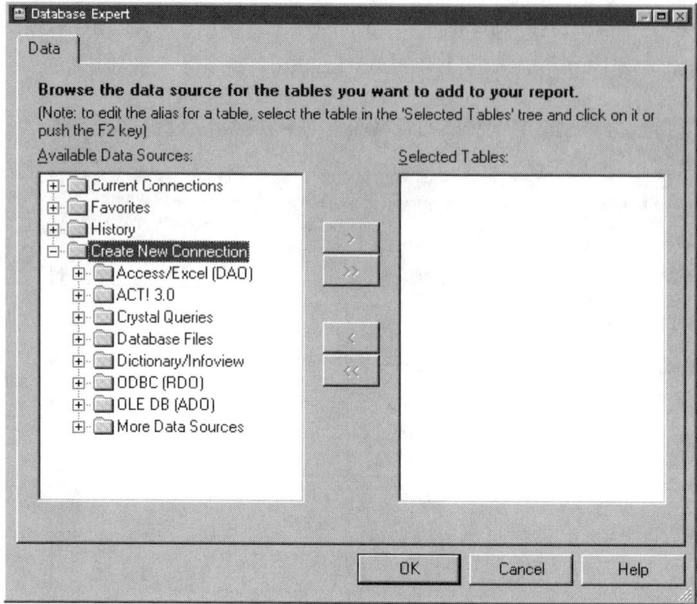

Figure 2-3. Data connection options of the Database Expert

Table 2-1. Create New Connection subfolders

Subfolder	Description
Access/Excel (DAO)	This folder creates a connection to a Data Access Object (DAO) data source. A *Data Access Object* is a data access interface that communicates with Microsoft Jet and ODBC-compliant data sources. DAO allows users to connect to and retrieve data from applications that use the Jet engine, including most Microsoft Office applications like MS-Word, MS-Access, and Excel.
ACT! 3.0	This folder creates a connection to data created within Symantec's ACT! contact management software. Crystal Reports can read this ACT! data, allowing you to create reports based on your contact information. You can create connections to earlier versions of ACT! (prior to version 3) by using a file called Crw.act. To use this file, you will need to access it from the Database Files folder. Check with your system administrator for connecting to versions of ACT! prior to version 3.

Subfolder	Description
Crystal Queries	This folder creates a connection to a Crystal SQL Designer (.qry) file. A *Crystal Query* file allows users to take a quick and easy look at a database (in other words, there is no formatting done to the data). You learn more about Crystal Queries in Chapter 15.
Database Files	This folder creates a connection to a local PC-style database, such as Microsoft Access. This is the type of connection that you use for the purposes of this book.
Dictionary/ Infoview	This folder creates a connection to a Crystal Dictionary (.dc5) file or a Crystal Infoview (.civ) file. A *Crystal Dictionary* file is a simplified view of a database, often useful to those unfamiliar with the complexity of their database. Crystal Dictionaries are useful, but they must first be created by one familiar with the database layout. A *Crystal Infoview* is a file that controls the tables, fields, and records that can actually be seen from a database and is often used to prevent access of classified or prohibited information.
ODBC (RDO)	This folder creates a connection to a Remote Data Object data source. A *Remote Data Object (RDO)* is an object-oriented data access tool, used only with databases complying with the most recent ODBC standard. ODBC (which stands for open database connectivity) is a program used to connect to popular databases. Most corporate databases (such as Oracle and Microsoft SQL Server) support this type of connection.
OLE DB (ADO)	This folder creates a connection to an ActiveX Data Object data source. An *ActiveX Data Object (ADO)* is an interface to the application programming interface known as *Object Linking and Embedding Database* (OLE DB). OLE DB accesses all kinds of data files on a computer network.
More Data Sources	This folder allows users to create a connection for the following data sources: Borland Database Engine, Btrieve, CDO, Field Definitions, File System Data, Outlook, and xBase.

Knowing the method of data connection can be tricky, it depends a lot on the type of data source from which you're reporting. Should you have questions about the connection to your real-world database, check with your system administrator. He or she will know best the correct method of how to access system data.

Creating a Data Connection to the Sample Database

In this book, you use a sample database provided with the Crystal Reports software. This database, xtreme.mdb, is a Microsoft Access database, with all the necessary drivers included with the Crystal Reports installation. You can use the database and begin designing reports immediately, even if you don't have Microsoft Access installed on your computer.

The xtreme.mdb database contains data about a mountain bike and accessory company. The data is an excellent model for real-world business activities and is useful in learning to develop usable reports.

To select this tutorial database, perform the following steps:

1. **Start up Crystal Reports (if you haven't done so already).**
2. **At the Welcome dialog box, select the As a Blank Report option.**
3. **Click the OK button. The Database Expert dialog box displays.**
   If the Database Expert dialog box is not displayed, go to the menu bar and select Database, Database Expert.
4. **Within the Database Expert dialog box, expand the Create New Connection folder.**
   If no items are found, you can double-click the folder. An Open dialog box displays, allowing you to search.
5. **Expand the Database Files folder and perform a search for the xtreme.mdb sample database.**
   You can perform a search by double-clicking the Find Database File option.
   By default, the xtreme.mdb database is located in the \Program Files\Crystal Decisions\Crystal Reports 9\En\Samples\Databases directory. This file is placed onto your computer during the Crystal Reports install.
6. **Double-click the xtreme.mdb database from the default location.**
   Voilà — you've made a connection to a data source! Your screen should look like Figure 2-4.

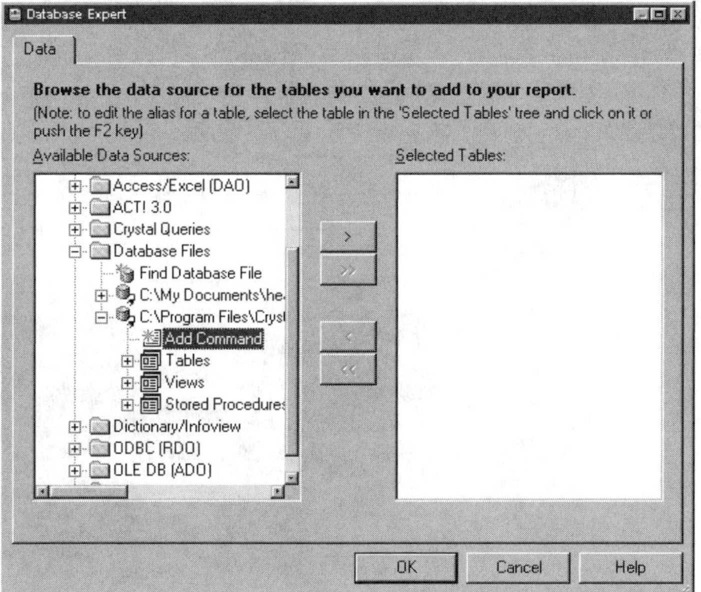

Figure 2-4. Selecting the sample database with the Database Expert

Note

To add a data source to the Favorites folder, first connect the data source (as you did in the steps above). Right-click on the data source when you see it in the Database Expert. A drop-down options menu displays.

Select the Add to Favorites option from this menu. The data source is now available within the Favorites folder.

After selecting your database, you usually begin selecting the database tables to use within your report. However, for now don't worry about selecting any tables or other database objects (you'll get your fair share of this in the next chapter). Press the OK button. You'll find yourself looking at the Report Design/Preview area.

Exploring the Report Design Area

The Report Design area (shown in Figure 2-5) is where most of your Crystal Reports development takes place. In this area, you select and format the objects that make up your report.

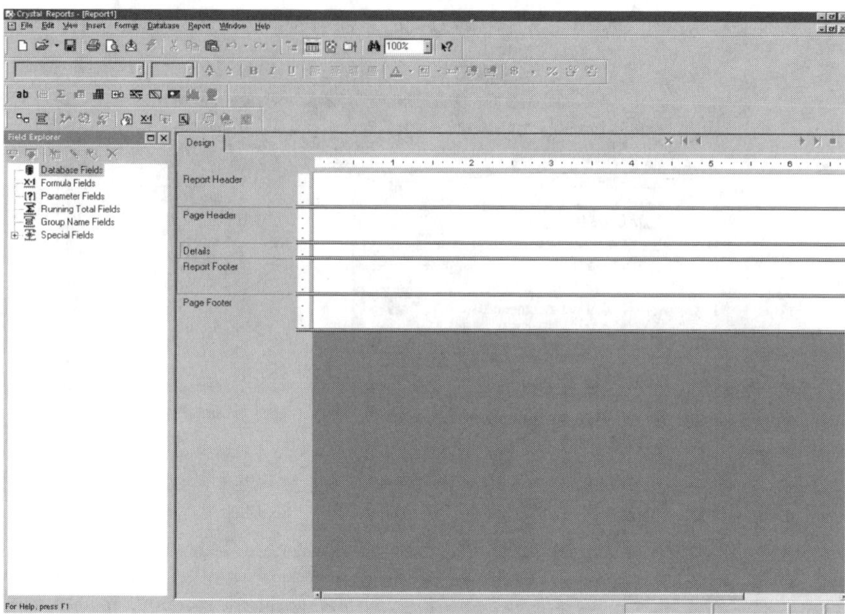

Figure 2-5. The Report Design area

Crystal Reports, like many report designing programs, uses a "banded" approach for designing reports. Each band (referred to in Crystal Reports as *sections*) reflects a particular type of content for the report. The following list summarizes the five sections used within Crystal Reports:

- **Report Header:** This section is generally used for the report title and other information that you want displayed on only the first page of a report (such as a company logo or a chart created from the report's data).
- **Page Header:** This section generally includes information at the top of every page in your report (such as descriptive labels that appear above your report data).
- **Details:** This section is where the body of the report occurs. It's here that all the retrieved data displays. This is the body of the report. This section prints once per record.
- **Report Footer:** This section is similar to the Report Header section. Information contained here displays only once at the end of the report. This section is used to display grand totals.

- **Page Footer:** This section is similar to the Page Header section. This section displays information at the bottom of every page of the report and is often used for page numbers.

Although these sections may seem confusing, they make more sense once you begin your report development.

Working with the Menu Bar

Perhaps the first thing you noticed on the Report Design screen was the menu bar — that rectangular bar displayed at the top of the screen as shown in Figure 2-6. The *menu bar* contains several drop-down options that represent different functionality you can use when designing your reports.

Figure 2-6. The Crystal Reports menu bar

Table 2-2 summarizes the different menus available within Crystal Reports.

Tip

While all the menus are useful, you'll find that the most widely used are the View, Insert, Database, and Report menus.

Table 2-2. Crystal Reports' menus

Menu	Description
File	This menu contains functionality such as opening, closing, and saving files, sending files to a printer, and creating new reports. This menu also contains additional options, such as setting page margins, exporting a report to a variety of file formats, adding summary information to the report, and customizing Crystal Reports' features to meet your personal preferences.
Edit	This menu allows you to modify your reports, including undo and redo action and cut/copy/paste/delete functionality. This menu also contains additional functionality, such as changing subreport links.
View	This menu allows you to modify Crystal Reports' user interface, as well as define which areas of this interface are to remain visible or hidden.
Insert	This menu allows you to add report objects, totals, groups, and subreports into your reports. This menu also provides the options to add additional reporting features, such as charts, maps, and graphics.

Menu	Description
Format	This menu allows you to change the look of elements within a report. These options include formatting various report objects, including charts and cross-tab reports. This menu also contains options that allow Crystal Reports to automatically arrange your report objects and apply template styles to your report.
Database	This menu allows you to utilize information from a database. Here you can add or delete the tables you wish to use in your report, define how various database tables link together, and browse the data within a table's field.
Report	This menu allows you to select the records or groups to include within a report, including grouping and sorting functionality, as well as creating formulas to use within your reports.
Window	This menu allows you to rearrange buttons and windows, as well as list what report windows are currently open.
Help	This menu allows you to access Crystal Reports' online help. The online help contains a variety of technical information and user questions related to Crystal Reports and report development.

Using the Crystal Reports Toolbars

Directly under the menu bar is a series of selectable buttons, better known as a toolbar. A *toolbar* is a block of on-screen buttons. When clicked with a mouse, these buttons activate some of the most widely used menu options. Toolbars provide another method of selecting some of the drop-down options found within the menu bar.

Crystal Reports contains four toolbars: Standard, Formatting, Insert Tools, and Expert Tools. Each is summarized in the following sections.

Note

You can turn on or off the Crystal Reports toolbars by selecting View, Toolbars from the menu bar.

When you select this option, a Toolbars dialog box displays with a check box next to each of the toolbars. A checked check box means that the toolbar displays; an unchecked check box means the toolbar does not display.

Use these check boxes to control which toolbars you wish to view.

Exploring the Standard Toolbar

The Standard toolbar (shown in Figure 2-7) contains buttons (such as Find, New, and Save) that are identical to buttons in several Windows programs. The Standard toolbar contains shortcuts to some of Crystal Reports' most widely used functionality.

Figure 2-7. The Standard toolbar

Tip

If you can't remember what a button stands for on any of the toolbars, try activating the Content Help tool.

To activate this tool, select Help, Content Help from the menu bar. Your Content Help tool is now activated. Rest your cursor pointer over a button. When Content Help is activated, a small label displays, explaining the name of the button.

To deactivate this tool, return to the Help, Content Help option within the menu bar. Simply unselect the option, and the Content Help will deactivate.

The following table summarizes the buttons available on the Standard toolbar.

Table 2-3. The buttons of the Standard toolbar

Button	Label	Shortcut Key	Description
	New	Ctrl+N	Creates a new report.
	Open	Ctrl+O	Opens an existing report.
	Save	Ctrl+S	Saves new changes.
	Print	Ctrl+P	Sends the report to the printer.
	Print Preview		Displays a preview of the report.
	Export		Exports the report to one of several popular file formats.
	Refresh	F5	Updates the report with new data.

Button	Label	Shortcut Key	Description
	Cut	Ctrl+X	Removes an object from the report, storing it in your computer's clipboard application.
	Copy	Ctrl+C	Copies an object from the report, storing it in your computer's clipboard application.
	Paste	Ctrl+V	Places an item cut or copied onto the report (retrieving this object from the clipboard application).
	Undo	Ctrl+Z	Enables users to return objects to a previous state by undoing the effects of an action. This key enables you to "undo" mistakes.
	Redo	Ctrl+Y	Redoes the last action that was previously undone.
	Group Tree		Activates (or deactivates) the Group Tree. The Group Tree enables you to drill down on groups to view the details of the underlying data.
	Field Explorer		Opens the Field Explorer dialog box, enabling users to insert database fields into a report.
	Report Explorer		Opens the Report Explorer dialog box, enabling users to view the contents of the report in a tree view.
	Repository Explorer		Activates the Repository Explorer, which enables you to view the contents of the repository. The repository contains report objects you can use within your current report.
	Find		Enables users to find a specific record.
100%	Zoom Control		Sets the magnification factor for viewing reports.
	Help		Activates the Content Help tool.

Exploring the Formatting Toolbar

The Formatting toolbar (shown in Figure 2-8) resides underneath the Standard toolbar and contains many self-explanatory buttons that you've probably seen in other applications, often associated with controlling the format of the objects within your report. For example, the Formatting toolbar allows you to control the size and style of your fonts, the alignment of text, and how many decimal places display within numerical information.

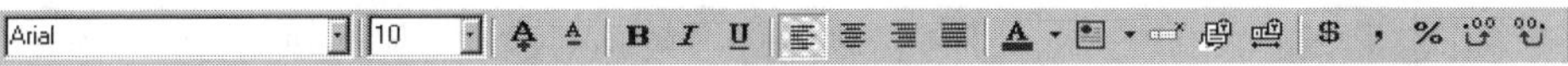

Figure 2-8. The Formatting toolbar

The following table summarizes the buttons available on the Formatting toolbar.

Table 2-4. The buttons on the Formatting toolbar

Button	Label	Description
 Arial	Font face	Changes the type of font used by a report object.
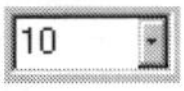 10	Font size	Changes the size of a font used by a report object.
	Increase font size	Increases a report object's text one point each time the button is pressed.
	Decrease font size	Decreases a report object's text one point each time the button is pressed.
 B	Bold	Changes a report object's text to boldface.
 I	Italics	Italicizes a report object's text.
 U	Underline	Underlines a report object's text.
	Align left	Aligns a report object's text flush left.
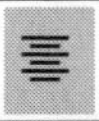	Align center	Centers a report object's text.
	Align right	Aligns a report object's text flush right.
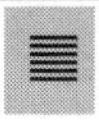	Align justify	Aligns a report object's text evenly along both the left and right margins of a column.
 A	Font color	Applies a chosen color to the selected report object.
	Outside borders	Applies a chosen border to the selected report object.

Button	Label	Description
	Suppress	Hides a report object.
	Lock format	Locks the formatting of the selected report object.
	Lock size/position	Locks the size and positions of a selected report object in relation to an adjacent report object.
$	Currency	Places a currency symbol next to a report object that is a number (or currency) data type.
,	Thousands	Places a thousands separator within a report object that is a number (or currency) data type.
%	Percent	Places a percent sign next to a report object that is a number (or currency) data type.
.00	Increase decimals	Adds one decimal place to a report object that is a number (or currency) data type.
00.	Decrease decimals	Removes one decimal place from a report object that is a number (or currency) data type.

Exploring the Insert Tools Toolbar

The Insert Tools toolbar (shown in Figure 2-9) resides underneath the Formatting toolbar. The Insert Tools toolbar contains shortcuts for adding a variety of report-enhancing features, such as text objects, groups, subreports, charts, and maps. We begin adding the features within this toolbar as early as the next chapter.

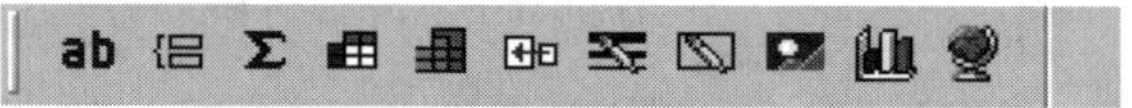

Figure 2-9. The Insert Tools toolbar

The following table summarizes the buttons available on the Insert Tools toolbar.

Table 2-5. The buttons of the Insert Tools toolbar

Button	Label	Description
ab	Insert text object	Inserts a text object into the report. A *text object* is a type of report field that can contain text written by you, the report designer. Text objects allow you to add labels (or larger portions of text if desired) to your reports. You'll learn about text objects in Chapter 5.
	Insert group	Inserts a group into the report. A *group* is a set of database records that are related to each other in some common way. For example, all customers residing in Texas could be a group. Groups can help organize report data so that it is presented in a meaningful manner. You'll learn more about groups in Chapter 8.
Σ	Insert summary	Inserts a summary object into the report. A *summary object* is a calculation performed on data within a group. You'll learn more about summary fields in Chapter 9.
	Insert cross-tab	Inserts a cross-tab object into the report. A *cross-tab object* is a format that presents data within rows and columns (similar to a spreadsheet). You'll find that inventory reports often work well in a cross-tab format. We look more at working with cross-tabs in the exercise at the end of Part II.
	Insert OLAP grid	Inserts an OLAP grid object into the report. *OLAP* is short for online analytical processing. Many databases utilize OLAP tools, which provide multidimensional analysis on data. For example, a database with OLAP tools might provide time series and trend analysis views. This button allows users to add an OLAP grid to the report.
	Insert subreport	Inserts a subreport into the report. A *subreport* is a self-contained report that displays within another report. Think of subreports as reports within a report. Often, subreports are existing reports that are imported into another report. You'll learn more about subreports in Chapter 13.
	Insert line	Inserts a line into the report. Lines are often added to reports in order to emphasize important data.

Button	Label	Description
	Insert box	Inserts a box into the report. Boxes are often added to reports to enclose data or create some other graphical effect.
	Insert picture	Inserts a picture into the report. *Pictures* are graphic files (such as company logos) that you may import into your report. We look more at working with pictures in the exercise at the end of Part II.
	Insert chart	Inserts a chart into the report. Crystal Reports provides the ability to generate colorful charts from a report's data. You'll learn about adding charts to your reports in Chapter 12.
	Insert map	Inserts a map into the report. In Crystal Reports, maps are similar to charts in that they're information presented in a graphical format. The information is obtained from a report's data. You'll learn about adding maps to your reports in Chapter 12.

Exploring the Expert Tools Toolbar

The last of Crystal Reports' toolbars is the Expert Tools toolbar (shown in Figure 2-10). The Expert Tools toolbar contains access to some of Crystal Reports' most advanced report-enhancing functionality. This advanced functionality is often made available through dialog boxes, better known as Experts.

Examples of some of Crystal's Experts include the Template Expert (explored in Chapter 4), the Database Expert (explored briefly in this chapter and in more detail in Chapter 6), the Select Expert (explored in Chapter 7), and the Group Expert (explored in Chapter 8).

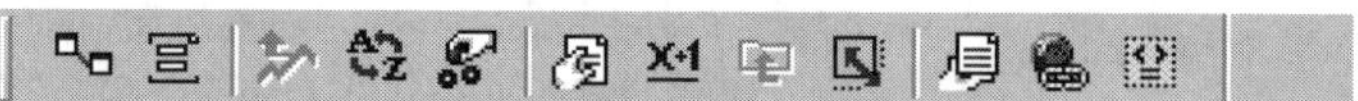

Figure 2-10. The Expert Tools toolbar

The following table summarizes the buttons available on the Expert Tools toolbar.

Table 2-6. The buttons of the Expert Tools toolbar

Button	Label	Description
	Database Expert	Allows users to access the Database Expert. The *Database Expert* lets users make additional database tables and fields available to a report. You'll learn more about the Database Expert in Chapter 6.
	Group Expert	Allows users to access the Group Expert. The *Group Expert* lets users define how a report groups and sorts data. You'll learn more about the Group Expert in Chapter 8.
	Group Sort Expert	Allows users to access the Group Sort Expert. The *Group Sort Expert* lets users sort Top *n* or Bottom *n* groups (with *n* representing the number you specify). This type of sorting is most commonly utilized in cross-tabs. You'll look more at working with the Group Sort Expert at the end of Part II.
	Record Sort Expert	Allows users to access the Record Sort Expert. The *Record Sort Expert* lets users define the sorting order of database records. You'll learn more about the Record Sort Expert in Chapter 8.
	Select Expert	Allows users to access the Select Expert. The *Select Expert* lets users define the records to display within a report, as well as filter the records that are not to display. You'll learn more about the Select Expert in Chapter 7.
	Section Expert	Allows users to access the Section Expert. The *Section Expert* lets users control various report section functionality (such as suppressing sections, inserting page breaks within a section, and adding multiple columns to a section). You'll learn more about the Section Expert in Chapter 3.
	Formula Workshop	Allows users to access the Formula Workshop. The *Formula Workshop* lets users create and modify formulas used within a report. You'll learn more about the Formula Workshop in Chapter 10.
	OLAP Report Settings	Allows users to access the OLAP Report Settings. The *OLAP Report Settings* changes the report settings of an OLAP grid. This option is available only in OLAP reports.

Button	Label	Description
	Template Expert	Allows users to access the Template Expert. The *Template Expert* lets users add a predesigned report appearance to a report. You'll learn more about the Template Expert in Chapter 4.
	Format	Allows users to access the Format Editor. The *Format Editor* lets users change the appearance of report fields and other report objects within a report. You'll learn more about the Format Editor in Chapter 5.
	Insert Hyperlink	Allows users to insert or define hyperlinks within a report. This button lets users access the Hyperlink tab of the Format Editor dialog box. The Hyperlink tab allows users to define and modify hyperlinks included within a report.
	Highlighting Expert	Allows users to access the Highlighting Expert. The *Highlighting Expert* lets users apply conditional formatting to report fields. Conditional formatting is essentially the following formula: If the value of field x meets condition A, then apply the specified formatting to the field selected. You'll look more at working with highlighting in the exercise at the end of Part II.

What's Next?

In this chapter, you've learned a lot about Crystal Reports' report environment, as well as many of the tools available at your fingertips. By the time you get to the end of Part I, you'll have utilized several of these tools in exercises that have you creating real-world reports!

The next chapter begins your familiarization with several of Crystal Reports' reporting tools, walking you through the steps of designing your first reports. By the end of the next chapter, you'll find yourself whipping around the Crystal Reports Design area like a pro!

Chapter 3

Designing Your First Report

Are you a control freak, taking control of an entire workload yourself? Or do you believe delegating duties is the most productive way to work? Neither work philosophy is necessarily correct or incorrect — it's all just a matter of personal preference.

Crystal Reports understands this. No matter what type of work personality you are, Crystal Reports has you covered. In Crystal Reports, you'll find building options for both the "control freak" and the "diligent delegator" in all of us.

In this chapter, we jump headfirst into the world of report design. As you begin your report building, you learn that Crystal Reports provides the following two options for developing reports:

- You can build a report from scratch.
- You can build a report using one of the Report Wizards.

Once you explore these two methods, you may use either one when designing reports. The choice is up to you. We look at both options before the end of Part I.

Blank Reports vs. Report Wizards

If you're of the control-freak-type personality, you'll probably enjoy building a report from scratch. We learn about that method in this chapter. For those of you who don't mind letting Crystal Reports do a portion of the work, the Report Wizards may be your choice. Both options have their advantages and disadvantages. The truth of the matter is that most Crystal Reports users find themselves using both methods, depending on their needs.

Building a report from scratch means that you start with a blank page and then add the fonts, color, data, and layout piece by piece. While this method may seem labor-intensive, it also provides the most flexibility. Even if you build reports using the Report Wizards, you'll still need to refine most reports, using concepts involved with building a report from scratch.

In comparison, the Report Wizards are utilities within Crystal Reports that lead you through the steps of producing different types of reports. Report Wizards simplify the process of report design by using a step-by-step approach. We explore Crystal Reports' Report Wizards in Chapter 4.

Your First Report

The first report that you create is a Customer Profile report. The purpose of this report is to display customer contact information. These types of reports typically include details such as the name of your customer's company, the name of an individual to contact, a physical address, and a telephone number. While developing this report, you'll learn about a number of Crystal Reports' features, which you'll find useful in most of your reporting design efforts.

To begin designing this report, start up your Crystal Reports program. At the Welcome to Crystal Reports dialog box, select the As a Blank Report option button. Then press the OK button. The Database Expert dialog box displays.

Tip

If no Welcome dialog box displays at initial startup, select File, New from the menu bar. A Reports Gallery dialog box displays. This dialog box contains the same options as the Welcome to Crystal Reports dialog box.

Selecting Your Reporting Database

Before creating any report, you'll need to select a data source. For the examples in this book, you'll use the sample xtreme.mdb database provided with Crystal Reports. Go ahead and connect to this database (as you did in the last chapter). You should see your connection display in the Database Expert dialog box.

Note

As mentioned in the last chapter, Crystal Reports allows you to connect to the same database using different methods. Check with your system administrator for your company's preferred method of database connection.

Selecting Database Tables for Your Report

Once you've connected to the xtreme.mdb file, click on the database's node. Notice that the database contains the following three nodes: Tables, Views, and Stored Procedures, as shown in Figure 3-1. These nodes represent the database's data structures.

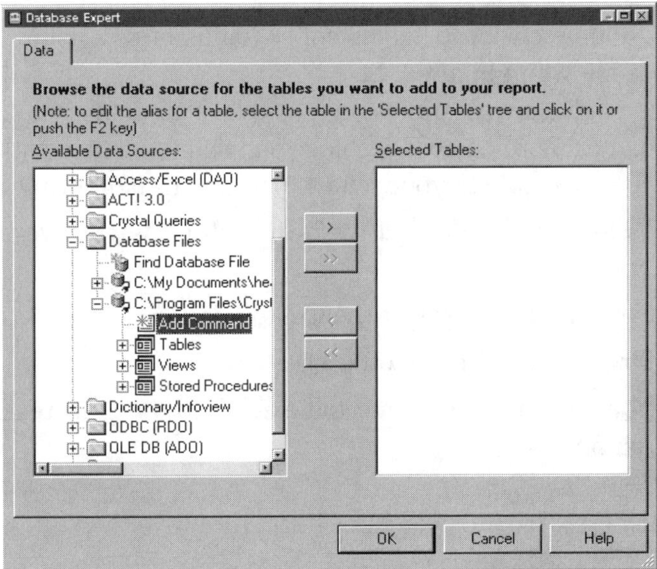

Figure 3-1. Viewing the data structures of your database

You learned about tables in Chapter 1. For most of your reporting needs, you'll find yourself working with tables more than any other database structure. However, it never hurts to familiarize yourself with these other database options available for reporting:

- **Views:** *Views* are tables created by grabbing certain fields from a number of tables and making them visible all within one table. Views can be useful in reporting. Rather than grabbing and linking multiple tables for a report (explored in Chapter 6), a single view might contain the only the needed information from multiple tables. Views are written in SQL and are typically created by a database administrator or other individual who has rights to manipulate the physical structure (not just the data) of a database.
- **Stored procedures:** *Stored procedures* are operations stored within the database server that are often used in the place of embedded SQL queries (written in the graphical user interface code). Stored procedures are developed by database developers/administrators to ease the management and display of information about that database (and its users). For the most part, you won't utilize many stored procedures within your reports.

For now, double-click the Tables node. You'll notice a list of tables display, as shown in Figure 3-2.

Once you've successfully connected to your database, you can choose one or more database tables you wish to include within your report. To add a table to your report, perform the following steps:

1. **Select the table you wish to include within your report.**

   For this report, select the Customer table.

2. **Press the Add button (>).**

   You'll see the Customer table move to the Selected Tables list box.

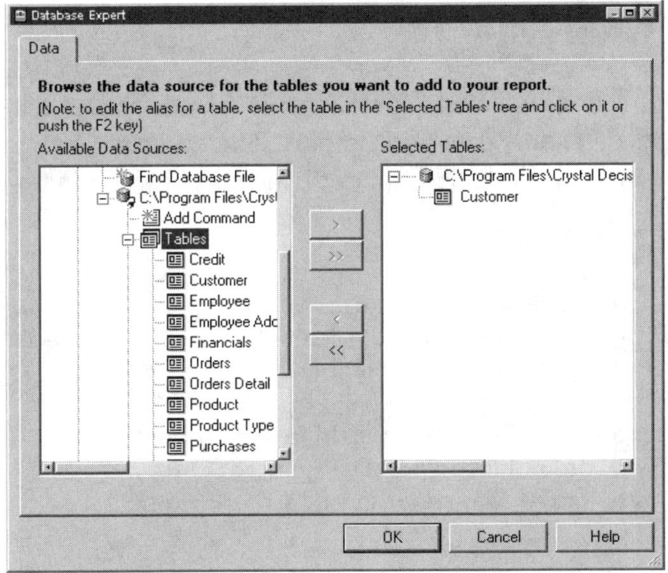

Figure 3-2. The Tables node displays all tables within a database.

3. **Press the OK button.**

   The Database Expert dialog box closes, and the Report Design area displays.

If you choose more than one table, you'll see a linking screen display. Using two or more tables within a report requires successfully linking the two tables together. Linking multiple tables is covered in Chapter 6.

Tip

You don't have to select all tables needed within a report right away. Once in the Report Design area, you can always access the Database Expert again and add tables as needed. To access the Database Expert within the Report Design area, select Database, Database Expert from the menu bar.

Using the Field Explorer

Now that you've selected your database and a database table, let's start inserting some data into a report. The easiest way to enter fields is through the Field Explorer pane (as shown in Figure 3-3).

Tip

You should notice this pane displayed within the left side of the Report Design area. If you do not see the Field Explorer, select View, Field Explorer from the menu bar. Make sure the Field Explorer option is selected.

You can dock and undock the Field Explorer pane by dragging it to any area of the Report Design area. Once the Field Explorer is unlocked, you can resize it by dragging any of its edges.

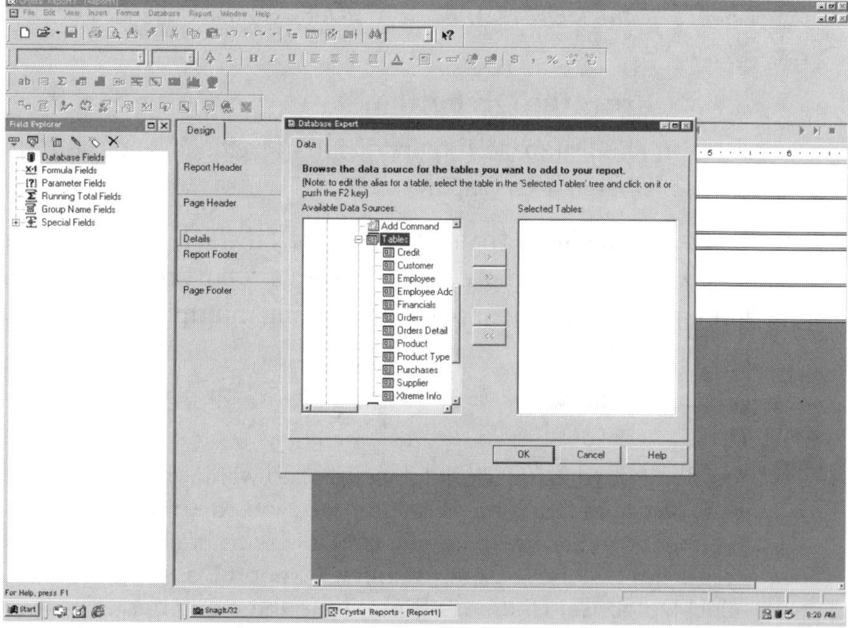

Figure 3-3. The Field Explorer pane is on the left side of the Report Design area.

The Field Explorer contains the different types of fields that you may place within your report.

In Chapter 1, you learned about database fields and how they're the main type of reporting object included within a report. However, there are other types of reporting fields that you may wish to include within your reports (besides just database fields). Table 3-1 summarizes the different types of reporting fields. The Field Explorer provides the ability to add these different fields to your reports.

Table 3-1. Crystal Reports' reporting fields

Reporting Field	Description
Database fields	*Database fields* are the columns of a database that contain one unit of information for a particular record. You learned about database fields in Chapter 1.
Formula fields	*Formulas* are mathematical statements that often perform "what-if" calculations by changing selected values and having Crystal Reports recalculate the results. Report designers (such as yourself) create these formulas. However, you can also use any of Crystal Reports' built-in functions, which are essentially pre-existing formulas. You'll learn more about formulas in Chapter 10.
Parameter fields	*Parameters* are values provided by the user and used as a constant value by a report. Parameters are used as a means of customizing the reporting operation. For example, a common use of parameters is to allow users to enter a date range (with this range being the parameter). When the report is run, only records that reside within this date range display. You'll learn more about parameters in Chapter 11.
Running total fields	*Running totals* are totals that calculate the sum of a group of records, as well as increment using values from previous groups of records within the report. You'll learn more about running totals in Chapter 9.
Group name fields	*Groups* are divisions of records that are related to each other in some way. For example, in a sales report, a group might consist of all sales generated within a particular sales region. You'll learn more about groups in Chapter 8.
Special fields	*Special fields* are system-generated information not part of the database table. Some examples of special fields include page numbers, the date the report was printed, and the report's file path. You'll learn more about special fields in Chapter 4.

You'll spend a lot of time in the Field Explorer pane, using it to add database fields, formula fields, and special fields. In fact, the bulk of information that you'll include within your reports is pulled from the Field Explorer pane.

Adding Database Fields to Your Report

Let's begin exploring the Field Explorer by adding database fields to your report. As you'll see, database fields tend to make up the majority of a report's content. No matter how snazzy and decorative a report looks, a report's main purpose is to display the records from a database.

To add database fields to your report, perform the following steps:

1. **In the Field Explorer pane, scroll down to the Database Fields node.**

   Expand this node. You'll see the Customer table you selected previously. Here, all tables that you've selected (for use within the report) display.

2. **Expand the Customer table node.**

   You'll see a list of all fields contained within the Customer table display, as shown in Figure 3-4.

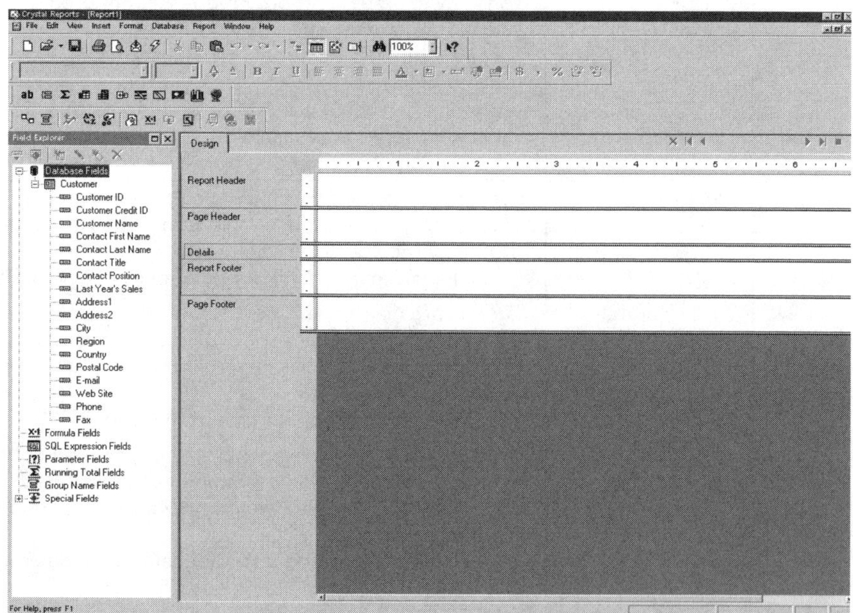

Figure 3-4. Adding database fields from the Field Explorer pane

3. **Select the Customer Name field from the Field Explorer pane.**

4. **To insert this field onto your report, drag the Customer Name field from the Field Explorer to the Report Design area.**

   To drag the field, you'll need to left-click and hold on the Customer Name field.

Tip

You'll notice that as you drag a field, a rectangular object frame appears at the tip of your cursor pointer. This object frame represents the field that you've selected to place on your report.

5. **Once you've added the database field to your report, drag the object frame to the far-left portion of the Details section.**

   Hold down your left mouse button as you drag the object frame. Release the mouse button to drop the Customer Name field.

Your screen should look something like Figure 3-5.

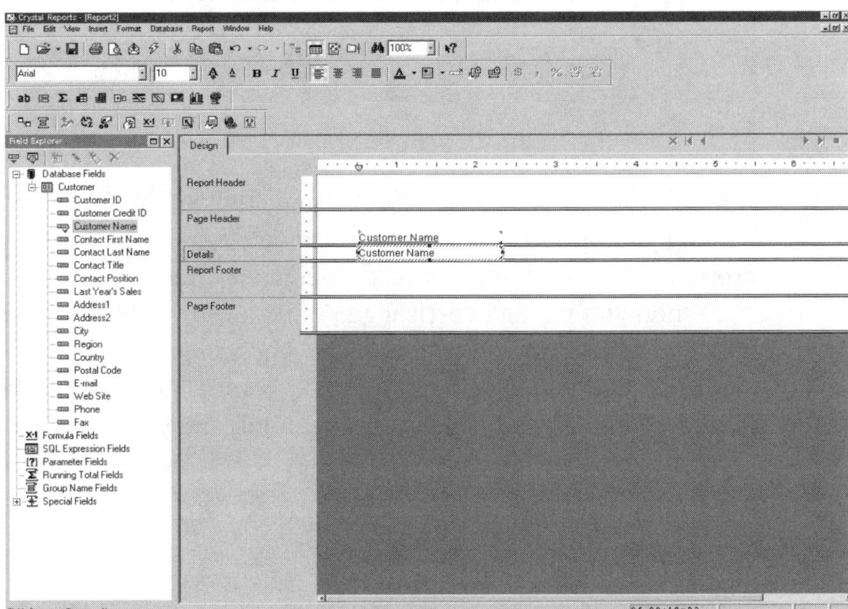

Figure 3-5. Adding a database field to a report

To move your objects within your report, you can use the same drag-and-drop procedure that you did when pulling the object from the Field Explorer. In other words:

1. **Click and hold your left mouse button on the object.**
2. **Drag the object where you want it.**
3. **Release the mouse button.**

You can also move objects by using vertical guidelines.

Moving Objects with the Vertical Guidelines

When you add a database field to the Details section, you may have noticed that an "upside-down pointer" object appears in the vertical ruler (which sits above the report). This "upside-down pointer" is a vertical guideline, as shown in Figure 3-6.

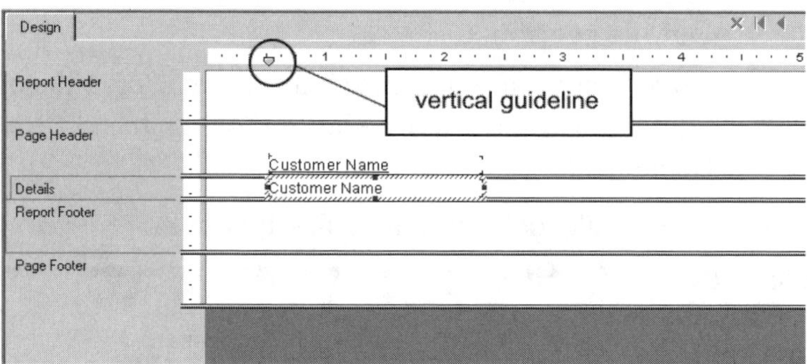

Figure 3-6. A vertical guideline

Vertical guidelines are non-printing lines that aid in alignment by helping you move objects with precision. Guidelines have a snap property that automatically snaps objects to them.

When you move a vertical guideline left or right, all objects attached to that guideline also move. Vertical guidelines are especially useful if you have a number of objects aligned with a database field (for example, a header and a subtotal) and you wish to move them all together.

Tip

Another trick you can use to move all objects at once is to hold down your Ctrl key and click multiple objects. You'll notice an elastic box appear around the objects as you click them.

Once several objects are selected, release the Ctrl key. You can now move all of the objects as a group.

Previewing Your Work

Now that you've placed a database field onto the Report Design area, you're probably looking at the results and thinking, "This is it? Where's all the data from my database?"

The reason you don't see any data is because you have not previewed your report yet. In Crystal Reports, there are two ways to see the Report Design area. You can work with objects in a Design mode (the one you're currently in). In this Design mode, report objects display using "placeholders."

You can also work in a Preview mode, which displays more of a WYSIWYG (what-you-see-is-what-you-get) environment. This means that in the Preview mode, you'll see exactly how the report displays when printed.

To enter the Preview mode, perform the following steps:

1. **Select File, Print Preview from the menu bar.**

   When you select this option, Crystal Reports begins its passes to the database server (described in Chapter 1). At the server, it gathers data and calculates formulas.

2. **A WYSIWYG environment of your report displays.**

   Also notice that Crystal Reports has created a Preview tab at the top of the Report Design area. This tab enables you to toggle between the Design tab (the view you've been working in up to this point) and the Preview tab.

Figure 3-7 displays your report, as viewed in the Preview tab.

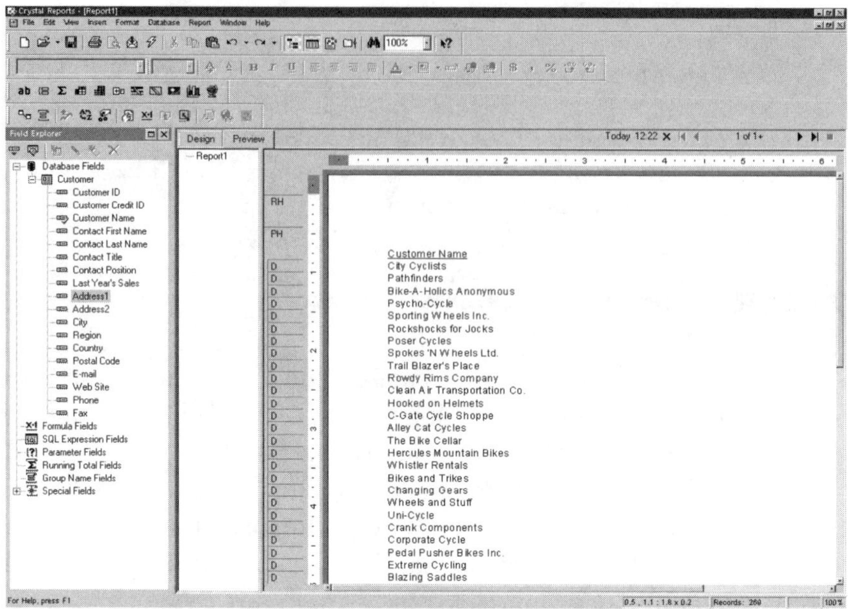

Figure 3-7. A report viewed from the Preview tab

The Design and Preview tabs both contain the same functionality, thus you can develop reports in whichever area you prefer. Both tabs are tied together internally, so any change in one automatically occurs in the other.

With that said, it is somewhat quicker to work in the Design tab. This is because the Design tab uses a single object "placeholder" to represent all data records. The Preview tab, in comparison, works with live data, where a single object placeholder might contain hundreds (perhaps even thousands) of records.

Adding Space to Your Sections

So, how useful is a report that only displays your customer names? Let's add some useful contact information, such as phone and physical address data. Of course, if you're adding more fields, you'll need to create some more space within the Details section of your report. You can accomplish this in two ways:

- The first method is to add more sections to your report (using the Section Expert).
- The second method is to manually resize the Details section by adding additional white space.

Both of these methods have their advantages:

- Adding multiple sections is often the best solution if you're adding more than one database field to a section.
- Adding additional white space is the best choice if you need to enlarge a section (such as making room for larger text). For example, you might stretch the Report Header section to make room for a title in a large font.

Let's look at both of these methods to see how they work and when they work best.

Creating Multiple Sections (Using the Section Expert)

Adding multiple sections provides much more control over your objects than simply resizing a section. For example, if a database field within your report contains no data, you can specify that the section not print, thus eliminating unnecessary blank sections from your report.

Note

A database record that contains no value is said to contain a NULL value. *NULL* literally means "nothing."

Although a NULL value is real in the sense of being recognizable, occupying space internally in a computer and being sent or received as a character, a NULL value character displays nothing and takes no space on the screen (or on a report).

Crystal Reports allows you to format entire sections of your report utilizing the Section Expert. Some of the functionality of the Section Expert includes:

- Inserting, deleting, merging, and moving report sections
- Hiding (suppressing) sections from printing
- Printing subtotals or group values only at the bottom of the page
- Inserting page breaks within the report
- Resetting page numbers to 1 after a group value prints
- Preventing blank records (or sections) from printing
- Printing sections that utilize overlying sections. In other words, a section prints and then all the following sections print on top of that first section. This is used often when printing maps, charts, or pictures within your reports.
- Formating a section so that it contains multiple columns (similar to newspaper style)

As you work through this book, you'll work with many of these different features of the Section Expert. For now, let's explore the Section Expert and see how it's used to add additional sections to your report. Perform the following steps:

1. **Select Report, Section from the menu bar.**

   The Section Expert dialog box displays, as shown in Figure 3-8.

2. **Select the Details section in the list box.**

   In the list box, you select the section for which you wish to format properties.

   In this example, you'll format properties for the Details section of your report. Therefore, you'll need to select the Details section within the list box.

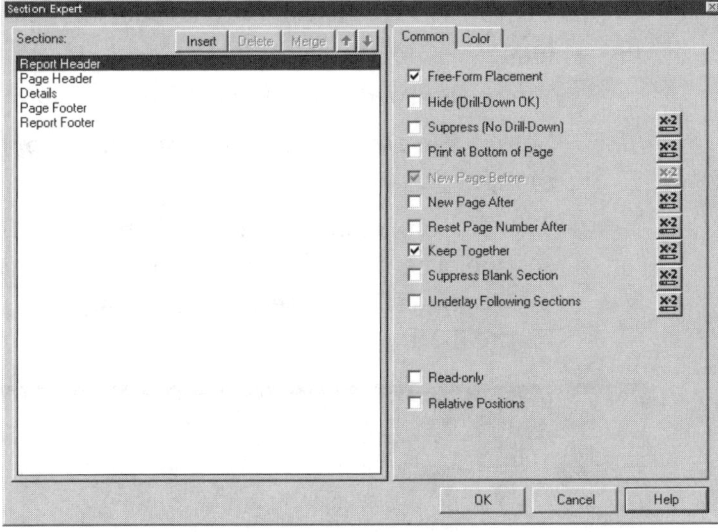

Figure 3-8. The Section Expert dialog

3. **When the Details section is highlighted, press the Insert button (toward the top of the dialog box) five times.**

   You'll notice additional Details sections are added, as shown in Figure 3-9. The last Details section should be Details f.

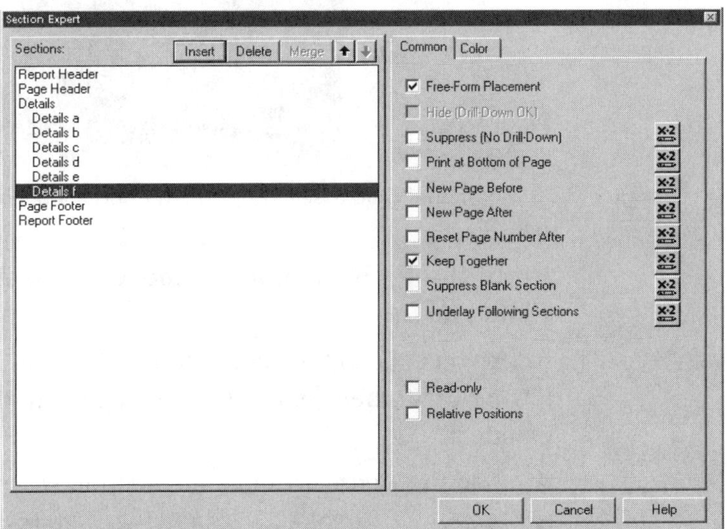

Figure 3-9. Adding multiple sections to your report

4. **Press the OK button on the Section Expert dialog box.**

   You're returned to the Report Design area.

5. **Select the Design tab to view your report in Design mode.**

   The Customer Name field should reside in the Details a section. The newly inserted sections reside underneath this section (Details sections b through f), as shown in Figure 3-10.

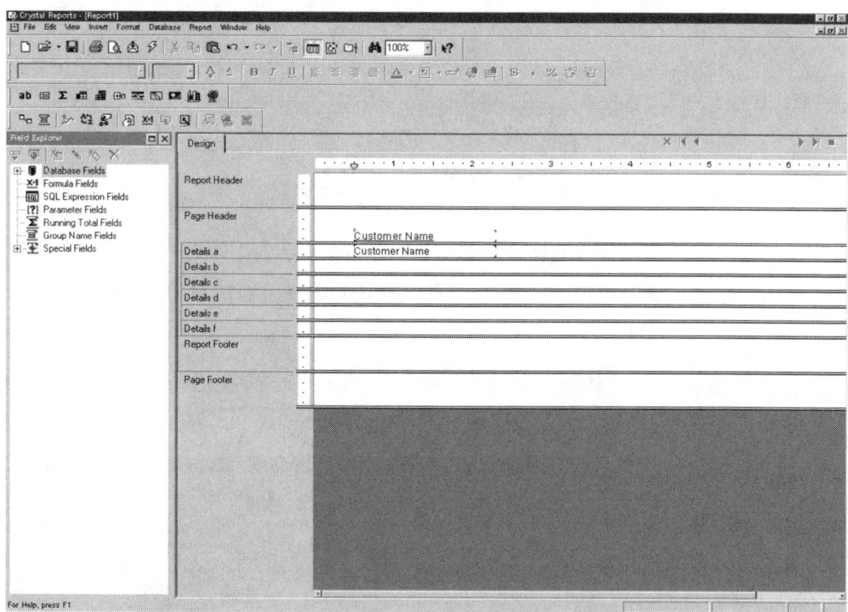

Figure 3-10. Additional Details sections (added using the Section Expert)

6. **From the Field Explorer pane, expand the Database Fields node.**

   After you expand the Database Fields node, insert the following Customer fields into your report, in the following manner:

   - Add the Address1 field into section Details b.
   - Add the City, Region, and Country fields into section Details c.

- Add the Postal Code field into section Details d.
- Add the Phone field into section Details e.
- Leave section Details f blank. Leaving this section blank creates some extra space between records.

7. **Select the Preview tab to preview the results of your work.**

   Your screen should look something like Figure 3-11.

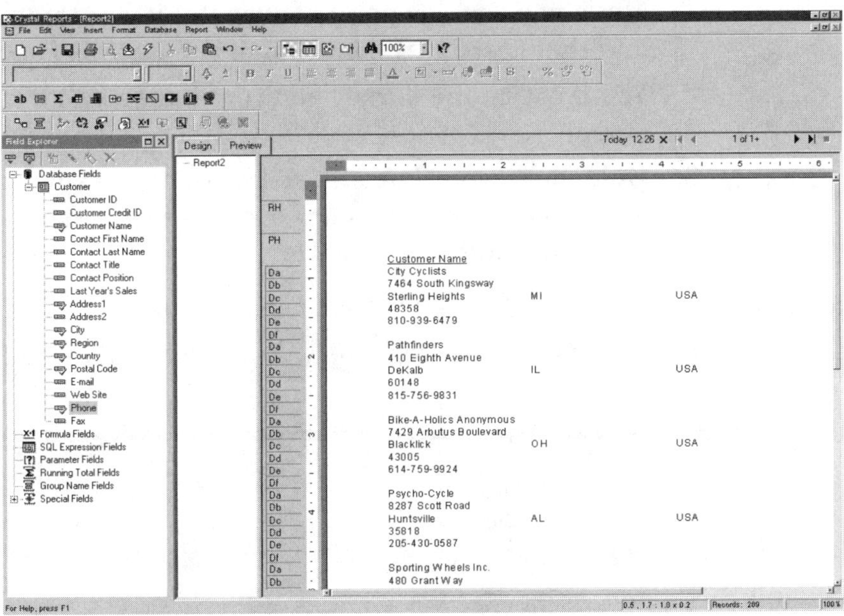

Figure 3-11. Adding multiple sections to your report

Looking at the results of your work, you may notice that the city, region, and country codes are spaced a little too far apart. Nothing screams "computer-generated report" louder than strange spacing of your data.

You can correct such spacing problems through the use of formulas in a process known as conditional formatting. You'll learn about conditional formatting, as well as more information on the Section Expert, in Chapter 10.

Adding White Space to Your Report

You may have noticed that Crystal Reports separates sections by thick, gray lines. These gray lines determine the default size of the sections. You can move these boundary lines around as you wish, physically controlling how large (or small) you want a report's section.

To add white space to a section, try the following:

1. **Move your cursor pointer over the lower thick, gray line that rests at the bottom of the Details f section.**
2. **You'll notice the cursor pointer change into a resizing cursor.**
3. **Hold down your left mouse button. With your mouse button held, drag the cursor down to stretch the boundary line.**

   You'll find the section enlarged.

Once you've done these steps, view your report within the Design tab.

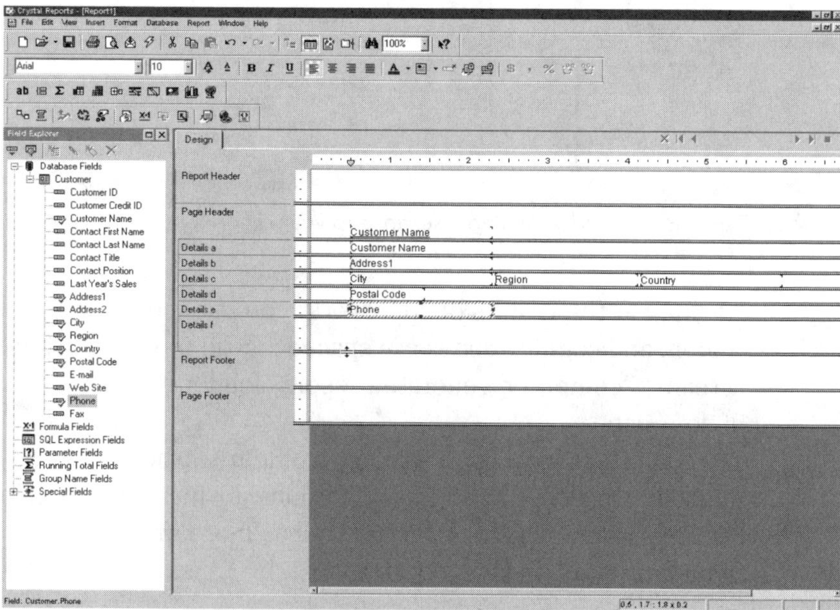

Figure 3-12. Dragging a section's border to create white space

Although dragging the bottom border of a section is the easiest way to add white space, there is another option available (in addition to using the Section Expert). You can add white space to your reports using a horizontal guideline.

Adding Space with Guidelines

We discussed vertical guidelines earlier in this chapter. Horizontal guidelines are similar in the sense that objects snap to them. However, there are two main differences between vertical and horizontal guidelines:

- Horizontal guidelines allow you to move objects *vertically* with precision (instead of horizontally, like the vertical guidelines).
- Horizontal guidelines are added manually to a report (rather than generated automatically, like the vertical guidelines).

Each time you add a horizontal guideline to a section, the section grows. Thus, horizontal guidelines are another way to increase the white space in a section. To add a horizontal guideline to a section (and therefore increase the amount of white space), perform the following steps:

1. **Right-click in the gray section name on the left side of the Report Design area. An options menu displays.**

   In this example, right-click in the gray portion of the Details f section (near the text that reads "Details f"). Figure 3-13 on the following page displays a menu of options available from the sections.

2. **This options menu contains four features for horizontal guidelines: Insert Line, Delete Last Line, Arrange Lines, and Fit Section. Select Insert Line.**

   Table 3-3 displays the horizontal guideline functionality available from the section's options menu.

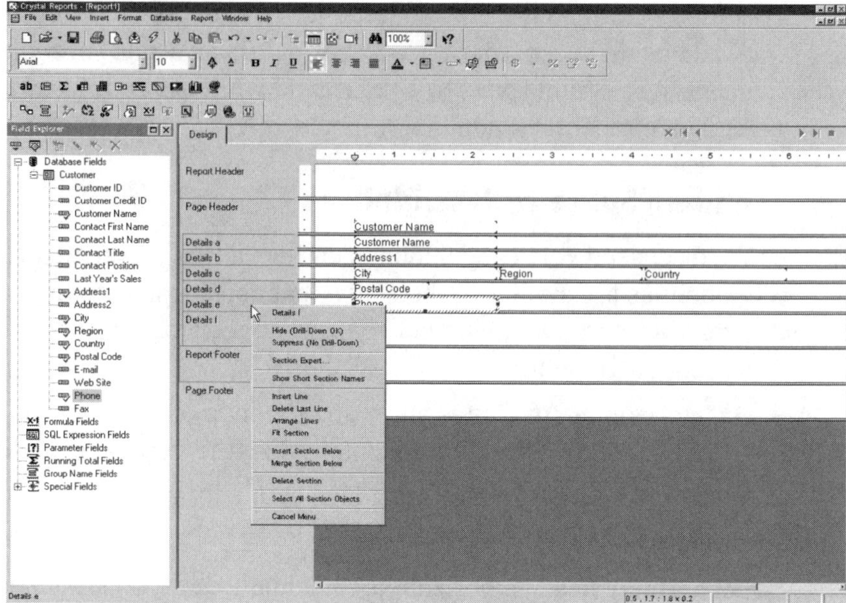

Figure 3-13. Accessing a section's options menu

Table 3-3. Horizontal guidelines options

Horizontal Guideline Option	Description
Insert line	Adds additional horizontal guidelines to a section, enlarging the size of the section.
Delete last line	Removes the last horizontal guideline within a section, shrinking the size of the section.
Arrange lines	Rearranges the horizontal guidelines within a section so that they contain equal space between.
Fit section	Shrinks the size of the section to the lowest object within the section. Any guidelines that exist below this lowest object are removed.

3. **Select the Insert Line option three times.**

   Your screen should look something like Figure 3-14.

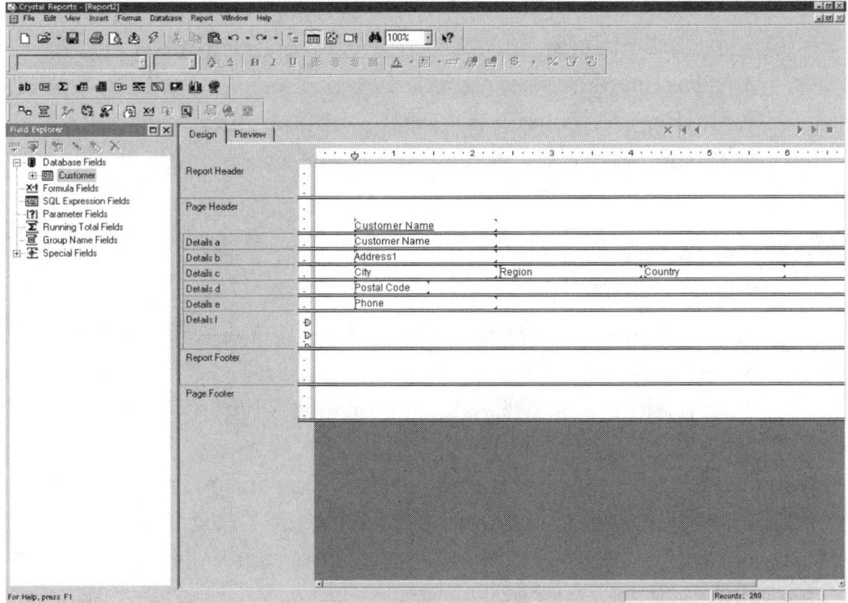

Figure 3-14. Using horizontal guidelines to add white space

Saving Your Work

With all this hard work that you've done, you'll want to save your work. Crystal Reports saves files in a fashion similar to most Windows applications. To save a report, perform the following steps:

1. **Select File, Save As from the menu bar.**
2. **A Save As dialog box displays, showing the default directory.**

   This directory designates where the file will be saved. A default filename also displays. You may change either of these defaults to your liking.
3. **When you're ready to save your work, press the Save button.**

   Your reports are saved to the directory specified.

You can designate whether you wish to save your report with or without data. If you save a report with data, the size of the file increases; however, you will not have to refresh the report the first time you open it. If you do not save data with the report, the file is a smaller file size but must refresh the first time it is previewed.

To toggle between these two options, select File, Save Data with Report. A check before this option means that data will save with the report. By default, data saves with a report.

What's Next?

You've come a long way in this chapter. Not only have you learned several useful design skills, but you're also on your way to creating a pretty impressive Customer Profile report — one you might one day tweak for use in the real world.

In the next chapter, we practice creating more reports, this time by familiarizing ourselves with the Crystal Reports creation wizards. These wizards are templates that walk you through the report design process.

Chapter 4

Writing Reports with the Report Wizards

No one likes to do more work than is necessary. The crew at Crystal Reports understands this. As a result, "Work smarter, not harder" is a philosophy that you'll find flowing throughout all the Crystal Decisions products.

One way Crystal Reports makes your life easier is through the use of Report Wizards. You're probably wondering, "Wizards? What in the world are *wizards*?"

If you're familiar with word processing programs, you've probably encountered wizards before. Software wizards are those nifty utilities in programs that help you perform a particular task.

The Report Wizards allow you to create reports by choosing options from different screens. By the time you finish with the last screen, you've developed a report with many of its features and information in place. You can then save and print your work or modify the report as needed.

Crystal Reports' Report Wizards

Crystal Reports contains four Report Wizards, each designed to help you create a different style of report. Table 4-1 summarizes each of the wizards.

Table 4-1. The Crystal Reports Report Wizards

Report Wizard	Functionality
Standard	The most flexible wizard, containing six screens that help you choose where and what data to use for your report. This wizard also helps with the grouping and sorting of data, chart creation, and selection of a template for your report.
Cross-Tab	Helps you design reports when you want your data displayed in a cross-tab format. A *cross-tab* is a format that presents data in a compact row and column format, similar to a spreadsheet. You'll find that inventory reports work well in a cross-tab format.
Mail Label	Allows you to create a report formatted to print data onto mailing labels. With this wizard, you can define the data to print on several commercial mailing label sizes. You can also define your own layout sizes for a custom mailing label.
OLAP	OLAP is short for *online analytical processing.* Many databases utilize OLAP tools, which provide multidimensional analysis of data. For example, a database with OLAP tools might provide time series and trend analysis views.

To access any of Crystal Reports' Report Wizards, perform the following steps:

1. **In Crystal Reports, select File, New from the menu bar.**

   The Crystal Reports Gallery dialog box displays, as shown in Figure 4-1.

2. **Select the Report Wizard that you wish to use as the basis for your report.**

   When you select each option button, you'll notice a thumbnail view of the report display in the Report Gallery. For now, select the Standard Wizard.

   To get a feel for how the Report Wizards work, you'll begin using the Standard Report Wizard to create an Employee Profile report. These types of reports usually contain contact and other miscellaneous information about company personnel.

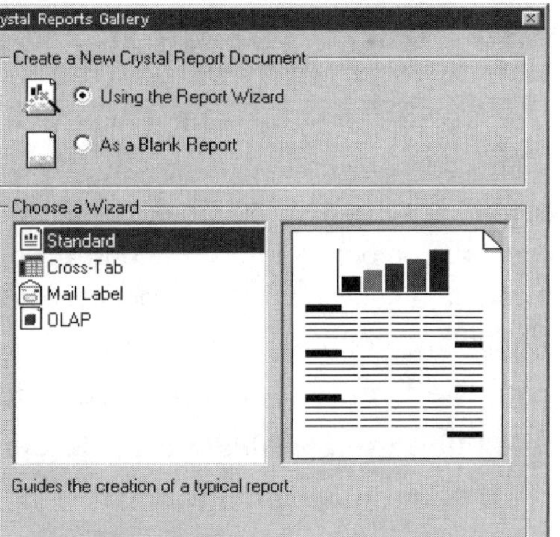

Figure 4-1. The Crystal Reports Gallery

3. **Press the OK button.**

   You'll now see a Creation Wizard dialog box display for that report, as shown in Figure 4-2.

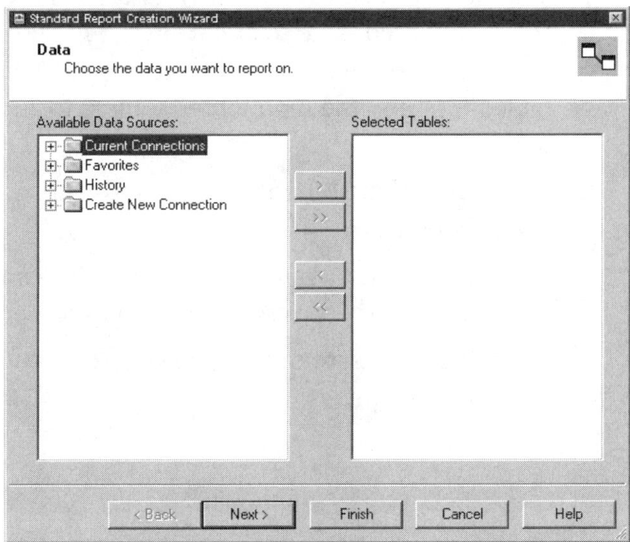

Figure 4-2. The Standard Report Creation Wizard dialog

Selecting a Data Source (Using the Wizards)

The first screen within the Standard Report Creation Wizard is the Data screen. This screen allows you to select the data source to use for your report. This screen should look familiar; it's similar to the Database Expert dialog box you first encountered in Chapter 2.

To select the data source for this report using a Report Wizard, perform the following steps:

1. **Expand the Create New Connection folder.**
2. **Double-click the Database Files folder.**
3. **Select the xtreme.mdb database.**

   Refer to Chapter 3 for more information.
4. **Double-click the xtreme.mdb node to display a list of tables.**
5. **Select the Employee table.**
6. **Press the Add (>) button to move this table to the Selected Tables list box, as shown in Figure 4-3.**

   The Add (>) and Remove (<) buttons allow you to move the highlighted table to and from the list boxes. The Add All (>>) and Remove All (<<) buttons allow you to move all tables (not just the highlighted tables) to and from the list boxes.
7. **Press the Next button to move to the next screen in the wizard.**

   As you work through these screens, you can also press the Back button to return to the previous screen if desired.

   Since the Data screen is the first screen, the Back button is not yet available.

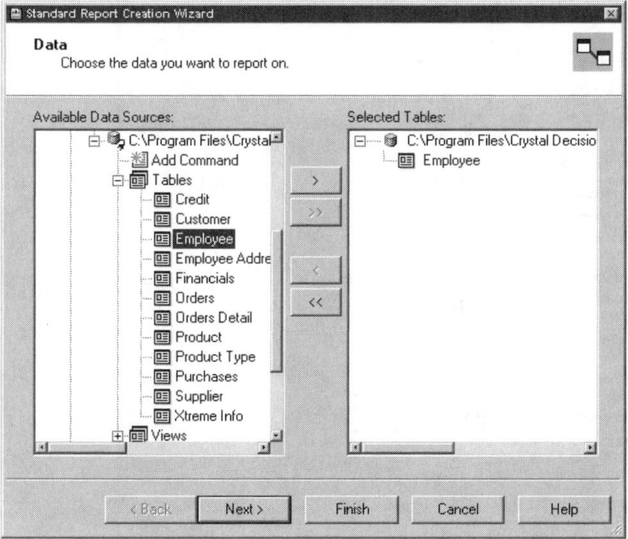

Figure 4-3. The Data screen (of the Standard Wizard)

If you add more than one table, you're taken to a Links tab, which allows you to define how multiple tables link together, based on their common fields. We learn more about linking multiple tables in Chapter 6. After successfully linking your multiple tables, a Fields screen displays.

If you select only one table (as you have in this example), you'll skip the Links screen, and the Fields screen immediately displays. The Fields screen allows you to choose which database field(s) to add to your report.

Adding Database Fields (Using the Wizards)

Once you've added the necessary tables to your report and pressed the Next button, you'll find yourself at the Fields screen. This screen enables you to choose the table information that you want to display in your report (see Figure 4-4).

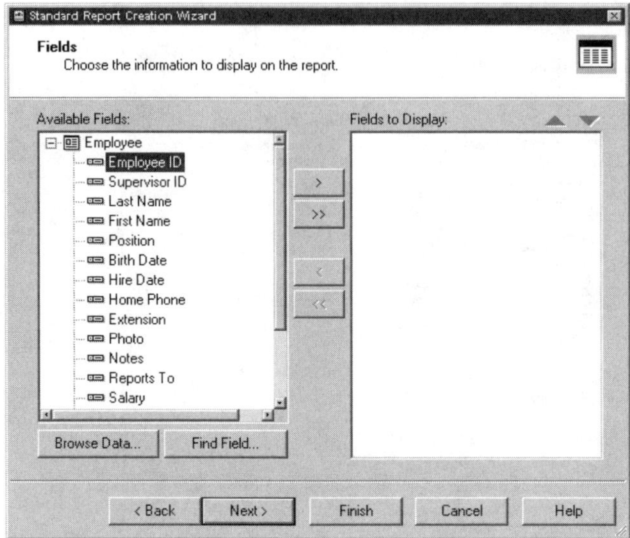

Figure 4-4. The Fields screen (of the Standard Wizard)

Perform the following steps to add database fields to your report:

1. **While in the Fields screen, hold down the Ctrl key on your keyboard. Select the following fields:**
   - Last Name
   - First Name
   - Position
   - Birth Date
   - Home Phone
   - Extension
   - Photo
   - Notes

Tip

You don't have to pick all the fields for your report within this area. Once you're finished with the tabbed screens, you can add additional information (such as database fields) from the Report Design screen.

2. **Click the Add button (>) to add the fields to the Fields to Display list box. Then click the Next button at the bottom of the screen.**

   Notice that you're now looking at a screen associated with grouping.

Browsing Data

Database tables can contain any number of fields. Often, you'll find it useful to browse sample records contained within these fields.

Crystal Reports makes browsing data easy. To view some data contained in a database field, perform the following steps:

1. **In the Fields screen, select the database field for which you wish to browse data.**

   You must select the database field from the Available Fields list box.

2. **Select the Browse Data button at the bottom of the Fields screen.**

   A sample of the data contained within the field displays, as shown in Figure 4-5.

3. **Once you view the sample data, press the Close button to close the Browse dialog box.**

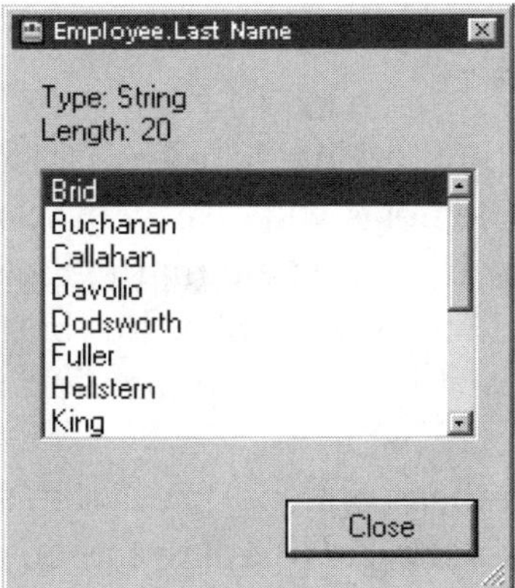

Figure 4-5. Browsing database field data

The Browse Data option is useful when trying to figure out which database fields contain the data you'd like your report to display.

Finding Fields

As your work with different reports increases, you may find some database tables containing possibly *hundreds* of fields. If this is the case, scrolling will probably prove painful and annoying in your search for different database fields. Another solution is to use the Find Field button, which is next to the Browse Data button.

To use the Find Field functionality, press the Find Field button. A search dialog box displays (shown in Figure 4-6), which allows you to type in and then search for the names of fields within a database table. You can type in either the full or partial name of a database table. Once you type in this information, press the OK button to initiate the search.

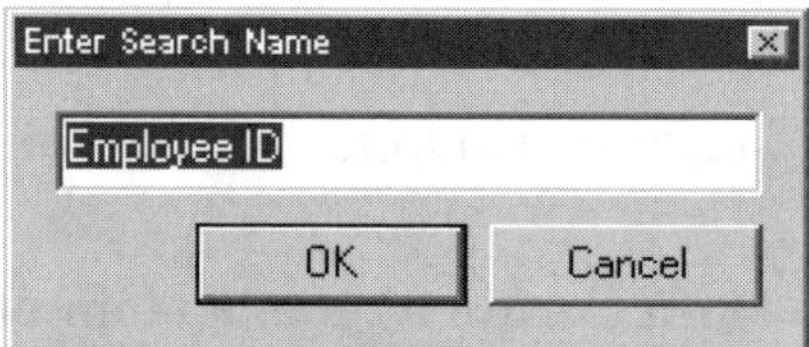

Figure 4-6. Crystal Reports' Finding Fields functionality

If your text matches the name (or part of the name) of a database table, you'll find that table highlighted within the Available Fields list box.

Changing the Field Order

The order of the fields within the Fields to Display list box represents the order in which the fields will display in your report. You can change this order by selecting a field (in the Fields to Display list box) and pressing the "up" or "down" arrow buttons above the list box, as shown in Figure 4-7. You'll see that field move up or down in the Fields to Display list box.

Once you've explored these options, press the Next button at the bottom of the Fields screen. A Grouping screen displays.

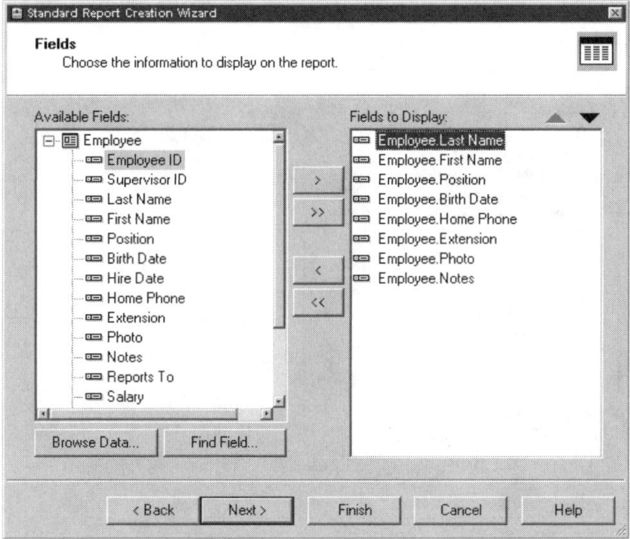

Figure 4-7. Changing the display order of database fields

Grouping Data (Using the Wizards)

In report writing, *groups* are a common relationship among records. For example, you could group all customers by state. The organization of your report might then list all states, followed by the customers within those states.

Crystal Reports offers a great deal of flexibility in how you can group data within a report. You'll learn more about grouping data in Chapter 8.

For now, let's create a group based on an employee's last name. To get an idea of how groups work, especially using the wizards, perform the following steps:

1. **Make sure that you're in the Grouping screen.**
2. **Select the Last Name field, and press the Add button.**

   The result is shown in Figure 4-8.

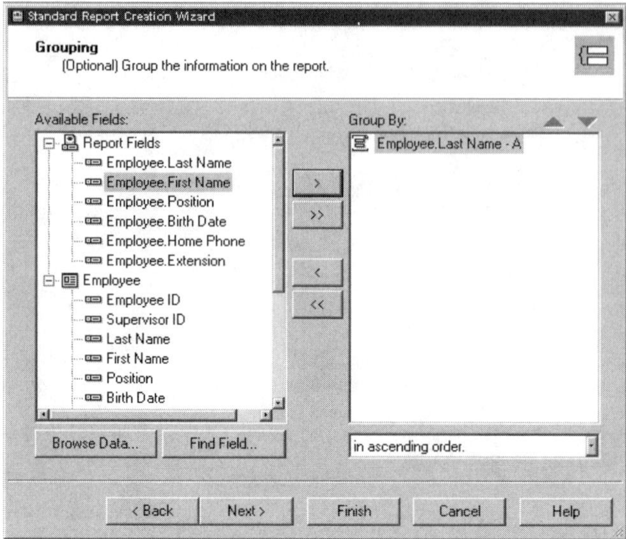

Figure 4-8. The Grouping screen (of the Standard Wizard)

Tip

When selecting a field as your group, you may notice that you can select the same field from the Report Field node or the Employee Table node.

The difference between these two nodes is that the Report Field node contains the fields you selected for your report. The Employee Table node, in comparison, contains all available fields from that database table.

You can use either option for grouping your reports. However, it's usually best to group using data you've selected for your report (available from the Report Field node).

3. **After you've selected a field to which you'll group data, press the Next button.**

   A Summaries screen displays.

Summarizing Data (Using the Wizards)

In report development, a *summary* is a count of all values within a group of records. From this count, a single value is tallied. Summaries are useful and powerful tools, especially in financial reports such as general ledgers or balance sheets.

In the Summaries screen, you can select fields for which to create summary totals. The Summaries screen (see Figure 4-9) is available only if you've specified a group in the Grouping screen.

Tip

Summary totals are also referred to as subtotals. The two terms are often used interchangeably.

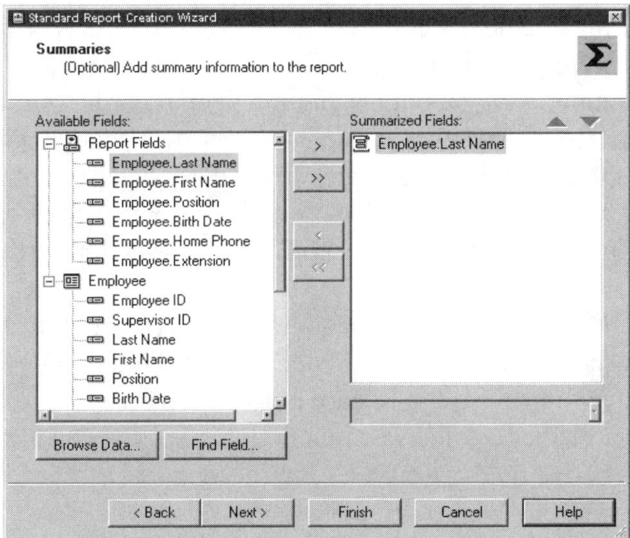

Figure 4-9. The Summaries screen (of the Standard Wizard)

Creating a summary field is one of those optional steps with the Report Wizards. Don't worry about creating any summary fields for now; we learn more about them in Chapter 9. Press the Next button to continue through the wizard.

Tip

When working through the screens within a Report Wizard, realize that you don't have to select information for every screen. Some of these screens contain the word *Optional* enclosed in parentheses. You can skip through optional screens by pressing the Next button (located at the bottom of each screen).

Filtering Records (Using the Wizards)

The Record Selection screen allows you to filter the fields that you selected earlier from the Fields screen. *Record selection* refers to the process of choosing the records to display within a report. In other words, record selection is a filtering process; you can have all records within a table display, or you can create a filter so that only a particular type of record displays.

For example, say you only want employee records from the Sales department to display within your report. Although an employee table contains employees from every department, a record selection statement will allow only employees from sales to display within your report. We discuss record selection further in Chapter 7.

The Record Selection screen allows you to control the records that your report should (or should not) display. Figure 4-10 (on the following page) displays the Record Selection screen.

You don't have to select records in this step; you can always filter your database fields after you're in the Report Design area. For now, just press the Next button.

Note

By not specifying any filters, you're stating that all records within your selected fields should display.

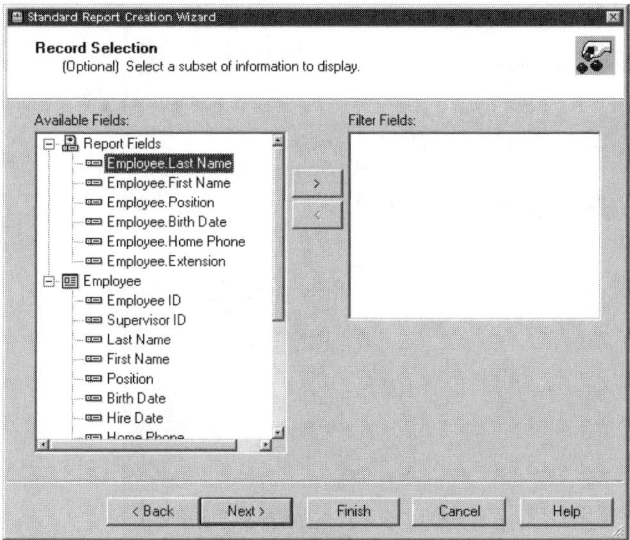

Figure 4-10. The Record Selection screen (of the Standard Wizard)

Applying Templates (Using the Wizards)

After you press the Next button, you'll find yourself at the Template screen. *Templates* are pre-existing formatting options available for your reports. Templates control the overall appearance of a report.

Just because you use a template doesn't mean that your report's appearance is set in stone. You can always customize a report further once you're at the Report Design area, as is the case with all the information you specify within the Report Wizards.

As you look through the Template screen, you'll notice several different options, as shown in Figure 4-11.

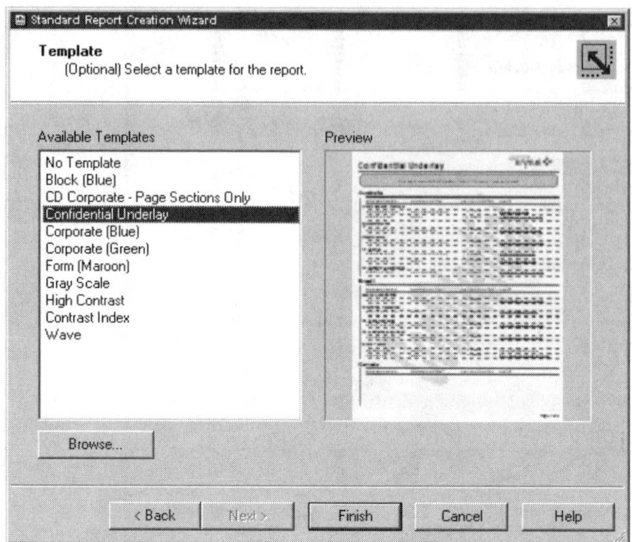

Figure 4-11. The Template screen (of the Standard Wizard)

To add a template using a wizard, perform the following steps at the Template screen:

1. **Select the Wave template.**
2. **Press the Finish button.**

   Figure 4-12 displays the results of your work.

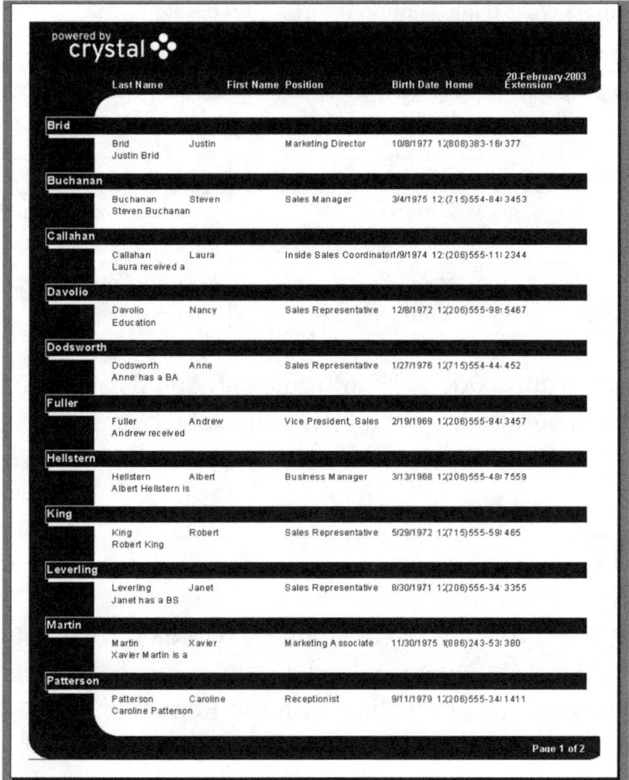

Figure 4-12. Using the Wave template

Once you've completed the screens within a wizard, you'll find yourself in the Report Design screen. You've seen this screen in Chapter 3, when you created a report from scratch.

Adding things like database fields, groups, and templates is easy with the wizards. But what if you finish with the wizard and realize that you want to add or modify the information defined from the wizard screens?

There's good news. You can access all the screens from the wizard in the Report Design area. The following table summarizes where to change various report wizard information from the Report Design area's menu bar.

Table 4-2. Report Wizard information (from within the Report Design area)

What to Change	Crystal Reports Tool	Location (from the menu bar)
The database selected	Database Expert	Database, Set Datasource Location
Database fields	Database Expert	Database, Database Expert
Groups	Group Expert	Report, Group Expert
Summaries	Summary dialog box	Insert, Summary
Filtering Records	Select Expert	Report, Select Expert
Report Template	Template Expert	Report, Template Expert

For now, save your work as EmpProfile.rpt. You'll return to this file in the next chapter when you address the subject of further defining the look and feel of your reports.

What's Next?

Crystal Reports provides the flexibility to develop what you want in a way that best suits your individual preference! You've already witnessed some of this flexibility with the Report Wizards.

Now that you're becoming more comfortable (and hopefully confident) with the process of report building, the next chapter explores some of Crystal Reports' tools for further formatting the look and feel of your reports. By the end of the next chapter, you should understand the basics of the Crystal Reports program and be ready to move on to the more advanced report-writing techniques covered in Part II.

Chapter 5

Report Formatting

So far in this book, you've worked with getting your reports up and running. You've learned to connect to a database and place database fields onto your report. With the knowledge you've gained, you can actually begin creating usable reports for you and your company.

The most important goal in report writing is the accuracy of the data that your report displays. However, almost equally as important is the presentation of your report. In order for your report users to make accurate business decisions, they must first be able to decipher the information within your report.

A report that contains all the correct information but has a format that is without any rhyme or reason isn't very useful to report users. An unformatted report is kind of the equivalent of searching for a needle in a haystack. You don't want your users scratching their heads, thinking to themselves, "What am I looking at?"

"Presentation of data" is known as report formatting. *Report formatting* is the specification of the visible properties of report objects. Some common examples of formatting are the specifying of a report object's font, color, and size.

In this chapter, we unleash the artist within as we explore some of Crystal Reports' formatting tools.

Changing Page Orientation

The first and foremost formatting decision that all report developers must make is whether a report should display in portrait (vertical) or landscape (horizontal) format. In other words, you must decide your page orientation. By default, Crystal Reports always prints in a portrait format.

Page orientation dictates how much information can display horizontally on a report page. Keep this in mind when deciding page orientation for your reports: A landscape format will allow you to fit more report objects on the report.

Try the following to change the page orientation of your report. You can create a new report and select any table you like for this exercise.

1. **Select File, Printer Setup from the menu bar.**

   A Print Setup dialog box displays, as shown in Figure 5-1.

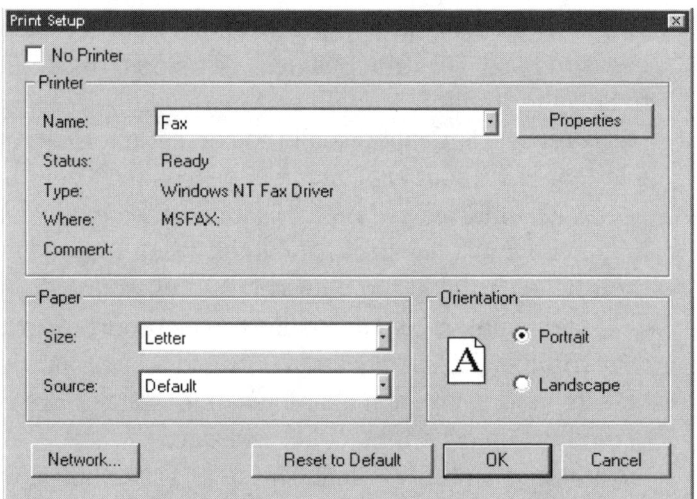

Figure 5-1. The Print Setup dialog box

2. **Select the Landscape or Portrait option button in the Orientation section.**
3. **Press the OK button to apply changes and return to the Report Design area.**

Your report's page print orientation is now changed. Changing the report layout is simple — even more so if you've used Microsoft products such as Word or Excel. The steps are identical.

Adding Text Objects

Once you've decided the orientation of your report page, it's time to focus on your report objects. You've spent the last two chapters adding database field objects to your reports. Let's explore another useful report object found in reports: the text object.

Text objects help describe information on your report and aid in improving presentation. Text objects don't pull anything from your database; essentially, text objects are labels for your report. A common use for a text object is as a title for your report.

To get an idea of how text objects work, let's continue with the report that you saved in the last chapter: EmpProfile.rpt. You can also pull up a copy of this report from the companion files (www.wordware.com/files/crystal).

Once you've pulled up this report and are looking at it in the Report Design area, perform the following steps:

1. **Select Insert, Text Object from the menu bar.**

   You'll notice a rectangular object frame appear at the tip of your cursor.

2. **Position the text object in the Report Header section.**

   Align the object frame to the 2.5" mark of this section.

3. **Release your mouse button to place the text object.**

   You should see a blinking cursor within this object frame. If not, click somewhere within the object frame to access the blinking cursor. A blinking cursor means that you may now begin typing text into the text object.

Note

The first time you add a text object, Crystal Reports automatically lets you begin adding text. After this initial placement, you'll need to click once within the text object to bring up the blinking cursor.

4. **Type the following into the object frame: Employee Profile Report.**

Once you've typed in the text, click outside the object frame. You're now out of the text-editing mode. Preview your report. Figure 5-2 displays the results of your work.

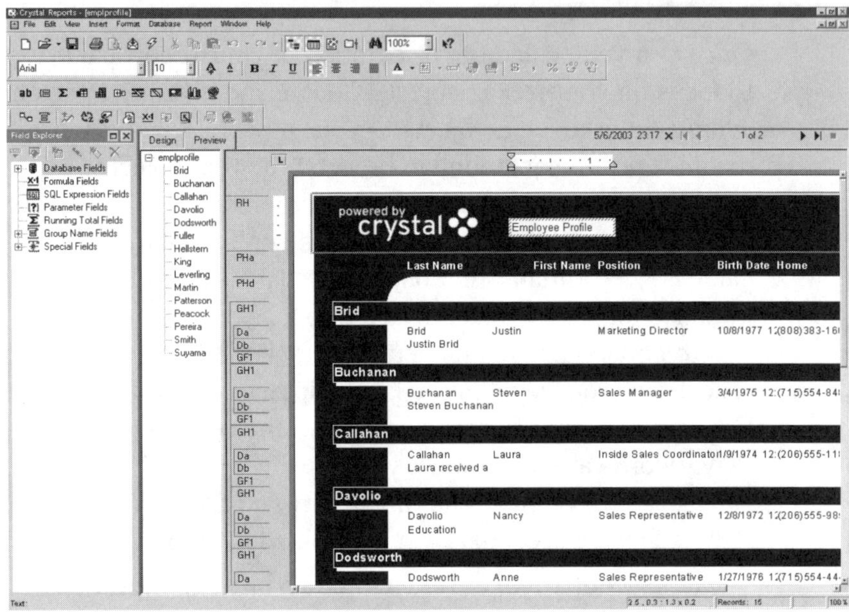

Figure 5-2. Adding a text object to your report

So, what do you think?

To be honest, you're probably thinking that the title isn't very impressive. The text object uses Crystal Reports' default settings, which makes the text appear in a black Arial font. This doesn't seem to work with your current report; the black is hard to see against the blue background.

Also, the title you typed in is too large for the text object. Instead of "Employee Profile Report," you're only seeing "Employee Profile."

Don't worry; these aren't huge problems. You just need to apply a little formatting to your report. The next sections look at formatting these and other report objects.

Formatting Report Objects with the Formatting Toolbar

As you learned in Chapter 2, Crystal Reports contains many easy-to-find formatting tools on the Formatting toolbar. These formatting tools are similar to many of those that you'll find in common Microsoft products, such as Word or Excel. If you've used either of those programs before, you'll have no problem with many of Crystal Reports' formatting tools.

Continue where you left off with the EmpProfile.rpt file. Try the following formatting exercise:

1. **Left-click once on the text object you just created.**
2. **Select the small arrow next to the Font Color icon.**

   This icon is located on the Standard toolbar. Once you select this small arrow, an options menu of colors displays, as shown in Figure 5-3.

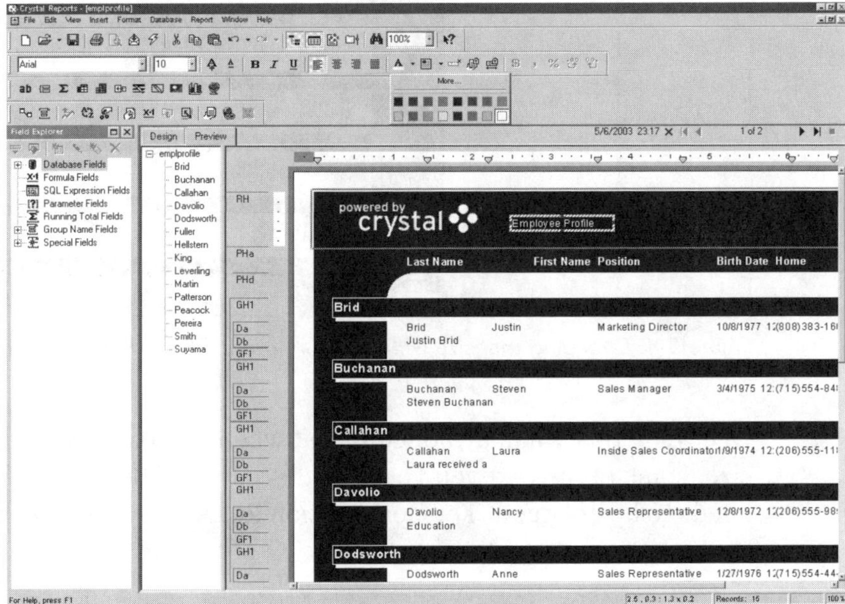

Figure 5-3. The Font Color options menu

3. **From this color options menu, select white.**

   You'll notice your text object displays now with a white font color.

4. **Press the Increase Font Size icon on the Standard toolbar four times.**

   You could also select the font size that you wish to increase your object to from the Font Size drop-down list, also located on the Standard toolbar.

   Figure 5-4 displays the results of your work.

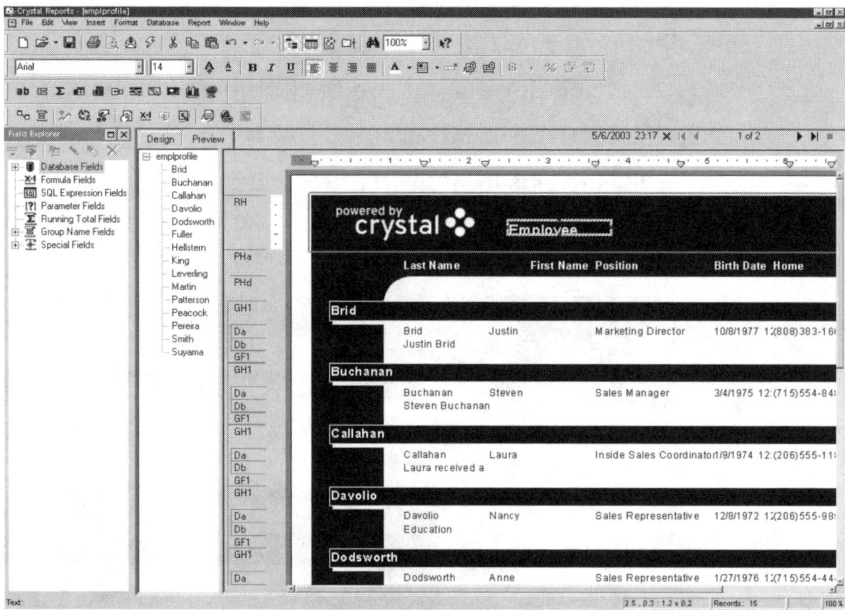

Figure 5-4. Changing font size with the Standard toolbar

One thing that you may notice is that when you increase the font size, some of the text you've created is cut off. The report object needs to be enlarged. The next section looks at correcting problems related to object size.

Resizing a Report Object

Resizing report objects is as easy as performing a drag-and-drop maneuver with your mouse. This maneuver may seem a little strange at first, but with some practice, you'll be resizing objects in no time.

The first thing you'll need to do is left-click on the object you wish to resize. For our purposes, left-click on the text object you've just created. You'll notice the selected object now contains four black squares. These squares are located at the center of each side of your report object, as shown in Figure 5-5.

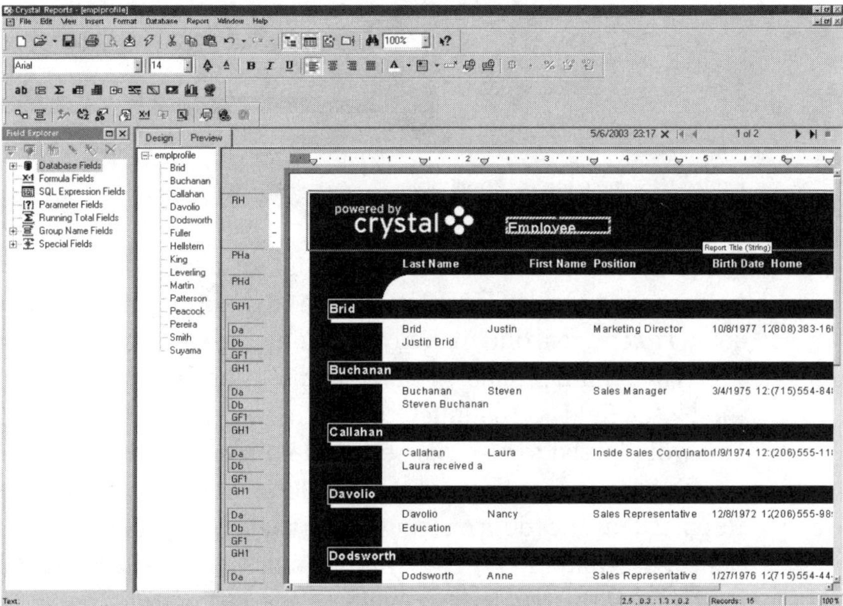

Figure 5-5. The resizing squares of a report object

Place your cursor over the right resizing square. Your cursor should turn into a double-headed arrow: ⟷

Once your cursor changes into the double-arrow, left-click and hold your mouse. Then, drag the text object to the 5.5" mark. Release your mouse. Go ahead and resize using the bottom resizing square on your text object. Voilà — you've just resized a report object. Figure 5-6 displays your work.

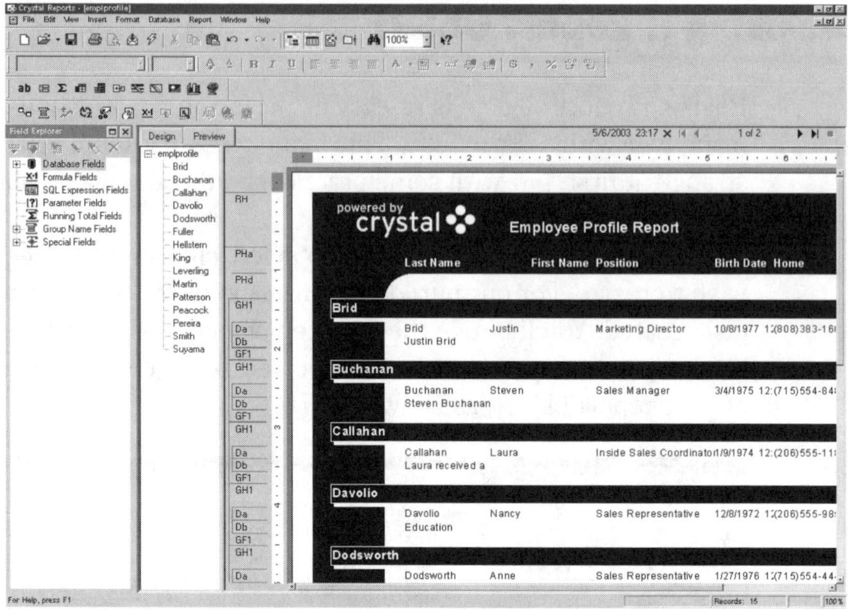

Figure 5-6. Resizing a report object

Looking at the EmpProfile.rpt, you might notice that the Notes field needs to be resized. Not all the text within this field is viewable. Try the resizing maneuver you just learned on the Notes field.

What you'll probably realize is that there's a lot of text within the Notes field — too much to handle by resizing the report object. You would need to also resize the Details b section.

To best deal with this problem, let's look at some of Crystal Reports' advanced formatting functionality. Crystal Reports contains a useful tool known as the Format Editor. The *Format Editor* contains all the options available on the Formatting toolbar, along with the more advanced formatting options available for a report object.

Working with the Format Editor

To access the Format Editor, right-click on the object you wish to format (for example, try right-clicking on the Notes field within your Details b section). An options menu displays. From this options menu, select Format Field. The Format Editor dialog box displays, as shown in Figure 5-7.

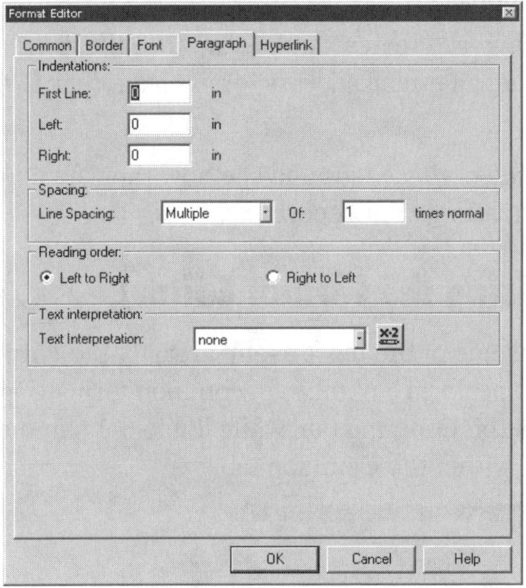

Figure 5-7. The Format Editor

Tip

If you're selecting a text object, the options menu will read Format Text instead of Format Field.

The Format Editor dialog box always contains a series of tabs, with some reporting objects containing more tabs than others. The tabs may differ slightly, depending on the reporting object you're formatting.

With database field objects (such as the Notes field), you'll notice a total of five tabs. These tabs are as follows:

- **Common:** This tab contains options that set properties such as suppressing an object or setting the horizontal alignment.

- **Border:** This tab contains options that control the formatting of borders, background, and drop shadows for an object. This is good to use when you want to highlight an object of importance in your report.
- **Font:** This tab contains options that control the look of an object's font, font size, or font style.
- **Paragraph:** This tab controls the formatting options for paragraphs in a text object.
- **Hyperlink:** This tab creates a link to another file, be it a web site, a data value, an e-mail address, or even another Crystal Reports file.

Let's jump into some of these tabs and see how their functionality can help you in formatting your reports.

Resize an Object (Using the Format Editor)

The Common tab is one of the most useful areas of the Format Editor, allowing you to perform a number of common formatting tasks. Figure 5-8 displays the Common tab, while Table 5-1 summarizes the fields available within the Common tab.

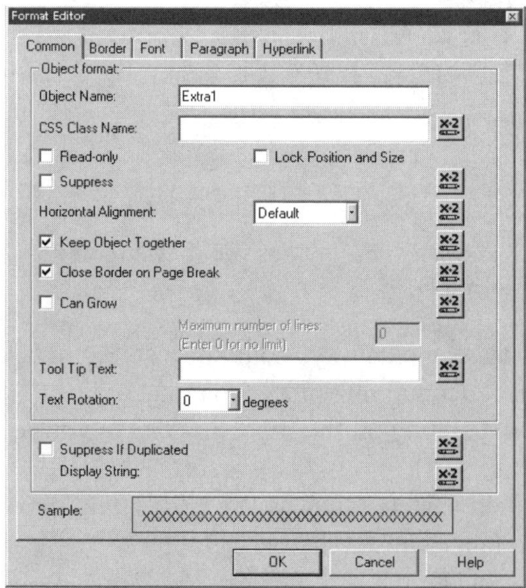

Figure 5-8. The Common tab of the Format Editor

Note

You may notice after certain fields the conditional formatting icon:

Conditional formatting is formatting that applies only under certain conditions. We explore conditional formatting in Chapter 10.

Table 5-1. The Format Editor's Common tab

Functionality	Description
Object Name	Defines a name for the report object you're formatting. A default name is created for each field within a report.
CSS Class Name	Defines a class name for the report object you're formatting. Class names are useful if you're using a Cascading Style Sheet (CSS) to indicate a unique style for the selected report object.
Read-only	Defines the report object as read-only so that the object cannot be formatted. If this option is selected, all other options within the Format Editor become inactive (as well as the formatting options available from the toolbars and shortcut menus).
Lock Position and Size	Defines the position of the report object so that the object cannot be moved. If this option is selected, the report object cannot be moved or resized.
Suppress	Defines whether a report object should be suppressed (in other words, the report object will not display within the Preview tab or when the report is printed).
Horizontal Alignment	Defines the horizontal alignment of a report object (for example: left, center, or right).
Keep Object Together	Defines that all report objects (within a given section) remain together on the same page. If there is not enough room to print these report objects on one page, Crystal Reports will move all report objects within that section to the next page. If the report objects within that given section are larger than a page, this property will not work.
Close Border on Page Break	If you define a report object to contain a border (available within the Border tab of the Format Editor), this option closes the border after each page, even if the report object is split over two pages.
Can Grow	Allows report objects to expand as necessary whenever the text within an object is larger than the object's frame.
Max Number of Lines	If the Can Grow check box is selected, this option allows you to define the maximum number of lines that Crystal Reports will expand an object frame. If you do not want a limit, enter a 0 (zero) in this field.

Functionality	Description
Tool Tip Text	This option is useful for reports that are viewed via a computer rather than printed. This option allows you to add text associated with a report object. This text displays when users leave their cursor over the report object for a few seconds. Tool Tip Text only displays within the Preview tab. In order for Tool Tip Text to display, go to File, Options. An Options dialog box displays. Make sure the Tool Tip check box is checked.
Text Rotation	Defines rotation options for the report object (for example, vertically aligning text).
Suppress If Duplicated	Defines the suppression of duplicate values on a report.
Display String	An advanced feature that allows you to define a formula to customize the formatting of a value. For example, if you wanted thousands to display as K, you could define that information in this area.
Sample	Displays a sample of the formatted object (if you add borders or boldfacing to the object, you will see these formatting actions represented in the Sample area).

To try your hand with the Common tab, let's use it to expand your report object frame. Perform the following steps. Make sure that you've accessed the Format Editor for the Notes field.

1. **Select the Common tab, and check the Can Grow check box.**

   This enables an object to expand so that all the information displays.

2. **Press OK on the Format Editor.**
3. **Resize the field by dragging the right resizing box to the 7.5" mark.**

Select the Preview tab (if you're not already there). In Figure 5-9, you'll see that the Details b section now expands to fit the Notes field.

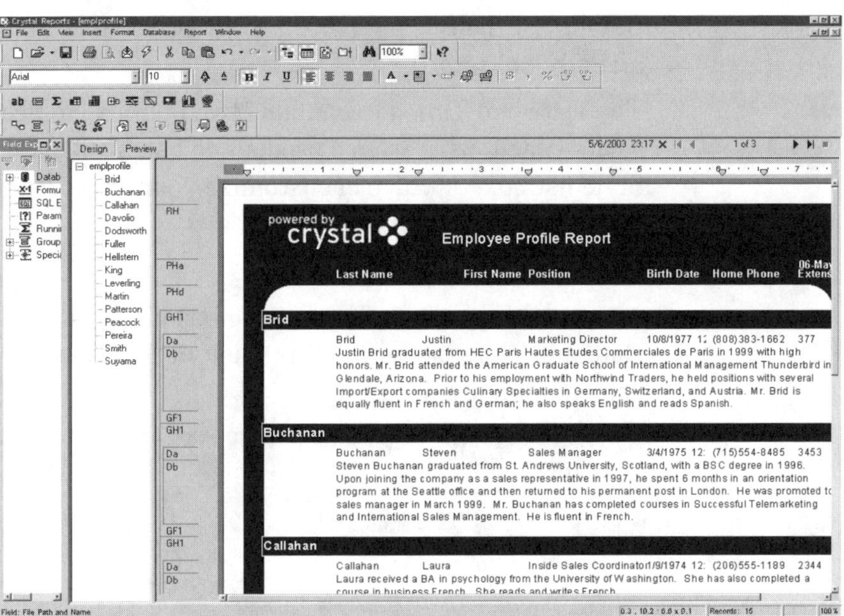

Figure 5-9. Using the Can Grow option to resize objects

Formatting Date Information

Take a look at the birth date information within this report. Notice that the birth date displays within a date/time format. You may need to resize the Birth Date field to see this.

Date information is often an area you'll need to clean up within your reports. Date information is often stored in a date/time format within databases. However, most reports usually only require the date. The Format Editor allows you to change the date/time format so that only the date displays.

In the report you've been working on in this chapter, try the following:

1. **Right-click on the Birth Date field (located within the Details a section.**

   An options menu displays.

2. **Select the Format Field option.**

   The Format Editor displays.

3. **Select the Date and Time tab (if this tab is not already selected).**

   The Date and Time tab contains two options. You can select a date/time format from a predefined list, available from the Style list box, or you can customize your own date/time format with the Customize button.

4. **Press the Customize button.**

   A Custom Style Date/Time dialog box displays. Select the Date and Time tab within this Custom Style dialog box, as shown in Figure 5-10.

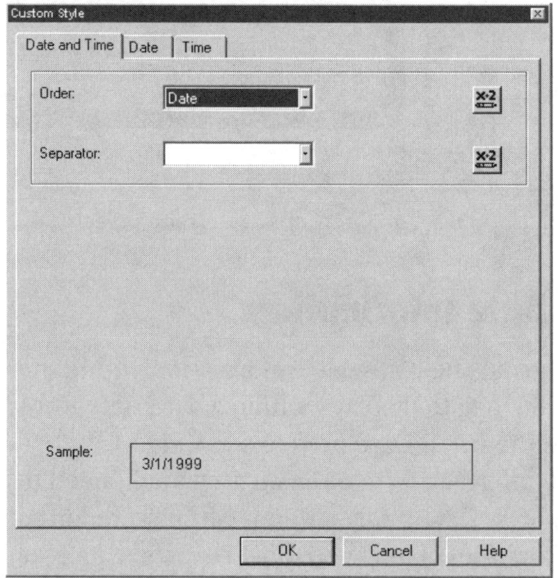

Figure 5-10. The Date and Time tab within the Custom Style dialog box

5. **In the Order drop-down field, select Date.**

   Notice the sample format at the bottom of this dialog box. This shows that only the date information will display within your report.

6. **Select the Date tab.**

This tab allows you to modify the format of the date information, if necessary. Feel free to experiment with this tab if you wish.

7. **Press the OK button on the Custom Style dialog box.**

   The Custom Style dialog box closes.

8. **Press the OK button on the Format Editor dialog box.**

   The Format Editor dialog box closes.

Preview your report. For some extra practice, try resizing and moving the Phone Number and Ext fields so that they display all information as necessary without overlap. Figure 5-11 displays what your report might look like.

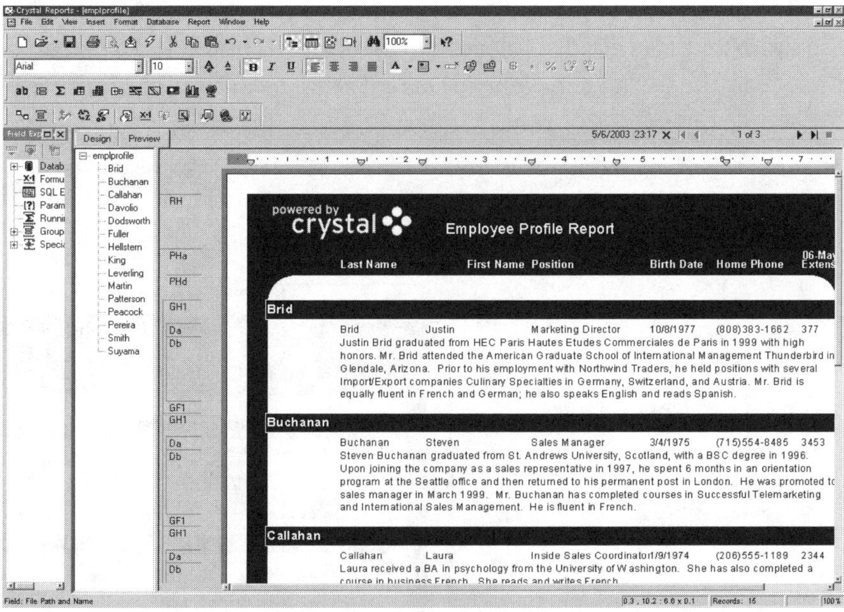

Figure 5-11. Formatting date information with the Format Editor

Adding Special Fields to Your Reports

When glancing through this report, you might notice a number of system-generated fields (such as page numbers or the location of the report file). These kinds of fields are entered automatically when you use Crystal Reports' templates. But what if you're creating your own report from scratch? How would you enter page numbers then?

The answer to that question is through system-generated data fields known as special fields. *Special fields* are not part of any database table.

Special fields are available from the Field Explorer, a tree view of various fields that you may add to your report. You first learned about the Field Explorer in Chapter 3. The Field Explorer is located to the left of the Report Design area, as shown in Figure 5-12.

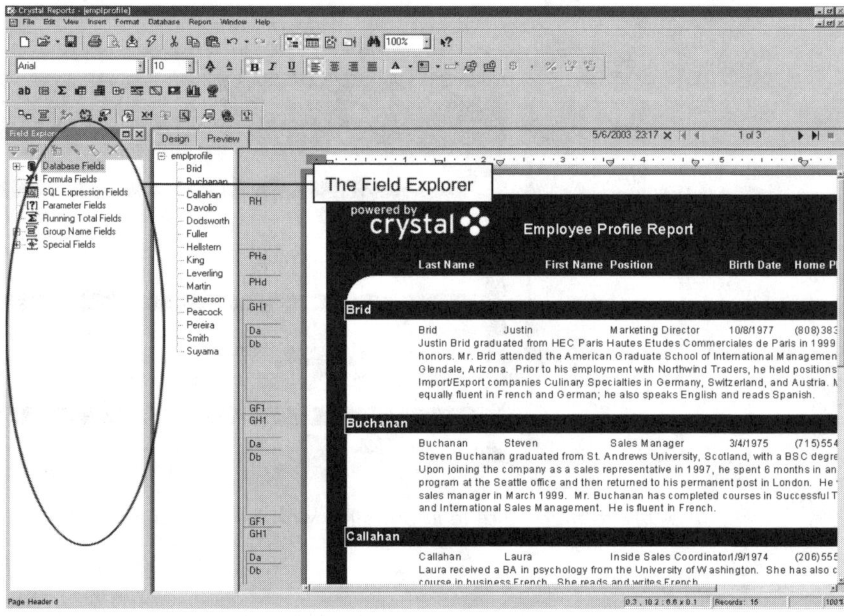

Figure 5-12. The Field Explorer

Tip

If the Field Explorer is not displayed, you may access it by selecting View, Field Explorer from the menu bar.

The following table summarizes the different special fields available within Crystal Reports.

Table 5-2. Special fields within Crystal Reports

Special Field	Description
Data Date	Displays the date the report data was last refreshed. This information is pulled from the system clock of the user's computer.
Data Time	Displays the time the report data was last refreshed. This information is pulled from the system clock of the user's computer.
File Author	Displays the name of the author of the report. This field pulls information from the Summary tab of the Document Properties dialog box. To access this dialog box, select File, Summary Info from the menu bar.
File Creation	Displays the date when the report was first created. This field pulls information from the Statistics tab of the Document Properties dialog box. To access this dialog box, select File, Summary Info from the menu bar.
File Path and Name	Displays the name of the file and where the file is located on a user's computer or network directory. This information is determined when a report is saved to a location.
Group Number	Displays a number (starting with 1) for each group in your report. You may place this special field only in the Group Header or Group Footer sections of your report.
Group Selection Formula	Allows you to insert a group selection formula field into your report. Group selection formulas allow you to filter the groups included within a report.
Modification Date	Displays the date the report was last modified. This information is determined from the user's system clock. Modification refers to any change to the report, followed by the report being printed. You do not need to save the report before printing for a new modification date to display.
Modification Time	Displays the time the report was last modified. This information is determined from the user's system clock. This field works in the same way as the Modification Date field.
Page N of M	Displays a page number for each page of the report (N) along with the total number of pages in the report (M). This number is generated when the report refreshes.
Page Number	Displays a page number for each page of the report. This number is generated when the report refreshes.
Print Date	Displays the date the report was printed. This information is pulled from the system clock of the user's computer.
Print Time	Displays the time the report was printed. This information is pulled from the system clock of the user's computer.
Record Number	Displays a number (starting with 1) for each record printed within the Details section of the report.

Special Field	Description
Record Selection Formula	Displays a record selection formula field in your report. Record selection formulas allow you to filter the records included within a report.
Report Comments	Displays comments about the report. This field pulls information from the Summary tab of the Document Properties dialog box. To access this dialog box, select File, Summary Info from the menu bar.
Report Title	Displays a title for the report. This field pulls information from the Summary tab of the Document Properties dialog box. To access this dialog box, select File, Summary Info from the menu bar.
Total Page Count	Displays the total number of pages in the report. This number is generated when the report refreshes.

As you can see from Table 5-2, special fields contain a lot of useful information that you might want incorporated into your reports.

Tip

At the very least, always make it a habit to include page numbers in your reports. There's nothing more aggravating to those reading reports than trying to figure out which page goes where. Page numbers eliminate this unnecessary headache.

Save the new work that you've done to this report, renaming this new version as EmpProfile2.rpt.

What's Next?

This chapter concludes the end of Part I. So far, you have learned the general workings of Crystal Reports and report writing and have enough tools in your arsenal to begin writing reports. Try your newfound skills on the examples provided on the next couple of pages before moving on to Part II of this book. You can find samples of the example reports in the companion files (www.wordware.com/files/crystal).

Part I Exercises

Mailing Label Report

See the companion files (www.wordware.com/files/crystal) for an example of this report. Create this report with the Mailing Labels Report Creation Wizard and the xtreme.mdb database.

Table(s)	Fields
Customer	Customer Name
	Address 1
	Address 2
	City
	Postal Code
	Country

When you get to the Label screen, choose User-Defined Label. In the Label Size section, define your labels with Width = 2 and Height = 2. Leave all other options as default. Figure P1-1 displays how your screen should look.

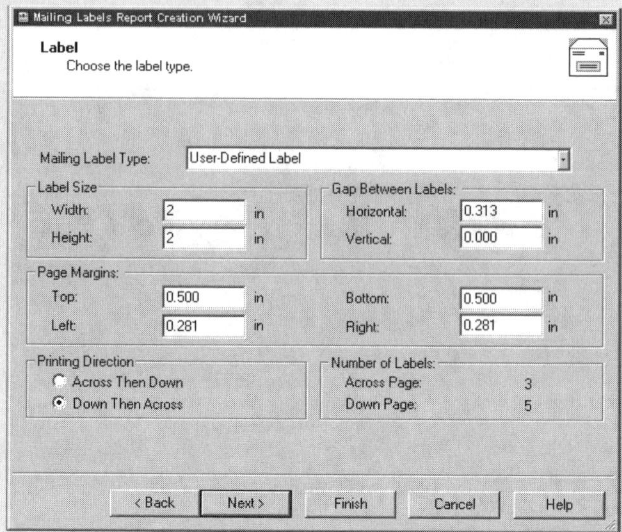

Figure P1-1. The Label screen of the Mailing Labels Report Ceation Wizard

Press the Finish button in the Mailing Labels Report Creation Wizard. The Report Design area displays.

Once in the Report Design area, perform the following:

1. **Right-click in the Details a section.**

   An options menu displays.

2. **Select the Insert Section Below option.**

   A new section is created.

3. **Move the Customer Name field from the Details a section to the Details b section.**

4. **Holding down the Ctrl key, left-click all report objects in the Details a through Details g sections.**

   All objects should be selected.

5. **With all objects selected, move them to the .5" mark.**

   Figure P1-2 displays the results of your work so far.

6. **Select Insert, Box from the menu bar.**

   Your cursor turns into a pencil.

7. **Draw a rectangle from the 0" mark to the .5" mark.**

8. **Right-click on your rectangle.**

   An options menu displays.

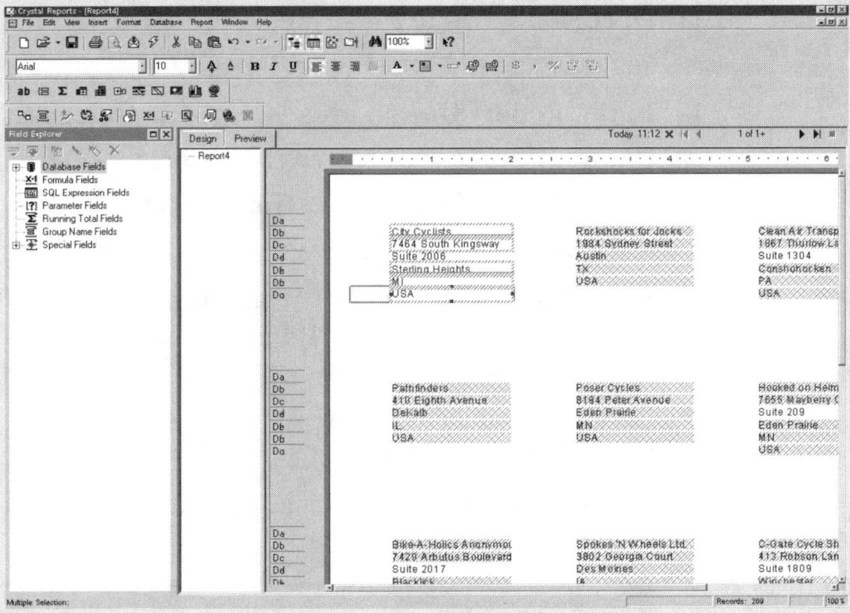

Figure P1-2. Moving all report objects at once

9. **Select the Format Box option.**

   The Format Editor displays.

10. **In the Format Editor, check the Color check box (located in the Fill section), and select Navy from the drop-down box next to this check box.**

    Your screen should look like Figure P1-3.

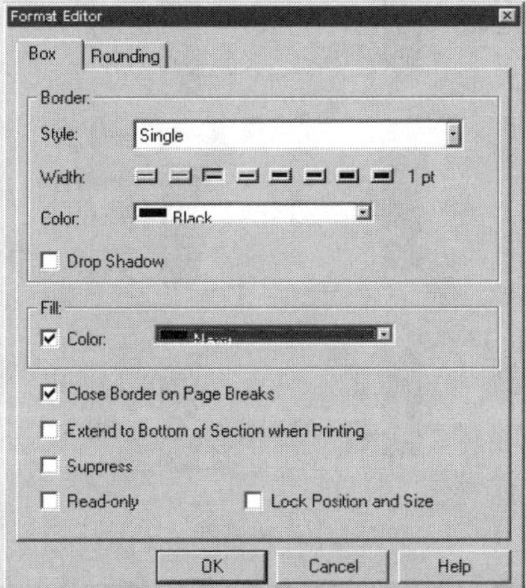

Figure P1-3. Filling in a box using the Format Editor

11. **Once you've done these steps, press the OK button.**

    You're returned to the Report Design area.

12. **In the Report Design area, select the Design tab.**
13. **Use your cursor to stretch the Details a section.**
14. **Select Insert, Text Object from the menu bar.**

    A text object is attached to your cursor.

15. **Place this text object in the middle of the Details a section. Then, press the Bold button in the Formatting toolbar.**

    Once you've done these steps, type the following into the text object: **Attn: Receiving.**

    Select the Preview tab. The final result of your work should look like Figure P1-4.

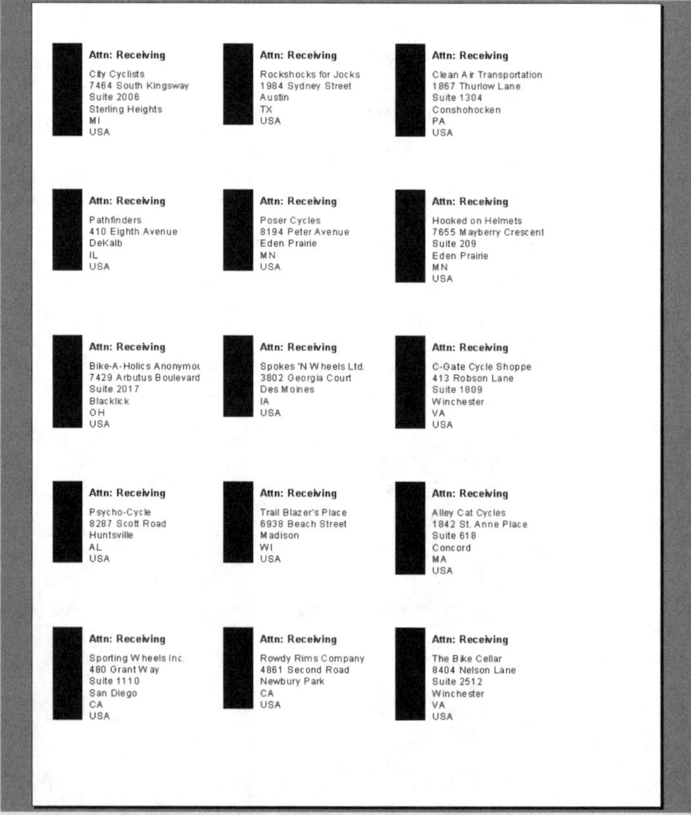

Figure P1-4. A mailing label report

Form Letter Report

See the companion files for an example of this report. Create this report starting as a blank report with the xtreme.mdb database.

Table(s)	Fields
Employee	Employee Name

Once in the Report Design area, perform the following steps:

1. **From the menu bar, select Insert, Picture.**
2. **Select the xtreme.bmp graphic from the following location: C:\Program Files\Crystal Decisions\Crystal Reports 9\Samples\En\Databases.**
3. **Place the xtreme.bmp graphic at the 0" mark in the Page Header section.**
4. **Right-click on the Report Header section.**

   An options menu displays.
5. **Select Suppress (No Drill-Down) from the menu.**

   Your screen should look like Figure P1-5.

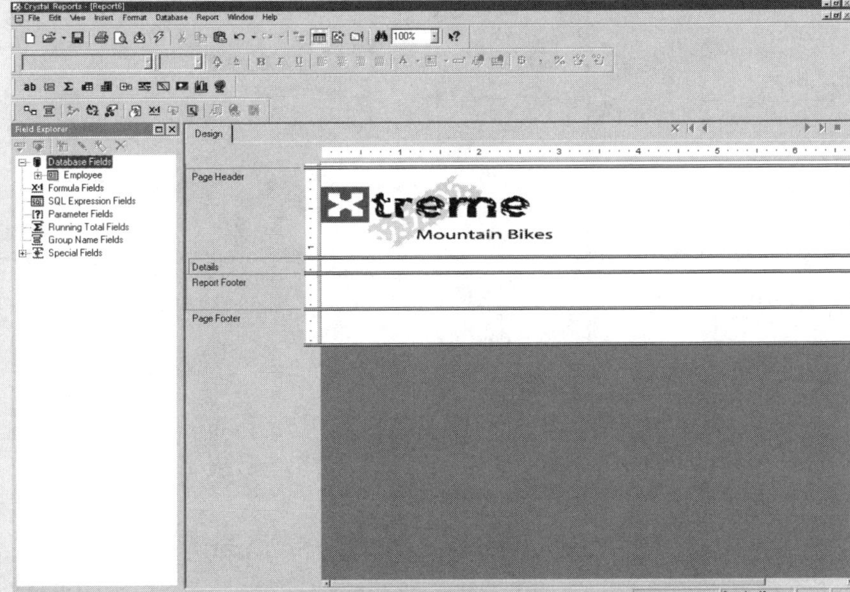

Figure P1-5. Adding a graphic to a report

6. **From the menu bar, select Insert, Text Object.**

   Place this text object in the Details section, at the 0" mark.

7. **With this text object selected, type in the following: Dear.**

   Shrink down this text object.

8. **From the Field Explorer, expand the Database Fields node.**

   The Employee table displays.

9. **Expand the Employee table node. Add the First Name field after the Dear text object.**

10. **Add the First Name field to the Details section. Delete the First Name header in the Page Header section.**

    Your screen should look like Figure P1-6.

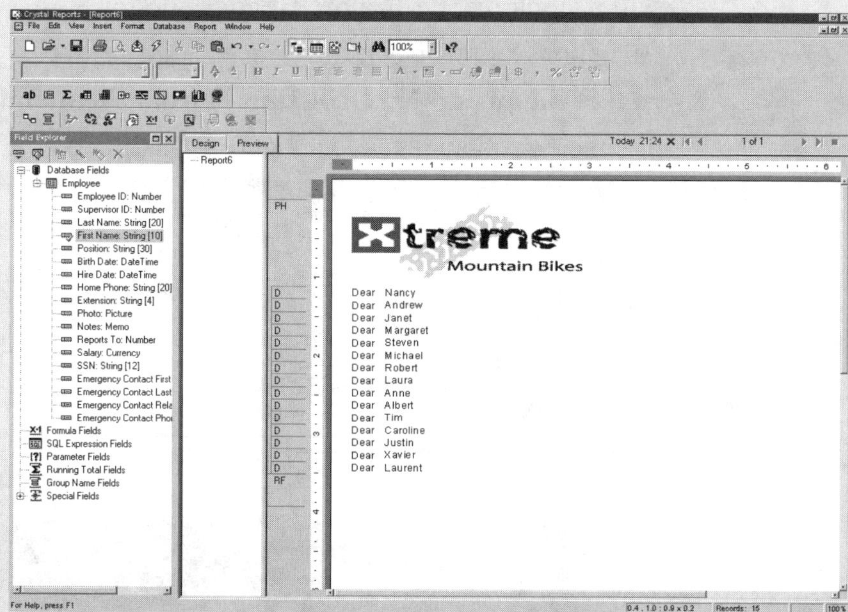

Figure P1-6. Adding a first name greeting to your report

11. **Right-click in the Details section.**

    An options menu displays.

12. **From the options menu, select the Section Expert option.**

    The Section Expert dialog box displays.

13. **In the Section Expert, check the New Page After check box.**

    This creates a separate page for each employee record. Your screen should look like P1-7.

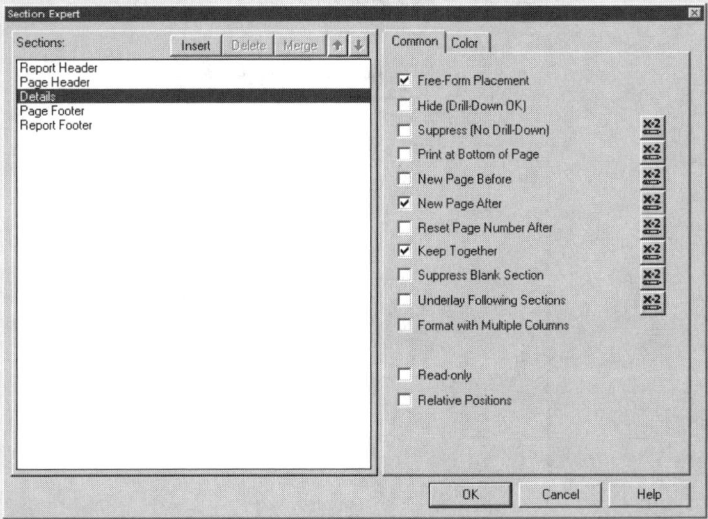

Figure P1-7. Defining each record to display as a separate page with the Section Expert

14. **Press the OK button in the Section Expert dialog box.**

    You're returned to the Report Design area.

15. **Select the Design tab.**
16. **Right-click in the Details section.**

    An options menu displays.

17. **From the options menu, select the Insert Section Below option.**

    A Details b section is created and the original Details section is now named Details a. Stretch the Details b section to make room.

18. **From the menu bar, select Insert, Text Object.**

Place this object within the Details b section. You can place this object at the 0" mark. Stretch the object to the 5.5" mark. Also, increase the height of this object.

19. **Type the letter's text into the text object.**

    Select the Preview tab. The final result of your work should look like Figure P1-8.

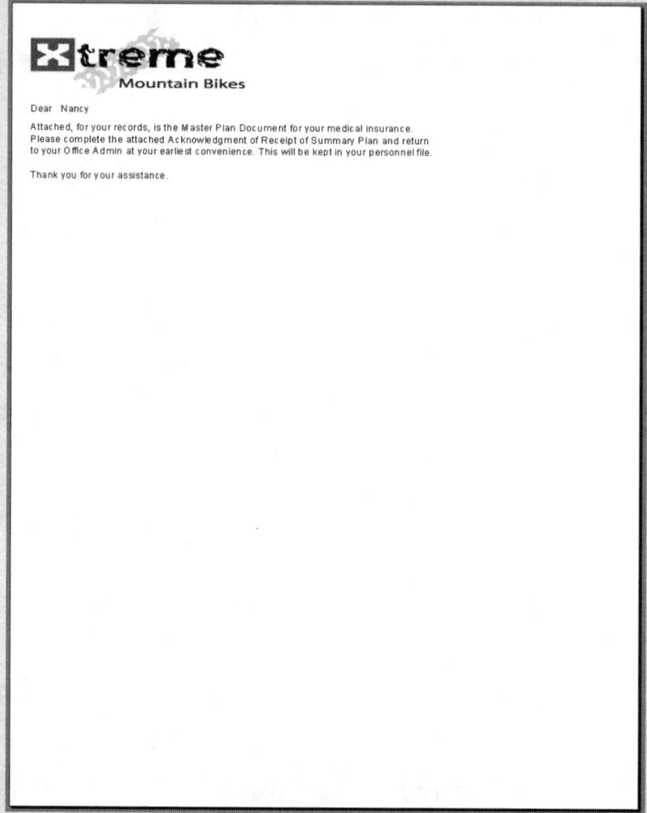

Xtreme
Mountain Bikes

Dear Nancy

Attached, for your records, is the Master Plan Document for your medical insurance.
Please complete the attached Acknowledgment of Receipt of Summary Plan and return
to your Office Admin at your earliest convenience. This will be kept in your personnel file.

Thank you for your assistance.

Figure P1-8. A form letter report

Part II

Working with Records

Chapter 6

Linking Tables

In Chapter 1 you learned how Crystal Reports works, often using databases as the reporting data source. In your reporting work, you'll probably find yourself using databases 99 percent of the time to create reports. Because of the frequency of which you'll use databases for reports, it's beneficial to explore databases in greater detail.

Most databases that you'll encounter are relational databases. Relational databases are modeled so that repetitive database information is separated into multiple tables. The reasons for this are to improve database efficiency and ease database maintenance.

Up to this point, you've created reports based on just one database table. However, most of the time, your reports will require two (and possibly more) database tables. In this chapter, we learn why most databases use multiple tables. We also discuss how to successfully link multiple tables for your reporting needs.

Why Multiple Tables?

As stated in the introductory paragraphs, a relational database separates information into multiple tables.

"So why break database information into multiple tables?" you might ask. "Why not contain everything in one table, like a spreadsheet? Isn't that a lot less complicated?"

To understand why relational databases use multiple tables, consider the following Employee table (see Table 6-1).

Table 6-1. An Employee table (without the relational model)

ID	Name	DeptID	DeptName	Loc
6000	Anderson	10	IT	Houston
6001	Andrzejewski	20	Accounting	Dallas
6002	Sims	30	Sales	Austin
6003	Burris	20	Accounting	Dallas
6004	Tull	10	IT	Houston
6005	Jensen	30	Sales	Austin

In Table 6-1, notice that there are the following:

- Six employee records
- Two employee records for each department

Looking at this table, you might notice a lot of duplicated information. For example, there is duplicate information in the Dept Name and Loc fields.

So what's so bad about duplicate information?

Well, for one, a lot of unnecessary memory is used because of this duplicate information. In Table 6-1, IT, Accounting, Sales, Plano, Austin, and Dallas are all records used twice. Six extra records might waste about 28 bytes on a database server. Now that doesn't seem so bad, does it?

But what if you have 5,000 employee records stored within this Employee table? Before you know it, your duplicate records might add up to about 13MB of wasted memory. Or worse.

Note

A byte is an abbreviation for *binary term*, which is a unit of storage capable of holding a single character. On almost all modern computers, a byte is equal to 8 bits.

A bit is an abbreviation for *binary digit* and is the smallest unit of information on a computer. A single bit can hold only one of two values: 0 or 1. Meaningful information (such as a single character) is obtained by combining consecutive bits into larger units.

Understanding the Relational Model

If you split the data shown in Table 6-1 into two different tables (for example, a Department *and* an Employee table), you'll improve the efficiency and maintainability of your database. Tables 6-2 and 6-3 summarize how a database might separate the information from Table 6-1 into two separate tables.

Table 6-2. An Employee table (within the relational model)

ID	Name	DeptID
6000	Anderson	10
6001	Andrzejewski	20
6002	Sims	30
6003	Burris	20
6004	Tull	10
6005	Jensen	30

Table 6-3. A Department table (within the relational model)

DeptID	DeptName	Loc
10	IT	Houston
20	Accounting	Dallas
30	Sales	Austin

In the world of relational databases, these multiple tables are joined (or linked) through a common field. This common field must contain identical information for both tables. In Tables 6-2 and 6-3, this common field is DeptID.

The following advantages occur by separating data into multiple tables:

- Relational databases are easier to maintain. For example, if a particular department (say, the Accounting department) moves from Dallas to Houston, all you would have to do is change one city in the Department table (you would change the Loc field for DeptID 20 to Houston).

  In a table that does not follow the relational model (such as the one displayed in Table 6-1), you would have to update all the individual employee records for those who worked in that department.

- Relational databases remove duplicate information (also known as *data redundancy*). Instead of duplicating the department name and location for every employee record, the new tables display the department name and location once. This conserves the server memory that a database uses.

The xtreme.mdb database is based on the relational model. Thus, you'll find multiple tables within this database, all linked together to reduce data redundancy. This method of organizing data in the least redundant manner is better known as *database normalization.*

Linking Tables

As you may already be deducing, there's a hard truth about report writing. Mainly, the data you need for your reports is probably not available within a single table, but rather a number of tables. When you correctly link two or more tables together, all the data in those tables is available for your reporting purposes. The link matches up the records from one database table with those from one or more other database tables.

And how does one know which tables and fields to link within a database? That's where your database documentation comes in.

Understanding Database Documentation

To successfully link tables together, you need to become familiar with your database and how your database accurately links tables and fields. You need to familiarize yourself with the relationships within your database.

The best place to find this information is to obtain two invaluable reference materials that are provided (usually) with every database system. These reference documents are:

- A data dictionary
- An entity-relationship diagram (also known as an ERD)

Your database administrator should know the locations of these documents for your system. Let's look briefly at how to understand and use these types of reference material.

What Is a Data Dictionary?

A *data dictionary* is a file that displays the basic organization of a database. In other words, a data dictionary tells you the relationships between the tables of a database. Data dictionaries usually contain information such as:

- All tables in the database
- The number of records in each table
- The data type of each field in the tables

Data dictionaries are usually text, Word, HTML, Excel, or PDF files and usually list information in alphabetical order.

Your system administrator should have a copy of the data dictionary. Most DBMSs provide a data dictionary upon delivery or installation of the system.

Note

Data dictionaries do not contain actual data from the database. A data dictionary's purpose is to provide information to aid in managing a database (such as understanding the relationships of database fields).

Let's take a look at the type of information contained in data dictionaries and how to decipher this information. The following looks at information from the xtreme.mdb data dictionary.

Tip

Appendix B, "The Xtreme.mdb Data Dictionary," contains a complete data dictionary of this database.

Tables 6-4 and 6-5 display information about the Customer and Orders tables, as found in a data dictionary. Table 6-4 pertains to the global customers of Xtreme Mountain Bikes, and Table 6-5 contains customer order information.

Table 6-4. The Customer table information (found within a data dictionary)

Field Name	Data Type	Field Size/ Format	Description
Customer ID	Number	Long Integer	Customer unique identification number.

Field Name	Data Type	Field Size/ Format	Description
Customer Credit ID	Number	Long Integer	Customer unique credit identification number.
Customer Name	Text	40	Name of the customer.
Contact First Name	Text	30	First name of the contact individual.
Contact Last Name	Text	30	Last name of the contact individual.
Contact Title	Text	5	Title of the contact individual.
Contact Position	Text	30	Position of the contact individual.
Last Year's Sales	Currency	Currency	Last year's total sales for the customer.
Address1	Text	60	The primary street address information for the customer.
Address2	Text	20	A line for secondary address information for the customer.
City	Text	20	The city of the customer's address.
Region	Text	30	The region with which the customer is associated.
Country	Text	30	The country of the cus-tomer's address.
Postal Code	Text	10	The postal code of the cus-tomer's address.
E-mail	Text	50	The customer's contact e-mail address.
Web Site	Text	50	The customer's web site.
Phone	Text	20	The customer's phone number.
Fax	Text	20	The customer's fax number.

Table 6-5. The Orders table information (found within a data dictionary)

Field Name	Data Type	Length	Description
Order ID	AutoNumber	Long Integer	Unique identification number assigned to each order.
Order Amount	Currency	Currency	Total amount of the order.
Customer ID	Number	Long Integer	Customer unique identifi-cation number.

Field Name	Data Type	Length	Description
Employee ID	Number	Long Integer	Employee unique identification number.
Order Date	Date/Time	General Date (MM/DD/YYYY HH:MM:SS AM/PM)	Date on which order was placed.
Required Date	Date/Time	Short Date (MM/DD/YYYY)	Date on which order is required to be received.
Ship Date	Date/Time	General Date (MM/DD/YYYY HH:MM:SS AM/PM)	Date on which order was shipped.
Courier Web Site	Hyperlink	h"ttp"://www. "up"s\.c\om	The courier's web site address.
Ship Via	Text	20	Comment regarding how product was shipped.
Shipped	Logical	Yes/No	Boolean that states "yes" or "no" to whether the product was shipped.
PO#	Text	50	The purchase order number.
Payment Received	Logical	Yes/No	Boolean that states "yes" or "no" to whether payment was received for the order.

Data dictionaries provide a lot of good information and are especially informative in looking at the detailed structure of a database.

In looking at these two tables, you might notice the Customer ID field within both. Data dictionaries are useful in finding common fields within different database tables.

However, as useful as a data dictionary might be, there is another type of file that better provides information about the relationship between tables. This type of file is known as an entity-relationship diagram (ERD).

ERDs are also usually provided with your database system. Check with your system administrator on obtaining a copy of your system's ERD.

Tip

Most databases (such as Access, Oracle, SQL Server) contain tools that can generate an ERD for you.

What Is an Entity-Relationship Diagram?

An *entity-relationship diagram (ERD)* is a graphical representation of the entities and the relationships between entities of a database. You're probably asking, "What are 'entities' and 'relationships'?" Let's break that definition down a little:

- An *entity* is the database object. In an ERD, entities are represented by a rectangle. For example, a database table is an entity.
- A *relationship* is the interaction between the entities or how the entities are connected. In an ERD, relationships are represented by lines, which join the entities.

Figure 6-1 displays an ERD for the xtreme.mdb database.

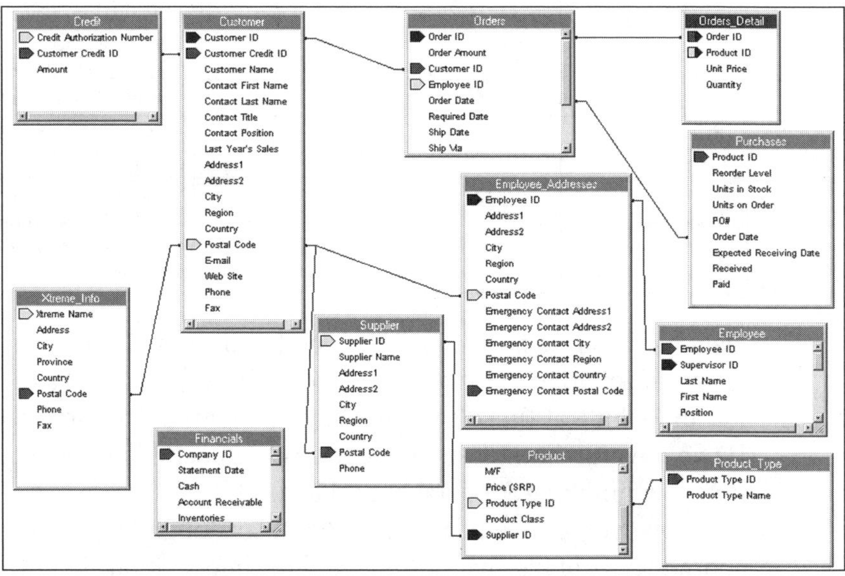

Figure 6-1. The ERD for the xtreme.mdb database

Understanding Table Relationships

Looking at the ERD in Figure 6-1, you may notice the database tables linked together by lines. In an ERD, the lines describe the matching fields within two tables. The lines also describe the type of relationship between two tables.

Although the xtreme.mdb file only uses one type of relationship, there are actually four types of relationships that may exist between database objects. These four types of relationships, known in database terminology as join types, define how two database objects match together. They are summarized in Table 6-6.

Table 6-6. The four join types

Join Type	Description
Inner	The most common type of join (also known as a *one-to-one* relationship). An inner join designates that a record in the parent table (the table you're linking from) is related to one and only one record in the child table (the table you're linking to). For example, you can use an inner join to view all customers and the orders placed. Only customers with placed orders will display within the report.
Left outer	A left outer join (also known as a *one-to-many* relationship) includes all records where the linked field value in both tables is an exact match (this being the same as an inner join). However, a left outer join also includes a row for every record in the primary (left) table for which the linked field value has no match in the secondary (right) table. For example, you can use a left outer join to view all customers and the orders they have placed. The report will display the customers with placed orders (as was the case with the inner join). However, you will also see a row of records for every customer who has not placed an order.
Right outer	A right outer join (also known as a *one-to-many* relationship) includes all the records where the linked field value in both tables is an exact match (this being the same as an inner join). However, a right outer join also includes a row for every record in the secondary (right) table for which the linked field value has no match in the primary (left) table. For example, you can use a right outer join to view all customers and the orders they have placed. The report will display the customers with placed orders (as was the case with the inner join). However, you will also see a row of records for every order without a customer.
Full outer	A full outer join (also known as a *many-to-many* relationship) includes all records in your linked tables. The result set includes all the records in which the linked field value in both tables is an exact match (this being the same as an inner join). It also includes a row for every record in the primary (left) table for which the linked field value has no match in the secondary (right) table and a row for every record in the secondary (right) table for which the linked field value has no match in the primary (left) table.

Note

In an ERD, a single line indicates a one-to-one relationship (as is the case in the xtreme.mdb ERD). A crow's foot (not displayed in the xtreme.mdb ERD) indicates a many (as in one-to-many or many-to-many relationship).

A crow's foot looks like this: /|\

Luckily for us, report writing does not involve designing relationships. Some poor database designer has already gone through the trouble of defining these table relationships.

Most databases utilize an inner (or one-to-one) join type, which is defined by the database designer when the database is first created. An inner join type means that two tables contain referential integrity.

Now that you're armed with some knowledge on database relationships, let's put this new-found knowledge to work by creating a report that utilizes two or more tables. Crystal Reports makes linking tables a breeze through the use of the Database Expert.

Working with Links in Crystal Reports

With all the background information in this chapter, you may worry that linking multiple tables is difficult. Actually, once you understand the relationships between your database tables, Crystal Reports makes the process of linking them together relatively easy.

In Crystal Reports, you link multiple tables together using a tool that you explored earlier in Chapter 2. This tool is none other than the Database Expert.

To get a feel for writing multi-tabled reports, let's create a product inventory report. To create such a report, you'll need to select a few tables from the xtreme.mdb database and then successfully link the matching fields within these tables.

To begin, start Crystal Reports and create a new blank report. Use the xtreme.mdb file as your data source. Once you're in the Database Expert, perform the following steps:

1. **Double-click the Tables node of the xtreme.mdb connection.**

2. **Add the Product, Product_Type, and Supplier tables.**

   Click the Add (>) button to move these tables to the Selected Tables list box. Once you add these three tables, you see two tabs display at the top of the Database Expert: the Data tab and the Links tab.

   The Data tab enables you to define your data source connection, whereas the Links tab enables you to define how your tables link together. Your screen should look like Figure 6-2.

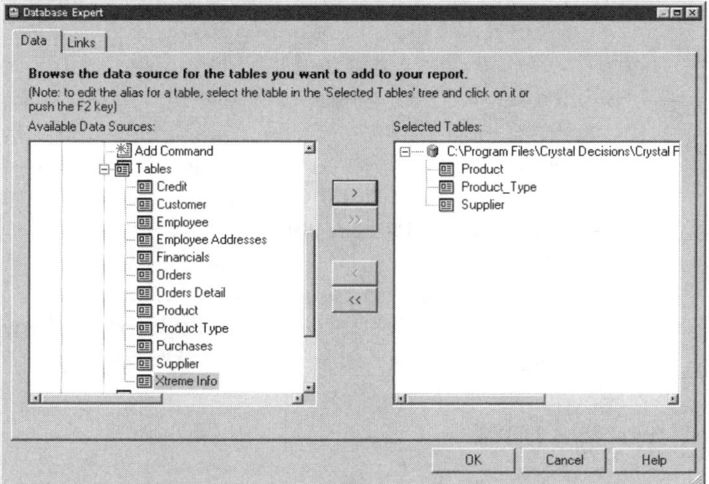

Figure 6-2. The Database Expert with the Data and Links tabs available

3. **Select the Links tab.**

By default, Crystal Reports creates links based on similar field names (a process known as Smart Linking).

The Smart Linking Feature

In this example, both the Product and Product Type tables have a Product Type ID, thus Crystal Reports' Smart Linking feature is applied. The Smart Linking feature automatically selects links for your tables, based on the following criteria:

- The field names are the same
- The field's data types are identical

- The field lengths are the same size (in the case of string fields)

The Smart Linking feature is a useful tool. However, you should still check with your database documentation to ensure that Crystal Reports has linked your tables correctly. Crystal Reports doesn't always guess correctly on how tables should link together.

Caution

As an example of how Crystal Reports might incorrectly smart link two tables together, consider a report that contains both Employee and Customer tables that might both include fields named Address, City, and State. These fields might very well have the same data types and field lengths in both tables. As a result, the Smart Linking feature would attempt to link the tables using these three fields.

The problem with these links is that just because the field names and data types are the same, it doesn't mean the fields are related. An employee's address is not the same as a customer's address.

Don't assume that the Smart Linking feature always links your reporting tables correctly. Make it a habit to always double-check how Crystal Reports links your tables together.

Removing Links

If for some reason you don't like the way Crystal Reports linked your database objects together, you can clear the links. To clear all links, perform the following steps:

1. **Press the Clear Links button.**
2. **A message box displays.**

   The message box asks if you're sure you want to remove all links.
3. **Press the Yes button on the message box.**

   You'll notice all links removed from your tables, as shown in Figure 6-3.

   When you're satisfied with the results, press the OK button. The links are now officially removed from your report.

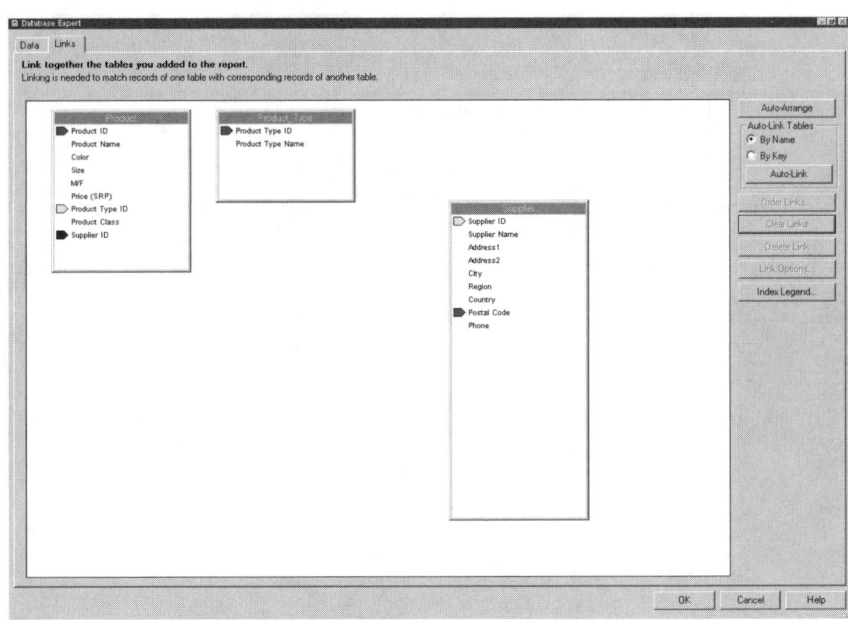

Figure 6-3. Clearing all links within the Database Expert

Of course, Crystal Reports also allows you to delete one link at a time, rather than removing all links at once. To delete one link at a time, perform the following steps:

1. **Press the Auto-Link button to have Crystal Reports smart link your tables.**
2. **Left-click on the link that joins the two Supplier ID fields.**

   This link joins the Product and Supplier tables. Notice that the Delete Link button now becomes active.
3. **Press the Delete Link button.**

   You'll notice only the Supplier ID link is removed, as shown in Figure 6-4.

Tip

You can also delete a single link by left-clicking on the link and then pressing the Delete key on your keyboard.

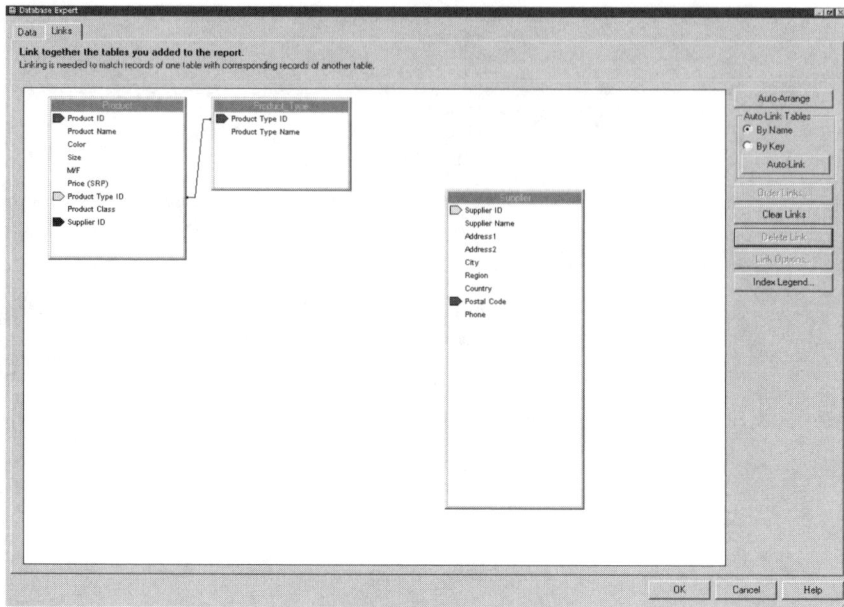

Figure 6-4. Deleting a single link within the Database Expert

Adding Links

While the Smart Linking feature is helpful, you can also add and remove links manually. Linking tables together in Crystal Reports is as easy as drawing a line with your mouse. To link two tables together, perform the following steps:

1. **Left-click and hold your cursor on the Supplier ID field.**

   This field is located in the Product table.

2. **Drag your mouse to the other Supplier ID field.**

   This field is located in the Supplier table. Notice a link being created as you drag your mouse.

3. **After you've connected these two fields, release the left mouse button.**

   Figure 6-5 displays the results of your work.

When you're satisfied with the results, press the OK button. The links are now officially added to your report.

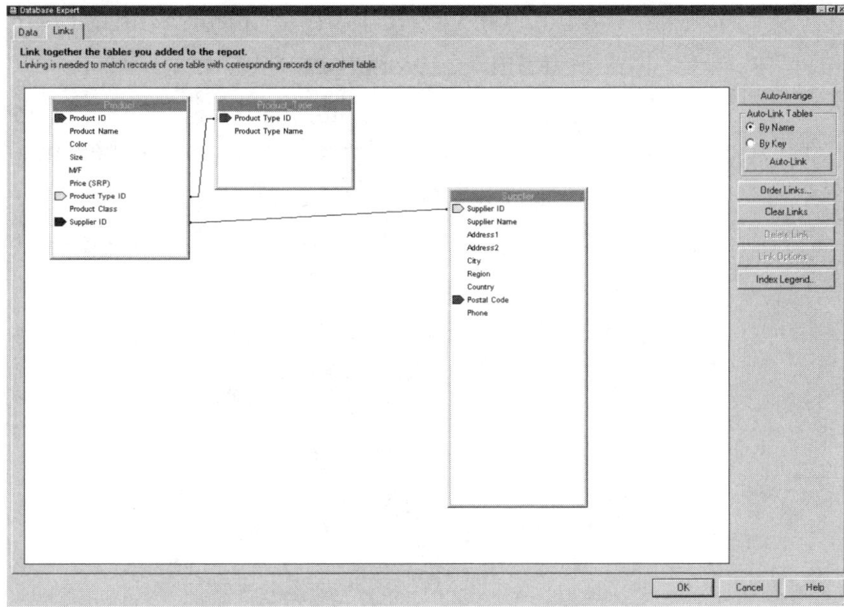

Figure 6-5. Adding links in the Database Expert

Note

The table from which you're linking is referred to as the *source* or *parent* table. The table to which you're linking is referred to as the *target* or *child* table.

Additional Linking Options

You're probably beginning to realize that the most challenging part of report development isn't the creation process but the correct linking of database objects. Not only do you need to link matching fields correctly, but you must also account for the relationship between the pair of tables (not every pair of database objects utilizes a one-to-one relationship). Hopefully your database documentation will steer you in the right direction regarding the relationships between your database objects.

If you should find that your database utilizes relationships other than one-to-one, you'll probably need to do a little tweaking of your links. You can find this ability with the Link Options button, available within the Database Expert.

To access the Link Options dialog box, perform the following steps:

1. **Select a link between two tables.**

   For example, select the link that joins the two Supplier ID fields. Notice that the Link Options button becomes active.

2. **Press the Link Options button.**

   The Link Options dialog box displays, as shown in Figure 6-6.

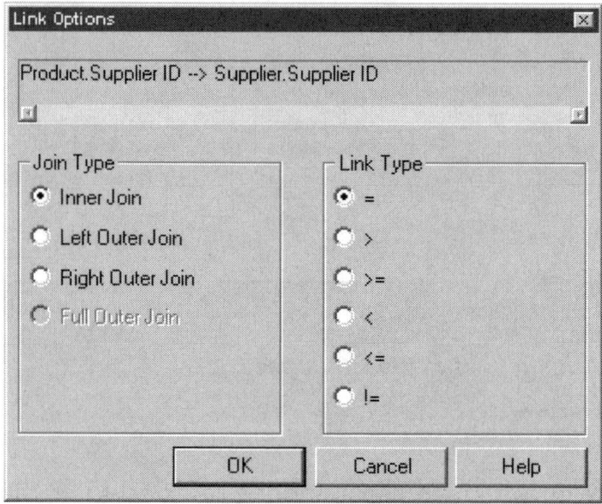

Figure 6-6. The Link Options dialog box

There are three areas of functionality associated with the Links Options dialog. These three areas are as follows:

- **From and To Table:** This section describes the linking fields used within the two tables. The source table is listed to the left of the arrow, and the target table is listed to the right of the arrow.
- **Join Type:** This section provides options that allow you to define the relationship between two tables (by default, Inner Join is selected). Refer to Table 6-6 for more information regarding these join types.
- **Link Type:** Link types are similar to parameters (discussed in Chapter 11). *Link types* allow you to filter the records that are returned within your report. Table 6-7 summarizes the available link types:

Table 6-7. The link types within Crystal Reports

Link Type	Abbreviation	Description
Equal	=	Links all the records that are an exact match.
Greater Than	>	Links all records in which the value from the source table is greater than the value from the target table.
Greater Than or Equal	>=	Links all records in which the value from the source table is greater than or equal to the value from the target table.
Less Than	<	Links all records in which the value from the source table is less than the value from the target table.
Less Than or Equal	<=	Links all records in which the value from the source table is less than or equal to the value from the target table.
Not Equal	!=	Links all records in which the value from the source table is not equal to field values within the target table.

Tip

The linking types are a way of creating an overall filter for your report records (in other words, defining even before the report generates what records should and should not display).

Creating parameter fields (which you'll learn about in Chapter 11) is a more flexible way to perform the same type of functionality. A good rule of thumb is that if you wish to filter the records that display within your reports, use parameter fields rather than link types.

Don't worry about tweaking your links — you'll find that the majority of databases that you use for your reporting purposes utilize inner joins. Thus, all you need to worry about is making sure that you're linking the correct fields from one database table to another. Crystal Reports will do the rest.

To get out of the Link Options dialog box, press the Cancel button. You're returned to the Database Expert.

Adding Tables

In the course of your report development, you'll often find the need to add additional tables to your report. For example, perhaps you need to add data not contained within the tables you've selected. Crystal Reports makes adding additional tables easy through the Database Expert.

To add another table to your report, perform these steps:

1. **In the Database Expert dialog box, select the Data tab.**
2. **In the Create New Connection folder, expand the Database Files folder.**

   You should see the connection to your xtreme.mdb database.
3. **Select and add the Purchases table to your report.**

   Press the Add (>) button to move these tables to the Selected Tables list box.
4. **Select the Links tab in the Database Expert.**

   You screen should contain the same links as Figure 6-7.

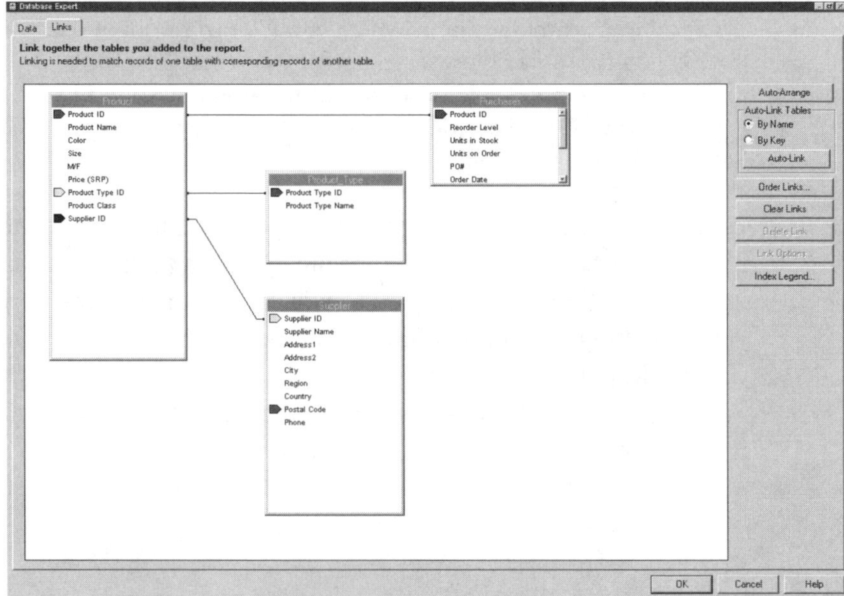

Figure 6-7. Adding tables within the Database Expert

When you're satisfied with the results, press the OK button. The table is now officially added to your report.

Tip

Sometimes, Crystal Reports displays linked tables in a compact format — so compact that it's difficult to tell what's linked to what.

To move tables around within the Links tab screen, click and hold on a table's title, and then move to where you wish the table to display. To resize a table, click and hold on a table's edge, and then use your mouse to resize the dimensions of the table.

With a little practice, you'll have no problem maneuvering things to your liking.

Deleting Tables

Crystal Reports makes removing unwanted tables and links from your report just as easy as adding a table. For example, let's say that you've decided you don't want to include supplier information within this report. Thus, there's no reason to keep this table. Perform the following steps to delete the Supplier table from your report.

Note

When you're deleting a table from Crystal Reports, you're only removing the table from the report. In no way whatsoever are you actually deleting the table from your database. Feel free to add and delete tables as much as needed. You can't harm or alter the database in any way with Crystal Reports.

1. **Select the Data tab on the Database Expert dialog box.**
2. **Select the Supplier table in the Selected Tables list box.**

   Press the Remove (<) button to remove these tables from the Selected Tables list box.
3. **Select the Links tab.**

Notice that the Supplier table is now removed. Your screen should look like Figure 6-8.

When you're satisfied with the results, press the OK button. The table is now officially removed from your report.

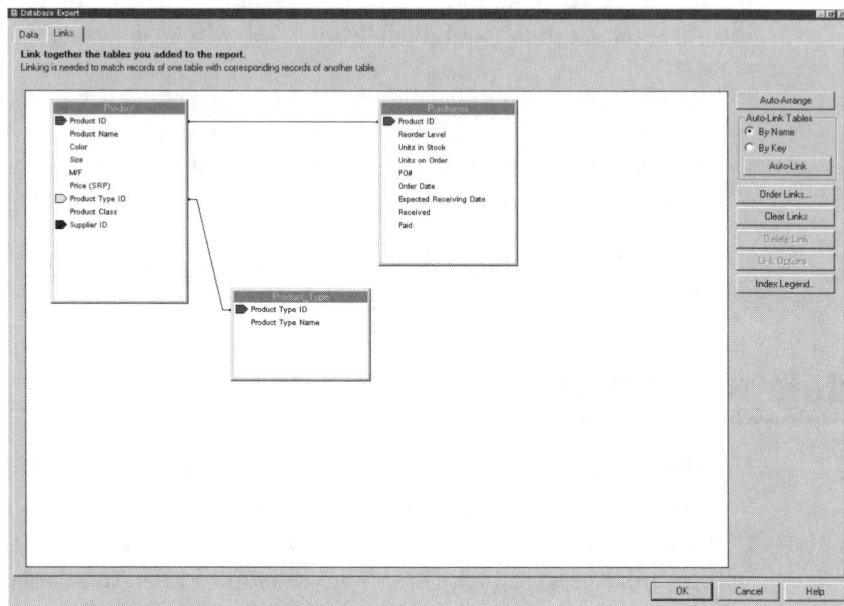

Figure 6-8. Deleting report tables within the Database Expert

Tip

If you remove a table that's linked to other tables, Crystal Reports not only removes the table but also all links used with the table.

What's Next?

Pat yourself on the back! In this chapter, you've familiarized yourself with one of the biggest obstacles in report designing — namely, table linking.

In the next chapter, we discuss filtering the records that you want included within your report. This filtering of records is better known as record selection, a powerful concept that will allow you to better create truly meaningful and effective reports.

Chapter 7

Filtering Records

So far in this book, you've been working with reports that require little to no manipulation of data. In other words, you grab a database field, throw it onto your report, and all records display.

While this is fine, the real power of Crystal Reports comes from its ease of manipulating data so that a report presents information in a meaningful manner for your users.

In this chapter, you'll learn how to filter the records you want included (or not included) within your report. This filtering of records is known in the world of report development as record selection. *Record selection* is the process of including specific records within a report.

Crystal Reports provides the following two tools for carrying out the process of record selection:

- **The Select Expert:** This tool provides a visual means of filtering data.
- **Record Selection Formula:** These are formulas that filter data, using some sort of filtering criteria. We learn more about record selection formulas in Chapter 11.

In this chapter, we learn about filtering through the Select Expert.

Exploring the Select Expert

To understand the concept of filtering, let's first create a new report, which you'll use throughout this chapter.

Start Crystal Reports and create a new blank report. Using the xtreme.mdb database, add the Customer and Orders tables. Allow the Smart Linking feature to link these tables, or refer to the ER Model diagram in Appendix A.

Once you're at the Report Design area, place the Customer Name and Region fields (from the Customer table) and the Order Date (from the Orders table) in the Details section. Once you've done this, preview your report. Your report should look something like Figure 7-1.

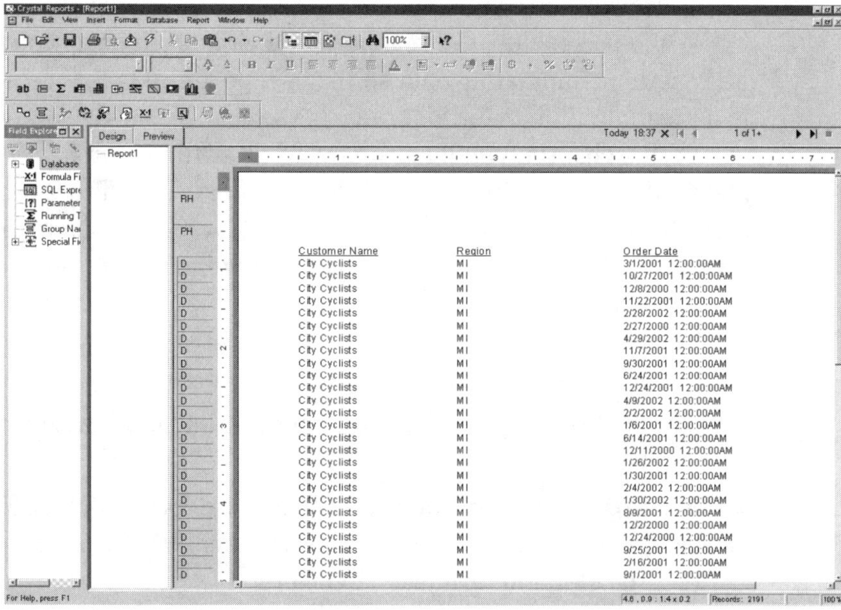

Figure 7-1. An unfiltered report

By default, Crystal Reports processes every record within a database table. Thus, in the report you've just created, all customers display. As you page through this report (all 37 pages or so), you'll see different customers from different states with different order dates.

The truth is, rarely does a report require all records to display. Usually, report users only wish to view a subset of a table's records. For example, a report user may only wish to view customer information that occurred on a particular date. Or perhaps a report user only wishes to view information for customers of a particular region.

The Select Expert allows you to create filters that define what records a report should (and should not) display.

Let's take a look at that Select Expert and see how it works. Working with the report that you just created, try the following:

1. **From the menu bar, select Report, Select Expert.**

   You may also press the Select Expert icon on the Standard toolbar (this button looks like a hand selecting one of three marbles).

2. **A Choose Field dialog box displays.**

   Figure 7-2 displays this Choose Field dialog box. This is not the Select Expert; you must first choose the field for which you wish to filter data.

Tip

If you forget which values are within any of the fields, you can always use the Browse button.

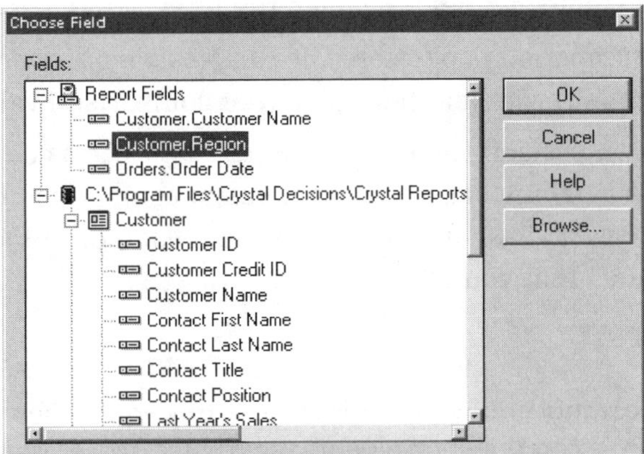

Figure 7-2. The Choose Field dialog box

3. **Expand the Customer table and select the Region field.**

   This field contains the data regarding whether a product is made by Xtreme or a competitor.

4. **Press the OK button on the Choose Field dialog box.**

   The Select Expert displays, as shown in Figure 7-3.

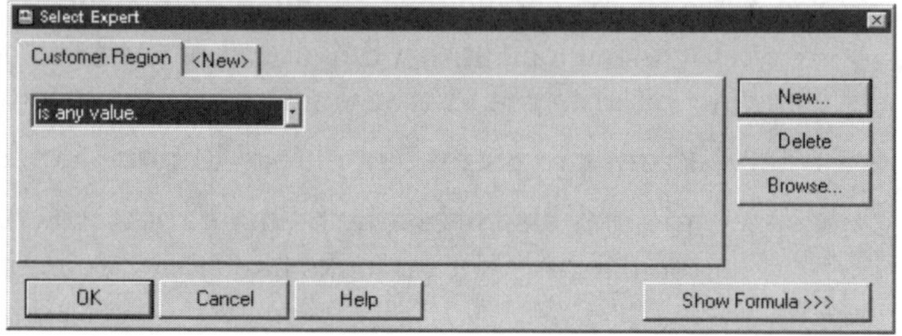

Figure 7-3. The Select Expert

Notice the tabs at the top of the Select Expert dialog box. These tabs represent the filters defined within your report. There's also a tab labeled <New>, which allows you to create additional filters.

Whenever you create a filter within Crystal Reports, there are three pieces of information you must define to perform a record selection. These pieces of information are:

- The table and field to which the filter is to be applied.
- A comparison operator. The *comparison operator* compares data in a field with another value (the comparison value).
- A comparison value. The *comparison value* is a value that is fixed and unchanging. Examples of comparison values include other database fields, a text string, data, or numeric or dollar values that you enter.

Note

If your comparison operator is set to *is any value*, then you will not have a comparison value (the third piece of information). This is because the *is any value* option returns all records. You'll need to change the comparison operator to another option (such as *is equal to*) in order to set the comparison value information.

Understanding the Comparison Operators

In SQL (the programming language used with Crystal Reports), *comparison operators* compare two values and then generate a true or false value from this comparison. This true or false value is known as a *Boolean* result. Crystal Reports uses this true or false value to determine which records display within a report.

The following table displays the available comparison operators available in the Select Expert. The Data Type column lists the data types that may use that comparison operator.

Table 7-1. The comparison operators of the Select Expert

Comparison Operator	Description	Data Type
Is Any Value	Returns all records within a field. There is no filtering done on the field.	Text, Numeric, Date
Is Equal To	Returns all records that EXACTLY match the comparison value.	Text, Numeric, Date
Is Not Equal To	Returns all records that DO NOT EXACTLY match the comparison value.	Text, Numeric, Date
Is One Of	Returns all records that MATCH one or more of a series of values you enter.	Text, Numeric, Date
Is Not One Of	Returns all records that DO NOT MATCH one or more of a series of values you enter.	Text, Numeric, Date
Is Less Than	Returns all records that are less than the comparison value.	Text, Numeric, Date
Is Less Than Or Equal To	Returns all records that are less than or equal to the comparison value.	Text, Numeric, Date
Is Greater Than	Returns all records that are greater than the comparison value.	Text, Numeric, Date
Is Greater Than Or Equal To	Returns all records that are greater than or equal to the comparison value.	Text, Numeric, Date
Is Between	Returns all records that FALL BETWEEN a range of values you enter.	Text, Numeric, Date
Is Not Between	Returns all records that DO NOT FALL within a range of values you enter.	Text, Numeric, Date
Starts With	Returns all records that START with a text comparison value (for example, if you define a record to start with the letter T, your report returns all records that begin with the letter T).	Text

Comparison Operator	Description	Data Type
Does Not Start With	Returns all records that DO NOT start with a text comparison value.	Text
Is Like	Returns all records that MATCH values you've entered that utilize a wildcard character. We learn more about wildcard characters later in this chapter.	Text
Is Not Like	Returns all records that DO NOT MATCH values you've entered that utilize a wildcard character.	Text
Formula	Returns all records that use filtering instructions from a formula. We learn more about selecting records with formulas in Chapter 11.	Text, Numeric, Date

Creating a Single Filter

The Select Expert allows you to define the filter that allows certain types of data to display within your report. This functionality is carried out through a *selection statement,* which is a formula that specifies the records or group of records that you want included within your report.

Selection statements are actually formulas written in the SQL language. What the Select Expert does is take the legwork (and headaches) out of writing these formulas.

To access the Select Expert and begin learning about filtering, let's create a new report.

1. **In the Select Expert, press the drop-arrow to open the Comparison Operator list.**

   You screen should look like Figure 7-4.

2. **Set the Comparison Operator option to Is Equal To.**

   When you select this value, a new drop-down field displays to the right. This new drop-down field allows you to define a comparison value.

3. **Select the Comparison Value drop-down field.**

   Click the down arrow in the right drop-down field. Select *TX* for Texas. You can type in TX, but make sure not to use quotation marks. Your screen should look like Figure 7-5.

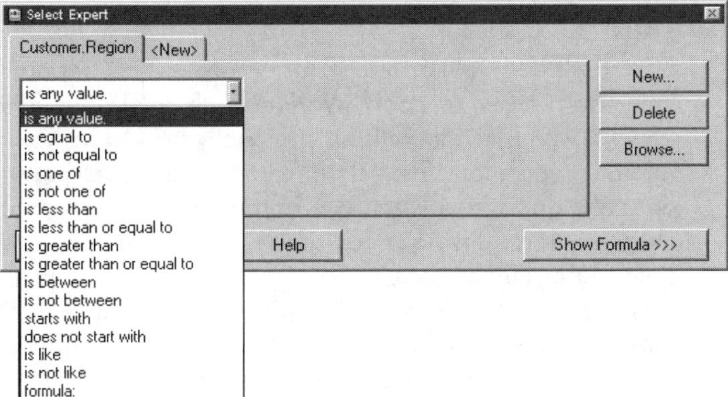

Figure 7-4. The Comparision Operator list

Caution

Databases are nitpicky when it comes to database values. A comparison value must appear *exactly* as it is in your report. You're usually safest choosing from the drop-down list (since these values are pulled directly from your database).

Unfortunately, these values do not always contain the comparison values you may need. If you do type in a value, make sure it exists within the database. Use the Browse button to view the values in the database.

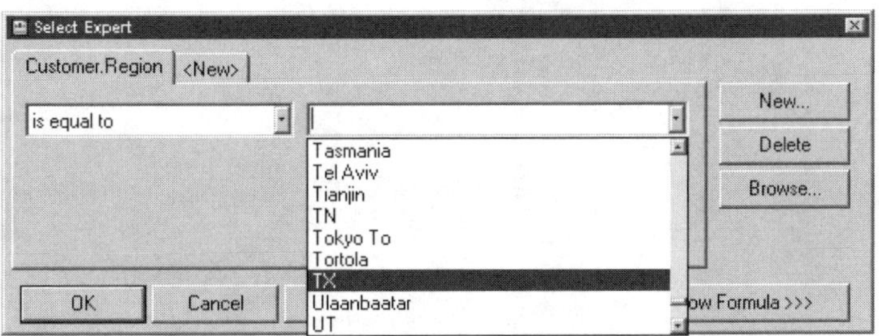

Figure 7-5. The Comparison Value field

4. **Press the OK button.**

   A message box asks if you wish to either use saved data or refresh your data.

5. **Select the Refresh Data button.**

   Your report refreshes, and you're returned to the Report Design area. Scroll through your pages.

Tip

By default, Crystal Reports saves records with a report the first time you preview a report. Working with saved data allows you to work with a report without constantly having to wait around for your report to refresh data from the server. Using saved data is a good idea when you're making simple formatting changes or modifying areas of the report that don't require the data to be refreshed.

However, if you're changing selection statement criteria (i.e., making changes within the Select Expert), it's a good idea to always refresh your report. Not doing so might result in your report showing too few records, even though they actually exist.

If you accidentally press the Saved Data button and your report doesn't return any records, press the F5 key (or Report, Refresh Report Data from the menu bar).

You've successfully created a selection statement within your report. You should only see customers with a region equal to TX, as shown in Figure 7-6.

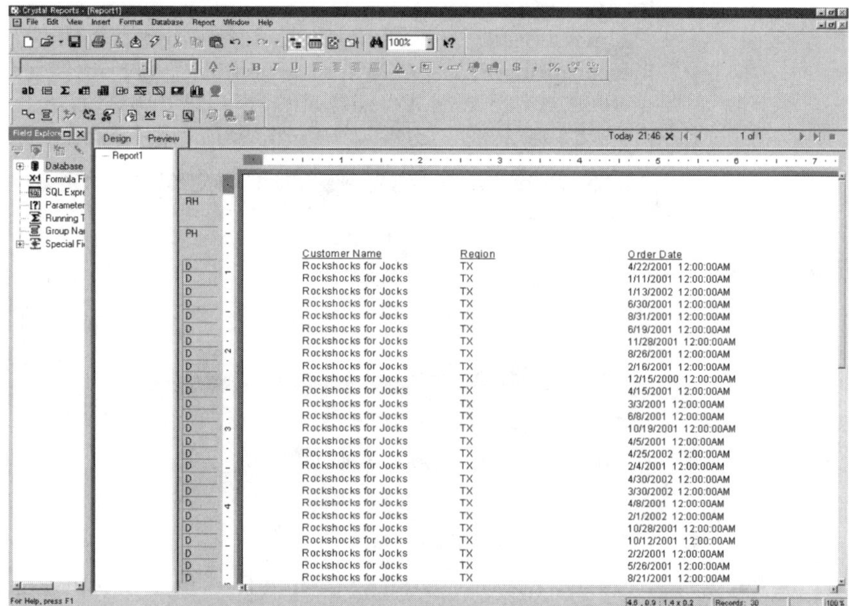

Figure 7-6. A report with a single filter

Removing Selection Statements

So what do you do if you wish to remove a selection statement? Crystal Reports makes removing your filters just as easy as adding them. To remove a selection statement, try the following. Use the report that you've been working on in this chapter.

1. **Access the Select Expert.**
2. **Select the tab that contains the Region filter.**
3. **Press the Delete button on the Select Expert dialog box.**

   That particular filter is now removed.
4. **Press the OK button on the Select Expert dialog box.**

   Crystal Reports asks if you'd like to refresh your data.
5. **Press the Refresh Data button.**

   You're returned to the Report Design area.
6. **Preview your report.**

Notice that Crystal Reports removes the region filter from your report. Thus, customer information from all regions now displays.

Creating Compound-Record Selection Statements

So far, you've created a record selection statement on a single field. Of course, you're not limited to only one filter per report. You can create as many filters as your report needs. A record selection statement with more than one filter is known as a compound-record selection statement. A *compound-record selection statement* is a selection statement that filters more than one field within a report.

When you're creating compound-record selection statements, you can create the first filter, test it out, reopen the Select Expert, and then add the second filter. You can also create both selection filters all at once within the Select Expert by using the <New> tab.

Either method works fine. However, sometimes creating one filter at a time and then previewing your work ensures that your report filters exactly the records you want.

Let's try an example, continuing with the report you've been creating in this chapter. Perform the following steps:

1. **Access Report, Select Expert from the menu bar.**

   The Choose Field dialog box displays.

2. **Select the Country field from the Customer table.**

   Just because a field isn't displayed within your report doesn't mean it can't act as a filter. In this example, you'll create a filter using the Country field, which is a field that's not displayed.

3. **Press the OK button.**

   The Select Expert displays.

4. **In the Comparison Operator drop-down field, select the Is Like operator.**

5. **In the Comparison Value drop-down field, select USA.**

   In this field, you're defining your filter to return only customers within the United States.

6. **Select the <New> tab.**

   The Choose Field dialog box displays again.

7. **Select the Order Date field from the Orders table.**

   The Select Expert displays.

8. **In the Comparison Operator drop-down field, select the Is Greater Than Or Equal To operator.**

9. **In the Comparison Value drop-down field, select 1/1/2001 12:00:00AM.**

   You screen should look like Figure 7-7.

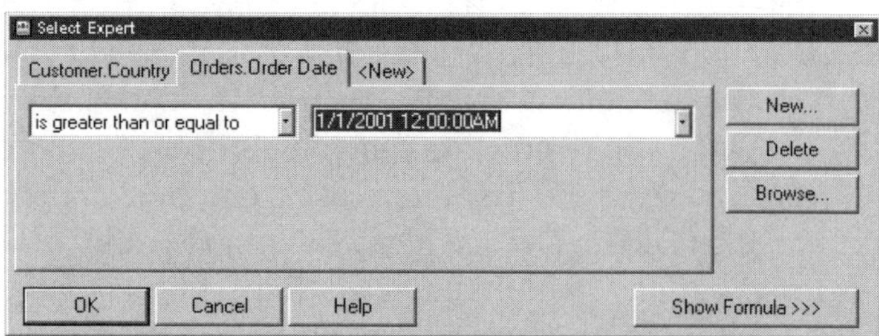

Figure 7-7. Creating a compound-record selection statement in the Select Expert

10. **Press the OK button on the Select Expert dialog box.**

    Crystal Reports asks if you'd like to refresh your data.

11. **Press the Refresh Data button.**

    You're returned to the Report Design area.

12. **Preview your report.**

    Scroll through the pages within your report. You should only see customers within the USA whose order dates are greater than or equal to 1/1/2001 12:00:00 AM.

    If you wish, add the Country field to your report to make sure the report displays customers from the USA only. Your report should look like Figure 7-8.

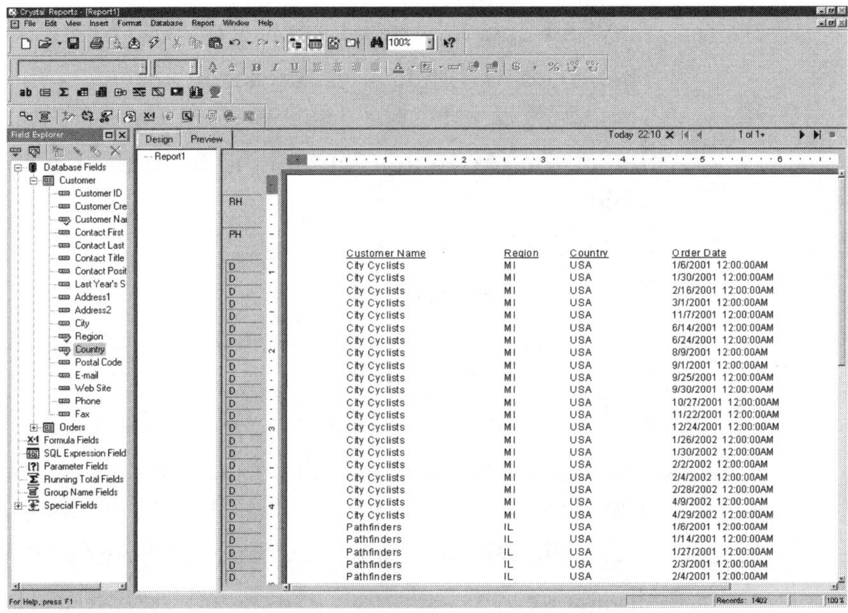

Figure 7-8. Your report with a compound-record selection statement

Creating Filters with Wildcard Characters

Many report developers prefer the use of wildcard characters when creating their filters. *Wildcard characters* are placeholders used to represent one or many characters. Wildcard characters are useful in that they allow you to filter records without having to define too specific of a comparison value.

The two wildcard characters are the asterisk (*) and the question mark (?). The asterisk represents one or more characters, while the question mark represents a single character.

Perhaps the easiest way to understand wildcard characters is to try an example. Continuing where you left off with the example in this chapter, perform the following steps:

1. **Access Report, Select Expert from the menu bar.**

   The Select Expert displays. Press the <New> tab. The Choose Field dialog box displays.

2. **Select the Customer Name field from the Customer table.**

3. **Press the OK button.**

   The Select Expert displays.

4. **In the Comparison Operator drop-down field, select the Is Like operator.**

5. **In the Comparison Value drop-down field, type P*.**

   Using this wildcard character means that only customers whose name begins with P shall display within your report.

6. **Press the OK button on the Select Expert dialog box.**

   Crystal Reports asks if you'd like to refresh your data.

7. **Press the Refresh Data button.**

   You're returned to the Report Design area.

8. **Preview your report.**

   Scroll through the pages within your report. You should only see customers whose name begins with P, are within the USA, and whose order dates are greater than or equal to 1/1/2001.

Figure 7-9 displays the results of your work.

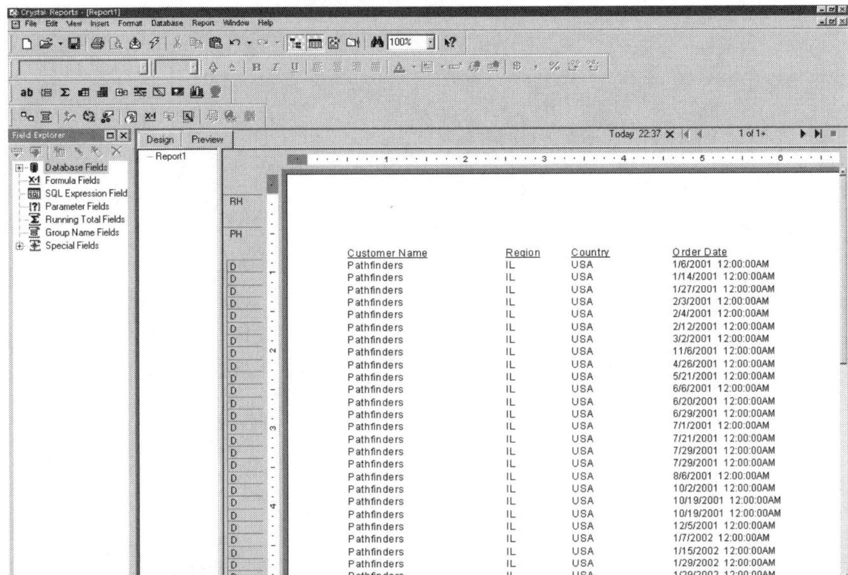

Figure 7-9. Creating filters using the wildcard character

You'll find that as you work more with reports, filters play a large part in how meaningful and useful your reports become. You'll get some more practice with creating filters in the report building exercise at the end of Part II.

What's Next?

In this chapter, you've familiarized yourself with the Select Expert, a Crystal Reports tool that allows you to extract and filter the data that you select from database tables.

In the next chapter, we explore the power of grouping and sorting data within your reports! Grouping and sorting are reporting concepts that not only make your reports pleasing to the eye but also easier to read and understand.

Chapter 8

Sorting and Grouping within Your Reports

Data doesn't always make sense when it's pulled from a database. Just because the correct data appears on a report doesn't mean the report is useful to your users.

For example, how useful is a general ledger report that displays a January 1, 2001 transaction after a September 1, 2001 transaction? Such a report would have your report users pulling their hair out (or worse, pulling *your* hair out).

To make sense of data, report designers define sorting and grouping functionality within their reports. *Sorting* is the method of organizing data in some defined order. *Grouping* is the method of separating records into categorical groups. In this chapter, we learn how to organize your data into logical units.

Understanding Sorting

When a report grabs records from a database, the records typically display in an order determined by data type. The sort order that most databases use for records is summarized in Table 8-1.

Table 8-1. The data type order of a database sort

Field Type	Sort Order
Single-character string fields	Blanks Punctuation Numbers Uppercase letters Lowercase letters
Multiple-character string fields	Two letters Three letters Four letters Five letters . . . *etc.*
Currency fields	Numeric order
Number fields	Numeric order
Date fields	Chronological order
DateTime fields	Chronological order Same-date values by time
Time fields	Chronological order
Boolean comparison fields	False values (0) True values (1)
NULL values	NULL values Non-NULL values

Unfortunately, this order is rarely useful. For example, check out Figure 8-1. In this figure, there's a report that pulls records from the Supplier table. Notice that there's no meaningful order as to how the records display (for example, the records don't display in alphabetical order).

Luckily, Crystal Reports allows you to sort text, numeric, and date fields in the two following orders:

- *Ascending*, which means records sort upward (such as from lowest to highest, earliest to latest, first to last, or A to Z)
- *Descending*, which means records sort downward (such as from highest to lowest, latest to earliest, last to first, or Z to A)

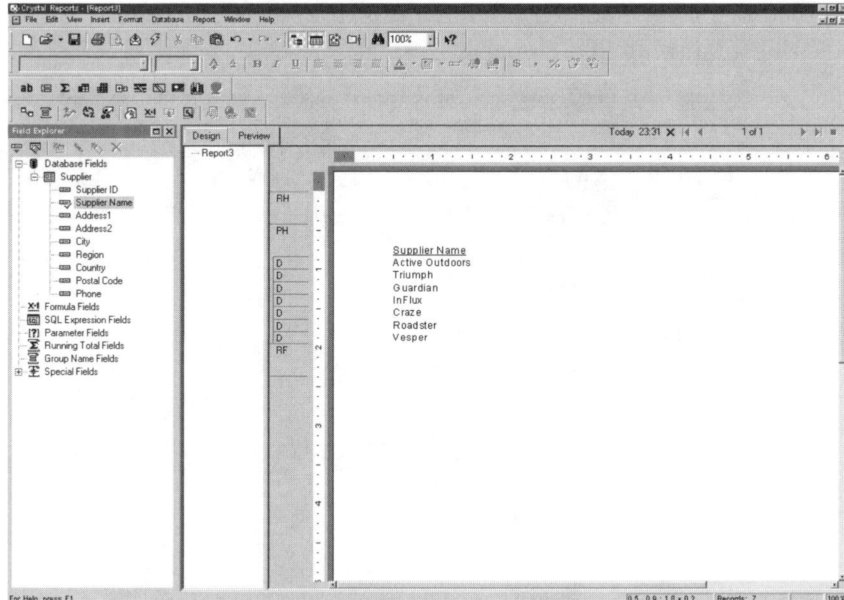

Figure 8-1. A report with no sorting order

In Crystal Reports, you also have the choice of sorting on only one field (known as *single field sorting*) or more than one field (known as *multiple field sorting*). In Crystal Reports, all sorting is handled through the Record Sort Order dialog box.

Sorting Single Fields

To understand the concept of sorting, let's first create a new report, which you'll use throughout this chapter.

Start Crystal Reports and create a new blank report. Add the Product, Product Type, and Purchases tables. Allow the Smart Linking feature to link these tables, or refer to the ER Model diagram in Appendix A.

Once you're at the Report Design area, place the Product Name and Product Class fields (from the Product table), the Product Type Name field (from the Product Type table), and the Units in Stock and Units on Order fields (from the Purchases table) in the Details section. Resize any of the fields as necessary so that all information displays. Once you've done this, preview your report; it should look something like Figure 8-2.

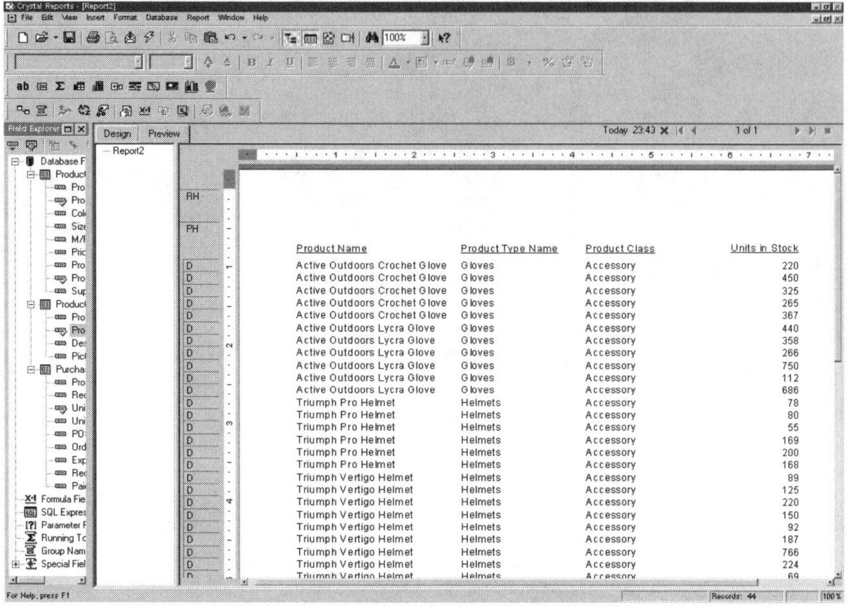

Product Name	Product Type Name	Product Class	Units in Stock
Active Outdoors Crochet Glove	Gloves	Accessory	220
Active Outdoors Crochet Glove	Gloves	Accessory	450
Active Outdoors Crochet Glove	Gloves	Accessory	325
Active Outdoors Crochet Glove	Gloves	Accessory	265
Active Outdoors Crochet Glove	Gloves	Accessory	367
Active Outdoors Lycra Glove	Gloves	Accessory	440
Active Outdoors Lycra Glove	Gloves	Accessory	358
Active Outdoors Lycra Glove	Gloves	Accessory	266
Active Outdoors Lycra Glove	Gloves	Accessory	750
Active Outdoors Lycra Glove	Gloves	Accessory	112
Active Outdoors Lycra Glove	Gloves	Accessory	686
Triumph Pro Helmet	Helmets	Accessory	78
Triumph Pro Helmet	Helmets	Accessory	80
Triumph Pro Helmet	Helmets	Accessory	55
Triumph Pro Helmet	Helmets	Accessory	169
Triumph Pro Helmet	Helmets	Accessory	200
Triumph Pro Helmet	Helmets	Accessory	168
Triumph Vertigo Helmet	Helmets	Accessory	89
Triumph Vertigo Helmet	Helmets	Accessory	125
Triumph Vertigo Helmet	Helmets	Accessory	220
Triumph Vertigo Helmet	Helmets	Accessory	150
Triumph Vertigo Helmet	Helmets	Accessory	92
Triumph Vertigo Helmet	Helmets	Accessory	187
Triumph Vertigo Helmet	Helmets	Accessory	766
Triumph Vertigo Helmet	Helmets	Accessory	224

Figure 8-2. Unsorted data within the Product Inventory Report

Looking at this report, you'll notice that there isn't any real order to how records display. For example, look at the Product Name information on the first page of your report. You have a number of glove products, followed by some helmet products, followed by more glove products.

Finding information within this report is like looking for a needle in a haystack.

To make this report more meaningful, let's add some sorting functionality. Perform the following steps to sort the report:

1. **Select Report, Record Sort Expert from the menu bar.**

   The Record Sort Order dialog box displays, as shown in Figure 8-3.

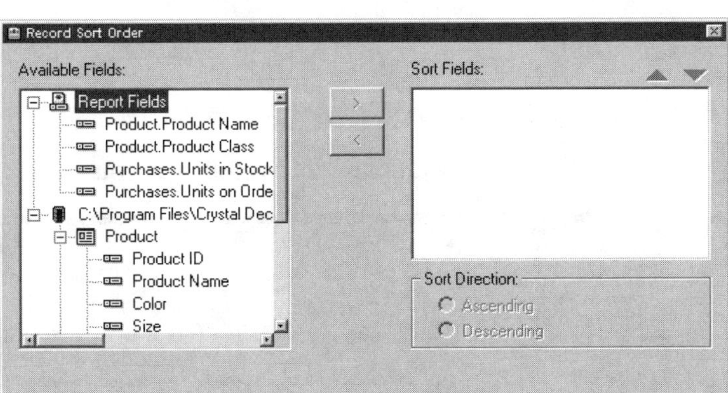

Figure 8-3. The Record Sort Order dialog box

2. **Select the Product Type Name field from the Available Fields list box.**

   This is the primary field that you wish your report to sort. This field is located in the Product Type table.

3. **Press the Add button (>).**

   You'll see the Product Type Name field display in the Sort Fields list box, as shown in Figure 8-4.

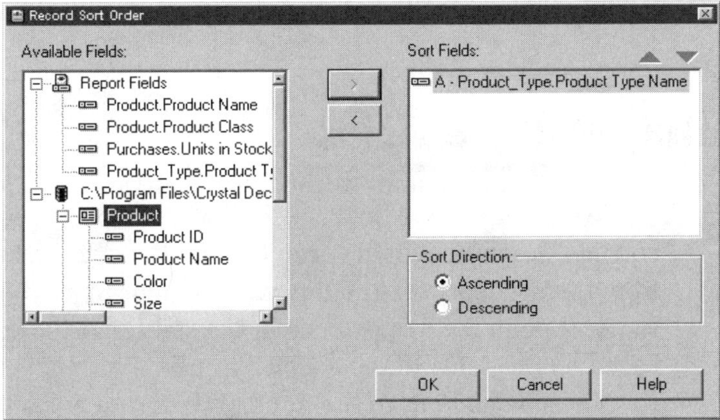

Figure 8-4. Sorting your report by the Product Type Name field

4. **Select the Ascending option button.**

This sorts records upward (in this case, alphabetically from A to Z).

5. **Press the OK button.**

   Figure 8-5 displays the results of your work.

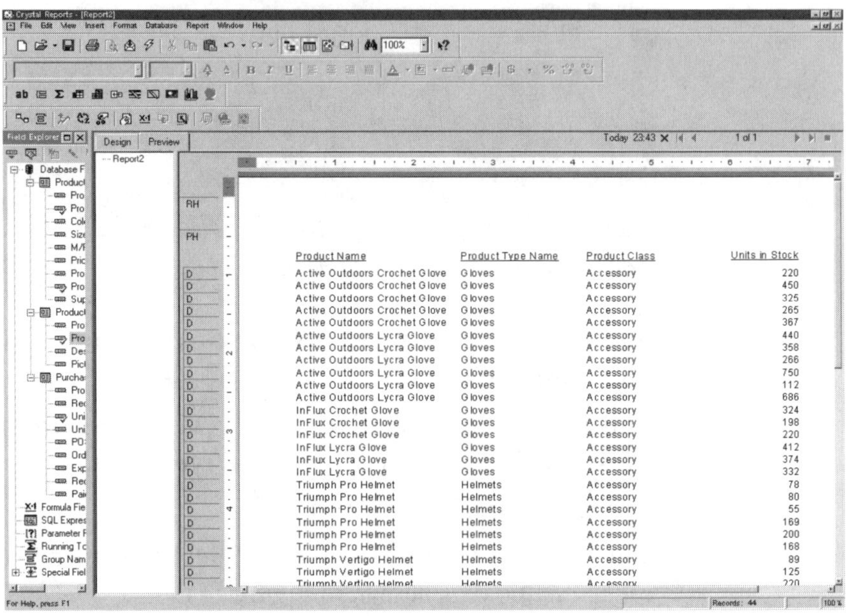

Figure 8-5. A report with single sorting functionality

Sorting Multiple Fields

While sorting on one field is useful, most reports require multiple sorting. In multiple field sorts, Crystal Reports first sorts records from the first sort field. Then, when two or more records have the same value in the first sort field, Crystal Reports sorts the records based on the value of the second sort field.

There is no limit to the number of sorted fields that a report may contain. However, a report will take longer to generate if it contains numerous sorting fields.

To get an idea of how multiple sorting works, try the following example. Continue using the report that you created earlier in this chapter.

1. **Select Report, Record Sort Expert from the menu bar.**
2. **Select the following fields.**

   Add them to the Sort Fields list box. These will appear after the Product Type Name field you've already created.

   - Product Name (from the Product table)
   - Units in Stock (from the Purchases table)
3. **Press the Add button (>) to add these fields.**
4. **Mark the Product Name field as Ascending and the Units in Stock field as Descending.**

   You can do this by first left-clicking on the field (when it's in the Sort Fields list box) and then checking the appropriate Sort Direction option button. Figure 8-6 displays what your screen should look like.

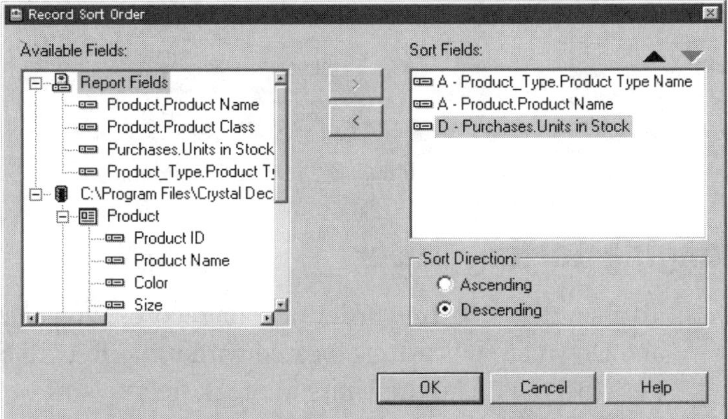

Figure 8-6. Defining multiple sorting with the Record Sort Expert

5. **Press the OK button.**

   Figure 8-7 displays the results of your work.

   You'll notice the report data display in the following sorted order:

   - The Product Type Name field sorts first, alphabetically from A to Z.
   - The Product Name field sorts second, alphabetically from A to Z.

- The Units in Stock field sorts third, numerically from large to small.

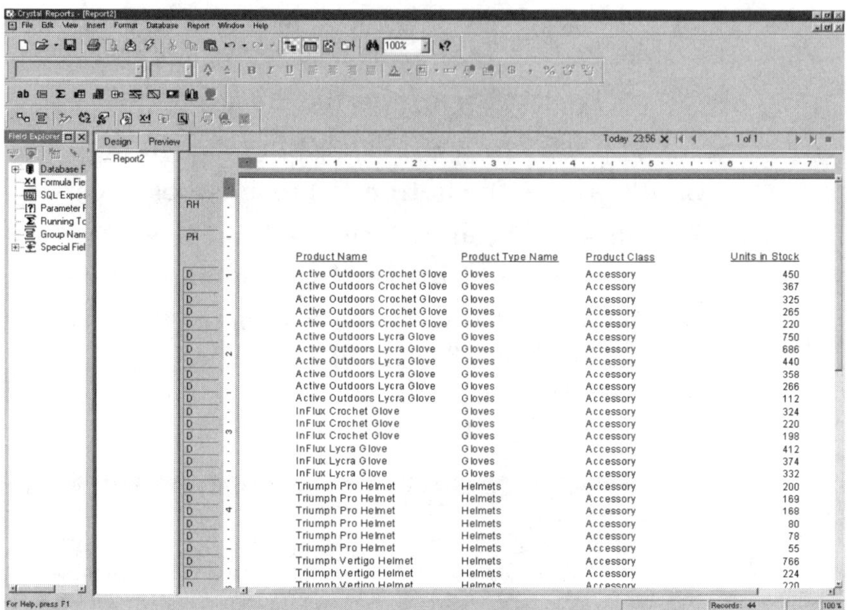

Product Name	Product Type Name	Product Class	Units in Stock
Active Outdoors Crochet Glove	Gloves	Accessory	450
Active Outdoors Crochet Glove	Gloves	Accessory	367
Active Outdoors Crochet Glove	Gloves	Accessory	325
Active Outdoors Crochet Glove	Gloves	Accessory	265
Active Outdoors Crochet Glove	Gloves	Accessory	220
Active Outdoors Lycra Glove	Gloves	Accessory	750
Active Outdoors Lycra Glove	Gloves	Accessory	686
Active Outdoors Lycra Glove	Gloves	Accessory	440
Active Outdoors Lycra Glove	Gloves	Accessory	358
Active Outdoors Lycra Glove	Gloves	Accessory	266
Active Outdoors Lycra Glove	Gloves	Accessory	112
InFlux Crochet Glove	Gloves	Accessory	324
InFlux Crochet Glove	Gloves	Accessory	220
InFlux Crochet Glove	Gloves	Accessory	198
InFlux Lycra Glove	Gloves	Accessory	412
InFlux Lycra Glove	Gloves	Accessory	374
InFlux Lycra Glove	Gloves	Accessory	332
Triumph Pro Helmet	Helmets	Accessory	200
Triumph Pro Helmet	Helmets	Accessory	169
Triumph Pro Helmet	Helmets	Accessory	168
Triumph Pro Helmet	Helmets	Accessory	80
Triumph Pro Helmet	Helmets	Accessory	78
Triumph Pro Helmet	Helmets	Accessory	55
Triumph Vertigo Helmet	Helmets	Accessory	766
Triumph Vertigo Helmet	Helmets	Accessory	224

Figure 8-7. A report with multiple sorting functionality

Changing Sorting Order

To change the sorting order of your records, you can use the Up and Down arrow buttons located within the Record Sort Expert. Perhaps you'd like the Units in Stock field to sort before the Product Name field.

Perform the following steps to change the order in which multiple fields sort within your report:

1. **Select Report, Record Sort Expert from the menu bar.**
2. **Select the Units in Stock field located in the Sort Fields list box.**

   This field is located in the Product table and is now highlighted.

3. **Press the Up arrow button above the Sort Fields list box, as shown in Figure 8-8.**

You'll now see this field move before the Product Name field. The report will now sort records by Units in Stock and then Product Name.

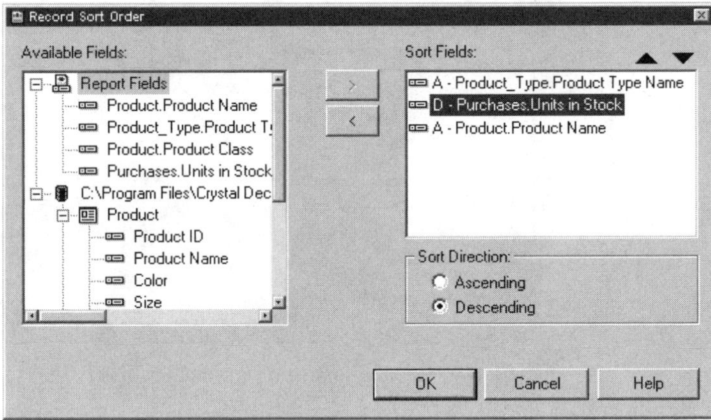

Figure 8-8. Changing the sorting order with the Record Sort Order dialog box

If for some reason you don't like the result of your sort, you can use the Undo feature (either from the menu bar or Standard toolbar). The Undo feature will return your report to the way it was before you entered information in the Record Sort Expert.

Removing Sorts

Removing sorting functionality from a field is as easy as adding sorting to your reports.

To remove a sort, perform the following steps:

1. **Select Report, Record Sort Expert from the menu bar.**
2. **Select the field from which you wish to remove sorting. You'll select this field within the Sort Fields list box.**

   In this example, select the Units in Stock field from the Sort Fields list box. This field is located within the Product table.
3. **Once the field you wish to remove is highlighted, press the Remove button (<) in the Record Sort Order dialog box.**

The sorting field is removed, as shown in Figure 8-9.

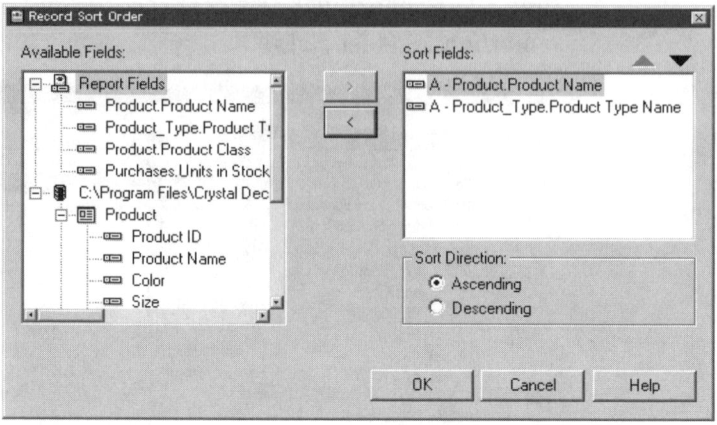

Figure 8-9. Removing sorting fields with the Record Sort Expert

The field is removed from the Sort Fields list box. As a result, the Units in Stock records are no longer sorted within your report (once you press the OK button).

Exploring Groups (Using the Group Expert)

Sorting allows you to define the order in which records are printed. Grouping records, in comparison, allows you to separate records into logical units that are related to each other in some way. For example, you'll often see reports group data by region or employee.

In Crystal Reports, all grouping is controlled through the Group Expert.

To access the Group Expert, make sure you're in the report that you've created within this chapter. From the menu bar, select Report, Group Expert. The Group Expert dialog box displays, as shown in Figure 8-10 (on the following page).

The Group Expert is a nice feature in that it provides a single location for adding and accessing all groups within a report.

In many ways, the Group Expert is similar to the Record Sort Expert. You use the Add (>) button to select the fields you wish to create as a group. You may define multiple groups and change the order in which fields are grouped using the Up and Down arrows (just as you did with the Record Sort Expert).

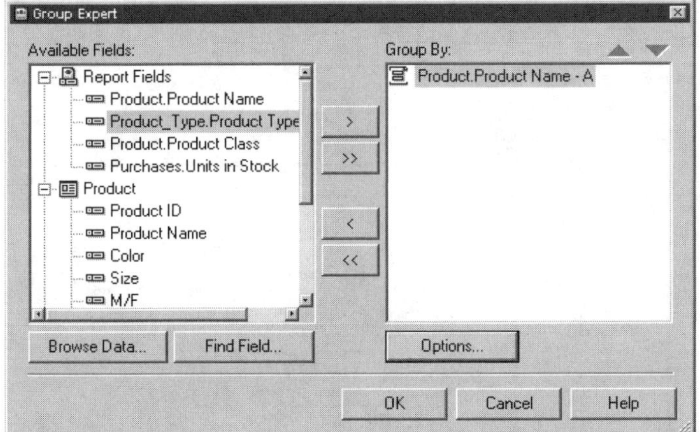

Figure 8-10. The Group Expert

To see how all this grouping stuff works, let's try an example. Continue using the report you've created within this chapter.

1. **Select Report, Group Expert from the menu bar.**

   The Group Expert dialog box displays.

2. **In the Available Fields list box, select the Product Type Name field.**

   This field is available from the Product Type table.

3. **Press the Add button (>) to add this field.**

   The Product Type Name field is listed within the Group By list box. By default, this group is sorted in ascending order.

4. **Press the OK button on the Group Expert.**

   You're returned to the Report Design area.

Preview your report. Your work should look something like Figure 8-11. Notice that your report now groups all data by the Product Type Name field. This information is sorted first, followed by Product Name (which you defined to sort earlier in this chapter).

Note

Whenever you create a group, that group's field always becomes the first to sort.

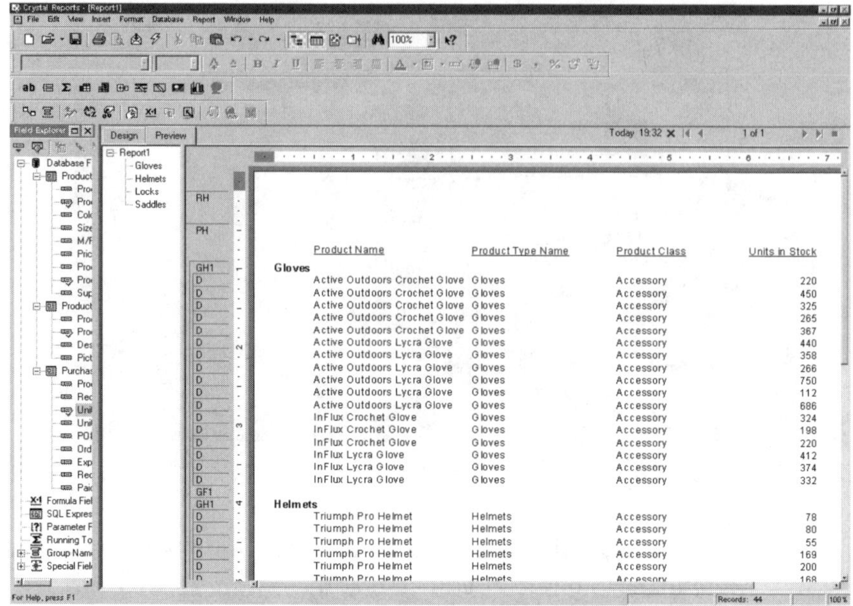

Figure 8-11. Creating a single group

Notice that there are now two new sections added to your Report Designer screen. These new sections are the Group Header and Group Footer (you can see these best in the Design tab). With each group you add, a subsequent group header and footer are also added.

Let's look at what both of these new additions can do for you.

Understanding the Group Headers and Footers

Select the Design tab and you'll see two new sections added to your report: a Group Header and a Group Footer (shown in Figure 8-12).

The Group Header section (labeled Group Header #1) prints when Crystal Reports processes the first record of each group. The Group Footer section (labeled Group Footer #1) prints when Crystal Reports processes the last record of each group.

Although the Group Footer is blank in this example, you'll find that it's often useful for subtotals and summary totals (you'll learn more about creating these values in Chapter 9).

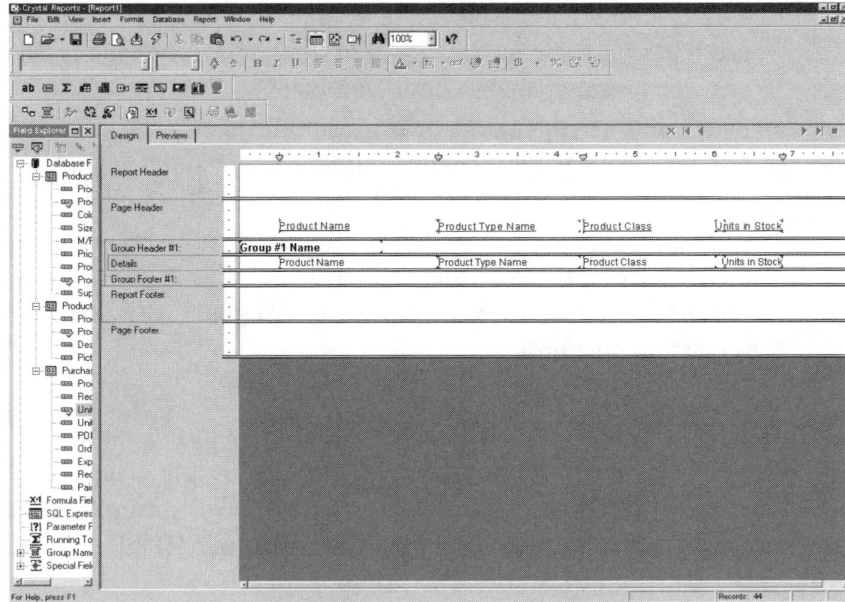

Figure 8-12. The Group Header and Group Footer sections

Grouping Options

Now that you've gotten a little practice with how groups work, let's look at some of the grouping options available to you. Using the example report that you've been working on in this chapter, access Report, Group Expert from the menu bar. When the Group Expert displays, press the Options button. A Change Group Options dialog box displays, as shown in Figure 8-13.

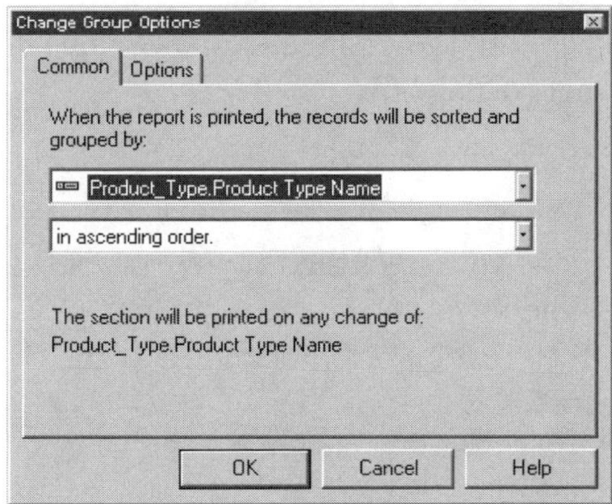

Figure 8-13. The Change Group Options dialog box

The Common tab displays the field upon which you're creating a group and the sorting direction of this group. By default, all groups sort in ascending order; however, you also have the option to sort in descending, specified, or original order.

You've already learned about ascending and descending sort order in this chapter. Specified order allows you to define a user-defined order. Crystal Reports places each record into this custom group that you specify. Original order is the order in which the data is pulled from the database. Original order essentially means no sort order.

Select the Options tab. You'll notice the following functionality:

- **Customize Group Name Field:** The group name field is what displays in the group header. By default, the group name field has the same value as the group field. For example, with this option, you could group on the Customer ID but display the Customer Name as the group name.
- **Keep Group Together:** This check box keeps groups from breaking across pages. By checking this option, Crystal Reports forces the group header, details, and group footer together.

  If there's not enough room for all this information to print on the current page, Crystal Reports moves this information to the next page. While this option is useful, realize that it may also create blank pages within your reports.
- **Repeat Group Header On Each New Page:** This check box allows you to repeat the group header when groups are spread over several pages.

For now, you can cancel out of the Change Group Options dialog box and the Group Expert dialog box.

The Group Tree

If you haven't already done so, select the Preview tab of the report you've been creating. Whenever you create a group in Crystal Reports, you'll notice the creation of a tool known as the Group Tree, as shown in Figure 8-14.

The *Group Tree* allows you to use smart navigation to quickly drill down on groups to view details of the group's underlying data. Essentially, the Group Tree is a navigation tool for dynamically getting around your reports. Your users will find this a great aid in finding and viewing information within a report.

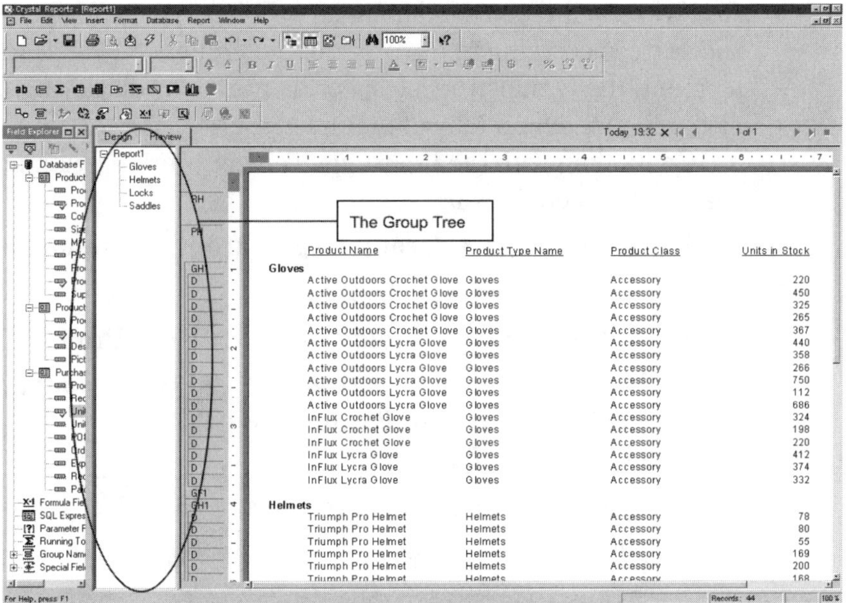

Figure 8-14. The Group Tree

You may repeatedly press the Group Tree button on the Standard toolbar to display or hide the Group Tree.

Tip

The Group Tree is only available within the Preview tab.

Working with Multiple Groups

As was the case with sorts, Crystal Reports does not limit the number of groupings that your report may contain.

Whenever you create multiple groups, a report hierarchy is created with each group containing its own header and footer sections and sorted according to the order of the groups. As you'll see in a moment, the Group Tree is especially useful for displaying (and navigating) the hierarchy of multiple groups.

Continuing with the report you've been working with in this chapter, try the following:

1. **Select Report, Group Expert from the menu bar.**

   The Group Expert displays.

2. **In the Available Fields list box, select Product Name.**
3. **Press the Add (>) button and add the Product Name field to the Group By list box.**

   The Product Name field displays underneath the Product Type Name field, which you've already added. Your screen should look like Figure 8-15.

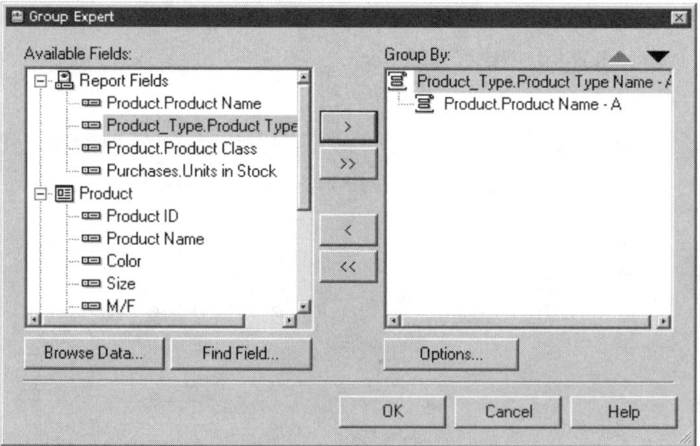

Figure 8-15. Adding multiple groups to your report

4. **Press the OK button.**

   Readjust your fields as necessary. Then preview your report. It should look something like Figure 8-16.

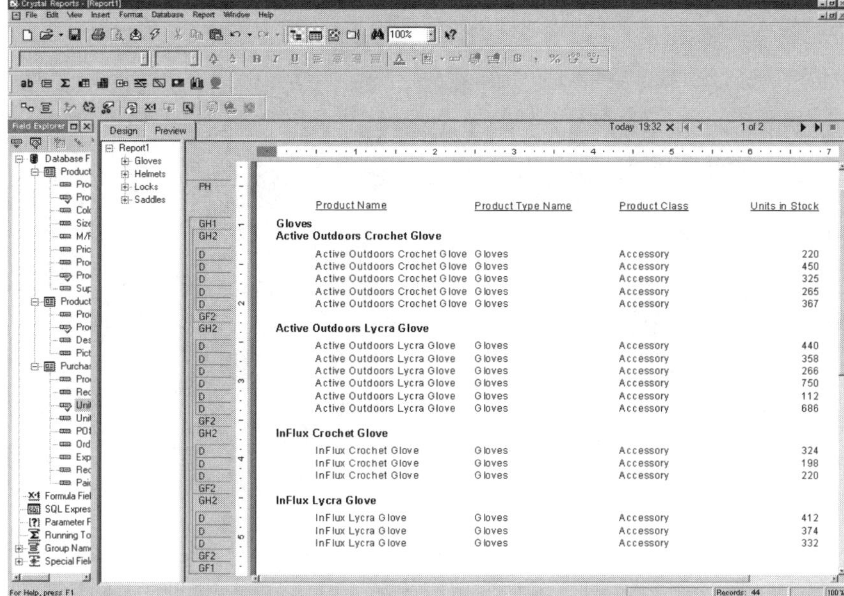

Figure 8-16. A report with multiple groups

What's Next?

In this chapter, you've learned about sorting and grouping and what these two concepts can do for your reports. Most real-world reports utilize sorting and/or grouping in some form or fashion.

In the next chapter, we learn about adding calculations to your report, such as different types of totals. Since most reports utilize numeric information, understanding how to add accurate totals information is a huge part of learning to develop reports successfully.

Chapter 9

Adding Summaries to Your Reports

So far, you've learned to filter, group, and sort your report data with the best of them. Yet perhaps more important than all of these is the ability to summarize data — in other words, to provide your report users with the bottom line. This is especially true of reports that use numbers.

In this chapter, we learn about adding calculations such as grand totals, subtotals, percentages, and averages to your report — information that emphasizes a summary and not the detail of the report.

As you delve further into the report-writing world, you'll find that most financial reports require the use of some (and probably all) of these types of summary calculations.

Understanding Totals

The most common calculations you'll use within your reports are totals. *Totals* are the sum of all values within a field.

Crystal Reports uses three types of totals. These totals are as follows:

- **Subtotals:** These are partial totals that summarize the data within a group.
- **Grand Totals:** These are summaries of all the values within a field for an entire report. Grand total values always display within the Report Footer (located on the very last page of your report).

- **Running Totals:** These totals display on a record-by-record basis. For example, if you have three records with values of 2, 3, and 4, the running total for each of these three records would be 2, 5, and 9.

  In other words, the first value is 2 because no other value is added, the second value is 5 because the 2 and 3 are added together, and the third value is 9 because the 2, 3, and 4 are added together.

There's good news: You don't have to be a mathematical whiz to include calculations within your reports. Crystal Reports will do the dirty work for you.

Exploring the Insert Summary Dialog Box

All summary calculations are created in Crystal Reports through the Insert Summary dialog box. Before accessing that tool, let's first create a sample report that you can utilize for the examples within this chapter.

From the xtreme.mdb database, select the Customer and Orders tables. Allow Smart Linking to link these tables, or refer to the ER Model diagram in Appendix A.

Once you're at the Report Design area, add the following fields to the Details section:

- Customer Name (from the Customer table)
- Order ID (from the Orders table)
- Order Date (from the Orders table)
- Order Amount (from the Orders table)

Create a group using the Customer Name field. Readjust any sections as necessary.

Once you've done this, select the Design tab. Left-click once on the Order Amount field. Then, select Insert, Summary from the menu bar. The Insert Summary dialog box displays, as shown in Figure 9-1.

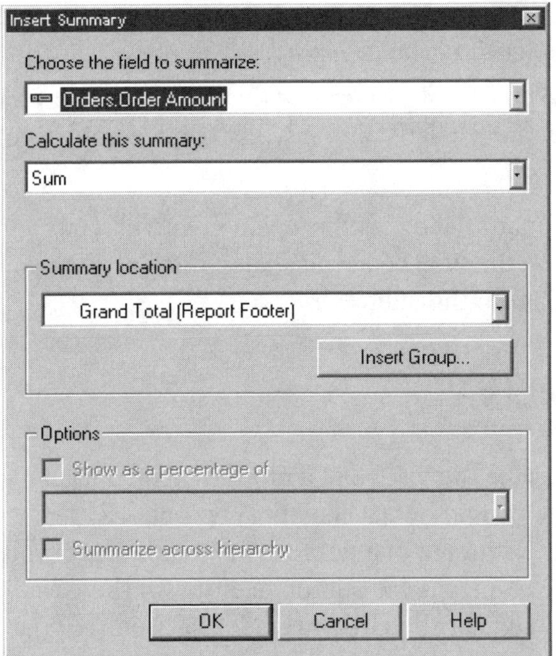

Figure 9-1. The Insert Summary dialog box

The Insert Summary dialog box contains the following functionality:

- **Choose the field to summarize:** Allows users to view the fields and formulas used within a report. This drop-down field also allows users to view fields available from the report's data source.

  Users select the field they wish to summarize here.

- **Calculate this summary:** Contains all the possible mathematical operations for use within your reports.

- **Summary location:** Displays the sections within your report where you may place this summary field.

- **Show as a percentage of:** Allows you to calculate the percentage of the group total. After selecting this check box, the drop-down field below the check box becomes active.

  You may use this drop-down field to select the group total that you wish to use as the comparison for your percentage.

- **Summarize across hierarchy:** Allows you to calculate a summary across hierarchical groupings.

  Hierarchical groupings are groups that show the relationship between two fields. This option won't display unless you create a hierarchy group.

The Insert Summary dialog is where you create all your summary calculations. Now that you're in this dialog box, let's try your first summary calculation: the subtotal.

Creating Subtotals

Subtotals summarize the values of a numeric field within a group and may use any variety of mathematical operations, such as the sum of a field, the average of a field, or the maximum or minimum value of a field. You may place subtotals either in the Group Footer (which is the default) or the Group Header sections of your groups.

Tip

Remember, groups are necessary in order to create summary calculations. Should you need to create a group for the field for which you're creating a subtotal, press the Insert Group button (in the Insert Summary dialog box). The Insert Group dialog box displays, allowing you to create a group. After you save your group, it appears within the Summary location list, which you may then select.

To add a subtotal to your report, perform the following steps. Make sure you're in the Insert Summary dialog box.

1. **In the Choose the field to summarize drop-down field, select the Order Amount field (from the Orders table).**
2. **In the Calculate this summary drop-down field, select Sum.**
3. **In the Summary location field, select the Group#1Customer.Customer Name — A field.**

Once you've done these steps, press the OK button. Preview your report. Figure 9-2 displays how your screen should look.

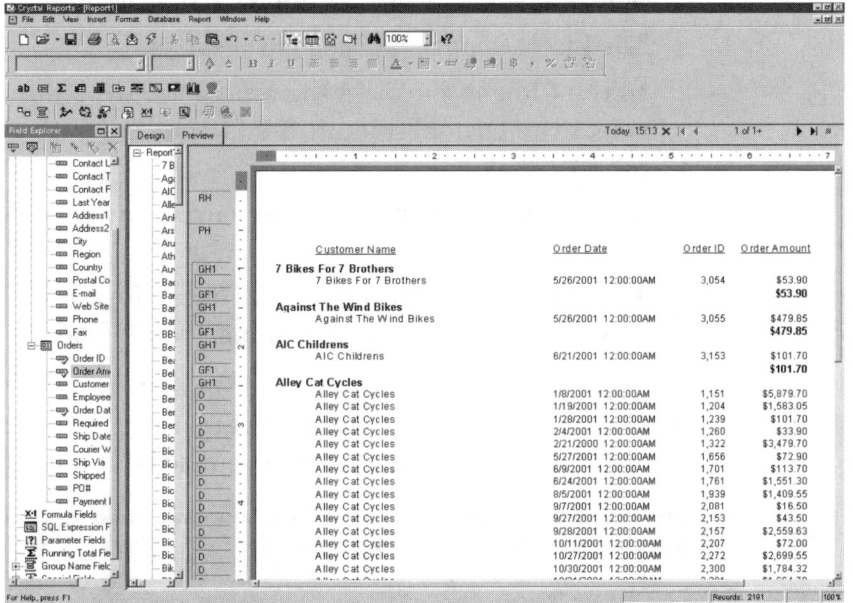

Figure 9-2. Adding subtotals to your reports

Note

The operations from the Calculate this summary drop-down field may vary, depending on the field's data type. For example, you won't find summary or average operations for a field that has character text or is a date/time data type.

Creating Grand Totals for Your Reports

Adding grand totals to your reports is nearly identical to adding subtotals. In many ways, it may be easier. A grand total takes a single field and creates a total value for those fields. That total value is then displayed on the last page of your report.

To insert a grand total into your report, try the following. Use the report you've been working on within this chapter.

1. **Select the Design tab.**

2. **Select the Order Amount field (from the Details section).**
3. **Select Insert, Insert Summary from the menu bar.**

   The Insert Summary dialog box displays.
4. **In the Choose the field to summarize drop-down field, select the Order Amount field (from the Orders table).**
5. **In the Calculate this summary drop-down field, select Sum.**
6. **To create grand totals, select Grand Total (Report Footer) from the Insert Summary dialog box.**

Once you've done these steps, press the OK button and preview your report. Press the Last Page arrow button to go to the last page of your report. Figure 9-3 displays how your screen should look.

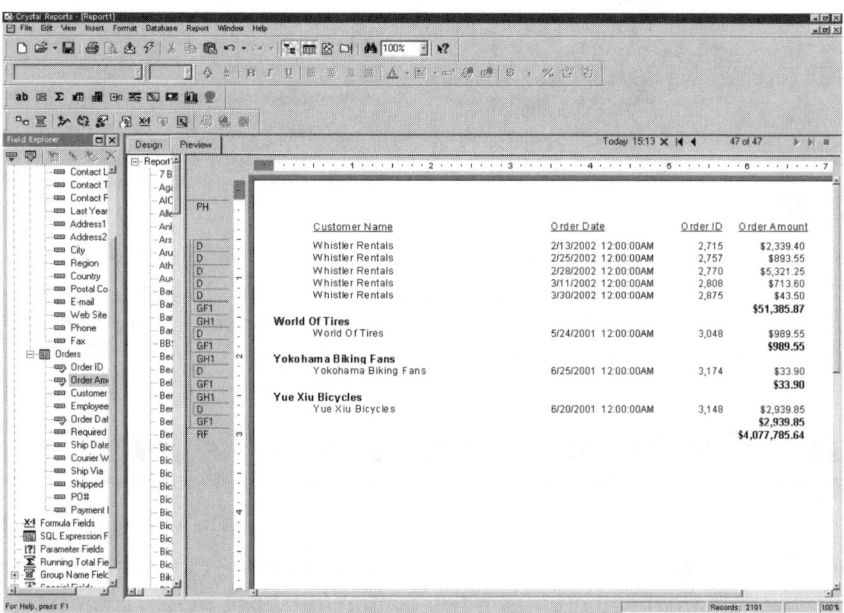

Figure 9-3. Adding a grand total

Tip

If for some reason you're not pleased with the result of your calculation, Crystal Reports makes it easy to change your work. Right-click on the value to display an Options dialog box. Select Edit Summary.

You're returned to the Insert Summary dialog box, where you can make changes as needed. Of course, you can always continue selecting the Insert Summary dialog box from the menu bar.

Defining Other Calculations

As your delve further into report development, you'll find yourself creating more and more calculations within your reports.

Calculations provide users with the ability to take data from a database and create mathematical representations of their data that is meaningful. For example, by creating a calculation that adds sales and cost information together, you might create a calculation that displays gross profit information — information that wasn't directly available from your database but available through the use of calculations.

As you've seen in the Insert Summary dialog box, Crystal Reports contains a number of "canned" calculations available at your fingertips. You've played around with the Sum calculation. Table 9-1 summarizes the rest of the predefined calculations available.

Note

Should you not see a specific calculation that you need in this table, don't sweat it. In the next chapter, we learn about creating our own unique calculations using the Formula Expert.

Table 9-1. The different calculations available within Crystal Reports

Calculation	Definition
Sum	Allows you to add the values that appear within a field.
Average	Allows you to average the values that appear within a field.
Sample variance	Allows you to print the average of the values within a field.
Sample standard deviation	Allows you to print the standard deviation of the values in the field (or group).
Maximum	Allows you to print the largest value within a field.
Minimum	Allows you to print the smallest value within a field.
Count	Allows you to print the number of entries within a field.
Distinct count	Allows you to print the number of unique records within a field.
Correlation with	Allows you to compare the values within two fields.
Covariance with	Allows you to measure the tendency two fields vary together (the linear relationship), according to a specific mathematical relationship.
Median	Allows you to print the middle value in a sequence of numeric values.
Mode	Allows you to print the most frequently occurring values within a field.
Nth largest, N is	Allows you to print the Nth largest value within a field. N is any integer from 1 to 100 (inclusive).
Nth smallest, N is	Allows you to print the Nth smallest value within a field. N is any integer from 1 to 100 (inclusive).
Nth most frequent, N is	Allows you to print the Nth-most-frequent value within a field. N is any integer from 1 to 100 (inclusive).
Pth percentile, P is	Allows you to print the value for a specified percentile (P) in a Number or Currency field. P is any integer from 0 to 100 (inclusive).
Population variance	Allows you to print the population variance of the data.
Population standard deviation	Allows you to print the population standard deviation of the data.
Weighted average with	Allows you to print the average of one field. You then use the values in another field to "weigh" the contribution of each value in the first field to the average.

Creating Running Totals

In the past, report developers loathed the creation of running totals. In older versions of Crystal Reports, there was no support for the creation of running totals — thus, developers found themselves needing to create custom formulas just to handle this type of calculation. Thankfully, Crystal Reports now includes the functionality to make adding running totals easy.

Running totals are commonly found in financial reports (such as account statements), where a total balance changes as each record is processed. In the case of an account balance report, the running balance changes after each transaction.

You may enter running totals anywhere within a report (unlike subtotals and grand totals, which are restricted to certain report sections). However, please note that where a running total is placed affects the value that returns.

For example, a running total placed in the Group Footer section creates a running total up to and including the last record of a group. A running total placed in the Details section creates a running total for every record.

Table 9-2 displays how running total values are affected depending on their placement within a section.

Table 9-2. How the different Crystal Reports sections calculate running totals

Section	How Running Total Is Calculated
Report Header	Returns only the first record of the report.
Page Header	Totals all values up to and including the first record of the current page.
Group Header	Totals all values up to and including the first record of the current group.
Details	Totals all values after every record.
Group Footer	Totals all values up to and including the last record of the current group.
Page Footer	Totals all values up to and including the last record of the current page.
Report Footer	Returns a grand total that includes all records.

To add a running total calculation to your report, perform the following steps. Continue using the report you've created in this chapter.

1. **Select the Design tab.**
2. **Right-click on the Order Amount field (in the Details section).**

   An Options dialog box displays.
3. **Select Insert, Running Total from the Options dialog box.**

   The Create Running Total Field dialog box displays, as shown in Figure 9-4.

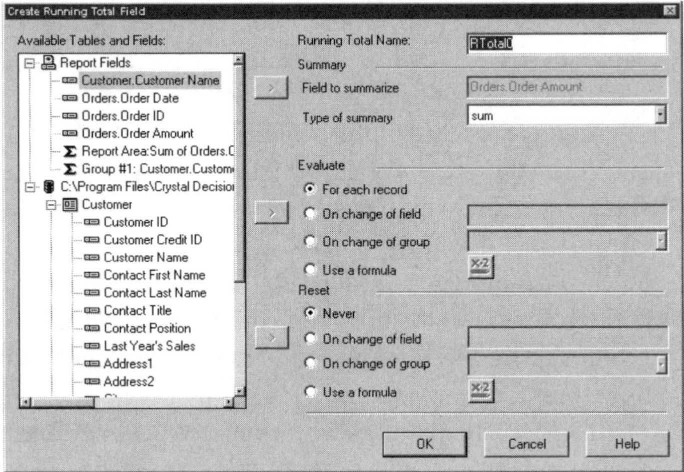

Figure 9-4. The Create Running Total Field dialog box

Note

You may also access the Create Running Total Field dialog box from the Field Explorer dialog box. Right-click on the Running Totals Fields node within the Field Explorer dialog box and select New.

You'll notice the Create Running Total Field dialog box contains the following functionality:

- **Available Tables and Fields:** Contains all tables and fields within the report. You may use this list box to select the field to base a running total upon.

- **Running Total Name:** Allows you to type a name for your running total. The name of the field may contain mixed-case characters and/or spaces. By default, Crystal Reports creates a unique field name for you.
- **Fields to summarize:** Displays the field you select from the Available Tables and Fields list box. This field is the one you'll base a running total upon.

  Use the Add button (>) to copy a field from the Available Tables and Fields list box to this field.
- **Type of summary:** Allows you to choose the type of calculation the running total shall perform (for example, sum or average).

  These options will change depending on the data type of the field that you select. For example, a field that contains text data will not contain the ability to calculate sums.
- **The Evaluate area:** Allows you to specify at what point in the report the records are incremented. The most common option (and the default) is to have the report increment "For each record."
- **The Reset area:** Allows you to specify when the running total accumulation should start over and reset to zero. The most common option (and the default) is to never have the report reset the running total within a report.

Although this dialog box may look complex, it's a lot less painless than creating a running total formula from scratch. Continuing with your report, try the following:

1. **In the Create Running Total Field dialog box, leave the Running Total Name as default.**
2. **In the Evaluate area, check the On change of group check box.**

   Make sure the drop-down field is set to Group#1: Customer.Customer Name. This setting defines that a running total will display at the end of each group.

Figure 9-5 displays this setting within the Create Running Total Field dialog box.

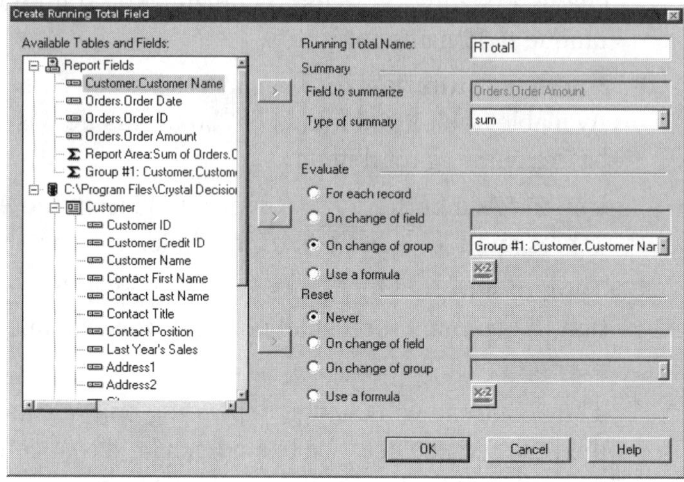

Figure 9-5. Defining a running total

3. **Press the OK button.**

   You'll notice your running total field display above the Order Amount subtotal (within the Group Footer #1 section).

4. **Move this running total field to the right of the Order Amount subtotal.**

5. **Create a header for this running total, and place it within the Page Header section.**

   Call this header Running Total. Figure 9-6 displays how your screen should look.

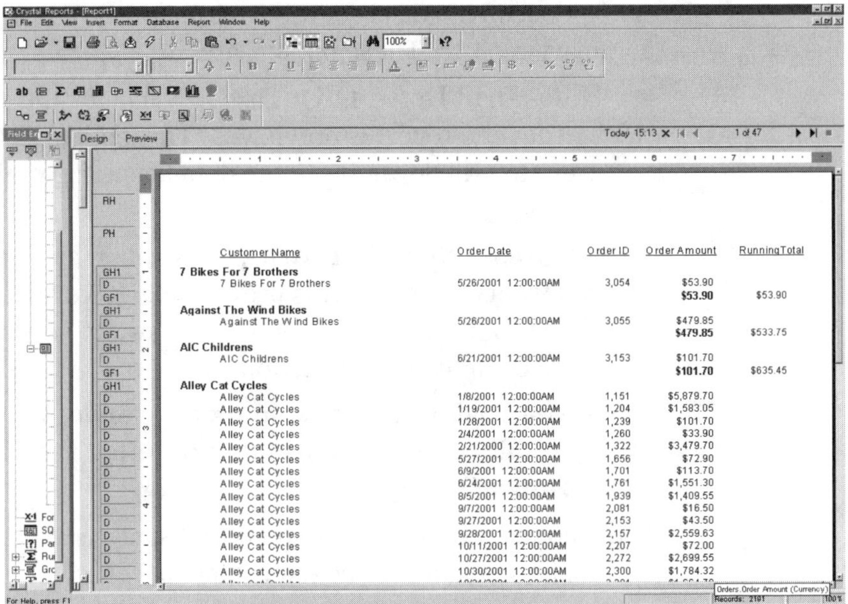

Figure 9-6. A report with a running total

Creating Summary Reports

So far in this chapter, you've created detailed reports that display every record that makes up your totals. However, you'll find that often your report users will desire two types of reports, one that shows detail (such as what you've created so far in this chapter) and one that provides a summary (just the totals and no details).

Crystal Reports makes creating summary reports easy. When creating a summary report, all grouping information displays; only the information within your Details section is suppressed.

The great thing about Crystal Reports is that it also provides the ability for your report users to view (on demand) any detail from a summary report. This technique is known as drill-down. *Drill-down* allows report users to expand view detail information.

Let's try the following to familiarize yourself with the creation of a summary report. Try the following exercise, using the report you've been creating within this chapter.

1. **Select the Design tab.**
2. **Right-click on the gray area of the Details section.**

An Options menu displays with two options available for summary reports. These options are:

- **Hide (Drill Down OK):** This option hides the section whenever a report is previewed. This option allows users to drill down to see the detail contents of this section.
- **Suppress (No Drill Down):** This option hides a section whenever a report is previewed. However, this option *does not* allow users to drill down to see the detail contents of this section.

3. **Since you wish to create a summary report with the ability to allow users to drill down, select the Hide (Drill Down OK) option.**

   You'll notice the Details section now displays slash marks. This indicates that the section is hidden.

4. **Select the Preview tab.**

   You'll notice the Details section is not displayed. Your screen should look something like Figure 9-7.

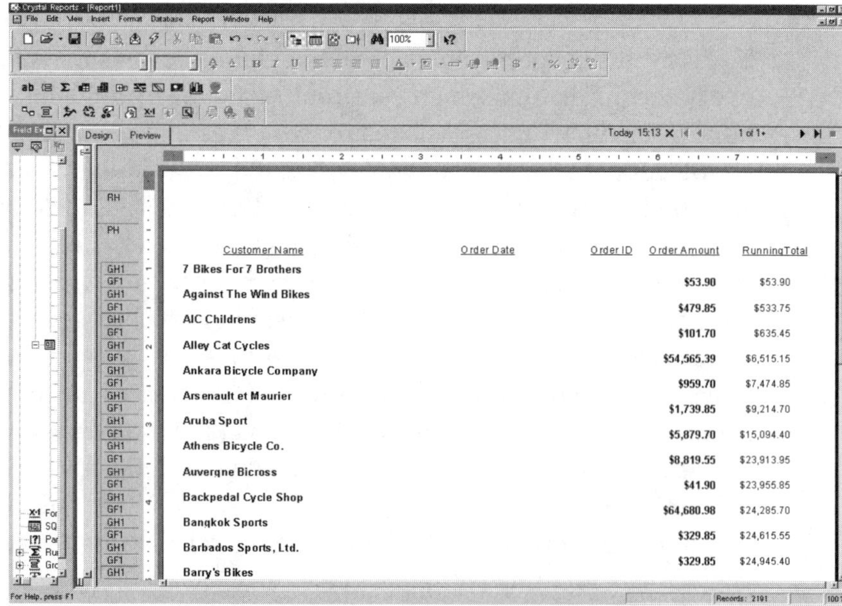

Figure 9-7. Creating a summary report within Crystal Reports

Drilling Down for Details

Once you've created a summary report, let's check out the drill-down functionality. The drill down is only available within the Preview tab.

To use the drill down, move your cursor over the Alley Cat Cycles group (specifically, the group for which you wish to view the detail records). The cursor will turn into a magnifying glass icon. When this happens, double-click. A new tab is created, which contains the group's supporting information. Figure 9-8 displays an example of the drill-down functionality.

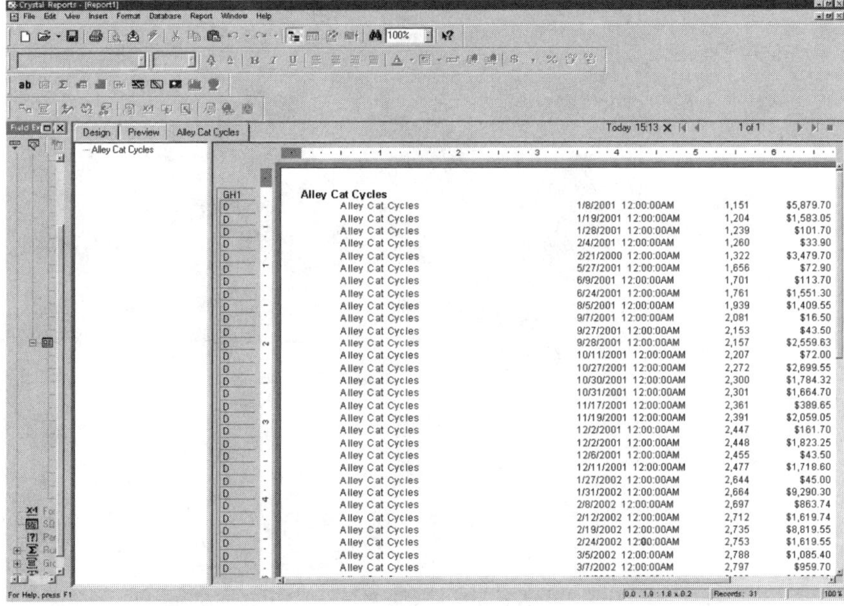

Figure 9-8. The drill-down functionality

Note

Crystal Reports will only print drill-down information when the drill-down tab is open. If you're in the Preview tab, your drill-down tab information will not print.

One thing you might notice when viewing a drill-down tab is that the headers above your information have disappeared. You can fix this with the following steps:

1. **Select the Preview tab.**
2. **Select File, Report Options from the menu bar.**

   You'll receive a warning message stating that your drill-down tabs will disappear. This is not a problem; you can recreate them if necessary. Press OK on the warning message.
3. **The Report Options dialog box displays. Check the Show All Headers On Drill Down option.**

   Your screen should look like Figure 9-9.

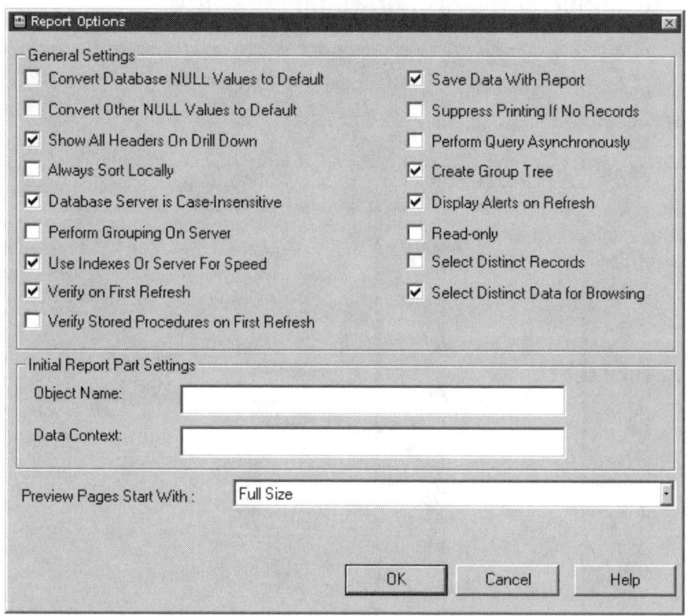

Figure 9-9. Modifying the Report Options dialog box for the drill-down functionality

4. **Press OK on the Report Options dialog box.**

Once you're back at the Report Design area, double-click on the Alley Cat Cycles group again. Notice the headers now display, as shown in Figure 9-10.

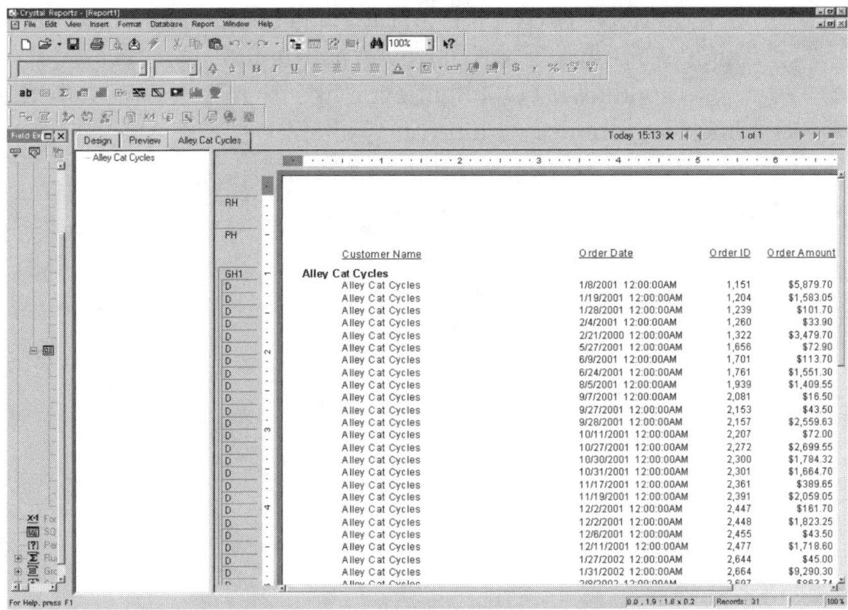

Figure 9-10. Drill-down functionality with the headers information displayed

Closing Drill-Down Tabs

After a while, the drill-down tabs might be getting in your way. That's not a problem; you can close them and then recreate them as necessary.

To close a drill-down tab, first make sure that you're in the tab you wish to close. Notice a red "X" near the page navigation buttons. Simply press this red "X" and the drill-down tab is closed.

What's Next?

In this chapter, you've learned some of the basics about manipulating your data. You've used many of Crystal Reports' predefined summary calculations to add subtotals and summary operations. You also learned about creating summary reports and the power of Crystal Reports' drill-down functionality.

In the next chapter, you learn to create other calculations (some mathematical, some not) to also suit your needs. If the words "math" and "programming" turn your stomach — don't worry.

Crystal Reports contains all the tools you need to make programming painless and perhaps even a little fun.

Who knows, you might even like it. Turn the page — the budding programmer within you awaits!

Part II Exercise

Cross-Tab Inventory Report

See the companion files (www.wordware.com/files/crystal) for an example of this report. Create this report with the Cross-Tab Report Creation Wizard. This report is created with the xtreme.mdb database.

Table(s)	Fields
Product	Product Name
Product_Type	Product Type Name
Purchases	Units in Stock Units on Order

Use the Smart Linking feature to link these tables. You'll want to make sure they're linked as follows:

- Product.Product ID = Purchases.Product ID
- Product.Product Type ID = Product_Type.Product Type ID

When you get to the Cross-Tab screen, place the Product Type Name field in the Rows list box, the Product Name field in the Columns list box, and the Units in Stock and Units on Order fields in the Summary Fields list box. Your screen should look like Figure P2-1.

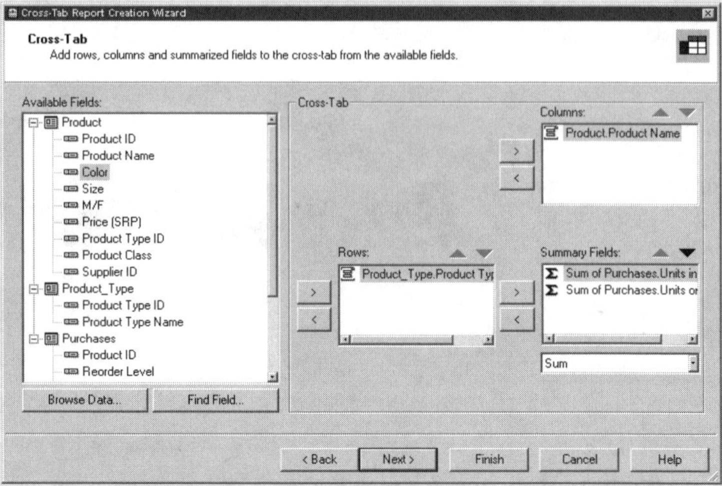

Figure P2-1. Defining a cross-tab report

Once you've defined the fields in the Cross-Tab screen, press the Next button. Then perform the following steps:

1. **In the Chart screen, select the No Chart option button.**

   Once you've done this, press the Next button.

2. **In the Record Selection screen, add the Product Type Name and the Product Class fields (both from the Product table) to the Filter Fields list box.**
3. **In the Record Selection screen, select the Product Type Name (located in the Filter Fields list box). Use the drop-down field below the Filter Fields list box and select the following: is not like.**
4. **In the second drop-down field, type in the following: Xtreme*.**

   Your screen should look like Figure P2-2.

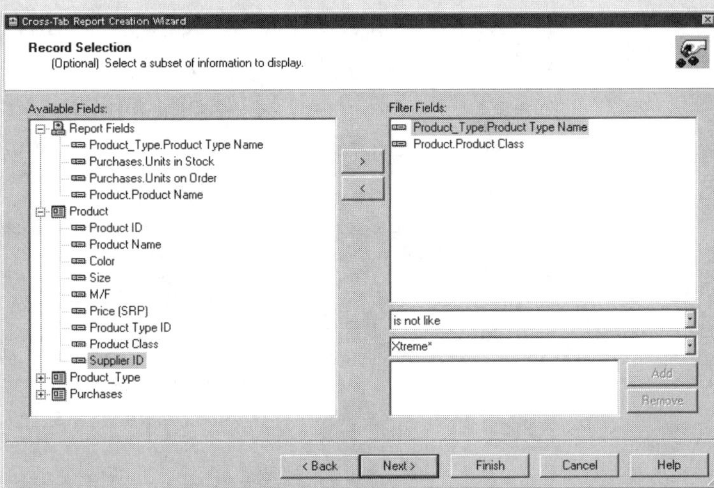

Figure P2-2. Defining a filter for the Product Type Name field

5. **In the Record Selection screen, select the Product Class (in the Filter Fields list box). Use the drop-down field below the Filter Fields list box and select the following: is equal to.**
6. **In the second drop-down field, select Accessory.**

   Your screen should look like Figure P2-3.

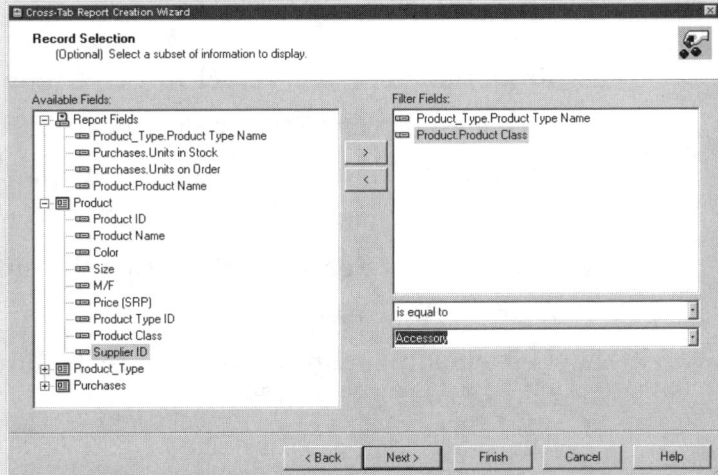

Figure P2-3. Defining a filter for the Product Class field

Once you've done these steps, press the Next button.

7. **In the Grid Style screen, select the Silver Sage 1 option.**

   Once you've done this, press the Finish button. Your report displays, as shown in Figure P2-4. (The Silver Sage 1 option places a pale green background behind the text.)

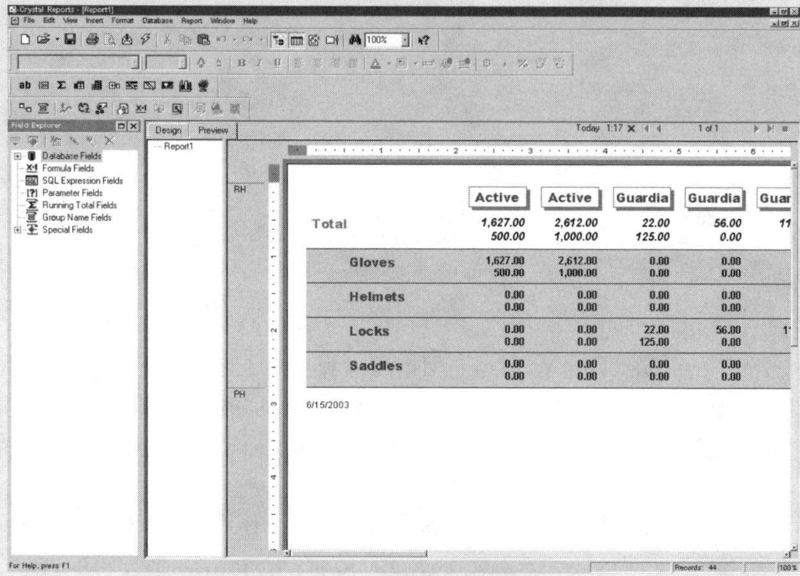

Figure P2-4. The start of a cross-tab inventory report

8. **From the menu bar, select Insert, Group.**

   Create a group using the Product Type Name.

9. **Right-click in the Group Header section.**

   An options menu displays.

10. **Select Insert Section Below from the options menu.**

    A Group Header b displays.

11. **Left-click in an area above the text "Total" (which is part of your cross-tab).**

    The entire cross-tab is selected.

12. **Drag the cross-tab into the Group Header b section.**
13. **Right-click in the Group Header a section.**

    An options menu displays again.

14. **From the options menu, select Suppress (No Drill Down).**

15. **Stretch the Product Type Name headers so that the entire name displays.**

    Figure P2-5 displays what your screen should look like.

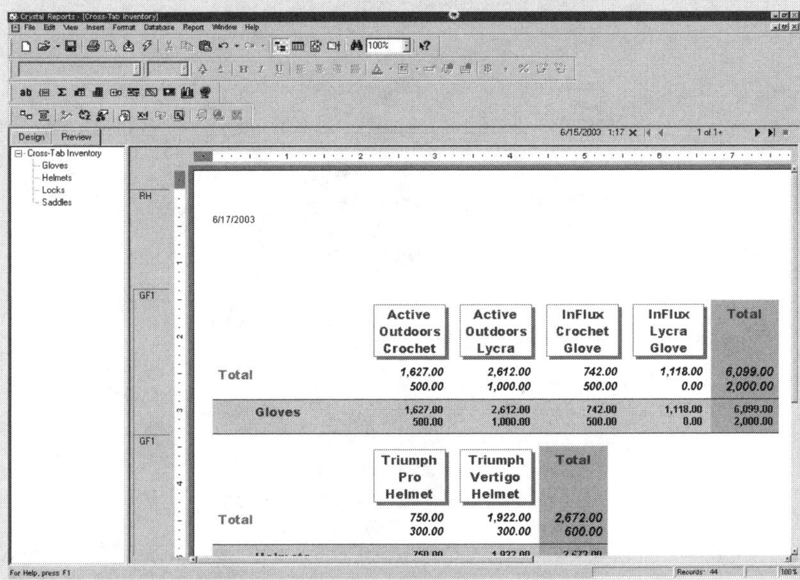

Figure P2-5. Formatting the cross-tab report

16. **Right-click the Sum of Purchases.Units in Stock object associated with the Product Name.**

    If you're not sure which object is the Units in Stock sum, select the Design tab. The names of your objects are displayed. This field has a white background.

    Once you right-click on this object, an options menu displays.

17. **Select Format Field from this options menu.**

    The Format Editor displays.

18. **In the Format Editor, select the Border tab.**

    In the Border tab, check the Background check box (located in the Color section), and select the color Yellow from the drop-down field next to the Background check box, as shown in Figure P2-6.

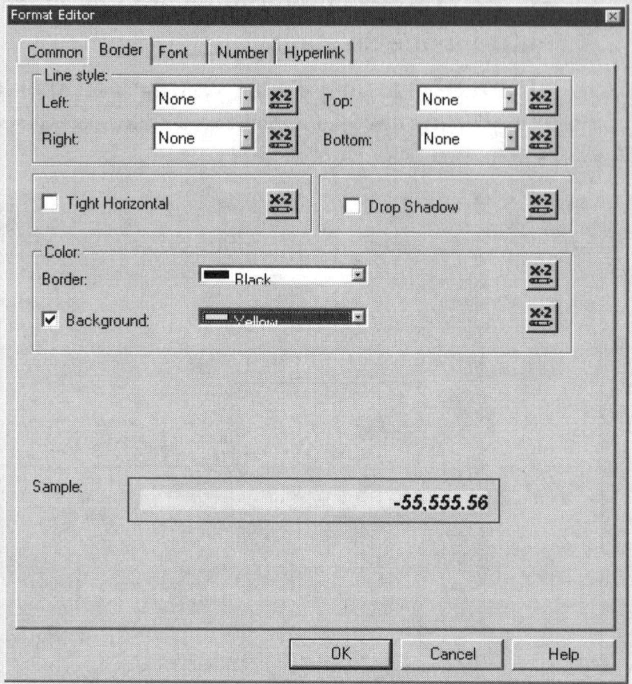

Figure P2-6. Defining a color for a report object

19. **Press the OK button on the Format Editor.**

    If you preview your report, you'll notice that all Units in Stock sums display with a yellow background.

20. **Right-click the Sum of Purchases.Units in Order object associated with the Product Type.**

    This field has a green background.

21. **With this object selected, select Format, Highlighting Expert from the menu bar.**

    The Highlighting Expert displays, as shown in Figure P2-7.

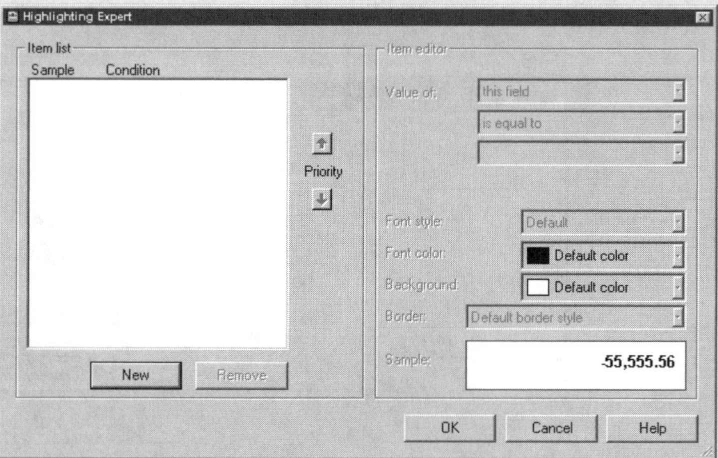

Figure P2-7. The Highlighting Expert

22. **In the Highlighting Expert, press the New button.**

    This creates a new highlighting item.

23. **In the Item Editor (located on the right side of the screen) define the following:**

    - The Value of section should read: this field is less than or equal to 0.00
    - Change the Background color to red

    Figure P2-8 displays what your defined Highlighting Expert should look like. This will highlight any values that meet the criteria you've just defined. In this example, should a Units in Stock number be less than or equal to 0.00, the number will display in red.

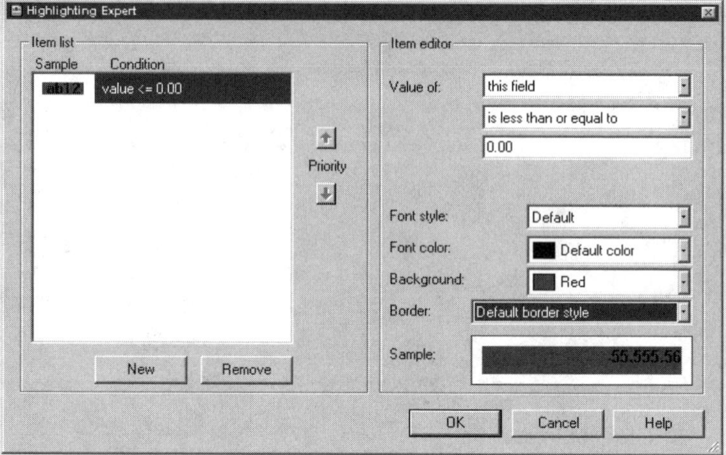

Figure P2-8. Defining the Highlighting Expert

24. **Press the OK button in the Highlighting Expert.**

    You're returned to the Report Design area.

To complete this report, you'll just need to perform a couple of formatting tasks. First, create a text object, and place this object within the Report Header section. This object will be your title. Type the following into this text object: Inventory Report. You'll probably want to stretch this object as necessary and also increase the size to about 18 and add a bold font.

Next, move the Print Date field into the Report Header section. You can place this field directly below your title. Finally, go to File, Printer Setup and change the type of paper this report uses to Legal. Once you've done that, preview your finished report. Figure P2-9 displays the result of this finished report.

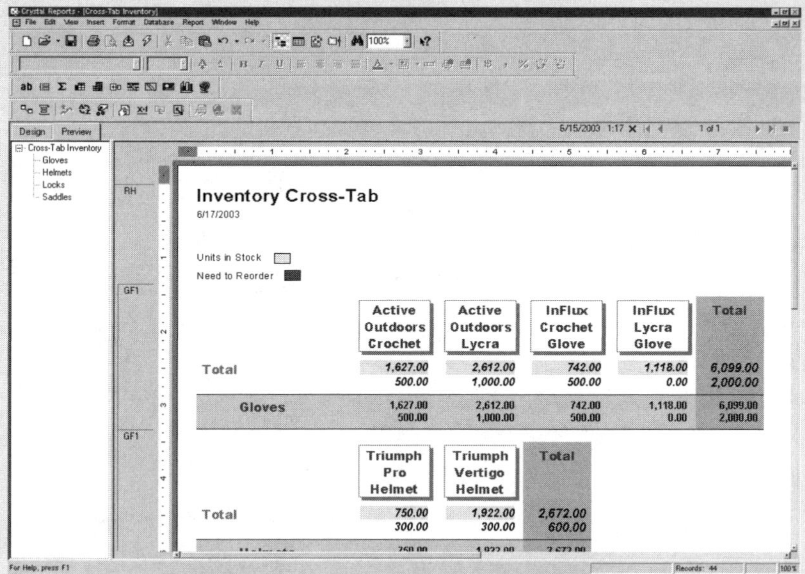

Figure P2-9. The finished Inventory Cross-Tab report

Part III

Advanced Report Writing

Understanding Formulas

Dynamic Reporting with Report Parameters

Visualizations with Charts and Maps

Creating Subreports

Distributing Reports

Exploring Crystal Reports' SQL Commands

Part III Exercise

Chapter 10

Understanding Formulas

Mention the word "mathematics," and most people become rigid with tension and terror (myself being no exception). Don't feel bad if you have these fears; you're not alone.

I hate to be the one to deliver bad news, but as you propel yourself further down the road of report development, you'll eventually find yourself needing to revisit the world of mathematics. Report development is a form of programming. And programming is truly nothing more than writing equations.

But there's good news. Crystal Reports takes into consideration that most users aren't mathematical wizards or programmers by trade. Crystal Reports contains a number of easy-to-use tools that makes programming in Crystal Reports painless. You might even find it kind of fun.

In this chapter, we discuss adding formulas to your reports. We learn not only what formulas are and the situations for which they're used in reports, but you should also come away equipped with some programming knowledge to get you through most programming obstacles you should run into.

If only high school algebra had been this easy!

The World of Formulas

So what are formulas?

Formulas are symbolic statements that control how data displays within your report. In Crystal Reports, you may create *formula fields*, which contain calculations based on existing database fields. Formula fields are a combination of two parts: the components and the syntax.

Components are the pieces that you add to create a formula. *Syntax* refers to the rules that dictate how you must organize the components. You'll learn about both components and syntax as you work your way through this chapter.

Once you've created formula fields, you may insert them within your reports, formatting them just as you have other objects (such as database fields or text objects).

Exploring the Formula Workshop

In Crystal Reports, you utilize the Formula Workshop to create formula fields. The Formula Workshop acts as a central location from where you may add, edit, or delete any formulas within your report.

Before we access the Formula Workshop, let's create a sample report to utilize within this chapter. Create a blank report, selecting the Employee and Orders tables. Allow the Smart Linking to link these tables, or refer to the ER Model diagram in Appendix A.

Once you're at the Report Design area, add the following fields to the Details section:

- Last Name (from the Employee table)
- First Name (from the Employee table)
- Order Date (from the Orders table)
- Order Amount (from the Orders table)

Create a group using the Last Name field. Use the Format Editor to change the Order Date field to adjust any sections as necessary. Once you've got this report created, select Report, Formula

Workshop from the menu bar. The Formula Workshop displays, as shown in Figure 10-1.

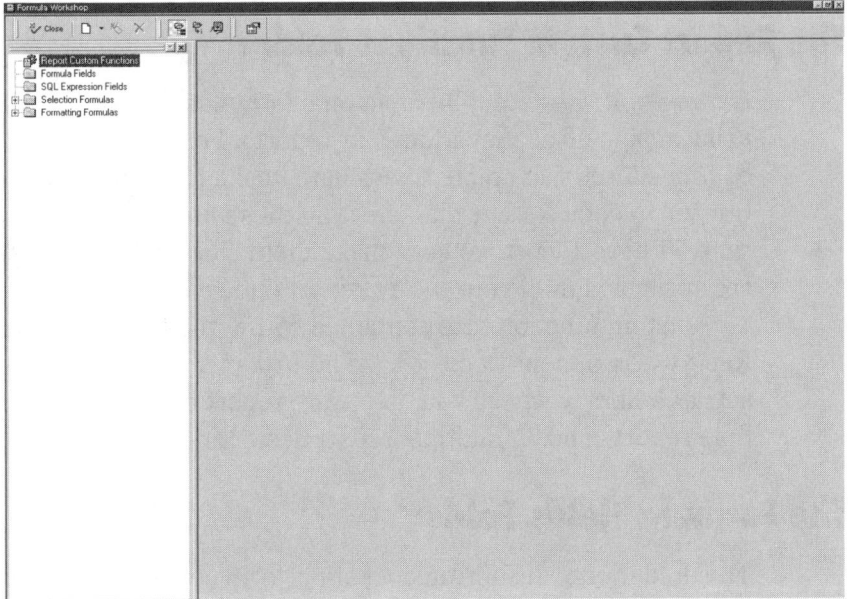

Figure 10-1. The Formula Workshop

The Workshop Tree is located on the left side of the Formula Workshop. The Workshop Tree contains a number of folders, each representing the different types of formulas that you can create in Crystal Reports.

Tip

To undock the Workshop Tree, click and hold your mouse button somewhere within the Workshop Tree's gray border. You'll find that you can drag and drop the Workshop Tree anywhere within your desktop. To dock the Workshop Tree again, drag it back to the left side of the Formula Workshop.

If you find that the Workshop Tree is not docking, right-click on the Workshop Tree title bar. In the Options menu that displays, make sure the Allow Docking option is checked.

The following sections summarize the different types of formulas that you can create within Crystal Reports. Whenever you create a formula, it is stored in the appropriate folder in the Formula Workshop for easy reference.

The Report Custom Functions Folder

Custom functions are fully functional formulas that you find yourself using again and again within your reports. For example, they might be procedures you create to evaluate, make calculations on, or transform data. Rather than creating these kinds of formulas every time within a report, you can make them custom functions so they are available for all your future report endeavors.

Custom functions are contained within the Crystal Reports' Report Component Repository. The *Report Component Repository* acts as a library where you may store report objects for use in multiple reports and by multiple report designers.

The Formula Fields Folder

This folder contains formulas that perform some sort of operation to the data that results in a new value. For example, a report formula might combine two text strings into one or perform a financial calculation on two numeric database fields to return some numeric result.

The SQL Expression Fields Folder

This folder contains formulas created exclusively with SQL rather than the Crystal Reports formula syntax. Often, users who are familiar with the SQL language prefer to write report queries and formulas through SQL statements rather than use Crystal Reports' "out of the box" functionality.

A full explanation of SQL is beyond the scope of this book. However, check out Chapter 15 for information about using SQL within your reports.

The Selection Formulas Folder

This folder contains formulas that limit (filter) the amount of data returned from the database. You created some selection formulas (with the Select Expert) in Chapter 7. In the next chapter, we look at expanding the functionality of selection formulas through the use of parameter fields.

The Formatting Formulas Folder

These formulas (better known as conditional formatting formulas) change the appearance of a report object (for example, changing the color of text or a database field or combining two database fields into one).

Formula Language: Crystal vs. Basic

In Crystal Reports, you have the option of using either Crystal or Basic syntax.

If you're familiar with Microsoft Visual Basic (or other versions of Basic), then you'll find Basic syntax quite familiar. Basic syntax is similar to Visual Basic, except it includes additional extensions to aid with reports.

In contrast, the Crystal syntax is similar to the Pascal or Delphi programming languages.

Note

Crystal syntax is the default formula language within Crystal Reports. In this book, you utilize Crystal syntax as your formula language. For more information about Basic syntax, check out "Creating Formulas with Basic Syntax" in the Crystal Reports online help.

Both languages are capable of performing the same jobs, and there are no performance issues associated with the languages. Thus, the choice is entirely based on your familiarity with the language. It is equally possible to create any formula within both the Crystal and Basic syntaxes.

No matter which language you choose to use, there are some fundamental concepts to formula creation found in both languages. The following sections summarize the most important areas of the language — enough to get your formulas up and running.

Common Operators

In the world of programming, *operators* provide some type of calculation on two values, resulting in the return of a single value.

Although Crystal Reports contains a plethora of operators that you may use within your formulas, there are essentially four basic operators you'll use over and over within your reports. These are summarized in the following table.

Table 10-1. The basic arithmetic operators used within report formulas

Operator	Operation	Description
+	Add	Returns the sum of the values within the formula.
–	Subtract	Returns the remainder of deducting one value from another.
*	Multiply	Returns the product of multiplying values together.
/	Divide	Returns the quotient of dividing one value by another.

Reserved Characters

Several keyboard characters are used by the Crystal and Basic languages and are thus considered reserved. The following table summarizes the different uses of these characters within report formulas.

Table 10-2. Reserved characters of the Crystal and Basic languages

Reserved Character	Name	Description
{ }	Curly brackets	Used to contain the report objects (such as the database or formula fields). For example: {Employee.First Name}
[ ]	Square brackets	Used to create computational formulas. Another common use for them is to return the character of a string field. For example: {Employee.First Name}[1] returns the first character of this string field.
( )	Parentheses	Used with operators to contain the different parts of a formula and define the order in which the calculations should take place.
.	Period	Separates the table name from the database field. For example: {Employee.Last Name}.

Reserved Character	Name	Description
" "	Quotation marks	Used to surround text that you wish to display within your formulas. For example, "USA" would display the text USA within your report. We look at adding text to your report formulas later in this chapter.
,	Comma	Used to separate multiple arguments within a formula. Arguments are values that exist within a formula. See page 202 for examples of arguments in your formulas.
@	Formula	Designates formula fields. For example: {@Name_of_Formula}
?	Parameter	Designates parameter fields. For example: {?Name_of_Parameter)
#	Running total	Designates running total field. For example: {#Name of Running Total}
Σ	Summary	Designates a summary field. For example: {ΣName_of_Summary_Field}
%	SQL Expression	Designates an SQL Expression field. For example: {%Name_of_SQL_Expression}

Syntax Differences between Crystal and Basic

Unfortunately, there are a couple of syntax differences between Crystal and Basic. These differences are summarized in the following table.

Table 10-3. Syntax differences between Crystal and Basic

Reserved Character (Crystal)	Reserved Character (Basic)	Name	Description
//	'	Comment	Designates a comment. *Comments* are text ignored by the formulas and used to help explain the code's functionality.
;	:	Semicolon	Allows you to separate multiple statements within a single formula.
Enter key	- (space followed by underscore)	New Line	Designates a new line within a formula. A new line may only start between a field or function and an operator.

III Part

Creating a New Formula

The creation of formulas is made easy through a part of the Formula Workshop known as the Formula Editor. The Formula Editor is where you actually create and modify the content of formulas. The Formula Workshop is simply a means of holding all your report's areas within one area.

To jump into the world of reporting formulas, try the following steps. Use the report that you've started within this chapter.

1. **Open the Formula Workshop by selecting Report, Formula Workshop from the menu bar.**
2. **To access the Formula Editor, select the arrow next to the New button.**

   This button is located within the toolbar of the Formula Workshop, as shown in Figure 10-2.

   From the arrow next to the New button, you'll see a list of different components that you can create.

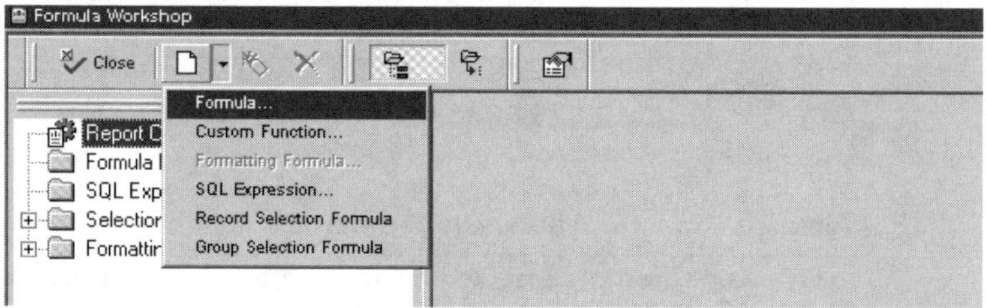

Figure 10-2. Creating a new formula from the Formula Workshop

3. **Select the Formula option from the drop-down menu.**

   A Formula Name dialog box displays.
4. **Enter the formula name EmplName.**

   Your screen should look like Figure 10-3.

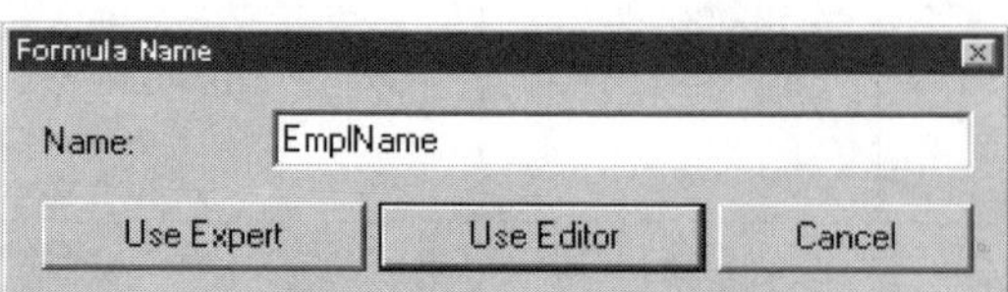

Figure 10-3. Naming a formula field

5. **Click the Use Editor button.**

   The Formula Editor displays.

Note

The Formula Expert allows you to create formulas based on existing custom functions. This is an advanced feature, useful for enhancing or editing already existing formulas. For the purposes of this book, you won't need to utilize the Formula Expert.

At first glance, the Formula Editor may seem a little scary. However, don't worry (be happy). Its bark is worse than its bite! Figure 10-4 displays the Formula Editor.

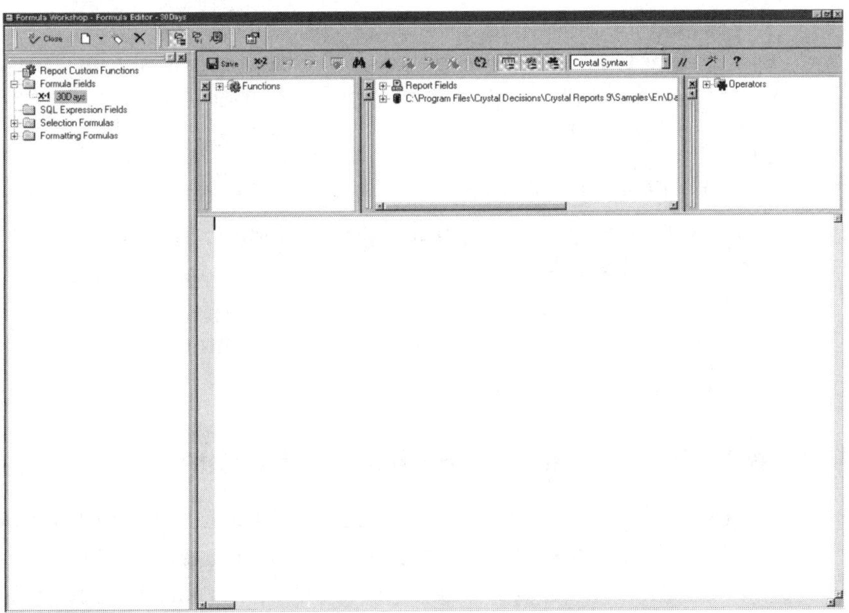

Figure 10-4. The Formula Editor

The Formula Editor allows you to add, edit, or delete the detail behind your formula fields. The Formula Editor consists of the following four windows:

- **Functions:** Contains the prewritten procedures included within Crystal Reports. These procedures perform a variety of calculations.

- **Report Fields:** Contains all the database fields available within your report. This window also contains any groups and other formulas already created within your report.
- **Operators:** Contains the symbols that represent a specific action. Think of operators as the "action verbs" that you use in formulas. Operators describe the action that takes place between two or more values.
- **Formula text window:** Contains the area where you write and edit the content of your formulas.

Note

The Workshop Tree displays to the left side of the Formula Editor.

Within the Formula Editor, you should see the different formulas that you create reside within the appropriate folder. The Formula Workshop is Crystal Reports' way of organizing your work.

In the Formula Editor, you create formulas by double-clicking any of the components within the Report Fields, Functions, or Operators windows. When you select a component, the required syntax is also inserted automatically.

Of course, if you're a glutton for punishment, you can also manually type every aspect of your formulas.

Creating a Concatenating String Formula

Now that you're somewhat familiar with where formula creation takes place, let's actually create some formulas.

At this point, you should have already created a new report and started the creation of a formula with the name EmplName. If you have not done these steps, flip back through this chapter to get yourself up to this point.

Once you've done these things, try writing your first formula. Notice that the Last Name and First Name information display in separate fields. This first formula combines these two fields into one and separates them with a comma, so the fields display in the format: *last name, first name*.

In the world of programming, this is known as concatenating fields. *Concatenating* means to link together or join. Thus, what this formula does is create a string field that links together the last name and first name fields from the Employee table.

Concatenating fields is useful. Often, you'll need to create such formula fields for addresses and your customers and employees.

Perform the following steps. Continue using the report example that you've been working on within this chapter.

1. **In the middle window, expand the Report Fields node.**

   You'll see the four fields that currently exist within your report.

2. **Double-click the Employee.Last Name field.**

   This field displays within the formula text window located in the lower half of the Formula Editor.

3. **After the (Employee.Last Name) field, type the following: +", "+.**

   This syntax states that you're adding a comma, followed by a blank space, between the Last Name and First Name fields.

4. **After you've typed in that information, double-click the Employee.First Name field, located in the Report Fields window.**

   The results of your work should look like Figure 10-5 on the following page.

After typing in your code, press Alt+C. You can also press the Check button next to the Save button (the Check button contains the text "x+2" with a green check mark below). Your formula should display the message "No Errors Found." Press OK on this message.

Finally, press the Save button and close the formula. You can close your formula using the Close button at the top left of the screen (above the Formula Workshop folders). Or you can press the X button at the top right of the screen to exit. You're returned to the Report Design area.

Congratulations — you've just become a programmer!

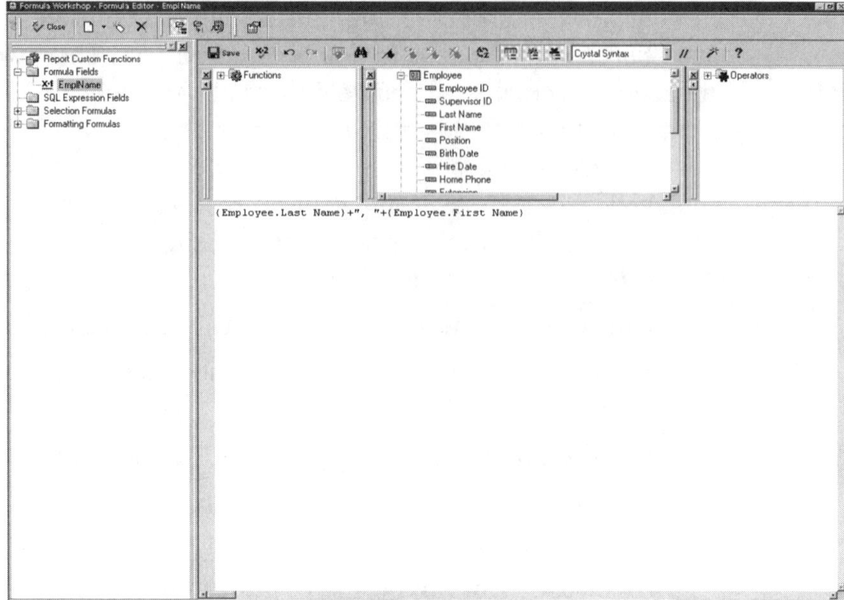

Figure 10-5. Creating a string formula

To see your work in action, try the following. Continue using the report that you've created within this chapter.

1. **Select the Design tab.**
2. **Delete the Last Name and First Name fields from the Details section.**
3. **From the menu bar, select Report, Group Expert.**

   The Group Expert dialog box displays.
4. **Press the Remove (<) arrow to remove the Employee.Last Name field as your group.**
5. **You'll notice the EmplName formula you just created now displays at the bottom of your report fields. Select this field, and press the Add (>) arrow button.**

   Your report will now group data by your formula field.

Press the OK button on the Group Expert. You may want to move the Order Date and Order Amount information slightly to the left to improve the appearance of your report.

Once you're satisfied with the report's look, try previewing your work. Your report should look something like Figure 10-6.

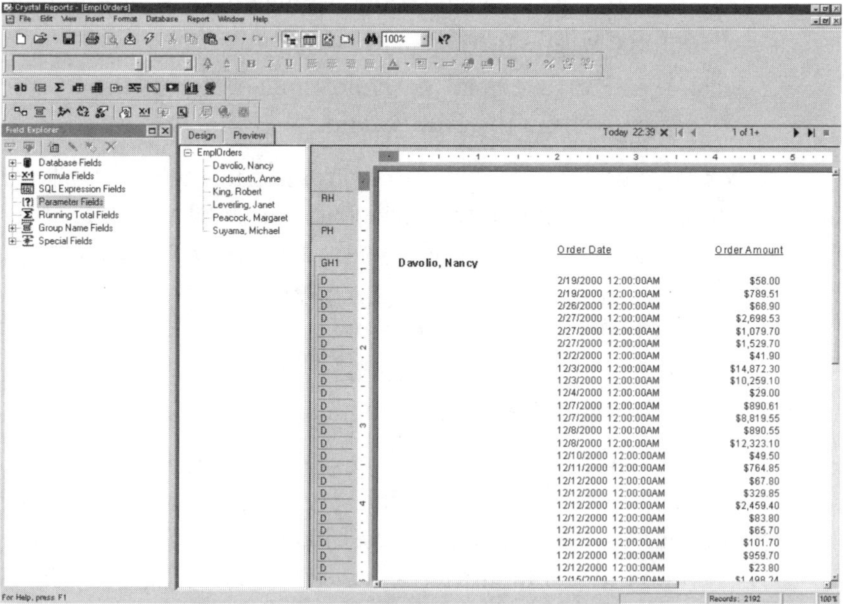

Figure 10-6. Grouping a report by a formula field

Of course, formula fields can be added to any section of your report (not just groups). Go to the Field Explorer window to add a formula field to another section (such as the Details section). Expand the Formula Fields node to display a list of all your formula fields. To add any formula field to your report, you can simply drag the formula field to the appropriate section.

Creating a Conditional Formula (Using Functions)

Up to this point, you've learned about creating formulas using arithmetic operators such as the plus sign (+) or the greater than or equal (>=) symbol.

There are two more operators that are just as useful, if not more so, than the arithmetic operators. These are the conditional operators. *Conditional operators* evaluate a statement's result as either true or false (known as the Boolean result). The two operators used with conditional statements are IF THEN and ELSE.

The IF THEN and ELSE operators work in the following manner:

- If the IF clause is true, the formula performs the functionality defined within the THEN clause.
- If the IF clause is false, the formula performs the functionality defined within the ELSE clause.

For example, say you wished to create a formula that alerts report users when an employee's sales are under $150,000 for the year. Your conditional expression would state something like this:

> IF an Employee's Sale Total for the Year were less than $150,000,
> THEN print the Order Total in red,
> ELSE print the Order Total in black.

If the previous conditional expression existed within your report, the formula would first check to see if an employee's order total (for the year) equals less than $150,000. If this IF clause is true, then the order total displays in red. If the IF clause is false, the employee's order total (for the year) must be greater than $150,000. Therefore, the order total prints normally (in black).

This concept is much easier to understand in practice. Try the following example, using the report you've created within this chapter:

1. **Select Report, Record Sort Expert from the menu bar.**

   The Record Sort Expert displays.

2. **Add the Orders.Order Date field (from the Report Fields node) to the Sort Fields list box.**

   The Order Date field displays underneath the @EmplName formula field.

3. **Press the OK button on the Record Sort Expert dialog box.**

   You're returned to your report.

4. **Open the Formula Workshop.**
5. **Select the arrow next to the New button and select the Formula option.**

6. **Call this new formula Quarter. Then, press the Editor button.**

   The Formula Editor displays.

7. **Type the following code within the Formula Edit window:**

```
IF Month({Orders.Order Date}) in [1, 2, 3] THEN "Quarter 1"
ELSE
IF Month({Orders.Order Date}) in [4, 5, 6] THEN "Quarter 2"
ELSE
if Month({Orders.Order Date}) in [7, 8, 9] THEN "Quarter 3"
ELSE
IF Month({Orders.Order Date}) in [10, 11, 12] THEN "Quarter 4"
```

The "Month" word is a function, available from the Functions window (expand the Functions node and then the Date and Time node). The Month extracts the month component of a date and converts it to a number.

You'll see the Month (x) function within this node, as shown in Figure 10-7.

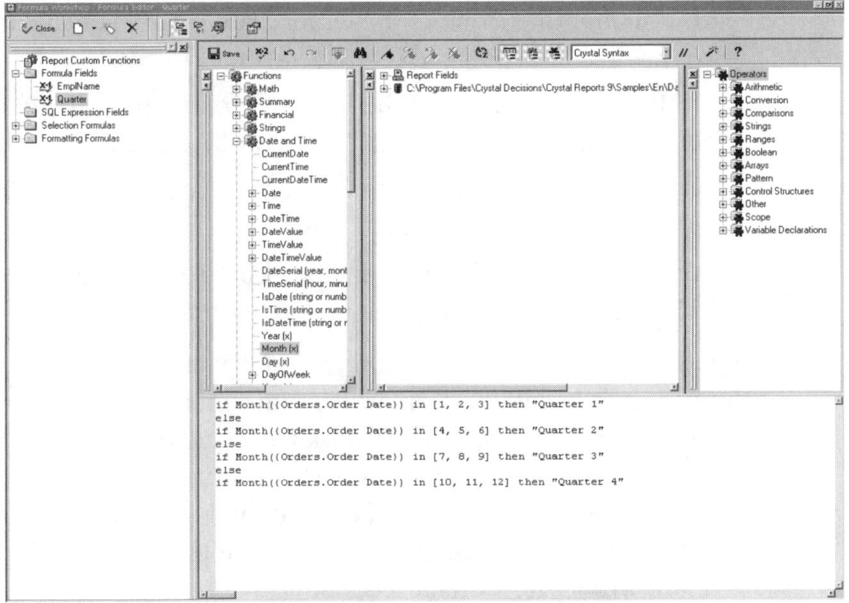

Figure 10-7. Expanding the Functions window

Once you've written this code, check the formula for correct syntax (by using the Check button). Then save the formula, and close the Formula Editor. You're returned to your report.

A Word about Functions

Most programming languages (Crystal included) come with a built-in set of procedures, known as functions. When a developer uses a function, the developer is using previously coded tasks rather than having to devise the code from scratch. Thus, functions are essentially prewritten code that you can use within your formulas.

Check out Appendix C for a summary of all of Crystal Reports' built-in functions.

The formula you've just written says the following:

> IF the month portion of the Order Date record is equal to 1, 2, or 3, THEN display the text "Quarter 1" ELSE
>
> IF the month portion of the Order Date record is equal to 4, 5, or 6, THEN display the text "Quarter 2" ELSE
>
> IF the month portion of the Order Date record is equal to 7, 8, or 9 THEN display the text "Quarter 3" ELSE
>
> IF the month portion of the Order Date record is equal to 10, 11, or 12 THEN display the text "Quarter 4"

If you're confused about how this formula works, maybe the best thing to do is see it in action. Check the syntax of your formula. If no errors are found, save your work and close the Formula Workshop. You're returned to your report.

In the Field Explorer pane, expand the Formula node. You'll see your newly created Quarter formula. Move this formula field to the .5" mark within the Details section.

Once you've done this, go to the menu bar and select Report, Group Expert. The Group Expert displays.

In the Group Expert, create a new group. This new group should reside underneath the EmplName group that you created earlier in this chapter. Once you've added this group, press the OK button on the Group Expert. You're asked if you wish to use saved or refreshed data. Press the Refresh Data button. Your report should look something like Figure 10-8.

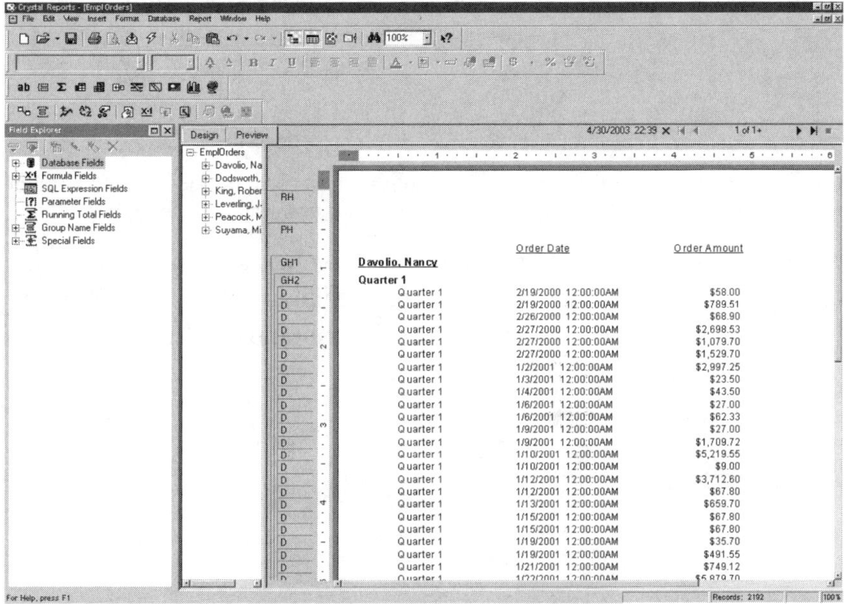

Figure 10-8. Adding a conditional formula to your report

Notice that your report now groups your data by quarter. Any months within January, February, or March are listed as Quarter 1, any months within April, May, or June are listed as Quarter 2, and so on.

Using the ToText and Year Functions

Unfortunately, most reports that display quarter information also display the year (for example, "Quarter 1, 2000" rather than just "Quarter 1"). So, how would one go about adding such information?

First, you need to extract the year from the Order Date data. To do that, you can use the Year function. The Year function extracts the year from a date and returns the value as a number.

From the menu bar, access Report, Formula Workshop. Then, expand the Formula node, and double-click the Quarter formula you created earlier. This formula displays within the Formula Editor. Change your formula in the Formula Edit window to look like the following:

```
IF the month portion of the Order Date record is equal to 1, 2, or 3, THEN
display the text "Quarter 1, " + Year({Orders.Order Date}) ELSE

IF the month portion of the Order Date record is equal to 4, 5, or 6, THEN
display the text "Quarter 2, " + Year({Orders.Order Date}) ELSE

IF the month portion of the Order Date record is equal to 7, 8, or 9, THEN
display the text "Quarter 3, " + Year({Orders.Order Date}) ELSE

IF the month portion of the Order Date record is equal to 10, 11, or 12, THEN
display the text "Quarter 4, " + Year({Orders.Order Date})
```

Once you've written this code, try checking the syntax.

Uh oh — there's an error (which is correct for this example; you'll see why in a moment). You should get the following error, as shown in Figure 10-9.

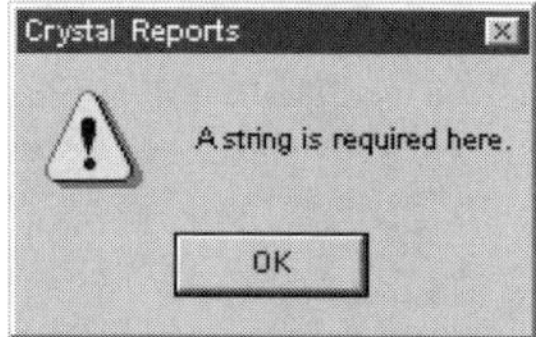

Figure 10-9. A formula syntax error

Whenever you receive an error, Crystal Reports describes the reason for the error within a message box and then highlights the problem area within your code.

The reason you received this error is that a formula cannot return a result made up of different data types. In other words, a formula result can't combine a text string (for example, "Quarter 1") with number data (for example, "2000"). So what can you do to correct this?

What you'll need to do is translate the year of the Order Date into a text string (to match the "Quarter 1" text string). A useful function that performs this is the ToText function. The ToText formula simply converts any data type into a string.

Caution

All results of your formula must end up as the same data type; otherwise you will receive errors.

If you haven't done so already, press the OK button in the error message box. Let's revisit your Quarter formula again. Type the following changes (marked in bold) into the formula. You can look at how this formula works in a moment — after writing it. Figure 10-10 displays how your screen should look.

IF the month portion of the Order Date record is equal to 1, 2, or 3, THEN display the text **"Quarter 1, " + ToText(Year({Orders.Order Date}), 0, "")**
ELSE

IF the month portion of the Order Date record is equal to 4, 5, or 6, THEN display the text **"Quarter 2, " + ToText(Year({Orders.Order Date}), 0, "")**
ELSE

IF the month portion of the Order Date record is equal to 7, 8, or 9, THEN display the text **"Quarter 3, " + ToText Year({Orders.Order Date}), 0, "")**
ELSE

IF the month portion of the Order Date record is equal to 10, 11, or 12, THEN display the text **"Quarter 4, " + ToText(Year({Orders.Order Date}), 0, "")**

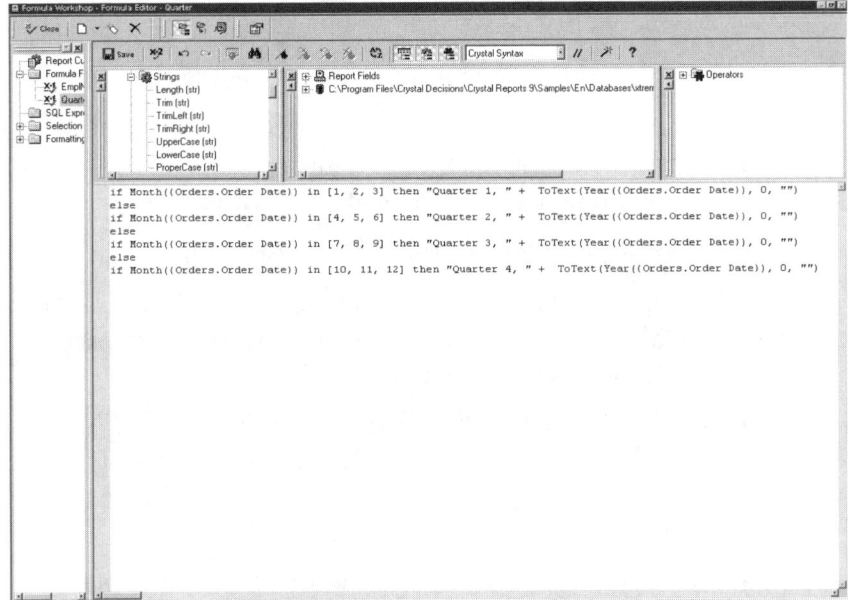

Figure 10-10. Adding the ToText function to a formula

Check the syntax of your formula. If you find no errors, save the formula and close the Formula Workshop. Figure 10-11 displays the results of this new formula. Notice the quarter information now displays the year.

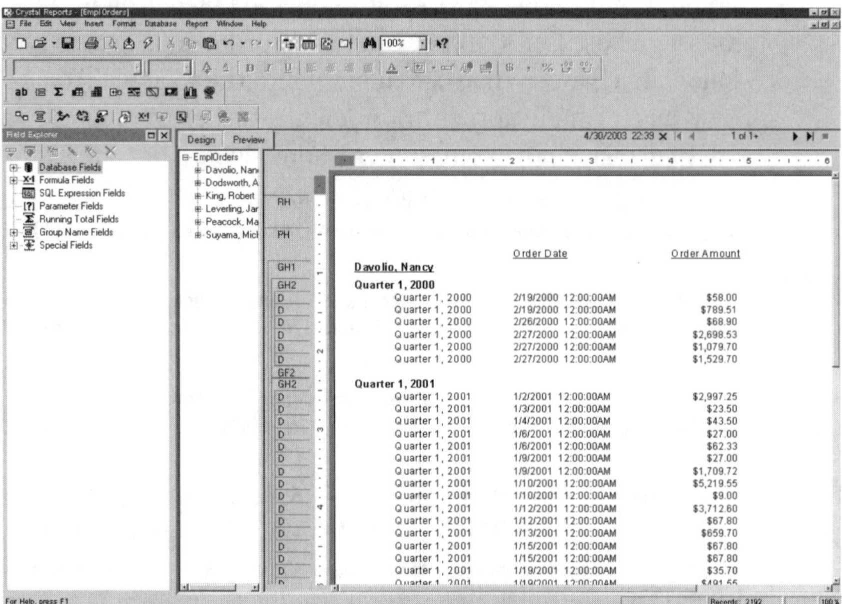

Figure 10-11. The results of your new Quarter formula

Before summarizing how this formula works, let's look briefly at the ToText function that you just used within this formula:

ToText(Year({Orders.Order Date}), 0, "")

While this looks confusing, it truly isn't. It's all part of the ToText function's syntax. Check out Appendix C for a summary of the syntax of all the Crystal functions.

The ToText function's syntax is as follows: ToText (x, y, z, w)

- x is the value you wish to convert to a text string. In the example in this chapter, the x value is the Year function, which contains the year of the Order Data field.
- y is a whole number that indicates the number of decimal places to use with the x value. In the example in this chapter, the y value is 0 (you don't want any decimal places with the year).

- z is a single-character text string that indicates the character to use to separate the thousand's place in the x value. In the example in this chapter, the z value is "". This represents no space. Thus, no character shall separate the thousand's place in the x value. Since the x value is a year, you want your year to read 2000, not 2,000.
- w is a single-character text string that indicates the character to use as a decimal separator in the x value. Since we designated 0 decimal places in the y value, we don't need to include this value.

  The default is the character specified in your International or Regional settings control panel.

With functions, you can use as many or as few of these values as you need.

There's just one final observation to note with this last formula. Notice that you changed the "Quarter *x*" text to read "Quarter *x*, ". The reason for this was to add a comma and space, so your ToText result displays correctly with the rest of your text string.

Save your work as **EmplOrders.rpt** and then take a breather — you deserve it. You've absorbed a lot in this chapter.

What's Next?

Don't worry if formulas have your head spinning. Just try to work them into your reports little by little. Eventually, you'll find yourself getting the hang of them and the power they can bring to your reports.

If you really want to get good at reporting formulas, check out a good book on SQL programming (some suggested titles are listed in Chapter 15). From there, study Appendix C to familiarize yourself with some of the Crystal Reports functions and operators that are at your fingertips. Follow this path, and you'll become a programming whiz in no time.

In the next chapter, we discuss dynamic reporting and how to put the power of selection criteria in the hands of your report users. Dynamic reporting allows different report users to control the data they wish to view, all from one report.

Chapter 11

Dynamic Reporting with Report Parameters

In Chapter 7 you learned about selection statements and how they narrow down the data that displays within a report.

Taking the concept of filtering one step further, what if you could allow report users to control how a report filters data — rather than you, the report developer, creating this filtering in advance? Perhaps a report user might wish to filter data differently each time he or she runs the report.

This ad hoc functionality is known as dynamic reporting. *Dynamic reporting* allows a user to filter a report exactly at the moment the report is run, rather than creating selection statements in advance.

To create this kind of flexibility, you utilize parameter fields (which we learn about in this chapter). *Parameter fields* are fields that use a value entered by the report user. Parameter fields prompt report users for information each time the report is generated.

The real power of parameter fields comes when the value entered by a report user is used within a selection statement (which you learn to do in this chapter). Using parameter fields in this manner allows your users to define the data a report displays.

Creating Parameter Fields to Display Text

The addition of parameter fields to your report actually consists of two parts. The first is to create the parameter field. The second is to then incorporate it into your report.

To create parameter fields, access the Field Explorer window. Then right-click on the Parameter Fields node. An options menu displays. Select New from the options menu. The Create Parameter Field dialog box displays, as shown in Figure 11-1.

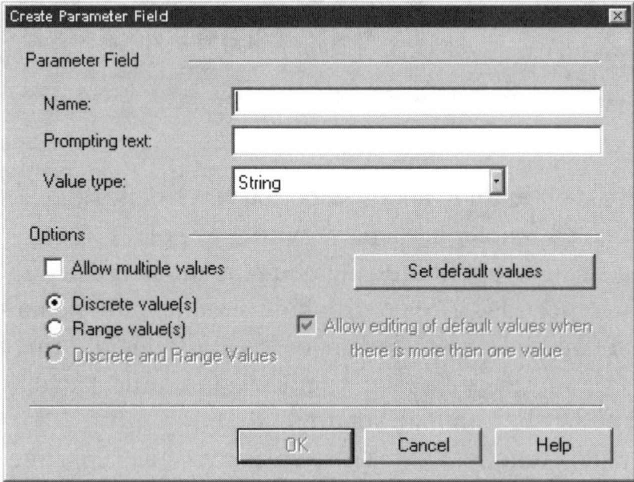

Figure 11-1. The Create Parameter Field dialog box

The following table summarizes the different functionality of the Create Parameter Field dialog box.

Table 11-1. The Create Parameter Field dialog functionality

Field	Description
Name	The name you create for your parameter field.
Prompting text	The text statement or question that displays to your report users at the parameter prompt.
Value type	The list of data types that define the type of records your parameter shall filter (for example: String, Boolean, Currency, Date, DateTime, Number, and Time).
Allow multiple values	Allows report users to enter multiple records at the parameter prompt.
Discrete value(s)	Allows report users to enter a single value at the parameter prompt.

Field	Description
Range value(s)	Allows report users to define a range, using starting and ending values, at the parameter prompt.
Discrete and Range Values	Allows report users to enter a single value, as well as a range (using the starting and ending values) at a parameter prompt.
Allow editing of default values...	Allows report users to edit any default values provided within the parameter prompt.
Set default values	Allows you (the report designer) to specify the default parameter values that display within the parameter prompt. These values may be based on a database field, an external pick list, or a manual entry.

To begin exploring parameter fields, use the report you created in the last chapter. Open the EmplOrders.rpt file you saved from Chapter 10 or access the report from the companion files (www.wordware.com/files/crystal). Make sure you're in the Create Parameter Field dialog box (found in the Field Explorer pane).

1. **In the Name field, type Report Title.**
2. **In the Prompting text field, type Please Enter the Report Title:.**

   This defines the text that displays each time the user refreshes the report.
3. **In the Value type drop-down field, select String.**

   Your screen should look like Figure 11-2.

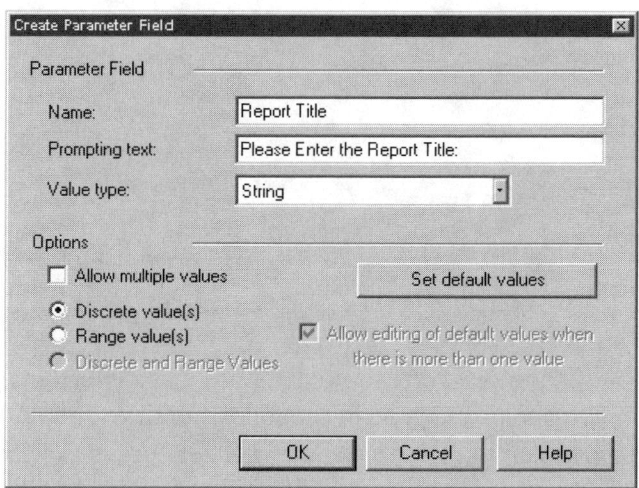

Figure 11-2. Creating a parameter field

4. **Press the OK button on the Create Parameter Field dialog box.**

   You're returned to the Report Design area.

5. **From the Field Explorer pane, expand the Parameter Fields node.**

   You'll notice the Report User parameter you just created now exists within this node.

6. **Drag the Report Title parameter field to the Report Header section.**

   You can place the field at the 0" mark, so that it's lined up with your report's left margin. Once you place this parameter field, you'll notice an Enter Parameter Values dialog box display, as shown in Figure 11-3.

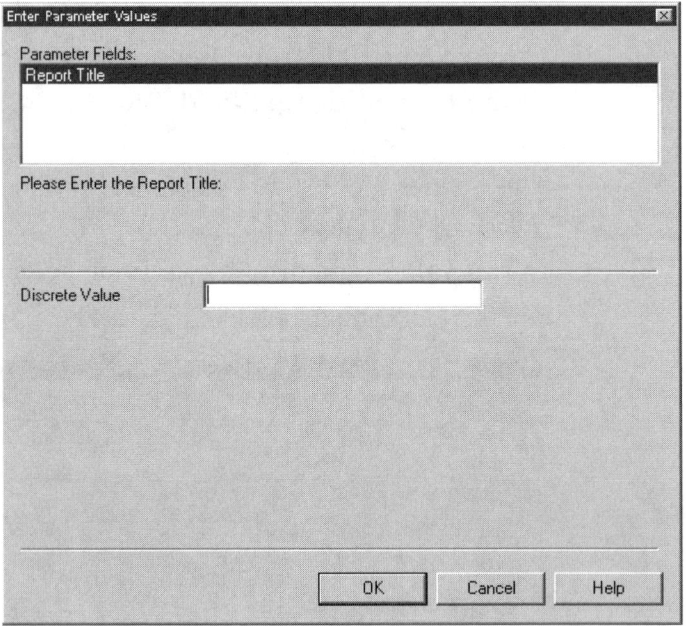

Figure 11-3. The Enter Parameter Values dialog box

Every time you refresh your report, this dialog box displays.

Go ahead and type in the following title: Employee Orders Report; run by *[your name here]*. Then, press the OK button. You'll need to resize and increase the title to make it look correct (as you learned in Chapter 5). Figure 11-4 displays what your report might look like.

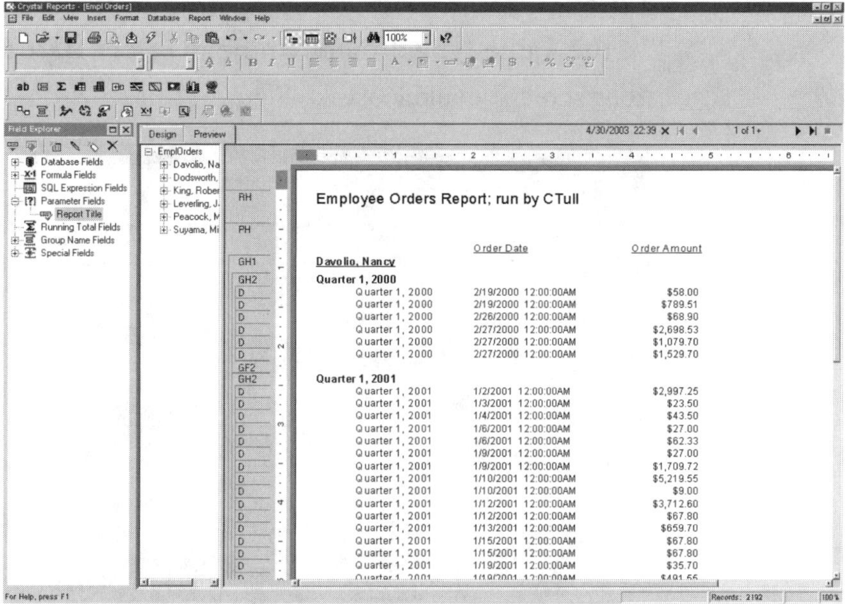

Figure 11-4. A parameter field within your report

Creating Parameter Fields to Select a Date

You'll find that one of the most common purposes of parameter fields is to select records based on a date (or some date range). In other words, the report will use the report user's defined value to select the desired records.

To perform this type of functionality, you'll need to:

- Create the parameter field
- Incorporate that parameter field into a selection statement

Continue working with the EmplOrders.rpt file.

1. **In the Field Explorer, right-click on the Parameter Fields node.**

   An options menu displays. Select New. The Create Parameter Field dialog box displays.

2. **In the Name field, type Order Date.**
3. **In the Prompting text field, type Please Enter Order Date:.**
4. **In the Value type drop-down field, select DateTime.**

   Your screen should look like Figure 11-5.

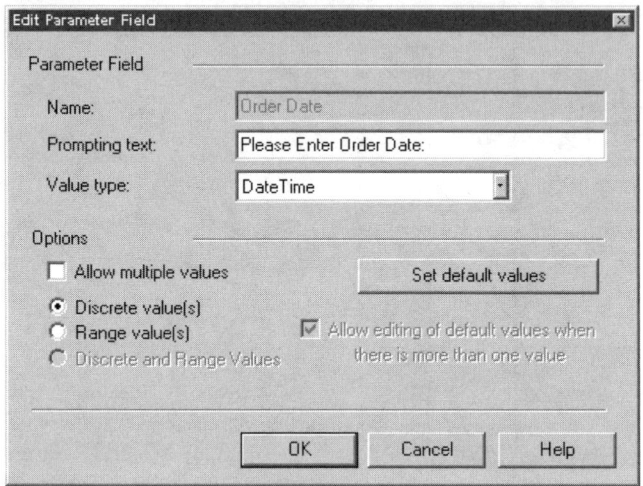

Figure 11-5. Defining a date parameter field

5. **Leave the Discrete value(s) option selected.**

   This means that the parameter value is to include only one value. If you wish to create a date range (which you learn later in this chapter), you would select the Range value(s) option.
6. **Press the OK button to close the Create Parameter Field dialog box.**

   You're returned to the Report Design area.

You're halfway there. You've created the date parameter field. Now try adding it to your report (below the title in the Report Header). You'll notice that the report date you define displays. However, none of the records in the report change, as shown in Figure 11-6. The reason there was no change in the report's data is because you have not defined the date parameter field within a selection statement.

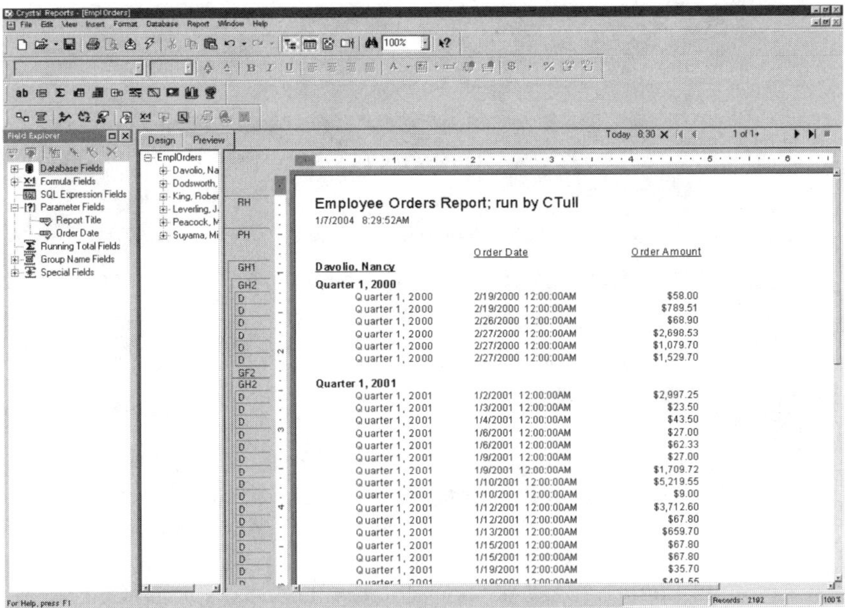

Figure 11-6. The date parameter field will not filter records until it is part of a selection formula.

Let's look now at the process of defining a parameter in a selection statement. Perform the following steps:

1. **From the menu bar, select Report, Select Expert.**

   The Choose Field dialog box displays.

2. **In the Choose Field dialog box, select the Orders.Order Date field from the Report Fields node.**

   Once you've done this, press OK. The Select Expert displays.

3. **In the Comparison Operator drop-down field, select Is Equal To.**

4. **In the Comparison Value drop-down field, select ?Order Date.**

   In Crystal Reports, all parameter fields are listed with a question mark (?) for identification purposes. Your screen should look like Figure 11-7.

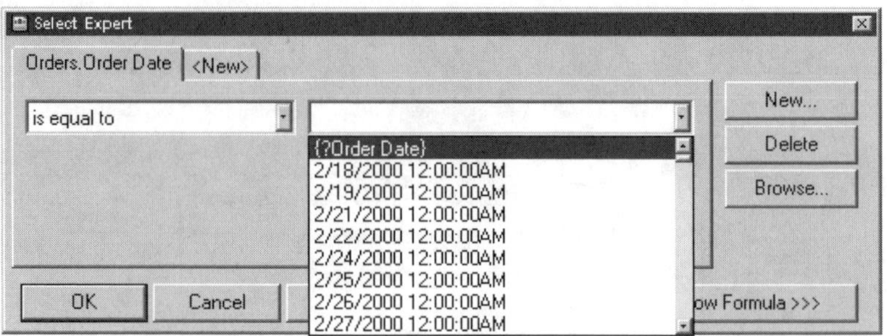

Figure 11-7. Defining a parameter value within a selection statement

Note

You don't have to create selection statements in the Select Expert; you can also create them in the Formula Editor.

Also, if you're in the Select Expert and curious about what your selection statement code looks like, press the Show Formula button. Your selection statement code displays. Once you press the Show Formula button, you'll also notice that a Formula Editor button displays, which takes you straight to the Formula Editor.

To hide this formula code, simply press the Hide Formula button on the Select Expert.

Once you've done these steps, press the OK button on the Select Expert. Refresh your data.

Your report shouldn't return any data, as shown in Figure 11-8. This is actually good. It shows that the selection statement is working.

The date that appears is the date parameter you entered earlier in this chapter. If you do not see any records display, it's because there are no records associated with the date you've entered.

Let's try again. Refresh your report by pressing the Refresh icon on the Standard toolbar. A Refresh Report Data dialog box displays, asking if you wish to use your current parameters or new parameter values. This dialog box displays every time a report with parameters is refreshed. Select the Prompt for New Parameter Values option box and press OK.

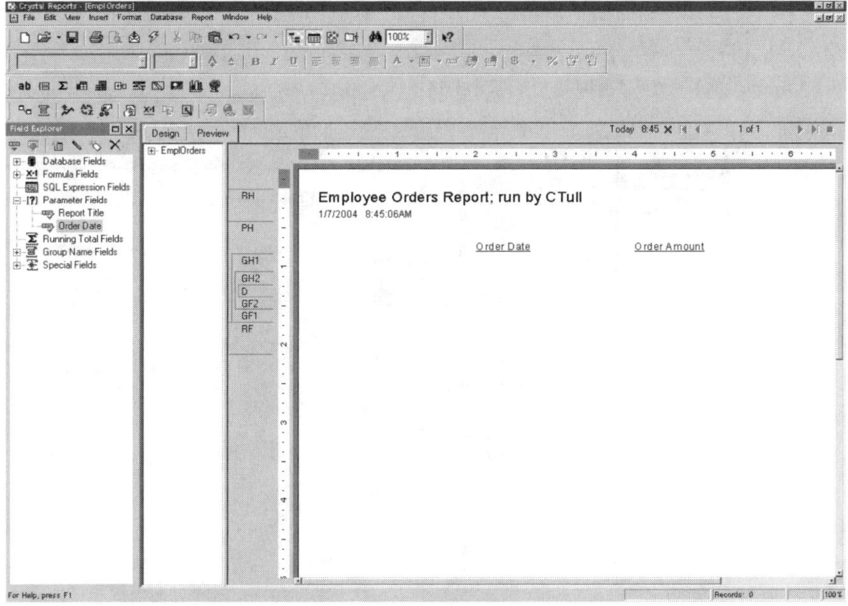

Figure 11-8. No records found for your parameter

An Enter Parameter Values dialog box displays, prompting you for the values for all report parameters:

- For the Report Title parameter, enter: Employee Orders Report; run by *[your name here].*

  Once you've done this, select with your cursor the Order Date parameter (within the list box at the top of the dialog box). If you press Enter or the OK button, Crystal assumes you wish to use the default for the second parameter.

- For the Order Date parameter, enter: 01/10/2001 12:00:00 A.M.

Once you've entered these values, press the OK button on the Enter Parameter Values dialog box. Your report refreshes with only orders that occurred on 01/10/2001, as shown in Figure 11-9.

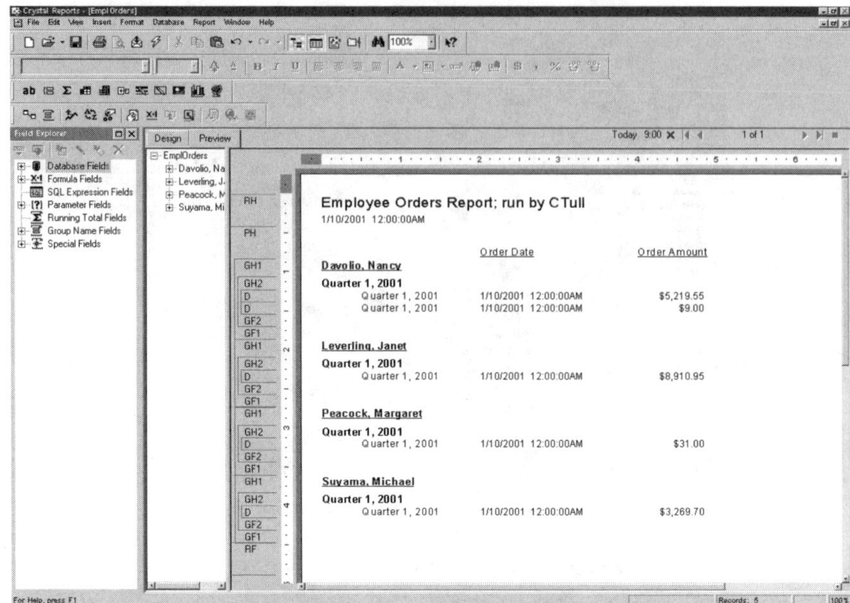

Figure 11-9. Record selection using a parameter field

Editing Parameter Fields

In the report in this chapter, you may have noticed that all the Order Date fields display in a format of DateTime. This is a default of the database. The time information isn't very helpful — it's simply defaulted to 12:00:00 A.M. with each record. Let's change this format to only display the date and then edit the parameter field to match this change. First, you'll need to change the format within the report. You learned about changing DateTime information in Chapter 5.

Right-click on the order date information within the Details section. Then, select Format Field from the options menu. The Format Editor dialog box displays. From the Format Editor, select the Date and Time tab. Then, from the Style list box, select the format that reads: 03/01/1999.

Once you've done this, press the OK button. You should now notice the Order Date information within your report change to a *mm/dd/yyyy* format.

You're now ready to edit your parameter field. Go to the Field Explorer. Then, expand the Parameter Fields node and right-click on the Order Date parameter. Select Edit from the options menu. The Edit Parameter Field dialog box displays.

Once you're at this dialog box, change the Value type to Date, as shown in Figure 11-10. You need to match the Value type to the newly changed Order Date format.

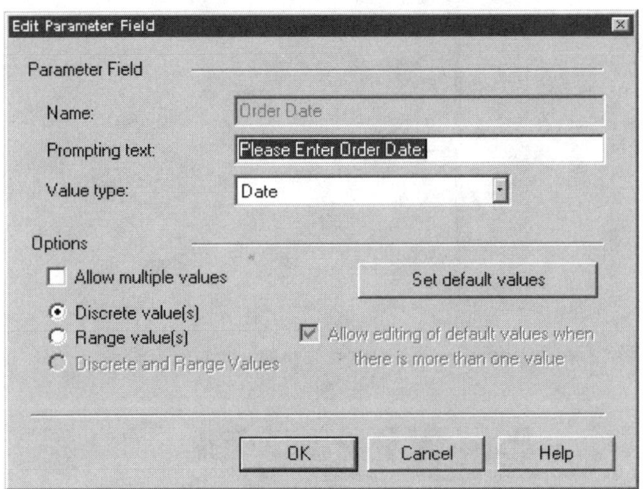

Figure 11-10. The Edit Parameter Field dialog box

Once you've made that change, press the OK button. Try refreshing your report. Notice at the Order Date parameter that you're only asked for Date information now. Type in 01/10/2001 as your date, and press OK. Your report should now look like Figure 11-11.

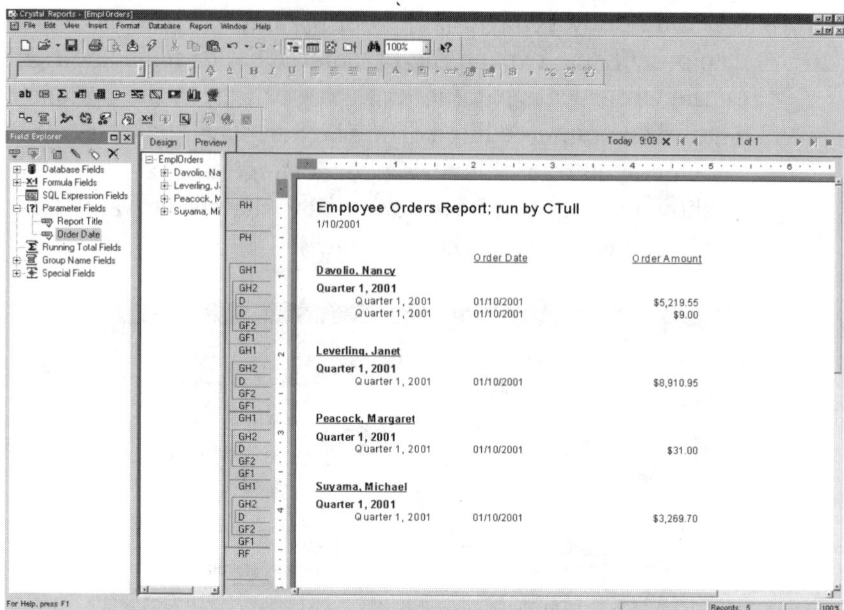

Figure 11-11. The results of editing a parameter field

Creating a Date Range Parameter

While this date parameter is useful, it's somewhat limiting. Only records that match the exact order date entered by report users displays. A better option is to create a date parameter that uses a date range. Date ranges are nice in that they allow users to select all records for a period of time that they define — be it a week, month, quarter, year, etc. Date range parameters are the most common found in reports.

Creating date ranges isn't much different from the creation of a single date parameter. In the Field Explorer, right-click on the Order Date parameter. Select Edit from the options menu. The Edit Parameter Field dialog box displays.

From this dialog box, change the following:

- Change the prompting text to Please Enter Order Date Range:.
- Select the Range value(s) option.

Your screen should look like Figure 11-12.

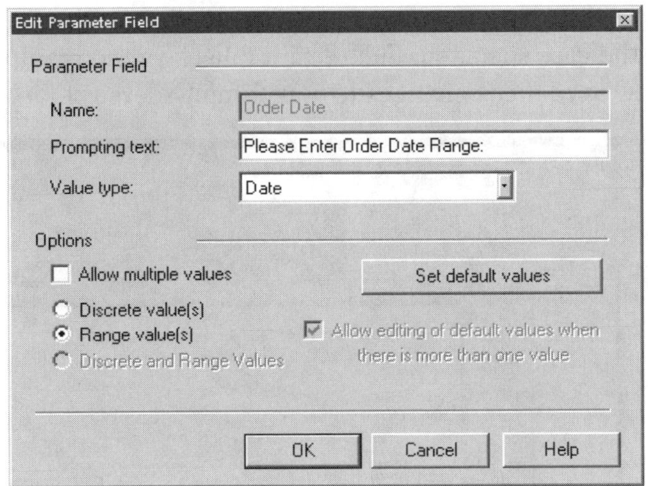

Figure 11-12. Changing a date parameter to allow for date ranges

Once you've done this, press the OK button. A Enter Parameter Values dialog box displays, asking you to enter the range of dates that you wish the report to display. Enter 01/01/2000 to 01/01/2001, as shown in Figure 11-13, and press OK.

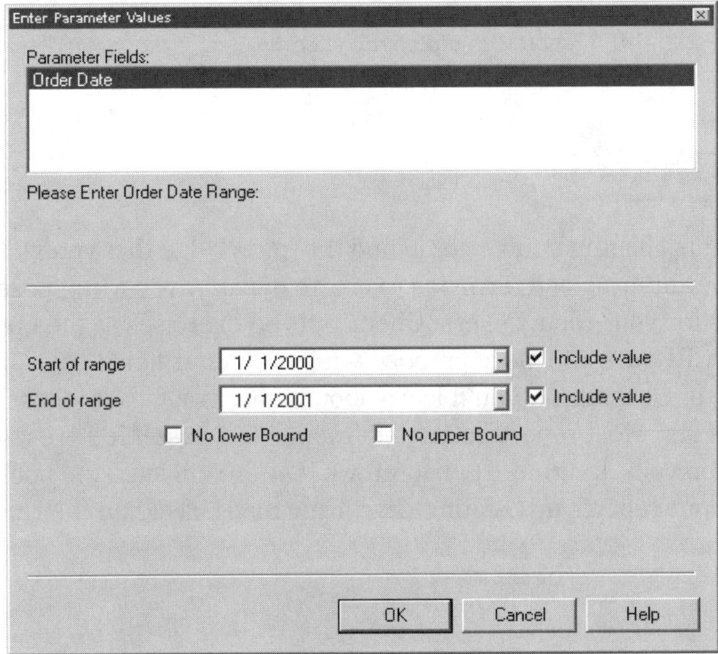

Figure 11-13. Entering date range values

Your report displays, only showing records with an order date between the date specified. Figure 11-14 displays the results of your work. Save these changes to your EmplOrders.rpt file.

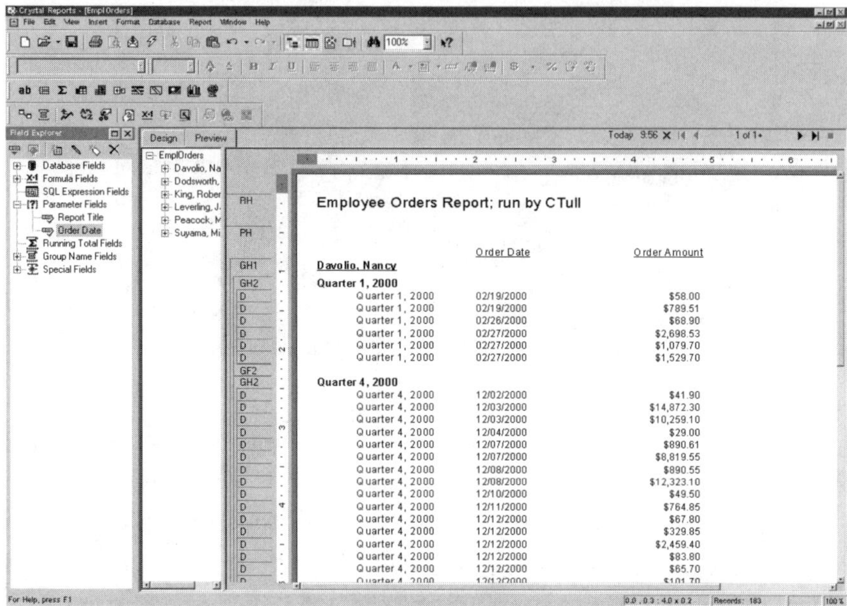

Figure 11-14. A report with a date range parameter

What's Next?

In this chapter, you've combined the knowledge that you've learned about filtering and formulas to create dynamic reporting possibilities for your report users. Check out the exercises at the end of Part III for some more practice with parameter fields.

In Chapter 12, you'll learn about using graphical tools with your reports. Most report users understand data best if it's presented graphically. In the next chapter, we learn to enhance the usefulness of your reports by creating charts and maps based on the report's data.

Chapter 12

Visualizations with Charts and Maps

Just because you're creating reports doesn't mean that you need to present your data in a dull, plain-vanilla format. Images such as graphs, charts, and maps will aid your report users in better understanding the relevant information of your reports. The truth is that for the majority of people, data is best understood if presented graphically.

In this chapter, we explore enhancing your reports through a variety of graphical means. Crystal Reports provides a number of different chart and graph templates (included newly added Gantt, Gauge, and Numeric Axis charts), as well as an impressive graphical mapping function (useful for identifying trends).

Understanding the Chart Expert

Crystal Reports contains 11 different chart types. *Chart types* define the kind of chart in which the data will display. Chart types include bar charts, line charts, and pie charts. To access these and other chart types, you utilize the Chart Expert. The *Chart Expert* is where you select a chart type and define how the data will be used to make up the chart.

To access the Chart Expert, go to the menu bar. Select Insert, Chart Expert. The Chart Expert dialog box displays, as shown in Figure 12-1.

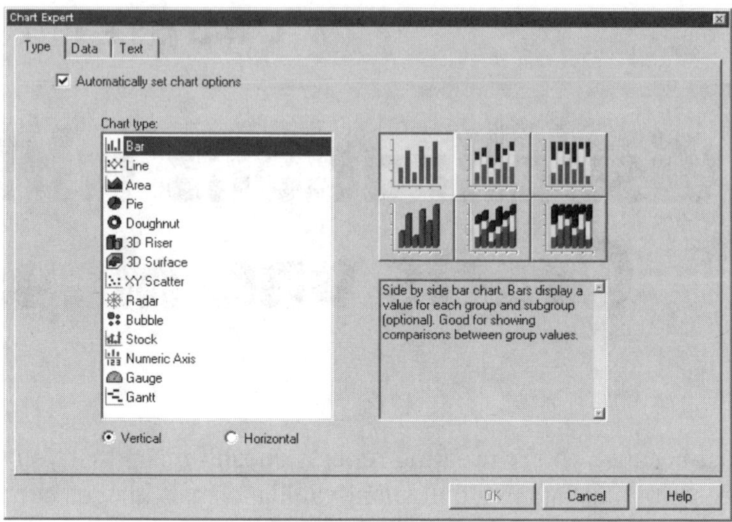

Figure 12-1. The Chart Expert

You'll notice three tabs at the top of the Chart Expert. These tabs perform the following functionality:

- **Type:** This tab allows you to choose the type of chart you wish to create.

  When you select one of these charts, you'll notice a set of chart options display to the right of the Chart type list box (these options display as thumbnails). These different options allow you to further specify the format of the chart. There's a description of each of these options below the thumbnails.

  Table 12-1 summarizes the different chart types and layouts available within Crystal Reports.

- **Data:** This tab allows you to choose the chart layout — in other words, where the data that makes up the chart comes from.

- **Text:** This tab allows you to define any text that should display within the chart, such as a chart title, subtitle, or titles on the group or data itself.

Before jumping into the creation of a chart, take some time to look through the functionality of these different tabs.

Working with the Type Tab

The Chart Expert Type tab allows users to select the type of graphical chart to create from your data. Considering the different chart types and their options, there are over 40 different charts that you may utilize within your report. Table 12-1 lists the basic chart types that Crystal Reports provides.

Table 12-1. The chart types of Crystal Reports

Chart Icon	Chart Type	Description
	Bar	Displays data using a series of vertical bars. This chart is also known as a column chart.
	Line	Displays data as a series of points connected by a line.
	Area	Displays data as an area filled with a color or a pattern.
	Pie	Displays data as a pie separated into slices that are filled with a color or a pattern.
	Doughnut	Displays data as sections of a circle (or doughnut). These sections are filled with a color or a pattern.
	3D Riser	Displays data in a series of three-dimensional objects. These objects display side by side.
	3D Surface	Displays data in a topographic view.
	XY Scatter	Displays a collection of plotted points, which represent data in a pool of information. These charts are useful for determining trends.
	Radar	Displays group data at the perimeter of the radar and then places numeric values that make up the group from the center of the radar to the perimeter.
	Bubble	Displays data as a series of bubbles, where the size of the bubble is proportional to the amount of data. This chart is an extension of the XY Scatter chart type.
	Stock	Displays the high and low values of data.
123	Numeric Axis	Displays a bar, line, or area chart that uses a number field (or date/time field) as its "on change of" field.
	Gauge	Displays a dial that shows a small number of data values.
	Gantt	Displays horizontal bars used to provide a graphical illustration of a schedule.

To get a feel for the Chart Expert, let's create a new report example. Create a new report using the Customer and Orders tables. Allow the Smart Linking feature to link these tables or refer to the ER Model diagram in Appendix A.

Once you're at the Report Design area, perform the following:

1. **Create a group using the Region field (available within the Customer table).**
2. **Add the following fields to the Details section:**
   - **Customer Name (from the Customer table)**
     Place this field at the 1" mark.
   - **Order Date (from the Orders table)**
     Place this field at the 3.5" mark.
   - **Order Amount (from the Orders table)**
     Place this field at the 5.5" mark.
3. **Create a subtotal for the Order Amount, adding the subtotal after each region.**

   You can create this Summary field by right-clicking on the Order Date field. From the options menu, select Insert, Summary. Here you can define this summary field. Check out Chapter 9 for more information.
4. **Change the Order Date format from date/time to just a date format.**

   From the Format Editor, select the Date and Time tab, and change the date format to *mm/dd/yyyy.* Check out Chapter 11 if you need a refresher on how to perform these steps.
5. **In the Field Explorer pane, right-click on the Parameter Fields node.**

   An options menu displays. From this menu, select New. The Create Parameter Field dialog box displays.
6. **In the Create Parameter Field dialog box, enter the following information:**
   - **In the Name field, type Order Date.**
   - **In the Prompting text field, type Please Enter Order Date:.**
   - **In the Value type drop-down list, select Date.**

- **Select the Range value(s) option.**

7. **Press the OK button in the Create Parameter Field dialog box.**
8. **From the menu bar, select Report, Select Expert.**

   The Choose Fields dialog box displays.
9. **From the Report Fields node (in the Choose Fields dialog box) select Orders.Order Date. Press OK.**

   The Select Expert displays.
10. **In the Comparison operator drop-down field, select Is Equal To.**
11. **In the Comparison value drop-down field, select ?Order Date.**

    If you don't see this value within your drop-down fields, you can always type {?Order Date} in the parameter field.

Once you've done these steps, press the OK button in the Select Expert. Then, preview your report. An Enter Parameter Values dialog box displays. In the date range fields, type in 12/1/2001 to 12/31/2001, as shown in Figure 12-2.

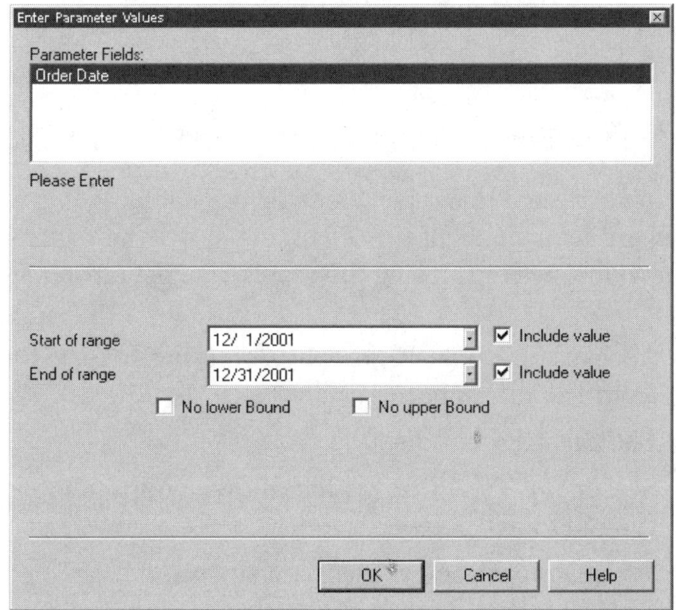

Figure 12-2. Dynamically selecting a date range for your report records

Once you've done this, press the OK button. You're asked if you'd like to use saved data or refresh your data. Refresh your data. You're returned to the Report Design area.

If you'd like, create a title for this report: Customer Sales by Region. This type of report is something utilized frequently by marketing departments. Figure 12-3 displays what your report should look like.

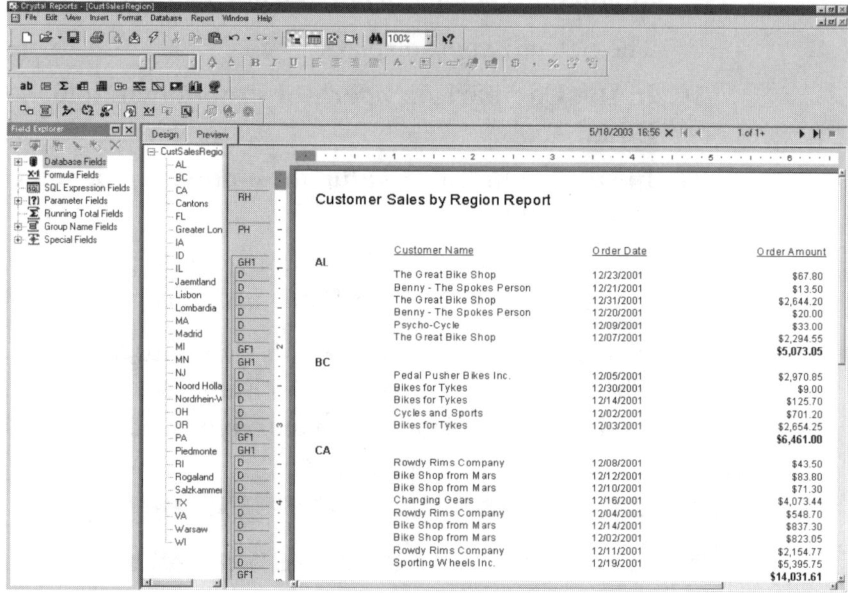

Figure 12-3. The start of Customer Sales by Region report

Once you've created this report, let's enhance it by adding a chart. In this chart, let's highlight the order amounts of the regions. Perform the following steps, using the report you just created in this chapter:

1. **Access the Chart Expert by selecting Insert, Chart from the menu bar.**

   The Chart Expert displays.

2. **Select the Type tab, which allows you to choose the type of chart you wish to use.**

   For this report, select the Bar chart type.

3. **Select the following bar chart option: Side by side bar chart with 3D visual effect.**

Figure 12-4 displays the bar chart option you should select for this example.

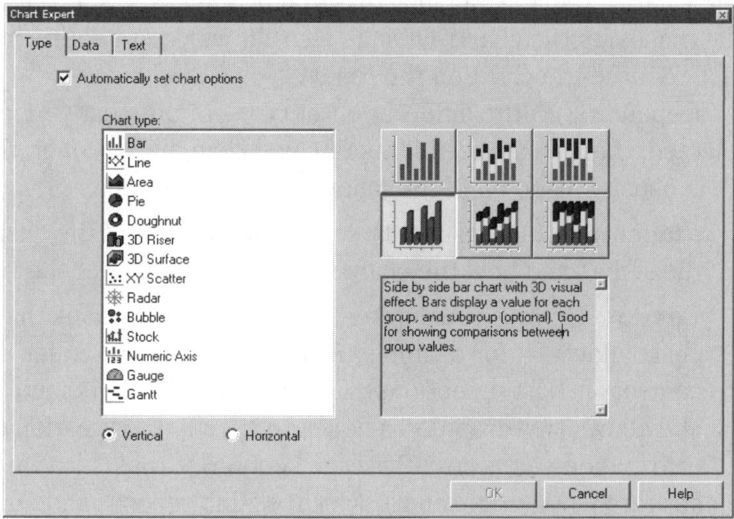

Figure 12-4. Selecting the side by side bar chart with 3D visual effect

Once you've selected this chart option, select the Data tab.

Note

Within the Type tab of the Chart Expert, notice that the Automatically set chart options check box is checked by default. Checking this check box allows Crystal Reports to use its default chart formatting options and hides the Options and Axes tabs.

If you wish to view and change the default chart options of Crystal Reports, uncheck this check box so you'll then have access to these two additional tabs.

Working with the Data Tab

The Chart Expert Data tab allows you to select the specific data that makes up the chart. This tab also allows you to define how you wish to place the chart on the report.

Depending on the different chart type options that you've selected, the appearance of this tab may change. However, the Data tab is usually made up of the following three sections:

- **Placement:** Allows you to select the location of the chart on the report and how the chart will recur throughout the report.
- **Layout:** Defines the different data selection options that the chart allows — for example, Advanced (which provides optimal control of charting options), Group (which is the default layout and allows two drop-down boxes to specify the creation of your chart when you access the Data section), Cross-Tab (which only appears when your report is a Cross-Tab report), and OLAP (which only appears when your report utilizes an OLAP data source).
- **Data:** Allows you to define the information that makes up the chart.

Continuing with your chart creation, select the following in the Data tab:

1. **Within the Placement section, make sure the following is selected in the Place chart drop-down field: Once per report.**
2. **Also in the Placement section, select the Header option button.**
3. **In the Data section, make sure the following is selected in the On change of drop-down field: Customer.Region.**
4. **Also in the Data section, make sure the following is selected in the Show drop-down field: Sum of Orders.Order Amount.**

Figure 12-5 displays what your Data tab should look like.

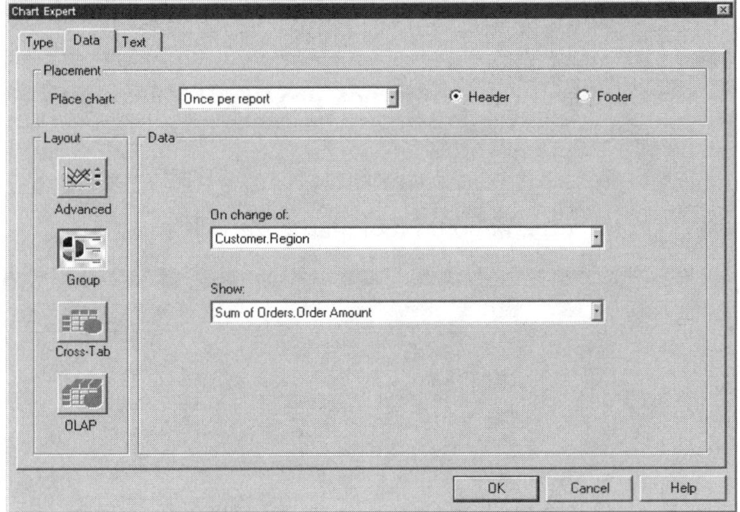

Figure 12-5. The Data tab

Once you've selected this information, select the Text tab at the top of the screen. The Text tab displays.

Working with the Text Tab

The Chart Expert Text tab allows you to define and format the titles that you wish to display within your chart. If you leave any of the text fields blank in this tab, that particular title will not display within your chart.

Before exploring this tab, notice that all check boxes are selected by default. Also, all the text fields next to these check boxes are dimmed. This means that Crystal Reports is automatically adding titles, based on the data within the chart. To change any of these titles, uncheck the check box. The text field then becomes active, allowing you to add or edit text.

To get a feel for this tab, continue with the chart that you've been creating within this chapter.

1. **Uncheck the check box next to the Title text field.**

   This text field now becomes active, allowing you to modify it as you wish.

2. **Change the Title text field to: Sum of Order Amount by Region.**
3. **Uncheck the check box next to the Group title text field.**
4. **Delete all text from the Group title text field.**

   Your screen should look like Figure 12-6.

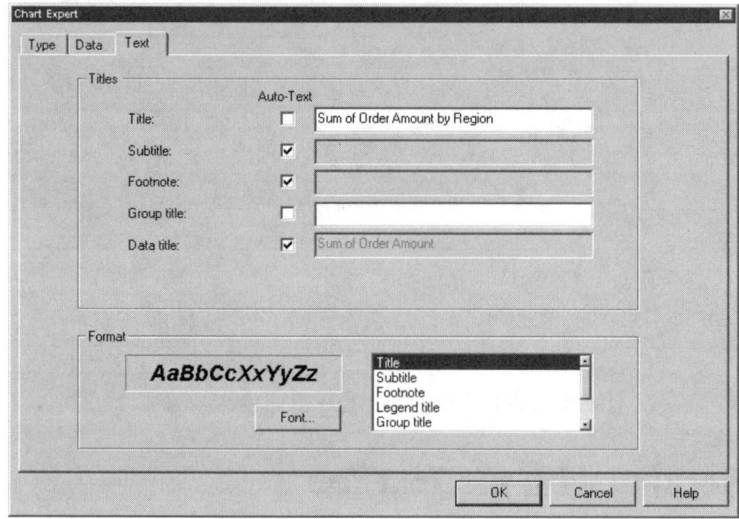

Figure 12-6. Modifying your chart within the Chart Expert Text tab

5. **To change the format of this title, go to the Format section of the Text tab.**

   Select Title from the list box (if it is not selected already).
6. **Press the Font... button.**

   The Font dialog box displays, as shown in Figure 12-7.

   If you're familiar with Microsoft Word or Excel, you've probably seen this Font dialog box before. The Font dialog box provides the functionality to determine a different text style for your chart text.

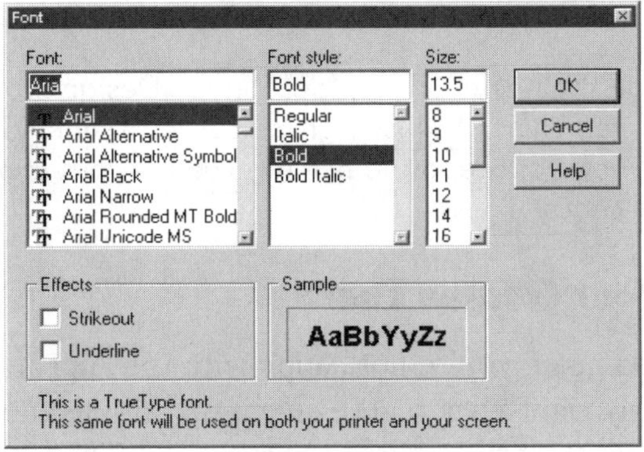

Figure 12-7. The Font dialog box

7. **In the Font dialog box, change the following:**
   - **Change Font style to Bold Italic.**
   - **Change Size to 14.**
8. **Press the OK button in the Font dialog box.**

   You're returned to the Chart Expert.
9. **Press the OK button in the Chart Expert.**

You're returned to the Report Design area. Preview your report. Your screen should look like Figure 12-8.

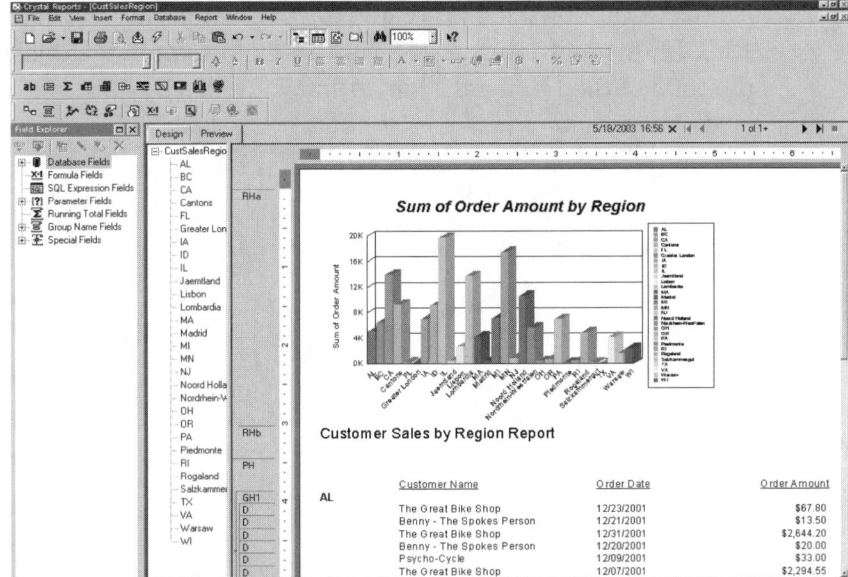

Figure 12-8. A report that utilizes a chart

Tip

Keep in mind that the chart displayed in the Design tab is not your completed chart; it's just a graphical representation. You'll need to preview your report to actually see the correct orientation of your chart.

Editing Your Created Chart

If for some reason you're not happy with the appearance of your chart, simply right-click on the chart. An options menu displays. From there, select the Chart Expert option. The Chart Expert dialog box displays, containing the information from your defined chart. From here, you can fine-tune your chart as needed.

Drilling Down on Chart Data

One of the nice features of charts created in Crystal Reports is that they contain drill-down functionality. In other words, you can double-click on a particular segment of your chart (basically, any area where the cursor turns into a magnifying glass), and a drill-down tab is created. This drill-down tab contains the detail that makes up that segment within your chart.

As an example, try double-clicking the "Lombardia" bar of your chart. A drill-down tab is created for Lombardia, as shown in Figure 12-9. In this new tab, you can view the information that makes up the total of the Lombardia bar within your chart.

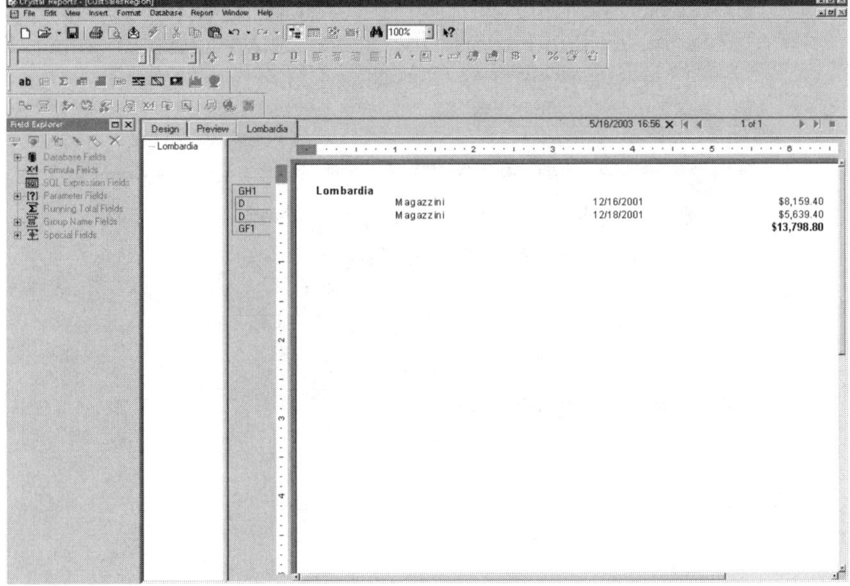

Figure 12-9. The drill-down tab of a chart

Creating Geographical Mapping

While the charting capabilities of Crystal Reports are useful, sometimes another graphical representation might better enhance the data trends of your report. Another useful visual tool is Crystal Reports' geographical mapping, which gives you the ability to create maps from geographically related information (such as Regions, as in the case of the report you've been creating in this chapter).

Tip

Crystal Reports creates maps utilizing a third-party product called MapInfo. While Crystal Reports comes with several useful map files, you may purchase more directly from MapInfo (they are then made accessible from Crystal Reports by adding them to the following folder: \Program Files\Map Info X).

Check out MapInfo's web site at www.mapinfo.com for more information about the additional map files that might be of benefit to you in your reporting endeavors.

In Crystal Reports, geographical mapping capabilities are created through the Map Expert. To access the Map Expert, select Insert, Map from the menu bar. The Map Expert dialog box displays, as shown in Figure 12-10.

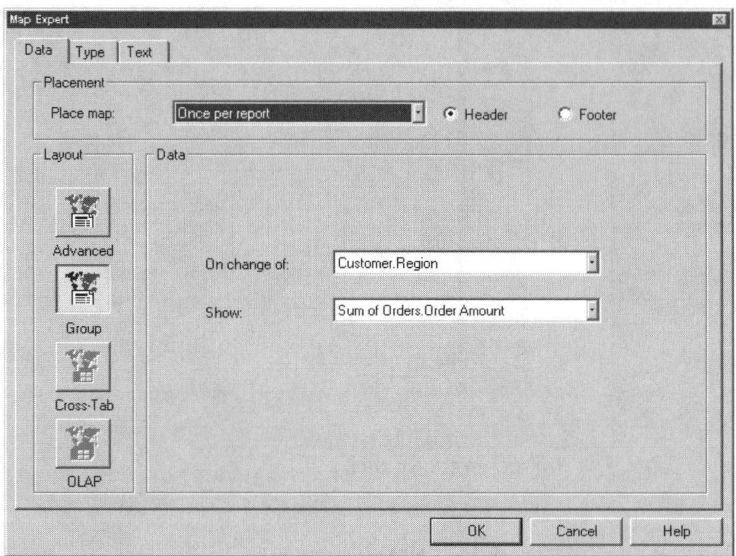

Figure 12-10. The Map Expert

Note

Make sure you have your Crystal Reports CD handy just in case the third-party mapping files were not added during initial install. Crystal Reports may ask for the CD to install the required mapping .dll files in order to use the Map Expert properly.

Working with the Data Tab

Like the Chart Expert Data tab, the Map Expert Data tab allows you to define the data that your map is to be based on and where it is to reside within your report. Also like the Chart Expert Data tab, the Map Expert Data tab contains the following three sections:

- **Placement:** Allows you to select the location of the map on the report and how the map will recur throughout the report.
- **Layout:** Defines the different data selection options the map allows — for example, Advanced (which provides optimal

control of mapping options), Group (which is the default layout and allows two drop-down boxes to specify the creation of your map when you access the Data section), Cross-Tab (which only appears when your report is a Cross-Tab report), and OLAP (which only appears when your report utilizes an OLAP data source).

- **Data:** Allows you to define the information that makes up the map.

Let's try an example. In the report you've created in this chapter, perform the following steps in the Map Expert Data tab:

1. **In the Placement section, make sure the following is selected in the Place map drop-down field: Once per report.**
2. **Also in the Placement section, select the Header option button.**
3. **In the Data section, make sure the following is selected in the On change of drop-down field: Customer.Region.**
4. **Also in the Data section, make sure the following is selected within the Show drop-down field: Sum of Orders.Order Amount.**

Once these settings are defined, select the Type tab at the top of the Map Expert dialog box.

Working with the Type Tab

The Map Expert Type tab provides five map options that you may select, each offering a different summarization category for your geographical mapping. Table 12-2 summarizes the different map types available within Crystal Reports.

Table 12-2. The map types of Crystal Reports

Map Icon	Map Type	Description
	Ranged	Divides data into ranges and then assigns a specific color to each range.
	Dot Density	Displays dots for each occurrence of a specified item in order to provide an overall impression of the distribution of that item.

Map Icon	Map Type	Description
	Graduated	Displays one symbol per instance of a specified item (such as a circle by default, although you can define any symbol you prefer). The symbol is proportional in size to the value of the item that it represents.
	Pie Chart	Displays a pie chart over each geographical area, with each slice within the pie representing individual data items.
	Bar Chart	Displays a bar chart over each geographical area, with each bar of the chart representing individual data items.

Within the Type tab, you'll notice an Options section. In this section, you can further define the appearance of the map values as they display within your map (such as the colors for the lowest and highest intervals on your map). For now, let's just stick with the defaults. Your screen should look like Figure 12-11.

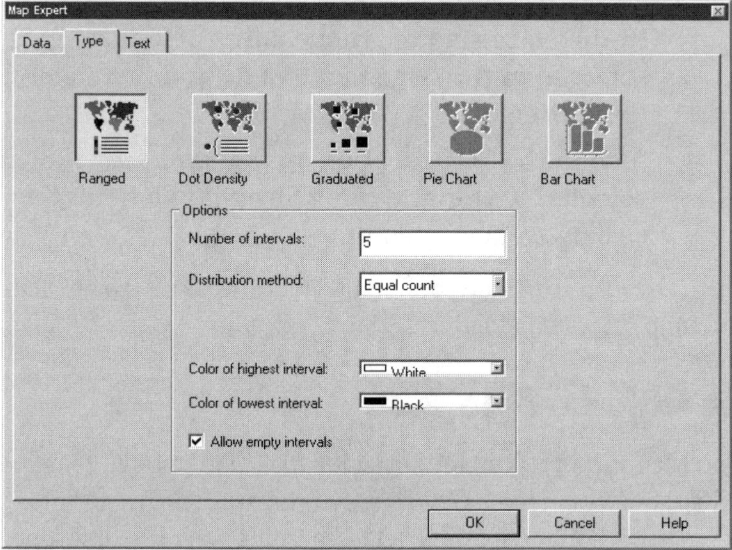

Figure 12-11. The Map Expert Type tab

Select the Text tab at the top of the Map Expert dialog box. You'll find yourself at the Text tab.

Working with the Text Tab

The Map Expert Text tab allows you to define a map title (if you wish) along with defining various display instructions for the title, subtitle, or legend information. To complete the map you've been creating, try the following:

1. **In the Text tab, type the following in the Map title field: Sum of Orders by Region Geographical Map.**
2. **Press the OK button in the Map Expert.**

You're returned to the Report Design area. Preview your report. You should see your newly created map above your chart. Figure 12-12 displays the results of your work.

Tip

As was the case with the Chart Expert, remember that the map displayed in the Design tab is not your completed map — it's just a graphical representation. You'll need to preview your report to actually see the correct orientation of your map.

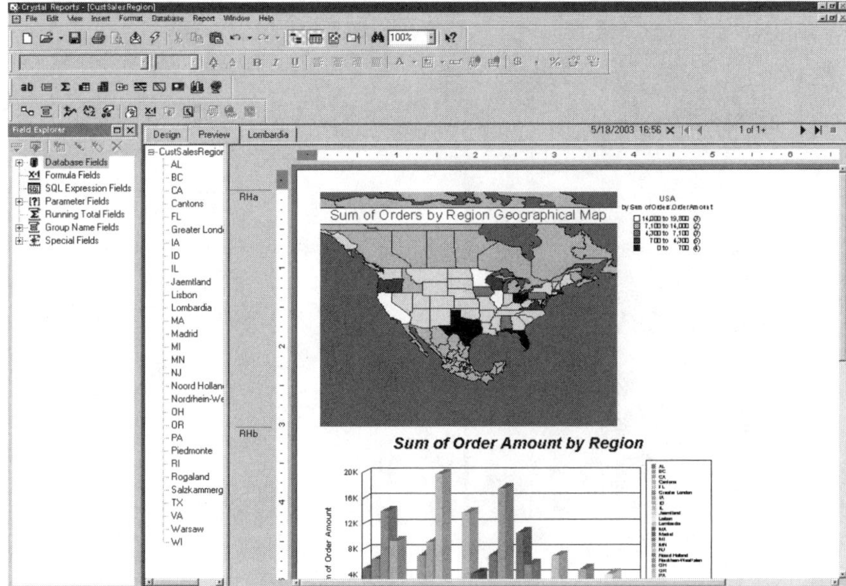

Figure 12-12. A report that utilizes a map

Editing Your Created Map

Like the Chart Expert, you can edit the appearance of your map by right-clicking on the map. An options menu displays. From there, select the Map Expert option. The Map Expert dialog box displays, containing the information from your defined map. You can now edit your map settings as needed.

Drilling Down on Map Data

Also like the Chart Expert, the Map Expert allows for drill-down functionality.

As an example, try double-clicking on "Texas" in your map. A drill-down tab is created for Texas, as shown in Figure 12-13. In this new tab, you can view the information that makes up the total of the Texas bar within your chart.

Save the work you've done in this chapter as CustSales-Region.rpt. We return to this report in the next chapter.

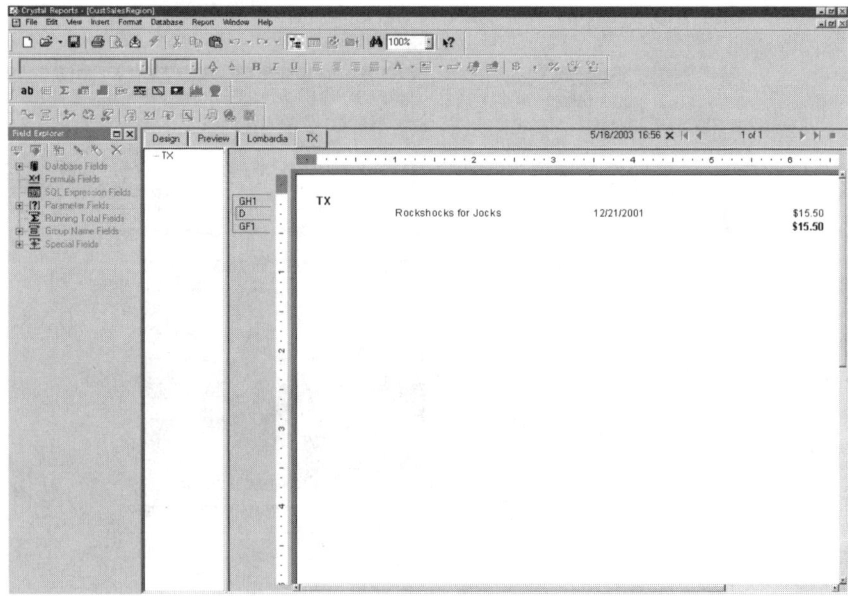

Figure 12-13. The drill-down tab of a map

What's Next?

In this chapter, you've learned about Crystal Reports' Chart and Map Experts and how to utilize them to create graphical visualizations based on your report's grouped data. The presentation of data in a visual manner is a powerful tool for conveying information effectively for your report users.

In the next chapter, we learn about adding reports within a report — better known as subreports. Subreports provide flexibility in creating reports that might be problematic if developed through traditional means. You'll come to think of subreports as your "get out of jail free" card!

Chapter 13

Creating Subreports

The time will come when a report user comes to you with a request to create an *impossible report.* For example, they may want something like:

- A report that includes information from a table that can't be linked to any other table within a database. Perhaps this information is from a different data source than the report uses.
- A report that displays the same data in two or more different ways.

To make matters worse, these report users are people you usually can't say "no" to. So, what do you do?

The answer to your *impossible* report problem is subreports. In this chapter, we explore subreports and how they allow you to display data that cannot be linked using a traditional report, as well as display different views of the same data within a single report.

Understanding Subreports

A *subreport* is a report within a report. Figure 13-1 displays a graphical representation of the structure of a subreport within a primary report.

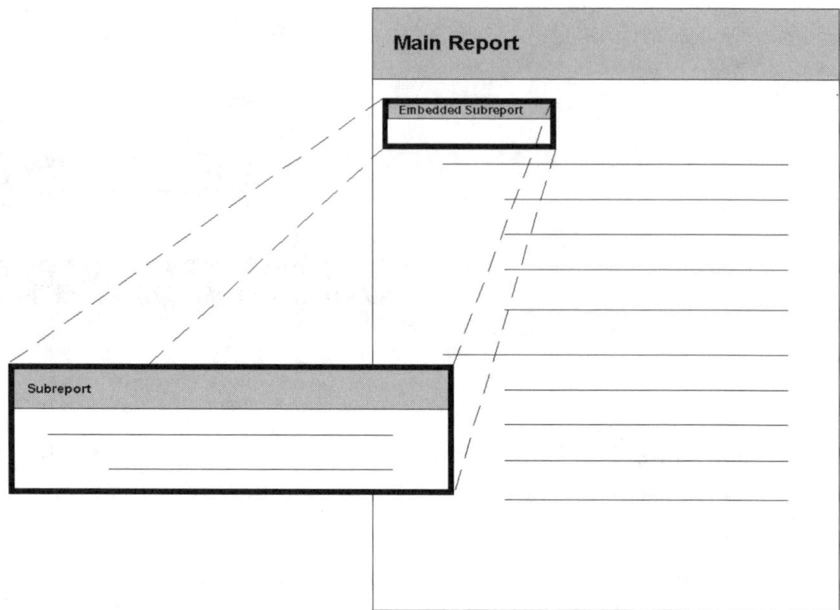

Figure 13-1. Graphical representation of a report that uses a subreport

Subreports have most of the characteristics of a regular report: They contain their own database tables and fields separate from the main report, they contain their own report design area where you may define the appearance of the report, and they contain their own selection criteria.

Generally, the only real differences between a subreport and a primary report are the following:

- A subreport may be placed within any report section. The entire subreport will then print in that section.
- A subreport may be inserted as an object into the primary report. A subreport may not stand on its own.
- A subreport may not contain another subreport.
- A subreport does not have a Page Header or a Page Footer section.

In Crystal Reports, there are two types of subreports — unlinked and linked. These are summarized in the following two sections. We explore both types of subreports within this chapter.

The Unlinked Subreport

Unlinked subreports do not attempt to coordinate their data with the primary report. In other words, an unlinked subreport does not match up records to the records within a primary report. Unlinked subreports do not need to use the same data as the primary report — in fact, an unlinked subreport often does not even share the same data source as the primary report.

The Linked Subreport

Linked subreports, in comparison to unlinked subreports, do share the same data source as a primary report. A linked subreport's data is linked and coordinated with the primary report's data. In other words, both reports contain records that are matched up.

As an example, say that your primary report contains employee information and your subreport contains order information (where this order information is linked to the employee information). For each employee record, a linked subreport would include all orders for that employee only. You can try your hand at creating a linked subreport later in this chapter.

Subreport Development

To get an idea of how subreports work, open the CustSales-Region.rpt that you created in the last chapter. You'll utilize that report as a main report to which you'll eventually add a subreport. You can also pull up a copy of this report from the companion files (www.wordware.com/files/crystal).

Once you've opened this report, select Insert, Subreport from the menu bar. The Insert Subreport dialog box displays, as shown in Figure 13-2. This is where you define your subreport functionality.

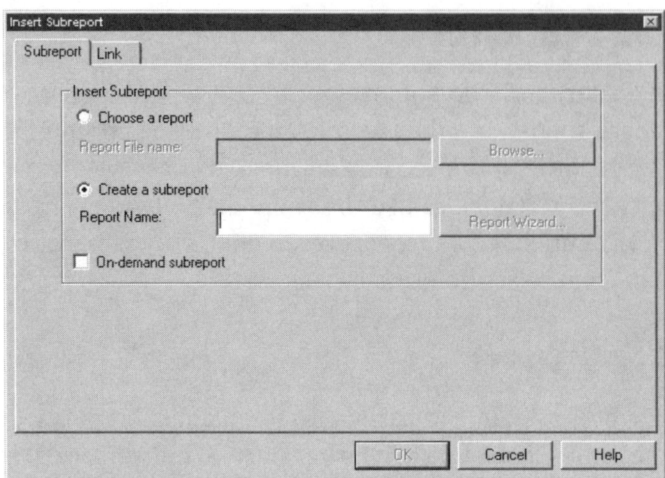

Figure 13-2. The Insert Subreport dialog box

From this dialog box, you have two options: You can choose a previously created report to embed within your primary report (CustSalesRegion.rpt), or you can create a new subreport from scratch.

Inserting an Unlinked Subreport

To get an idea of how subreports can resolve a number of report development challenges, let's consider the following scenario. Say that someone in upper management would like to see the following changes in the Customer Sales by Region report:

- Remove the geographical map from the report.
- Move the bar chart to the last page of the report.
- Add a pie chart that summarizes Xtreme's top five selling products.

At first glance, these may seem easy tasks — until you get to the third request. In this example, upper management wants two reports in one. Sounds like a complicated task, huh? It would be complex (if not impossible) without Crystal Reports' subreport functionality.

Let's walk through this example to get an idea of how subreports allow you to create seemingly impossible reports. Perform the following steps:

1. **Within the CustSalesRegion.rpt, select the Design tab.**

   The Design view displays.

2. **Right-click in the gray portion of the Report Header a section.**

   An options menu displays.

3. **From this options menu, select the Delete Section option.**

   If you have any drill-down tabs within this report, you may receive a message stating that your drill-down tabs will be closed. Press the OK button in this dialog box to continue.

   The Report Header a section with the geographical map is deleted. The bar chart now displays in a new Report Header a section.

4. **Right-click on the bar chart (located in Report Header a).**

   An options menu displays.

5. **Select the Cut option from the options menu.**

   The bar chart is cut from the Report Header a section.

6. **Right-click in the gray portion of the Report Header a section.**

   Again, an options menu displays.

7. **From this options menu, select the Delete Section option.**

   Your title text object now displays within the Report Header a section.

8. **Move your cursor into the white portion of the Report Footer section and right-click.**

   An options menu displays.

9. **Select the Paste option from the options menu.**

   You'll see the outline of your subreport connected to your cursor.

10. **Move your cursor (with the outline of your chart) to the top of the Report Footer section.**

    Left-click once to place the chart within the Report Footer section. Then, stretch the bottom border of this section. You'll need the extra room in a moment.

Notice that you've accomplished the first two requests from upper management: You've removed the geographical map from your report, and you've moved the bar chart to the last page of your report. Figure 13-3 displays what your report should look like within the Design view.

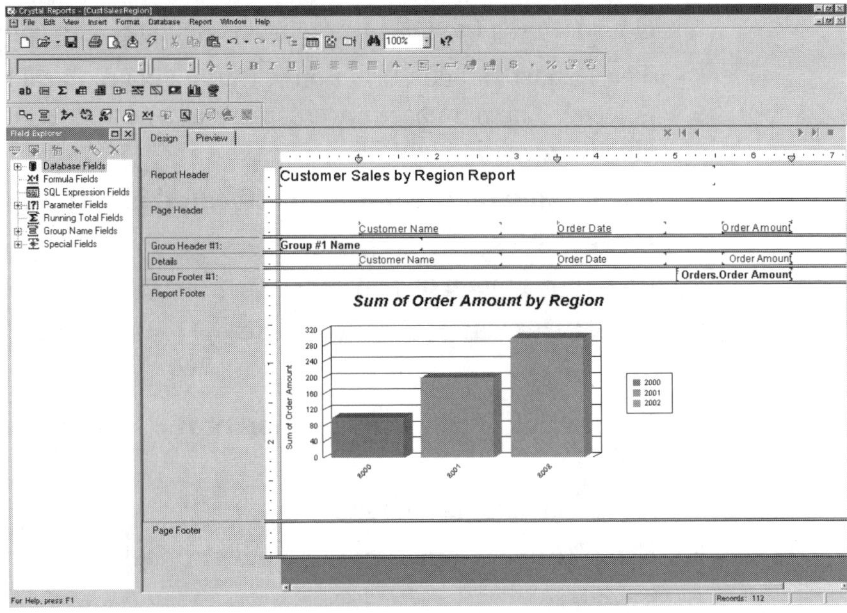

Figure 13-3. Modifying the Customer Sales by Region report

Now all that's left is to add that pie chart that summarizes Xtreme's top-selling products. A subreport is the perfect solution for that challenge. Make sure that you're still in the CustSalesRegion.rpt, and perform the following steps:

1. **Select Insert, Subreport from the menu bar.**

   The Insert Subreport dialog box displays.

2. **Select the Create a subreport option button.**

If you have created a report previously and would like to use it as a subreport, you can select the Choose a report option and then use the Browse button to select the location of that report within your computer or network.

For this example, there is not a report you've created in this book that displays the top five products. Thus, you'll need to create that subreport now.

3. **In the Report Name field, type the following: TopFiveProducts.**

   Your screen should look like Figure 13-4.

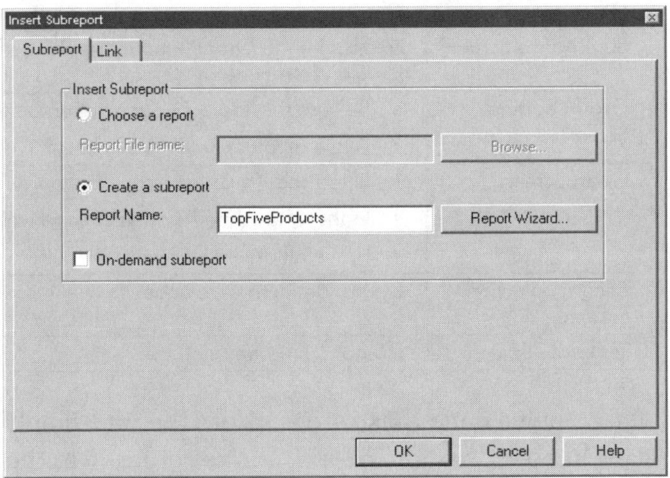

Figure 13-4. Creating a new report as your subreport

4. **Press the Report Wizard... button.**

   The Standard Report Creation Wizard dialog box displays (as you learned about in Chapter 4).

Refer to the following table for the information to define within the Standard Report Creation Wizard.

Table 13-1. The information to define within the Standard Report Creation Wizard

Screen	What to Define
Data Screen	Select the Orders, Order Details, and Product tables.
Links Screen	• Link the Orders_Details.Order ID field to the Orders.Order ID field. • Link the Product.Product ID field to the Orders_Details.Product ID field.
Fields Screen	Select the Product.Product Name and Orders.Order Amount fields.
Groupings Screen	Create a group with the Product.Product Name field.
Summaries Screen	Make sure the Order Amount field is summarized (it should already be by default).
Group Sorting Screen	• Be sure the Top 5 Groups option button is selected. • Leave all other settings as default.
Chart Screen	• Select the Pie Chart option button. • In the Chart Title field, type: Top Five Products. • Leave all other settings as default.
Record Selection Screen	Do not define any settings.
Template Screen	Do not define any settings.

Once you've done these steps, press the Finish button in the Standard Report Creation Wizard. You're returned to the Insert Subreport dialog box. Press the OK button in the Subreport dialog box. You'll notice the outline of a subreport object attached to your cursor.

Left-click the subreport outline in the Report Footer section (place this subreport underneath the original bar chart). Once you've done this, you'll see the name of the report display as a report object, as shown in Figure 13-5.

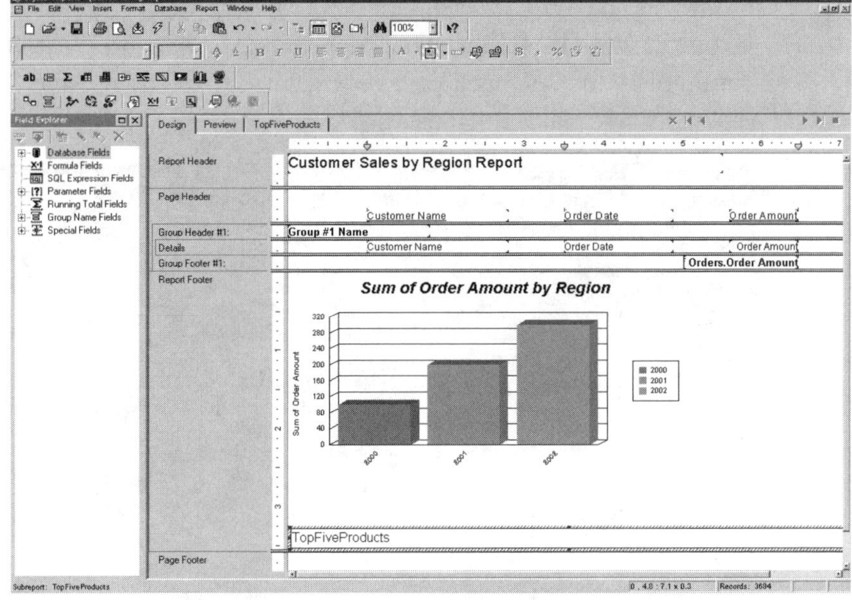

Figure 13-5. The TopFiveProducts.rpt as a subreport of the CustSalesRegion.rpt

When you add a subreport to another report, a new tab displays. This new tab contains the name of the subreport. You can select this tab and edit the subreport just as you would any other regular report.

You can also access a subreport by double-clicking the subreport object. When you perform either of these tasks, you're taken to the subreport's tab. Go ahead and select the TopFiveProducts tab now.

Tip

The subreport tab always displays details in the Design view. If you wish to view the subreport in the Preview view, select the Preview button while in the subreport tab.

Once you're in the TopFiveProducts tab, suppress every section except the Report Header a section. Remember, you can suppress by right-clicking in the gray area of each section. Once you right-click, an options menu displays. From this options menu, select the Suppress (No Drill Down) option.

Once you've suppressed these sections, select the Preview tab.

If you go to the last page of your report, you'll see two charts — one created by the primary report and the second created by the TopFiveProducts subreport, as shown in Figure 13-6. Save this report as CustSalesRegion2.rpt.

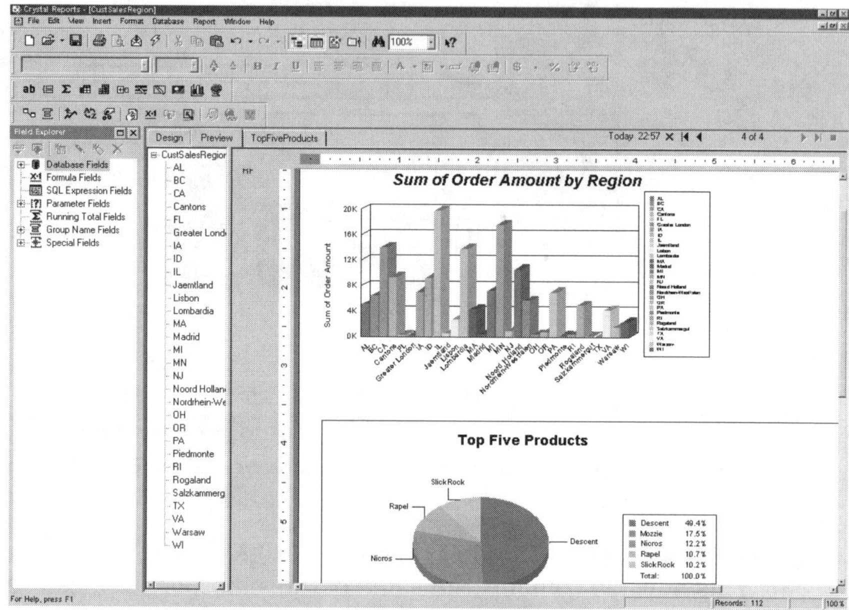

Figure 13-6. A primary report using an unlinked subreport

Inserting a Linked Subreport

You've learned that in unlinked subreports, the primary report does not have any specific data links to its related subreport. As a result, an unlinked subreport is independent from the primary report. Unlinked subreports are useful when you wish to display different views of either the same or different data within a single report. However, sometimes you'll need to match up (link) the data in the primary report and in the subreport in order for your report to make sense. These types of matched up subreports are known as linked subreports.

Creating a linked subreport is nearly identical to creating an unlinked subreport. The only difference is that you'll need to utilize the Link tab in the Insert Subreport dialog box.

1. **Open the EmplOrders.rpt you updated in Chapter 11.**

   You can also access this file from the companion files.

2. **Select Insert subreport from the main menu.**

   The Insert Subreport dialog box displays.

3. **Select the Create a subreport option.**

   In the Report Name field, type: EmplOrdersDetails. Also, check the On-demand subreport check box. Your screen should look like Figure 13-7.

Tip

The On-demand subreport check box allows the subreport to appear as a hyperlink within your report. The actual data is not read from the database until the report user drills down on this hyperlink.

On-demand subreports are a useful way to handle sections that might contain a large number of records.

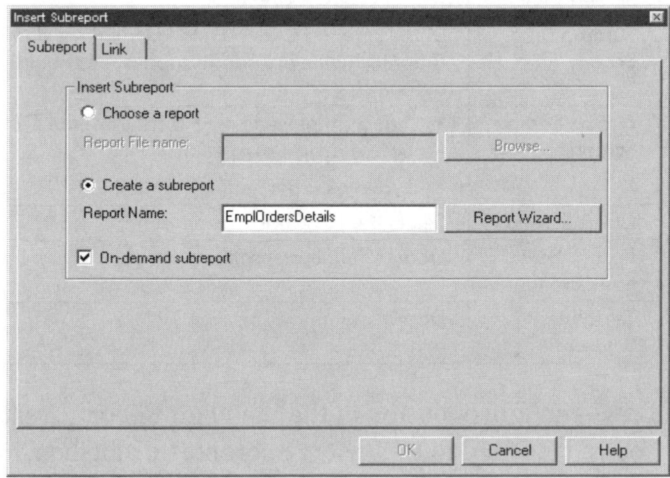

Figure 13-7. Creating a linked subreport

4. **Press the Report Wizard... button.**

   The Standard Report Creation Wizard dialog box displays (as you learned about in Chapter 4).

Refer to the following table for the information to define within the Standard Report Creation Wizard:

Table 13-2. The information to define within the Standard Report Creation Wizard

Screen	What to Define
Data Screen	Select the Customer, Employee, Orders, Order_Details, and Product tables.
Links Screen	• Link the Orders.Employee ID field to the Employee.Employee ID field. • Link the Customer.Customer ID field to the Employee.Customer ID field. • Link the Orders_Details.Order ID field to the Orders.Order ID field. • Link the Product.Product ID field to the Orders_Details.Product ID field.
Fields Screen	Select the following fields: • Employee.Last Name • Order_Details.Unit Price • Order_Details.Quantity • Orders.Order Date
Groupings Screen	Create a group with the Employee.Last Name field.
Summaries Screen	Make sure the Order_Details.Unit Price and Order_Details. Quantity fields are summaried (they should already be by default).
Group Sorting Screen	• Select Employee.Last Name from the Group That Will Be Sorted drop-down field. • Leave all other settings as default.
Chart Screen	Select the No Chart option button.
Record Selection Screen	Do not define any settings.
Template Screen	Do not define any settings.

Press the Finish button in the Standard Report Creation Wizard. You're returned to the Insert Subreport dialog box. Select the Link tab. This tab allows you to match the subreport to your primary report.

The Link tab contains an Available Fields list box, which contains the fields from the main report to which your subreport may link. You can select one or more fields for linking. For the purposes of this example, press the Add button (>) to move the

Orders.Order Date field from the Available Fields list box to the Field(s) to link to list box.

Your screen should look like Figure 13-8.

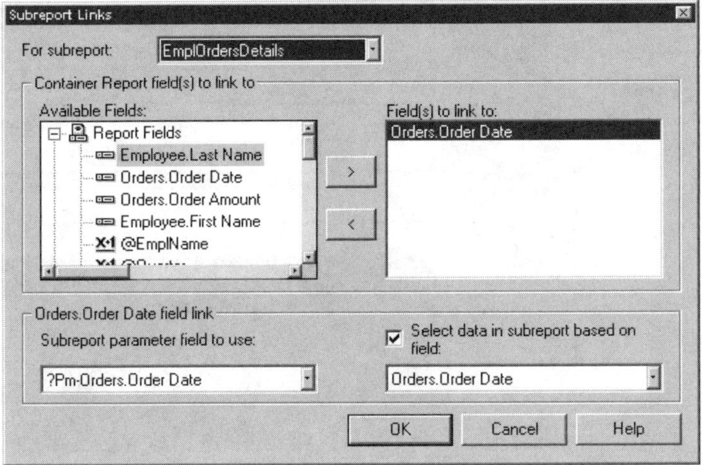

Figure 13-8. Linking a subreport to a primary report

Note

For each linked field, Crystal Reports automatically creates a parameter field in your subreport. These parameter fields are listed at the bottom of the Link tab screen and contain the prefix *"?Pm-"*. You won't need to worry about these parameter fields; they're just the mechanism for how Crystal Reports links data between subreports and primary reports.

Once you've defined these two links, press the OK button. You'll notice the outline of a subreport object attached to your cursor. Left-click the subreport outline in the Group Header #1 section. You can set this object at the 2" mark. Your screen should look like Figure 13-9.

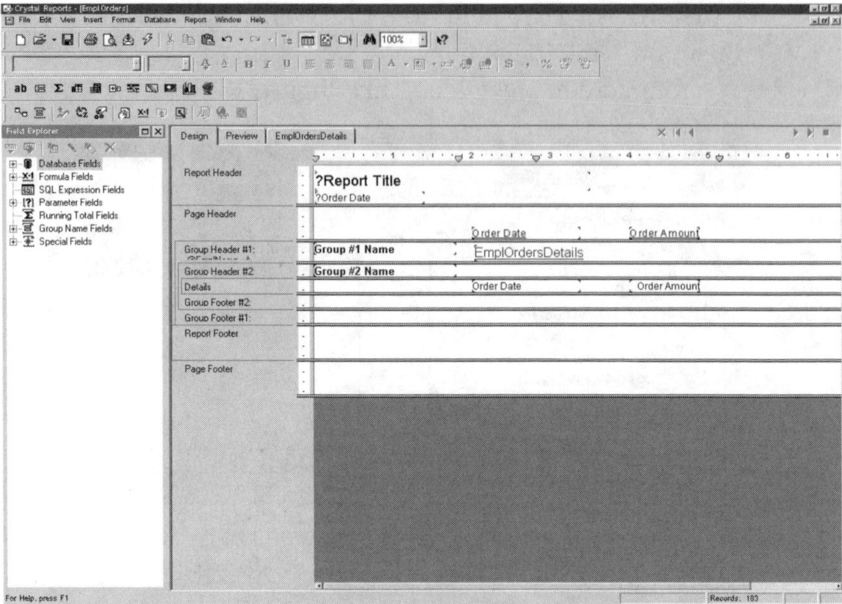

Figure 13-9. Adding a linked on-demand subreport

Try previewing your report. The primary report should display with your on-demand hyperlink, as shown in Figure 13-10. If you select the hyperlink, a drill-down detail report displays. This drill-down report is the EmplOrdersDetails report you just created, as shown in Figure 13-11.

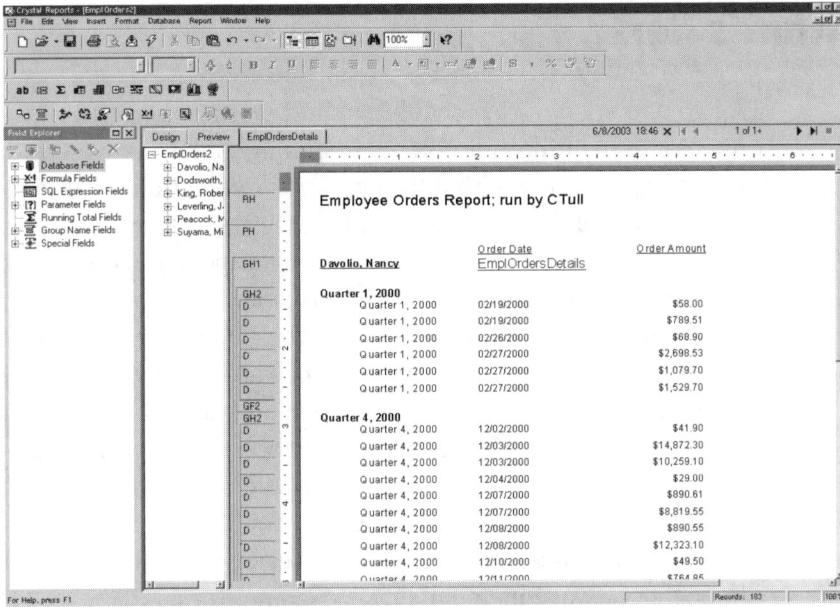

Figure 13-10. The primary report with a link to the on-demand subreport

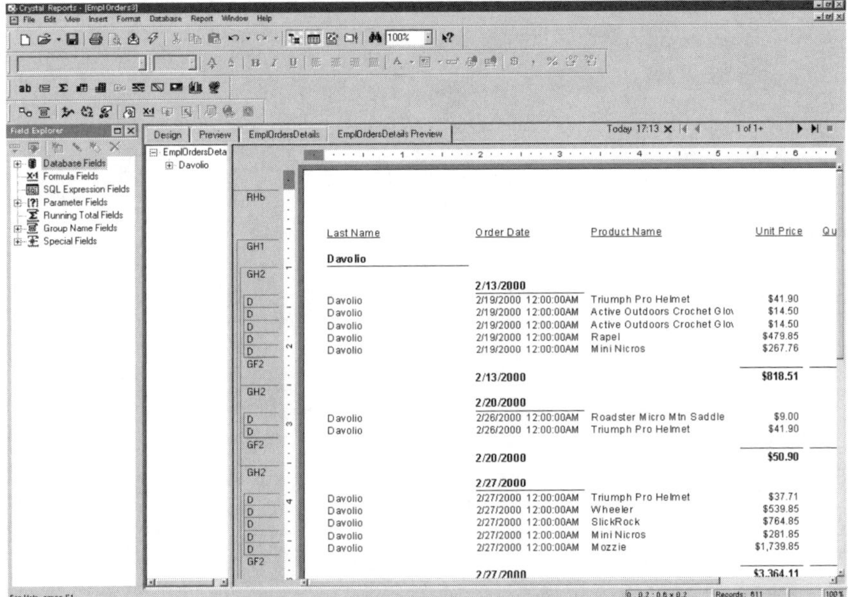

Figure 13-11. The on-demand subreport

What's Next?

As you've seen in this chapter, subreports are a useful way to overcome mammoth problems in linking tables, as well as display report information with different sort or selection criteria than that defined in a primary report. Subreports are created using nearly the same methods for creating a traditional report and contain most of the same characteristics of a main report.

In the next chapter, we explore the functionality of exporting and distributing your reports. Chances are the reports that you create aren't just for your use but are probably also for the use of several other individuals. You'll learn about exporting your reports into different file formats, such as spreadsheets and word processing documents, for easy distribution. You'll also learn how to provide reporting functionality for users without the Crystal Reports software installed on their computers.

Chapter 14

Distributing Reports

Chances are that if you've come this far in the book, you've become somewhat proficient in using Crystal Reports. But now that you have a number of saved report files, you're probably interested in learning how to distribute them to other users.

The majority of your report users won't necessarily have Crystal Reports installed on their computer. This chapter looks at the variety of methods available to you for report distribution.

In this chapter, we first explore report exporting options, such as a spreadsheet or word processing document. These options provide the best methods for distributing static versions of a report. A *static version* means that the report's data becomes fixed at the time of the report generation. In other words, these static versions of a report provide an easy means for providing data at a certain period of time. However, static versions of a report cannot have their data refreshed.

Should you wish to provide your report users dynamic versions of your report (meaning your users can view and refresh a report), one of the following options must be available:

- Your report users will need to have a version of Crystal Reports installed on their computer. However, doing so also means that the user can edit a report, which may be functionality that you do not want report users to have.
- You (or a developer) will need to create a custom application that delivers reports. Developing such applications is beyond the scope of this book. To do so, you'll also need to have the Developer or Advanced editions of Crystal Reports.

- You can use the Report Application Server (which is provided with the Professional and Developer version of Crystal Reports), an out-of-the-box web interface for real-time reporting.
- You can use Crystal Enterprise (another Crystal Decisions product) as a prebuilt report distribution system.
- You can use a third-party software report viewer. Viewers provide your report users with the ability to run (but not edit) reports from any computer. Some of these are discussed in Appendix D.

This chapter looks at each of these options. For the purposes of this book, we assume that you are using the Crystal Reports Standard Edition. Thus, in this book, you mainly focus on using a third-party software report viewer for report distribution.

Note

Report distribution is typically a system administration function. There are factors such as security that come into play when considering how reports should be distributed. Check with your system administrator to determine which distribution method works best for your organization.

Exporting Reports into Different File Formats

So your reports are written and now you wish to make them available for those without access to Crystal Reports. Not a problem. Crystal Reports provides exporting options that allow you to convert your reports into a number of different file formats.

You can convert your finished reports into a number of spreadsheet or word processor file formats, such as those used by Microsoft Excel or Word. You can also convert your files into HTML and make your report a web page or convert your report into a PDF (Portable Document Format) file, which is a file format developed by Adobe Systems.

The following summarizes Crystal's different file exporting formats:

- Adobe format (PDF)
- Crystal Reports (RPT)
- HTML 3.2
- HTML 4.0
- Microsoft Excel 97-2000
- Microsoft Excel 97-2000 (data only)
- Microsoft Word
- ODBC
- Record style (columns without spaces)
- Record style (columns with spaces)
- Report definition
- Rich text format (RTF)
- Comma-separated values (CSV)
- Tab-separated text
- Text
- XML

Tip

As you'll see in exporting examples in this chapter, Crystal Reports does a good job of retaining much of your report formatting when exporting reports into the different file formats. However, exporting into certain files may result in this formatting being lost.

Defining the Exporting Destination

When you export a report into a file format, you must define the exporting location of files. You can define one of six destinations. Table 14-1 summarizes these exporting destinations.

Table 14-1. Crystal's exporting destinations

Exporting Destination	Description
Application	Allows you to export a report to a "temp" file. The appropriate application may then utilize this temp file.

Exporting Destination	Description
Disk File	Allows you to save the report to any location you specify (either on your computer or a drive on a network). This location is the default exporting destination.
Exchange Folder	Allows you to export a report to a Microsoft Exchange folder. Microsoft Exchange folders can contain standard notes (mail), files, and instances of Microsoft Exchange forms.
Lotus Domino	Allows you to export a report to a Lotus Domino client, version 3.0 or higher (you must also have, at a minimum, depositor access).
Lotus Domino Mail	Allows you to export a report to a Lotus Domino Mail Server.
MAPI (Microsoft Mail)	Allows you to export a report to a Microsoft mail client installed (such as Outlook, Mail, or Exchange). The exported file is attached to an e-mail file.

The procedures are nearly the same, no matter what file format you export your report into.

Whenever you're exporting a report, you want to refresh the data to make sure you're using the most recent data. Also, you can only export one Preview view of a report at a time. Thus, if you're exporting a report that contains drill-down tabs or subreports, only the current tab you're viewing is exported.

Exporting into an Excel Spreadsheet

You can practice exporting with any report that you've created so far. The examples in this chapter use the CustSalesRegion2.rpt report that you created in the last chapter.

To export this report to an Excel spreadsheet, perform the following steps:

1. **Open the CustSalesRegion2.rpt.**

   You can also access this report from the companion files.

2. **From the menu bar, select File, Export.**

   The Export dialog box displays. You can also access this dialog box by pressing the Export button on the Standard toolbar. Figure 14-1 displays the Export dialog box.

3. **In the Export dialog box, select MS Excel 97-2000 from the Format drop-down field.**

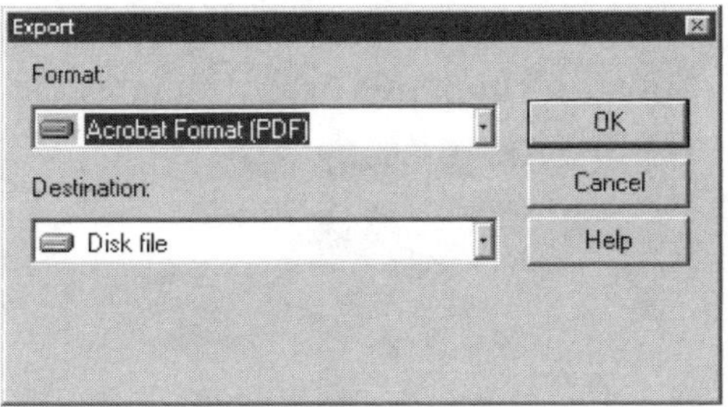

Figure 14-1. The Export dialog box

4. **In the Export dialog box, select Disk file from the Destination drop-down field.**
5. **Press OK.**

   An Excel Format Options dialog box displays, as shown in Figure 14-2.

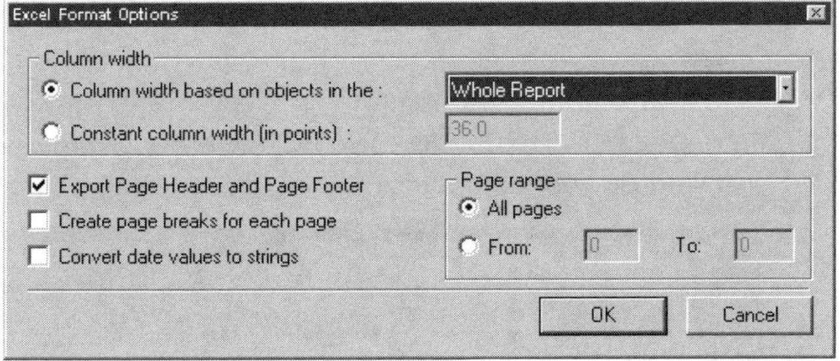

Figure 14-2. The Excel Format Options dialog box

Tip

Depending on the file format that you choose, you may receive an additional options dialog box, asking you for additional exporting information (as is the case when exporting into Excel). Unless you wish to customize the way your report exports, it's best to leave all options as default.

To complete your export, press OK on the Options dialog box. A Select Export File dialog box displays, asking you to define the name of your exported file, as well as the location where you wish to save it. Rename your report if you wish and define a location for your report. Then press the OK button. An Exporting Records dialog box displays, as shown in Figure 14-3. This will run for a few seconds and disappears when the exporting process is complete.

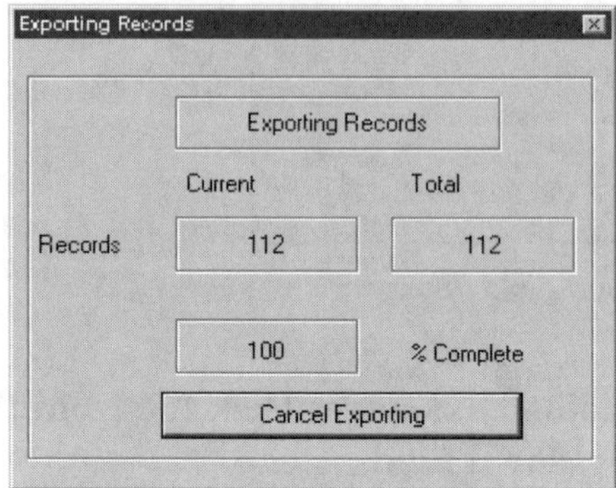

Figure 14-3. The Exporting Records dialog box

Go to the location where you saved your exported file (it will be an Excel file with the extension .XLS) and try opening it. Figure 14-4 displays an example of your exported Excel file.

Caution

To access this exported file, you will need Microsoft Excel installed on your computer.

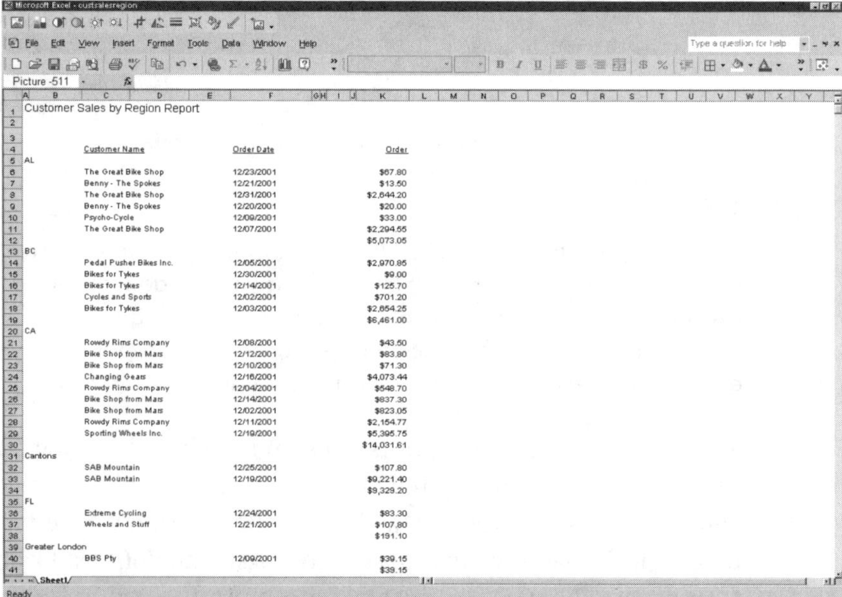

Customer Sales by Region Report

	Customer Name	Order Date	Order
AL			
	The Great Bike Shop	12/23/2001	$67.80
	Benny - The Spokes	12/21/2001	$13.50
	The Great Bike Shop	12/31/2001	$2,644.20
	Benny - The Spokes	12/20/2001	$20.00
	Psycho-Cycle	12/09/2001	$33.00
	The Great Bike Shop	12/07/2001	$2,294.55
			$5,073.05
BC			
	Pedal Pusher Bikes Inc.	12/05/2001	$2,970.85
	Bikes for Tykes	12/30/2001	$9.00
	Bikes for Tykes	12/14/2001	$125.70
	Cycles and Sports	12/02/2001	$701.20
	Bikes for Tykes	12/03/2001	$2,654.25
			$6,461.00
CA			
	Rowdy Rims Company	12/08/2001	$43.50
	Bike Shop from Mars	12/12/2001	$83.80
	Bike Shop from Mars	12/10/2001	$71.30
	Changing Gears	12/16/2001	$4,073.44
	Rowdy Rims Company	12/04/2001	$548.70
	Bike Shop from Mars	12/14/2001	$837.30
	Bike Shop from Mars	12/02/2001	$823.05
	Rowdy Rims Company	12/11/2001	$2,154.77
	Sporting Wheels Inc.	12/19/2001	$5,395.75
			$14,031.61
Cantons			
	SAB Mountain	12/25/2001	$107.80
	SAB Mountain	12/19/2001	$9,221.40
			$9,329.20
FL			
	Extreme Cycling	12/24/2001	$83.30
	Wheels and Stuff	12/21/2001	$107.80
			$191.10
Greater London			
	BBS Pty	12/09/2001	$39.15
			$39.15

Figure 14-4. The Customer Sales by Region report, exported into an Excel spreadsheet

If you scroll down to the end of this Excel file, you'll see that Crystal Reports exports all charts (shown in Figure 14-5).

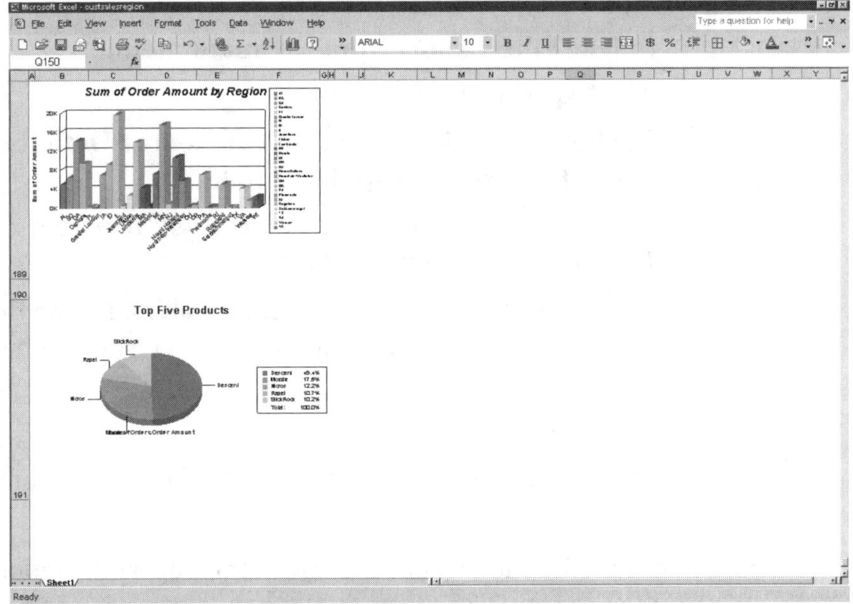

Figure 14-5. The exported file containing all report charts

Try experimenting with the different file formats to see which provides the best export for your reports. You'll find that sometimes some file formats export better than others, depending on the layout of your report.

Creating a Report Definition File

Another useful exporting technique is to export your reports into a report definition file. A *report definition file* acts as a blueprint for your report design, containing such information as the tables that the report uses and the formulas it utilizes. Report definition files are something you should create for all your reports. They're especially useful for other report developers who might need to work on a report you created. A report definition file will provide other developers with a summary of how your report works.

The following example describes the process of creating such a file. In this example, you continue using the CustSales-Region2.rpt.

1. **Select File, Export from the main menu.**

   The Export dialog box displays.

2. **In the Export dialog box, select Report Definition from the Format drop-down field.**

3. **In the Export dialog box, select Disk file from the Destination drop-down field.**

   The Select Export File dialog box displays. Define the name of your report definition and the location where you wish to save the report definition.

4. **Press OK.**

   An Exporting Records dialog box displays quickly and then disappears.

Check out the location where you saved this report definition file. It's saved in a text (.TXT) format. Open the report definition file. It should look like Figure 14-6.

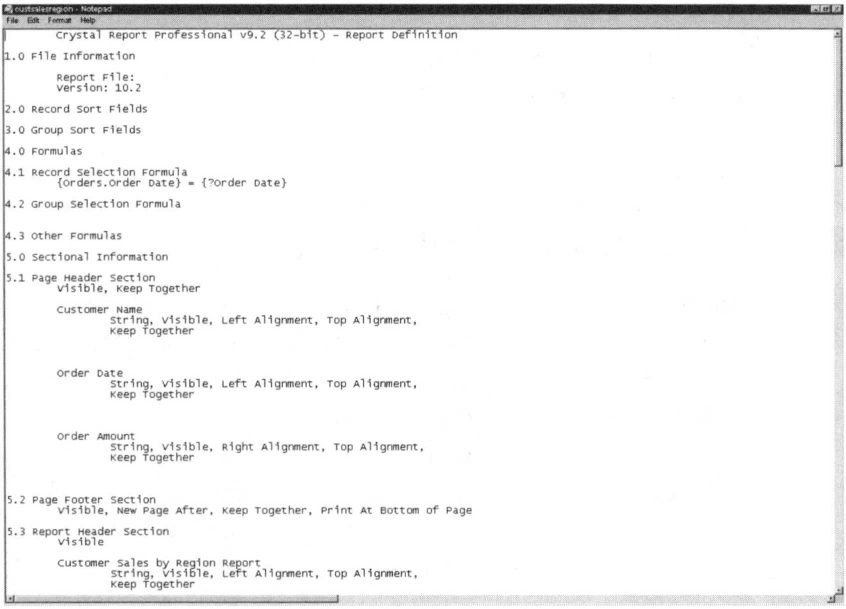

```
custsalesregion - Notepad
File  Edit  Format  Help
        Crystal Report Professional v9.2 (32-bit) - Report Definition

1.0 File Information

        Report File:
        Version: 10.2

2.0 Record Sort Fields

3.0 Group Sort Fields

4.0 Formulas

4.1 Record Selection Formula
        {Orders.Order Date} = {?Order Date}

4.2 Group Selection Formula


4.3 Other Formulas

5.0 Sectional Information

5.1 Page Header Section
        Visible, Keep Together

        Customer Name
                String, Visible, Left Alignment, Top Alignment,
                Keep Together


        Order Date
                String, Visible, Left Alignment, Top Alignment,
                Keep Together


        Order Amount
                String, Visible, Right Alignment, Top Alignment,
                Keep Together


5.2 Page Footer Section
        Visible, New Page After, Keep Together, Print At Bottom of Page

5.3 Report Header Section
        Visible

        Customer Sales by Region Report
                String, Visible, Left Alignment, Top Alignment,
                Keep Together
```

Figure 14-6. A report definition file

Viewing Real-Time Reports

So far in this chapter, you've looked at exporting reports into a static format in which your data is essentially frozen at the time you ran the report. But what if you wish for your users to view real-time reports — providing them with the ability to refresh reports to ensure they're viewing the most current data?

One solution is to provide report users with a copy of the report file (.RPT) you created and have them open and refresh the report with their own copy of Crystal Reports. Unfortunately, doing so requires that they have a copy of the software on their computers. This method may not be the most cost-effective solution for an organization.

Essentially, you have four other choices to provide real-time reports to your users. You can:

- Use a custom application that delivers the reports to your users. You'll need to have the Developer or Advanced editions of Crystal Reports to utilize this option.
- Use the Report Application Server (which is provided with the Professional and Developer version of Crystal Reports), an out-of-the-box web interface for real-time reporting.
- Use Crystal Enterprise (another Crystal Decisions product supported by Crystal Reports Developer and Advanced editions) as a prebuilt report distribution system.
- Use a third-party software report viewer (such as some of the products discussed in Appendix D).

In this book, we look briefly at the use of third-party products as a solution for report deployment.

The Crystal Reports Distributor

One excellent third-party product for successful report distribution is Crystal Reports Distributor, provided by ChristianSteven Software, Ltd. (www.christiansteven.com). This product allows you to automate the production of your Crystal Reports, including:

- Automating the scheduling of batch reports and sending them all out in the same e-mail

- Automating the sending of a report output to a folder, printer, or fax machine
- Automating the sending of a report output to Microsoft Word, Excel, Adobe Acrobat (PDF), and other popular file formats

Figure 14-7 displays an example of the Crystal Reports Distributor. This and other third-party products are discussed in Appendix D.

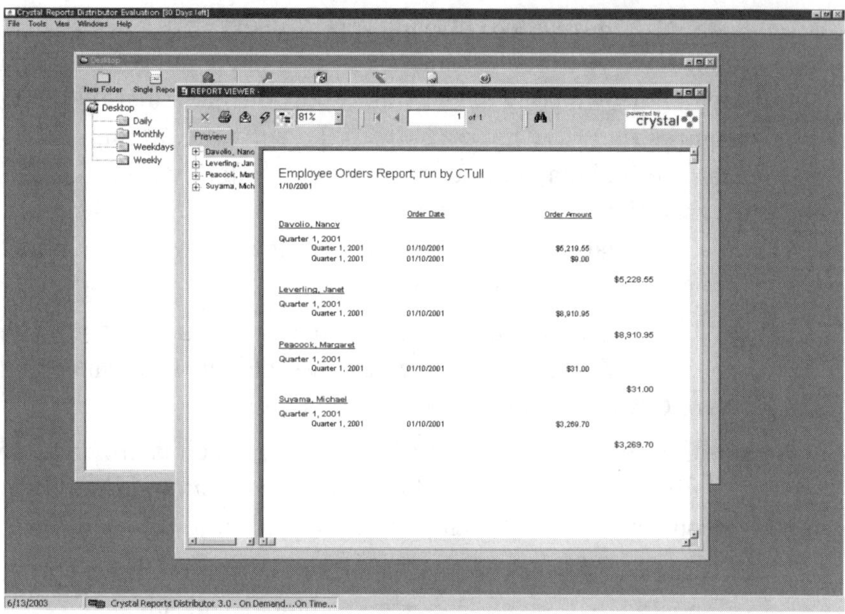

Figure 14-7. The Crystal Reports Distributor from ChristianSteven Software, Ltd.

The following steps present report viewing with the Crystal Reports Distributor:

1. **To view a report in real time, select File, Report from the menu bar.**

   An Open dialog box displays. Select the location of the report that you wish to view. Note, you do not need to have Crystal installed on your computer to view these reports.

2. **Once you select the file, the report displays in a Report Viewer dialog box.**
3. **Explore the Standard toolbar located on the Report Viewer.**

   You can expand the Group Tree, refresh your data, scroll through the pages of your report, print, e-mail, and even export the report to other formats.

   Figure 14-7 displays how your screen might appear when viewing one of the reports that you've created within this book.

Of course, this is only scratching the surface of what Crystal Reports Distributor can do. There's a plethora of functionality that provides scheduling, mailing, and other distribution options. You can find more information regarding this product in the online help that ships with the trial software.

What's Next?

This chapter has given you some ideas on how to share your reports with your business users. It's also given you some important considerations to think about, including which report distribution method works best for you. In this chapter, you've looked at the functionality within Crystal Reports to create static report distribution and a third-party package as a solution for dynamic report distribution. However, keep in mind that Crystal Decisions does provide numerous options and products to meet your report distribution needs. Check out www.crystaldecisions.com for more information regarding the various products available for your report distribution.

Chapter 15

Exploring Crystal Reports' SQL Commands

In Chapter 1 you learned that the Crystal Reports program essentially provides an easy-to-use method of creating a query against a database. *Queries* request information from a database in the SQL query language. In this chapter, we look at writing SQL queries within Crystal Reports.

A question is probably ringing in your head: If Crystal Reports goes through all the trouble of querying your database in a user-friendly manner, why would you want to delve into writing SQL yourself? Why not just have Crystal Reports do the dirty work for you?

As a report writer, you'll find writing queries useful. You can create query files and connect your reports to these files. Using query files in your reports eliminates much of the data-generating tasks performed by Crystal Reports on a database server. Query files result in much quicker report generation for your users.

A SQL Overview

As you explore Crystal's SQL commands, you'll explore some of the areas of the SQL language. The subject of SQL is huge (not to mention a little on the dry side) and could easily fill volumes of books. Rather than explore the whole of SQL (which is beyond the scope of this book), this chapter explores the most frequently used areas of SQL, especially those areas of most interest to the report developer.

Where Did SQL Come From?

SQL (or structured query language) began as an IBM language. In 1988, the American National Standards Institute (ANSI) and the International Organization for Standardization (ISO) standardized SQL. The standard became known as ISO-ANSI SQL.

In 1992, a new version of the ANSI-ISO standard was released, containing a much richer set of functionality for commercial implementations. The U.S. National Institute of Standards and Technology (NIST) has required that most database vendors be compliant with the 1992 ANSI-ISO SQL (known as ANSI 92 Entry Level).

Thus, when talking about SQL, we're talking about the 1992 version of the language.

To get you started in the world of SQL programming, there are four basic SQL statements:

- SELECT
- INSERT
- UPDATE
- DELETE

With Crystal Reports' SQL commands, the only one of the above commands that you can use is SELECT. The SELECT statement allows you to retrieve (or view) data from a database.

Note

The other statements modify the database, which is functionality that is not available in Crystal Reports. As stated in Chapter 1, in no way can Crystal Reports alter the data within your database.

With that said, let's jump into Crystal Reports and get you building your first query files.

Exploring the SQL Commands

To access Crystal Reports' SQL commands, begin creating a blank report. Select the xtreme.mdb file. Once you select your database, notice the Add Command node above the Tables node in the Database Expert, as shown in Figure 15-1.

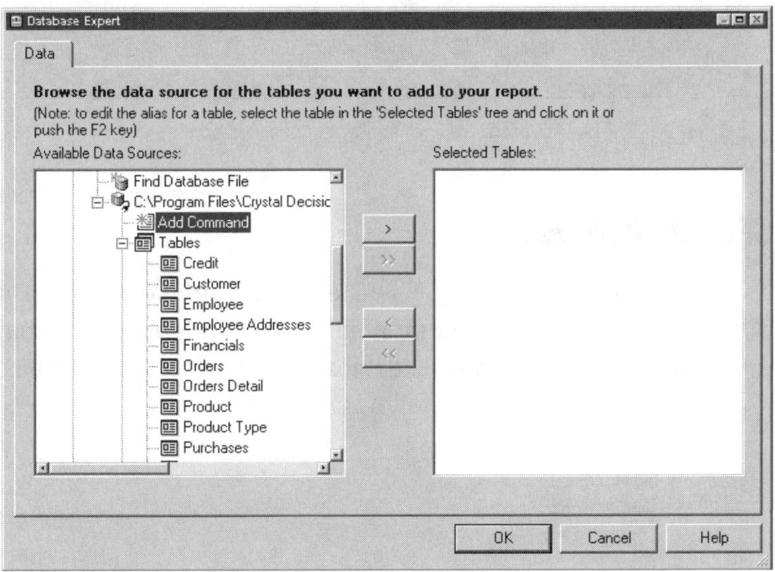

Figure 15-1. The Add Command node

Double-click this Add Command node. The Add Command To Report dialog box displays, as shown in Figure 15-2. This dialog box is where you create SQL commands.

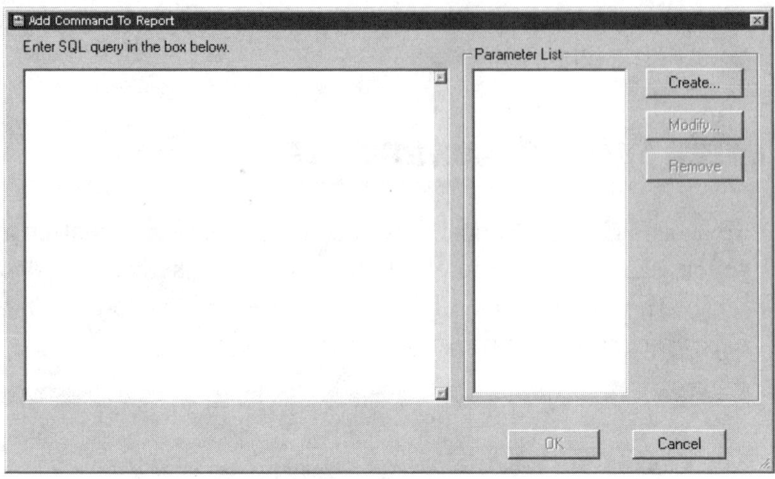

Figure 15-2. The Add Command To Report dialog box

The SELECT Statement

To get used to creating queries, let's try a simple SELECT statement. The SELECT statement allows you to obtain information from the tables within your database. The format for the basic SELECT statement is as follows:

```
SELECT fields
FROM table
[WHERE condition]
[ORDER BY sort-fields]
```

Note

In the above SELECT statement, the square brackets ([]) indicate that this content is optional.

Perhaps the best way to get a feel for how SQL works is to see it in action. Say you wish to create a SELECT statement that allows you to view all records within the Product table. In the Add Command To Report dialog box, try the following:

1. **In the Enter SQL query box in the Add Command To Report dialog box, type the following:**

   ```
   SELECT *
   FROM Product
   ```

   Your screen should look like Figure 15-3.

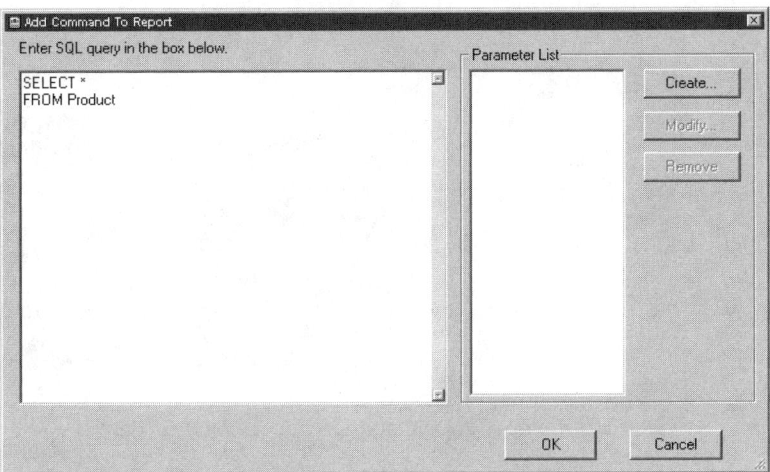

Figure 15-3. Creating a SELECT statement

Tip

The asterisk (*) represents a wildcard character, which is a placeholder used to represent one or more characters. Using the wildcard character in this instance means that you wish to select all fields within the Product table.

You first learned about the wildcard character in Chapter 7.

2. **After typing in the SQL, press the OK button.**

   You'll see your SQL command display in the Selected Tables list box of the Database Expert, as shown in Figure 15-4.

If you press the OK button in the Database Expert, the Report Design area displays. In the Field Explorer pane, expand the Command node. You'll notice the query displays all fields within the Product table, as shown in Figure 15-5 on the following page.

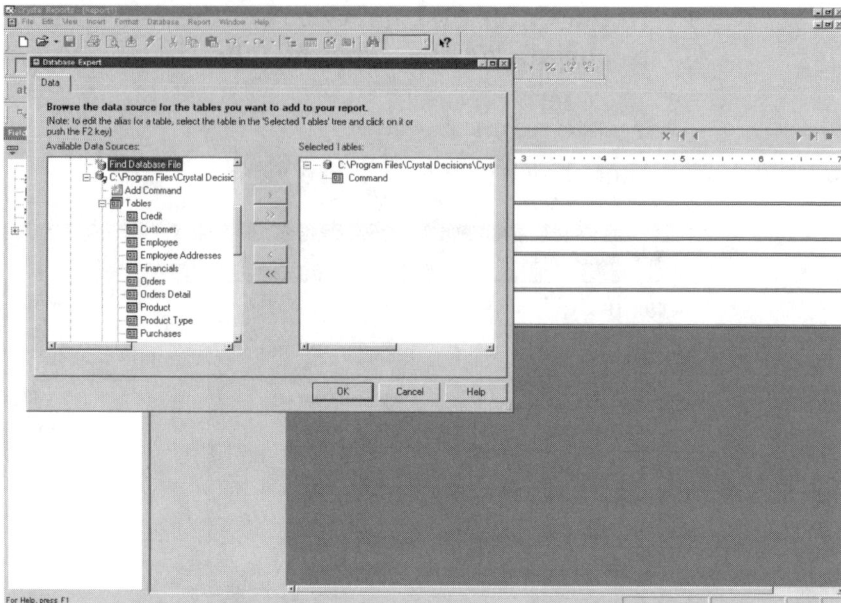

Figure 15-4. The SQL command in the Selected Tables list box

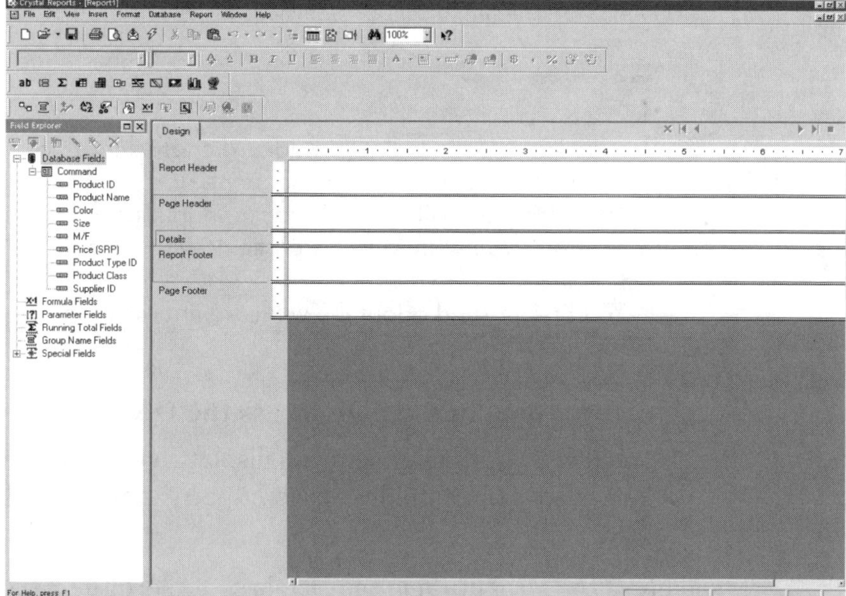

Figure 15-5. The SQL query you created returns all fields in the Product table (as shown in the Field Explorer).

The WHERE Clause

Of course, the real power of a SQL statement comes from the ability to restrict (or filter) records returned with the query. If you recall from your previous reports, the Product table contains information regarding several different products.

To limit your query to products that meet certain conditions, you can utilize a WHERE clause. The WHERE clause allows you to filter the records returned by your SELECT statement.

Tip

Although the WHERE clause is optional, it's usually included with most SELECT statements.

Say you wish to limit the previous SELECT statement to only include products that are classified as bicycles. Perform the following to get a feel for the WHERE clause:

1. **In the report you've been working with in this chapter, select Database, Database Expert from the menu bar.**

   The Database Expert displays.

2. **Left-click on the command that resides in the Selected Tables list box.**

   The command should now be highlighted.

3. **Press the F2 key on your keyboard.**

   Notice that you can now edit the name of this command. Type the following: Product_qry. Your screen should look like Figure 15-6 on the following page.

4. **Right-click on the Product_qry command.**

   An options menu displays.

5. **Select Edit Command from the options menu.**

   The Modify Command dialog box displays.

6. **Modify your SELECT statement as follows:**

```
SELECT *
FROM Product
WHERE 'Product Class' = 'Bicycle'
```

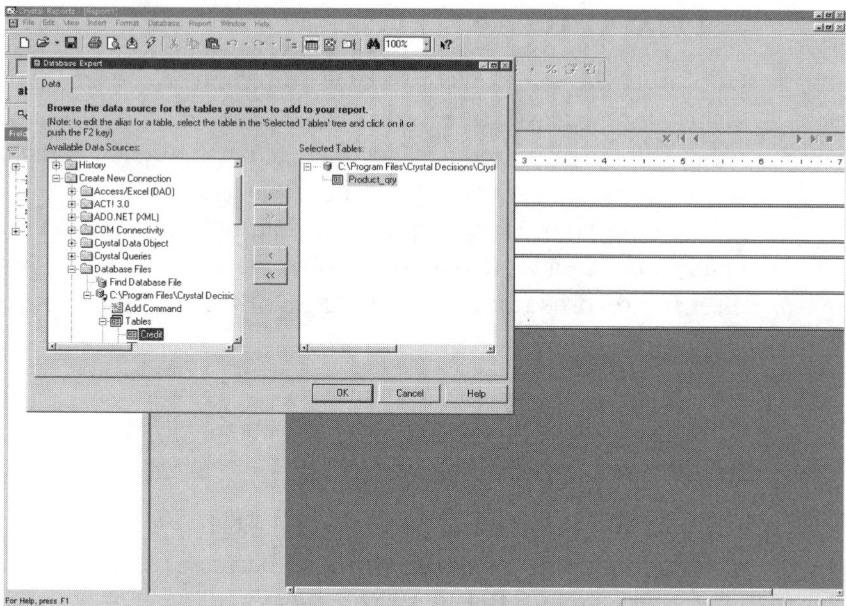

Figure 15-6. Renaming a SQL command

Your screen should look like Figure 15-7.

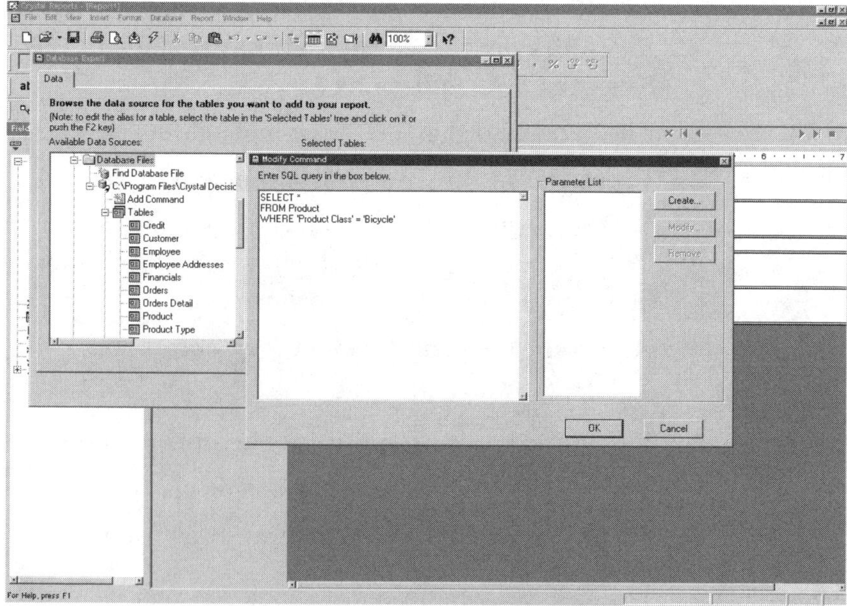

Figure 15-7. Adding a WHERE clause to your SELECT statement

Tip

Whenever you are referring to a specific field and record within Crystal Reports SQL, you must enclose the name of the record in quotes.

If you were to run this query, only products that are classified as bicycles would display.

A common practice with WHERE clauses is to combine conditions using the Boolean operators AND, OR, and NOT. For example:

```
SELECT *
FROM Product
WHERE 'PRODUCT CLASS' = 'Bicycle' AND 'Product Name' =
'Descend'
```

This SQL statement would return only Descend products from the Products table where the products are classified as bicycles.

The ORDER BY Clause

Relational databases do not use a built-in ordering of records. If a new record is added to your database and then retrieved by a report, that new record might display at the beginning of your report, at the end of the report, or anywhere in between. Basically, relational databases do not have a built-in rhyme or reason of how they'll order your records.

To order your records within a query, you can use the ORDER BY clause within your SELECT statements. For example, say in the report you're working on that you wish to display all products alphabetically by the product name. Try the following example:

1. **In the report you've been working on in this chapter, select Database, Database Expert from the menu bar.**

   The Database Expert displays.

2. **Right-click on the Product_qry command.**

   An options menu displays.

3. **Select Edit Command from the options menu.**

   The Modify Command dialog box displays.

4. **Modify your SELECT statement as follows:**

```
SELECT *
FROM Product
WHERE 'Product Class' = 'Bicycle'
ORDER BY 'Product Name'
```

Your screen should look like Figure 15-8.

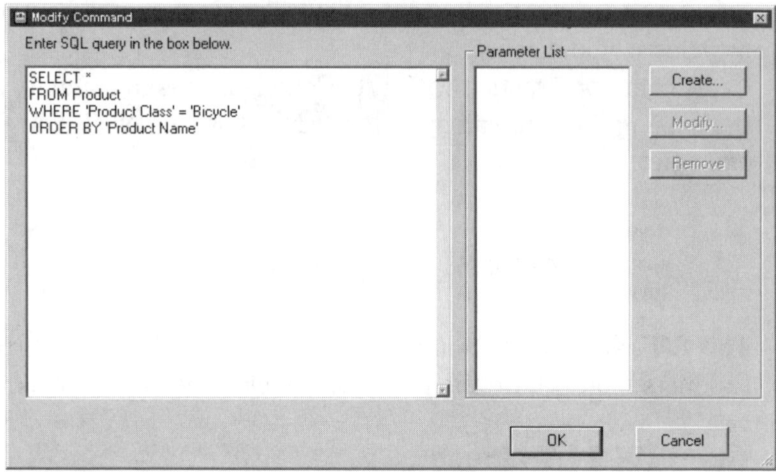

Figure 15-8. Adding an ORDER BY clause to your SELECT statement

This statement returns all products listed in ascending order (which is the default in SQL) by product name. You can define whether the ORDER BY clause lists records in ascending or descending order by using the keywords ASC (for ascending order) or DESC (for descending order). For example:

```
SELECT *
FROM Product
WHERE 'Product Class' = 'Bicycle'
ORDER BY 'Product Name' DESC
```

This SELECT statement returns all products by product name in descending order (or Z to A). Also, only products classified as bicycles display.

Tip

Even though the ASC keyword is the default, it's still a good idea to show either the ASC or DESC keyword whenever you use the ORDER BY clause. These keywords act as a reminder for your design decision and keep you from forgetting how the data sorts.

The JOIN Clause

So far, you've been creating queries using only a single table. But as you've learned in this book, most reports are developed from two or more tables. In Chapter 6 you explored this concept through the Database Expert. But how do you create a SQL query that performs this same functionality? The answer is through SQL's JOIN clause. JOIN allows you to define how two tables within a database are to match up.

There are a number of syntaxes for the JOIN clause, but the easiest is to utilize an equal sign (=) within your WHERE clause:

```
SELECT fields
FROM table1, table2
WHERE table1 table1 INNER JOIN table2 table2 ON
field = table2.field
```

Try the following to see this in action. In this example, you'll be linking the Customer and Orders table. Instead of selecting all fields after the SELECT statement, you're defining specific fields that you wish to use.

1. **In the report you've been working on in this chapter, select Database, Database Expert from the menu bar.**

   The Database Expert displays.

2. **Right-click on the Product_qry command.**

   An options menu displays.

3. **Select Edit Command from the options menu.**

   The Modify Command dialog box displays. This is the same dialog box as the Add Command to Report dialog box.

4. **Modify your SELECT statement as follows:**

```
SELECT
    Customer.`Customer Name`,
    Customer.`Last Year's Sales`,
    Customer.`Region`,
    Customer.`Country`,
    Orders.`Order Amount`,
    Orders.`Order Date`

FROM

    Customer Customer INNER JOIN Orders Orders ON
```

Part III

```
        Customer.`Customer ID` = Orders.`Customer ID`

    ORDER BY
        Customer.`Country` ASC,
        Customer.`Region` ASC
```

Your screen should look like Figure 15-9.

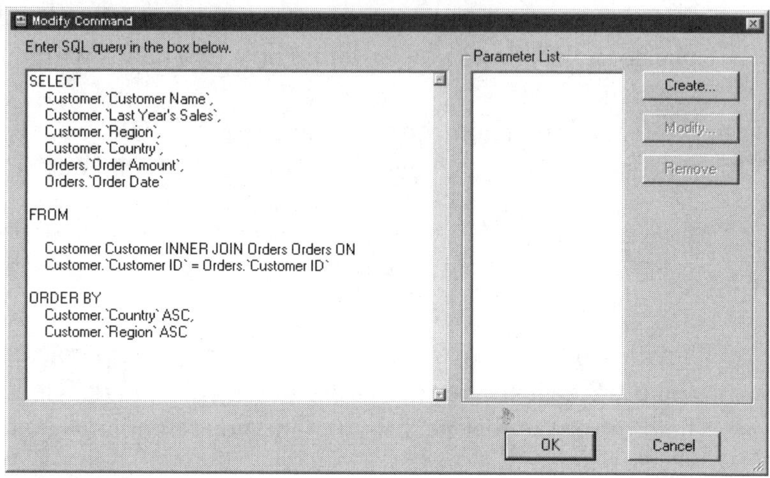

Figure 15-9. Joining multiple tables within your SQL command

What's Next?

In this chapter, you've explored creating SQL queries for use within Crystal Reports. Learning the SQL language is a great skill for any report writer to possess; the more you understand about SQL, the greater command you'll have with report writing software such as Crystal Reports. Should you be interested in learning SQL, two excellent books to get you started are *Sams Teach Yourself SQL in 10 Minutes* by Ben Forta and *The Guru's Guide to Transact-SQL* by Ken Henderson.

You've come a long way in this book, learning many of the reporting techniques required for real-world report development. By now, you probably have a strong understanding of Crystal Reports and are familiar with the possibilities available within this exciting and usable software.

Keep plugging away, and remember that the only way to learn how to develop usable reports is by doing.

Part III Exercise

Balance Sheet Report

See the companion files (www.wordware.com/files/crystal) for an example of this report. Create this report with the Standard Report Creation Wizard. This report is created with the xtreme.mdb database.

Table(s)	Fields
Financial	Statement Date Cash Account Receivable Inventories Other Current Assets Land Buildings Machinery etc. Accumulated Depreciation Other Assets Accounts Payable Accrued Liabilities Accrued Income Taxes Notes Payable Deferred Income Taxes Preferred Stock Common Stock Retained Earnings

Since there is only one table, you won't have to worry about linking multiple tables. Once you've selected your table and fields within the Standard Report Creation Wizard, perform the following:

1. **In the Grouping screen, create a group for every field except the Statement Date field.**

   Your screen should look like figure P3-1. Once you've defined these groups, press the Next button. The Summaries screen displays.

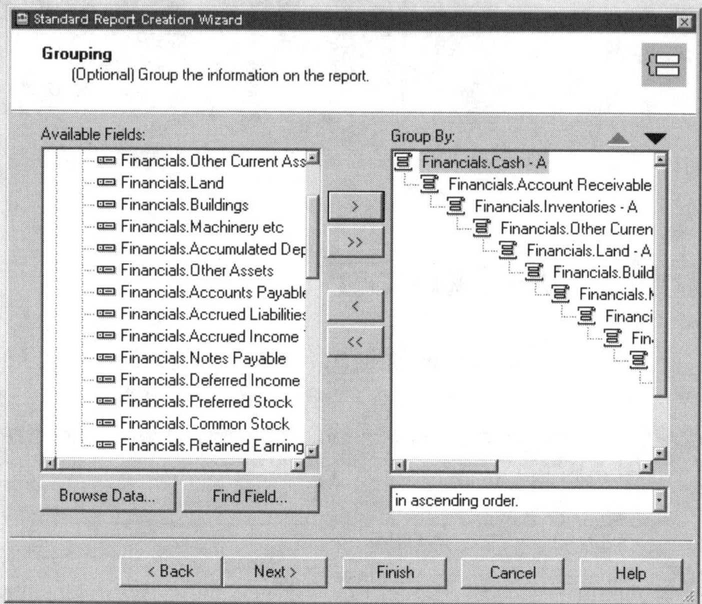

Figure P3-1. Defining groups within your Balance Sheet report

2. **In the Summaries screen, leave everything as default.**

   Press the Next button. The Group Sorting screen displays.

3. **In the Group Sorting screen, leave everything as default.**

   Press the Next button. The Chart screen displays.

4. **In the Chart screen, leave everything as default.**

   Press the Next button. The Record Selection screen displays.

5. **In the Record Selection screen, press the Next button.**

You do not need to create any record selection statements at the moment. After pressing the Next button, the Template screen displays.

6. **In the Template screen, select the No Template option.**

   Press the Finish button. Your screen should look like Figure P3-2.

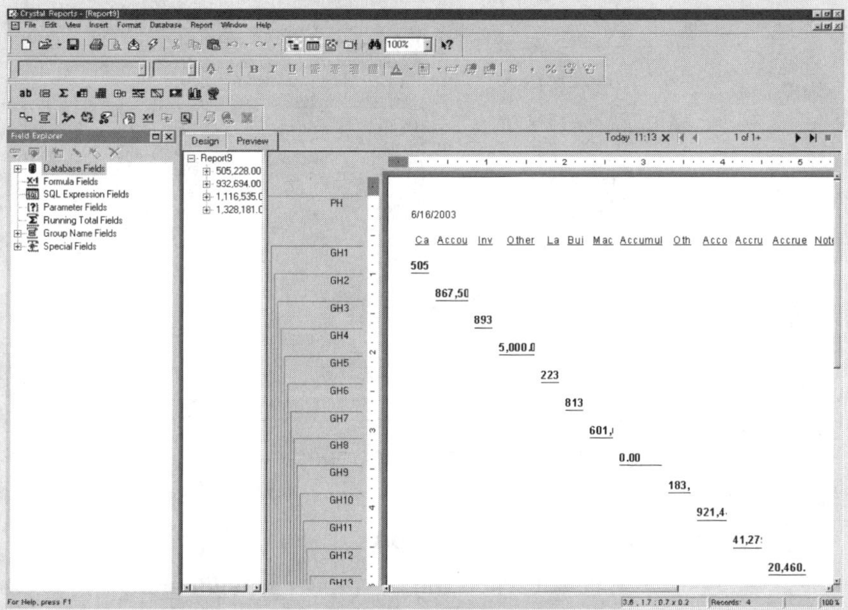

Figure P3-2. Creating a Balance Sheet report with the Standard Report Creation Wizard

Continue with the following steps to continue defining your Balance Statement report:

1. **From the Field Explorer, right-click on the Parameter Fields node.**

   An options menu displays.

2. **From this options menu, select the New option.**

   The Create Parameter Field dialog box displays.

3. **Define your parameter as follows:**

   - In the Name field, type the following: Report Period.

- In the Prompting text field, type the following: Please define your reporting period:.
- In the Options section, select the Range value(s) option.

Your screen should look like Figure P3-3.

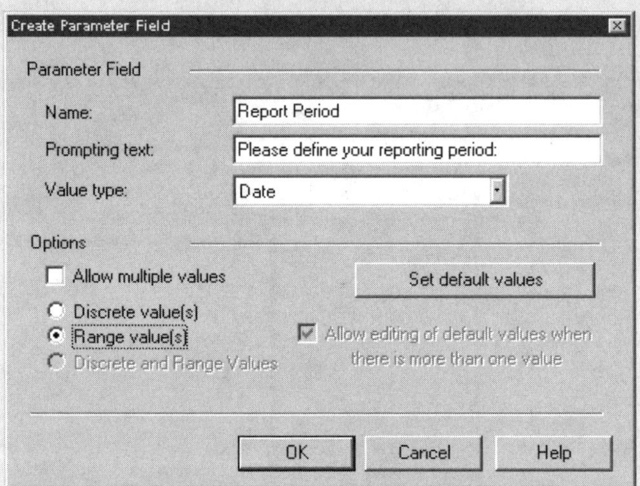

Figure P3-3. Defining a report parameter

4. **Press the OK button.**

   You're returned to the Report Design area.

5. **From the menu bar, select Report, Select Expert.**

   The Choose Field dialog box displays.

6. **Select the Statement Date field within the Choose Field dialog box.**

   Once you've done this, press OK. The Select Expert dialog box displays.

7. **Define your select statement as follows:**

   - In the Comparison operator drop-down field, select Is Equal To.
   - In the Comparison value drop-down field, type the following: {?Report Period}.

   The Enter Parameter Values dialog box displays.

8. **Type in the following report period in the Enter Parameter Values dialog box: 03/01/2001 to 03/31/2001.**

   This dialog box should look like Figure P3-4.

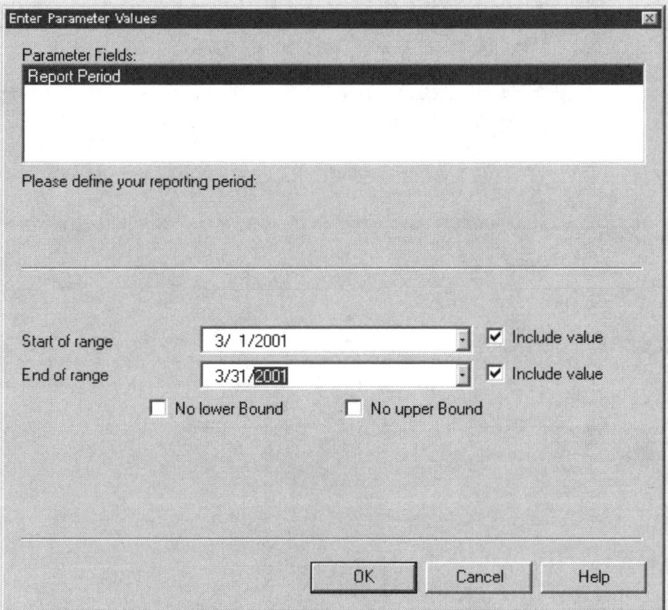

Figure P3-4. Entering a report date range for your report

Once you've pressed OK, you're asked if you want to use saved data or refresh your data. Select to refresh your data. Your report refreshes, and you're returned to the Report Design area. Let's now focus on the format of your report.

1. **Within the Group Headers, align all fields at the 3.5" mark. Stretch these fields so that all data displays.**
2. **Drag all headings within the Page Headers into their respective Group Header sections.**

   For example, the Cash header is placed in Group Header 1, the Accounts Receivable header is placed in Group Header 2, etc.

   Align the right edge of the headers at the 3" mark. Then stretch the left edge of the header to the 1.5" mark.

Once you've done this, change the alignment so that all headers are left aligned.

Finally, double-click into the Account Receivable field and rename it Accounts Receivable.

3. **Suppress all Group Footer sections. Also, suppress the Report Footer section.**
4. **Select all headers and fields. Change their font size to 8.**

   Your screen should look like Figure P3-5.

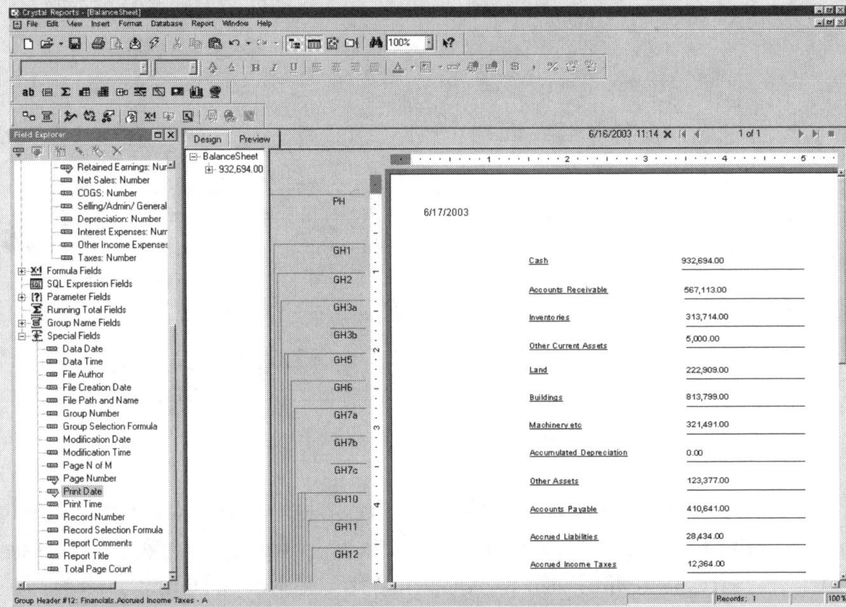

Figure P3-5. Formatting the Balance Sheet report

5. **From the menu bar, select Report, Formula Workshop.**

   The Formula Workshop displays.
6. **Right-click on the Formula Fields folder.**

   An options menu displays.
7. **From this options menu, select New.**

The Formula Name dialog box displays. In this dialog box, type Total Current Assets. Then, press the Use Editor button. The Formula Editor displays.

8. **Type the following code within the formula edit window:**

```
{Financials.Cash} +
{Financials.Account Receivable} +
{Financials.Inventories} +
{Financials.Other Current Assets}
```

9. **Check your formula for errors.**

   If no errors are found, press the Save button.

While you're in the Formula Editor, create the rest of the formulas you'll need for this report. These are summarized in the following table. To create a new formula, right-click on the Formula Fields folder. Make sure you check for any errors, and save your work before creating a new formula.

Table P3-1. Additional formulas of the Balance Sheet report

Formula Name	Formula
Net Fixed Assets	{Financials.Land}+ {Financials.Buildings}+ {Financials.Machinery etc}+ {Financials.Accumulated Depreciation}
Total Fixed and Other Assets	{Financials.Land}+ {Financials.Buildings}+ {Financials.Machinery etc}+ {Financials.Accumulated Depreciation}+ {Financials.Other Assets}
Total Assets	{Financials.Cash}+ {Financials.Account Receivable}+ {Financials.Inventories}+ {Financials.Other Current Assets}+ {Financials.Land}+ {Financials.Buildings}+ {Financials.Machinery etc}+ {Financials.Accumulated Depreciation}+ {Financials.Other Assets}
Total Current Liabilities	{Financials.Accounts Payable}+ {Financials.Accrued Liabilities}+ {Financials.Accrued Income Taxes}
Total Long Term Liabilities	{Financials.Notes Payable} + {Financials.Deferred Income Taxes}

Formula Name	Formula
Total Shareholders' Equity	{Financials.Preferred Stock}+ {Financials.Common Stock}+ {Financials.Retained Earnings}
Total Equity and Liabilities	{Financials.Accounts Payable}+ {Financials.Accrued Liabilities}+ {Financials.Accrued Income Taxes}+ {Financials.Notes Payable}+ {Financials.Deferred Income Taxes}+ {Financials.Preferred Stock}+ {Financials.Common Stock}+ {Financials.Retained Earnings}

Once you've created these formulas, add them to the following areas of your report, as defined by Table P3-2. If you have any confusion, check out Figure P3-6 to see what your screen should look like when finished.

Table P3-2. Adding the formulas to your report

Formula Name	Location	Text Object	Formatting
Total Current Assets	Stretch the Group Header 4 section. Place the formula at the 2-inch mark.	Create a text object with the following text: Total Current Assets. Place this object in line with the formula, starting at the 0-inch mark.	Bold, Left Align, and change font color to navy for both text object and formula.
Net Fixed Assets	Stretch the Group Header 8 section. Place the formula at the 2-inch mark.	Create a text object with the following text: Net Fixed Assets. Place this object in line with the formula, starting at the 0-inch mark.	Bold, Left Align, and change font color to navy for both text object and formula.
Total Fixed and Other Assets	Stretch the Group Header 9 section. Place the formula at the 2-inch mark.	Create a text object with the following text: Total Fixed and Other Assets. Place this object in line with the formula, starting at the 0-inch mark.	Bold, Left Align, and change font color to navy for both text object and formula.

Formula Name	Location	Text Object	Formatting
Total Assets	Place the formula at the 2-inch mark, slightly under the Total Fixed and Other Assets formula.	Create a text object with the following text: Total Assets. Place this object in line with the formula, starting at the 0-inch mark.	Bold, Left Align, and change font color to maroon for both text object and formula.
Total Current Liabilities	Stretch the Group Header 12 section. Place the formula at the 2-inch mark.	Create a text object with the following text: Total Current Liabilities. Place this object in line with the formula, starting at the 0-inch mark.	Bold, Left Align, and change font color to navy for both text object and formula.
Total Long Term Liabilities	Stretch the Group Header 14 section. Place the formula at the 2-inch mark.	Create a text object with the following text: Total Long Term Liabilities. Place this object in line with the formula, starting at the 0-inch mark.	Bold, Left Align, and change font color to navy for both text object and formula.
Total Shareholders' Equity	Stretch the Group Header 17 section. Place the formula at the 2-inch mark.	Create a text object with the following text: Total Shareholders' Equity. Place this object in line with the formula, starting at the 0-inch mark.	Bold, Left Align, and change font color to navy for both text object and formula.
Total Equity and Liabilities	Place the formula at the 2-inch mark, slightly under the Total Shareholders' formula.	Create a text object with the following text: Total Equity and Liabilities. Place this object in line with the formula, starting at the 0-inch mark.	Bold, Left Align, and change font color to maroon for both text object and formula.

Figure P3-6 displays the results of your work so far.

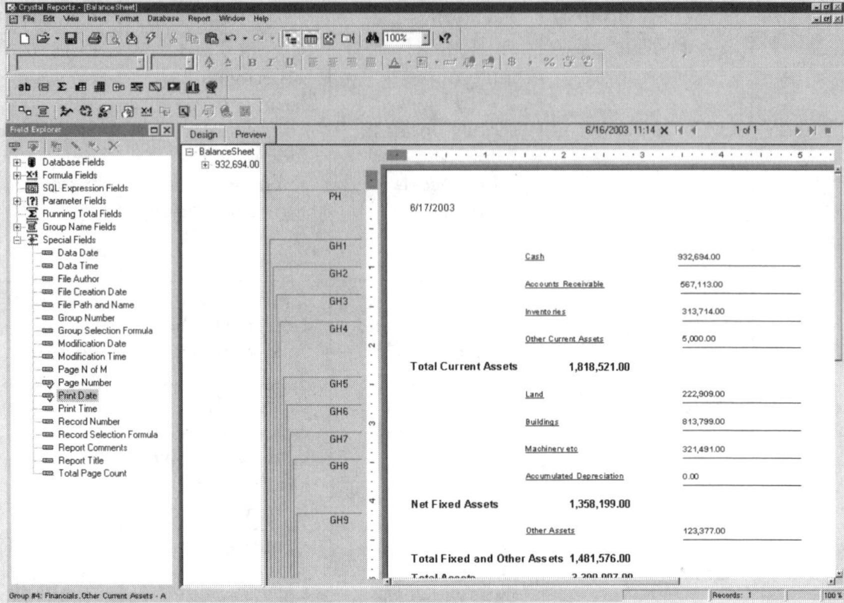

Figure P3-6. Adding formulated totals to the Balance Sheet report

To complete this report, add a title (Consolidated Balance Sheet) and place it in the Page Header section at the top of your report. This title should be bold and in a font size of around 18.

Also, delete the print date and replace with the Statement Date field. Change the Statement Date field so that it displays in a format of *mm/dd/yyyy*. Figure P3-7 displays the final version of the Consolidated Balance Sheet report.

Consolidated Balance Sheet

03/31/2001

		Cash	932,694.00
		Accounts Receivable	567,113.00
		Inventories	313,714.00
		Other Current Assets	5,000.00
Total Current Assets	**1,818,521.00**		
		Land	222,909.00
Total Current Assets	**1,818,521.00**		
		Land	222,909.00
		Buildings	813,799.00
		Machinery etc	321,491.00
		Accumulated Depreciation	0.00
Net Fixed Assets	**1,358,199.00**		
		Other Assets	123,377.00
Total Fixed and Other Assets	**1,481,576.00**		
Total Assets	**3,300,097.00**		
		Accounts Payable	410,641.00
		Accrued Liabilities	28,434.00
		Accrued Income Taxes	12,364.00
Total Current Liabilities	**451,439.00**		
		Notes Payable	698,568.00
		Deferred Income Taxes	14,258.00
Total Long Term Liabilities	**712,826.00**		
		Preferred Stock	230,640.00
		Common Stock	1,905,192.00
		Retained Eamings	0.00
Total Shareholders' Equity	**2,135,832.00**		
Total Equity and Liabilities	**3,300,097.00**		

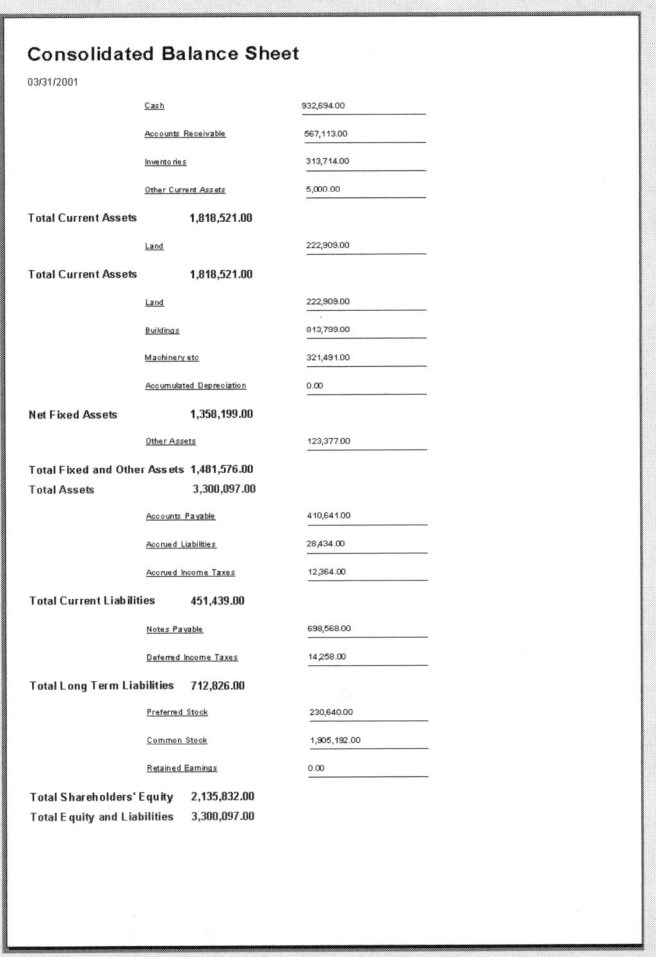

Figure P3-7. The final version of the Consolidated Balance Sheet report

Part IV

Reference

Appendix A

The Xtreme.mdb ER Model

The following entity-relationship model displays the different relationships between the tables of the xtreme.mdb database. These relationships utilize primary keys, which contain the following restrictions:

- The value of the primary key must contain a unique value. In other words, no two different rows within a table can have the same value within the primary key field.
- The value of the primary key cannot contain a NULL value. A *NULL* value represents missing, unknown, or inapplicable data. A NULL value is not the same thing as a zero value.

Entity-relationship models are especially useful when linking multiple tables together for use within a report. Remember, when linking tables together in Crystal Reports, the linking relationships must match the relationships of the tables within the database. An entity-relationship model will tell you how different database tables link together.

The following diagram summarizes the referential integrity constraints required by the tables of the xtreme.mdb database.

Note

In the xtreme.mdb database, the Financials table does not contain any links to any other tables.

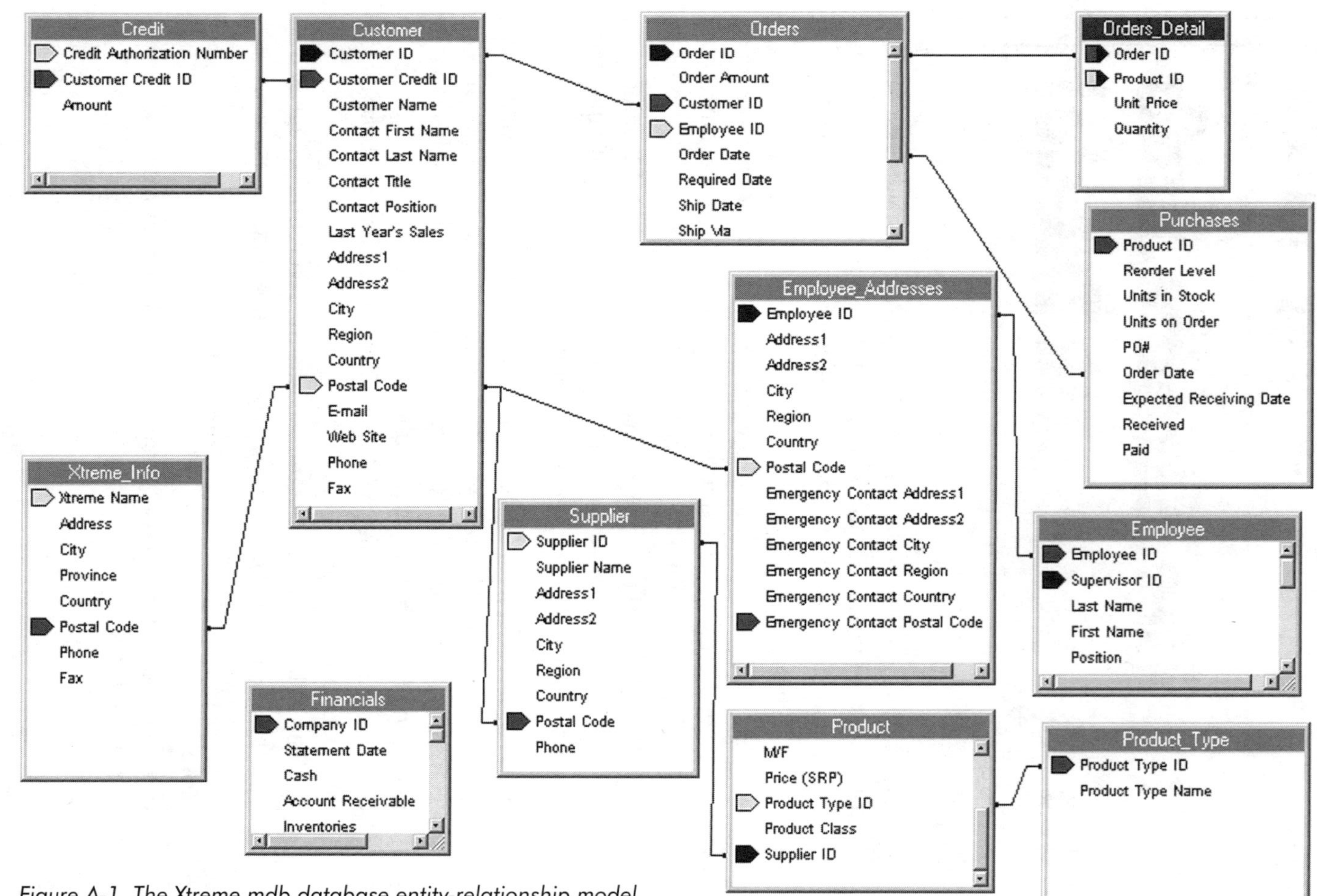

Figure A-1. The Xtreme.mdb database entity-relationship model

Appendix B

The Xtreme.mdb Data Dictionary

The following is a data dictionary of Crystal Reports' xtreme.mdb database. Xtreme.mdb is a Microsoft Access database with all the necessary drivers included. The data types listed within this appendix are associated with Microsoft Access databases.

Xtreme.mdb is a database that contains data for Xtreme Mountain Bikes, a fictitious Canadian wholesale company that operates worldwide. Xtreme Mountain Bikes fills orders for retail stores that specialize in mountain bikes and accessories.

The following information describes the attributes of the xtreme.mdb database and the constraints imposed on these attributes.

Credit

The Credit table contains data regarding the customer credit information.

Table B-1. Credit data

Field Name	Data Type	Field Size/Format	Description
Credit Authorization Number	Text	10	Customer's unique credit authorization ID.
Customer Credit ID	Number	Long Integer	Customer's credit ID.
Amount	Currency	(undefined)	Customer's total credit amount.

Customer

The Customer table contains data regarding the global customers of Xtreme Mountain Bikes.

Table B-2. Customer data

Field Name	Data Type	Field Size/Format	Description
Customer ID	Number	Long Integer	Customer unique identification number.
Customer Credit ID	Number	Long Integer	Customer unique credit identification number.
Customer Name	Text	40	Name of the customer.
Contact First Name	Text	30	First name of the contact individual.
Contact Last Name	Text	30	Last name of the contact individual.
Contact Title	Text	5	Title of the contact individual.
Contact Position	Text	30	Position of the contact individual.
Last Year's Sales	Currency	Currency	Last year's total sales for the customer.
Address1	Text	60	The primary street address information for the customer.
Address2	Text	20	A line for secondary address information for the customer.
City	Text	20	The city of the customer's address.
Region	Text	30	The region with which the customer is associated.
Country	Text	30	The country of the customer's address.
Postal Code	Text	10	The postal code of the customer's address.
E-mail	Text	50	The customer's contact e-mail address.
Web Site	Text	50	The customer's web site.
Phone	Text	20	The customer's phone number.
Fax	Text	20	The customer's fax number.

Employee

This table contains data regarding the employees of Xtreme Mountain Bikes.

Table B-3. Employee data

Field Name	Data Type	Field Size/Format	Description
Employee ID	Number	Long Integer	Unique identification number assigned to each employee.
Supervisor ID	Number	Long Integer	Unique identification number assigned to the employee's supervisor.
Last Name	Text	20	Last name of the employee.
First Name	Text	10	First name of the employee.
Position	Text	30	Employee's position.
Birth Date	Date/Time	Short Date (MM/DD/YYYY)	Employee's birth date.
Hire Date	Date/Time	Short Date (MM/DD/YYYY)	Employee's hire date.
Home Phone	Text	20	Phone number includes country code or area code.
Extension	Text	4	Internal telephone extension number.
Photo	OLE Object	(N/A)	Picture of employee.
Notes	Memo	64,000	General information about employee's background.
Reports To	Number	Long Integer	Employee's supervisor.
Salary	Currency	Currency	Employee's salary.
SSN	Text	12	Employee's social security number.
Emergency Contact First Name	Text	20	First name of the employee's emergency contact.
Emergency Contact Last Name	Text	20	Last name of the employee's emergency contact.
Emergency Contact Relationship	Text	20	Relationship between the employee and the emergency contact.
Emergency Contact Phone	Text	20	The emergency contact's phone number.

Employee Addresses

The Employee Addresses table contains data regarding the address information of Xtreme Mountain Bikes' employees.

Table B-4. Employee address data

Field Name	Data Type	Length	Description
Employee ID	Number	Long Integer	Number automatically assigned to a new employee.
Address1	Text	60	The primary street address information for the employee.
Address2	Text	20	A line for secondary address information for the employee.
City	Text	15	The city of the employee's address.
Region	Text	15	The region with which the employee is associated.
Country	Text	15	The country of the employee's address.
Postal Code	Text	10	The postal code of the employee's address.
Emergency Contact Address1	Text	60	The primary street address information for the employee's emergency contact.
Emergency Contact Address2	Text	20	The secondary address information for the employee's emergency contact.
Emergency Contact City	Text	15	The city of the emergency contact's address.
Emergency Contact Region	Text	15	The region with which the emergency contact is associated.
Emergency Contact Country	Text	15	The country of the emergency contact's address.
Emergency Contact Postal Code	Text	10	The postal code of the emergency contact's address.

Financials

This table contains data regarding the financial information of Xtreme Mountain Bikes.

Table B-5. Financial data

Field Name	Data Type	Length	Description
Company ID	Text	5	Unique identification assigned to each company. In the case of this table's data, the only company is Xtreme Mountain bikes.
Statement Date	Date/Time	(undefined)	Financial statement date.
Cash	Number	Double	The company's cash amount (a current asset).
Account Receivable	Number	Double	The company's accounts receivable amount (a current asset).
Inventories	Number	Double	The company's inventory amount (a current asset).
Other Current Assets	Number	Double	The company's other current assets amount.
Land	Number	Double	The company's land amount (a net fixed income).
Buildings	Number	Double	The company's building amount (a net fixed income).
Machinery etc.	Number	Double	The company's machinery amount (a net fixed income).
Accumulated Depreciation	Number	Double	The company's accumulated depreciation amount.
Other Assets	Number	Double	Other asset amounts.
Accounts Payable	Number	Double	The company's accounts payable amount (a current liability).
Accrued Liabilities	Number	Double	The company's accrued liabilities amount (a current liability).
Accrued Income Taxes	Number	Double	The company's accrued income taxes (a current liability).
Notes Payable	Number	Double	The company's notes payable amount.
Deferred Income Taxes	Number	Double	The company's deferred income taxes amount.
Preferred Stock	Number	Double	The company's preferred stock amount (a shareholder's equity).
Common Stock	Number	Double	The company's common stock amount (a shareholder's equity).
Retained Earnings	Number	Double	The company's retained earnings amount (a shareholders equity).

Field Name	Data Type	Length	Description
Net Sales	Number	Double	The company's net sales amount.
COGS	Number	Double	The company's COGS amount.
Selling/Admin/ General Expenses	Number	Double	The company's selling/admin/general expenses amount.
Depreciation	Number	Double	The company's depreciation amount.
Interest Expenses	Number	Double	The company's interest expenses amount.
Other Income Expenses	Number	Double	The company's other income expenses amount.
Taxes	Number	Double	The company's taxes amount.

Orders

The Orders table contains data regarding customer orders of Xtreme Mountain Bikes' products.

Table B-6. Order data

Field Name	Data Type	Length	Description
Order ID	AutoNumber	Long Integer	Unique identification number assigned to each order.
Order Amount	Currency	Currency	Total amount of the order.
Customer ID	Number	Long Integer	Customer unique identification number.
Employee ID	Number	Long Integer	Employee unique identification number.
Order Date	Date/Time	General Date (MM/DD/YYYY HH:MM:SS AM/PM)	Date on which order was placed.
Required Date	Date/Time	Short Date (MM/DD/YYYY)	Date on which order is required to be received.
Ship Date	Date/Time	General Date (MM/DD/YYYY HH:MM:SS AM/PM)	Date on which order was shipped.
Ship Via	Text	20	Comment regarding how product was shipped.
Courier Web Site	Hyperlink	h"ttp"://www".up"s \.c\om	The courier's web site address.
Shipped	Logical	Yes/No	Boolean which states "yes" or "no" to whether the product was shipped.
PO#	Text	50	The purchase order number.

Field Name	Data Type	Length	Description
Payment Received	Logical	Yes/No	Boolean which states "yes" or "no" to whether payment was received for the order.

Orders Detail

The Orders Detail table contains data regarding the detail of customer orders.

Table B-7. Order detail data

Field Name	Data Type	Length	Description
Order ID	Number	Long Integer	Unique identification number assigned to each order.
Product ID	Number	Long Integer	Unique identification number assigned to each product.
Unit Price	Currency	Currency	The unit price of each product within an order.
Quantity	Number	Long Integer	The quantity of products within an order.

Product

The Product table contains data regarding each of Xtreme Mountain Bikes' products.

Table B-8. Product data

Field Name	Data Type	Length	Description
Product ID	Number	Long Integer	Unique identification number assigned to each product.
Product Name	Text	50	Name of the product.
Color	Text	20	Color of the product.
Size	Text	10	Size of the product.
M/F	Text	10	States whether product is for men or women specifically.
Price (SRP)	Currency	Currency	The price of the product.
Product Type ID	Number	Long Integer	Unique identification number assigned to each product type.
Product Class	Text	50	The product class.
Supplier ID	Number	Long Integer	Unique identification number assigned to each product supplier.

Product Type

The Product Type table contains data regarding the different series of Xtreme Mountain Bikes products. Examples of product types include the Competition series, the Hybrid series, and the Kids series.

Table B-9. Product type data

Field Name	Data Type	Length	Description
Product Type ID	AutoNumber	Long Integer	Unique identification number assigned to each product type.
Product Type Name	Text	50	Name of the product type.
Description	Memo	64,000	Description of the product type.

Purchases

The Purchases table contains data regarding the purchase information of Xtreme Mountain Bikes products.

Table B-10. Purchase data

Field Name	Data Type	Length	Description
Product ID	Number	Long Integer	Unique identification number assigned to the product.
Reorder Level	Number	Long Integer	Minimum number of products left in inventory before a reorder is made.
Units in Stock	Number	Long Integer	Current number of product units in stock.
Units on Order	Number	Long Integer	Current number of products on order.
PO#	Number	Long Integer	Purchase order number.
Order Date	Date/Time	Date/Time	Date an order for products was made.
Expected Receiving Date	Date/Time	(undefined)	Expected receiving date for the product.
Received	Logical	Yes/No	Boolean which states "yes" or "no" to whether the product was received.
Paid	Logical	Yes/No	Boolean which states "yes" or "no" to whether payment was made for the product shipment.

Supplier

The Supplier table contains data regarding the supplier of Xtreme Mountain Bikes products.

Table B-11. Supplier data

Field Name	Data Type	Length	Description
Supplier ID	AutoNumber	Long Integer	Unique identification number assigned to the supplier.
Supplier Name	Text	50	Name of the supplier.
Address1	Text	50	The primary street address information for the supplier.
Address2	Text	50	A line for secondary address information for the supplier.
City	Text	50	The city of the supplier's address.
Region	Text	50	The region with which the supplier is associated.
Country	Text	50	The country of the supplier's address.
Postal Code	Text	50	The postal code of the supplier's address.
Phone	Text	20	Supplier's phone number.

Xtreme Info

The Xtreme Info table contains data regarding the Xtreme Mountain Bikes company.

Table B-12. Company data

Field Name	Data Type	Length	Description
Xtreme Name	Text	50	Unique string given to the Xtreme company.
Address	Text	255	Xtreme's street address.
City	Text	50	Xtreme's city information.
Province	Text	50	Xtreme's province information.
Country	Text	50	Xtreme's country information.
Postal Code	Text	20	Xtreme's postal information.
Phone	Text	20	Xtreme's phone number.
Fax	Text	20	Xtreme's fax number.

Appendix C

Crystal Report Functions

As you've learned in this book, functions are predefined formulas that perform some sort of calculation. Functions perform these calculations using specific values, also known as arguments. An *argument* can be a number, text, a logical value (such as TRUE or FALSE), a formula, or another function. Arguments can also be constants or arrays.

Note

A *constant* is a numeric or text value that you type directly into a cell or formula or is represented by a name.

An *array* is used to build a formula that produces multiple results. Arrays are also used to build formulas that operate on a group of arguments arranged in rows and columns.

Function Structure

The structure of a function begins with the function name. The function name is then followed by an opening parenthesis, the arguments for the function (separated by commas), and a closing parenthesis. Figure C-1 displays an example of a function structure:

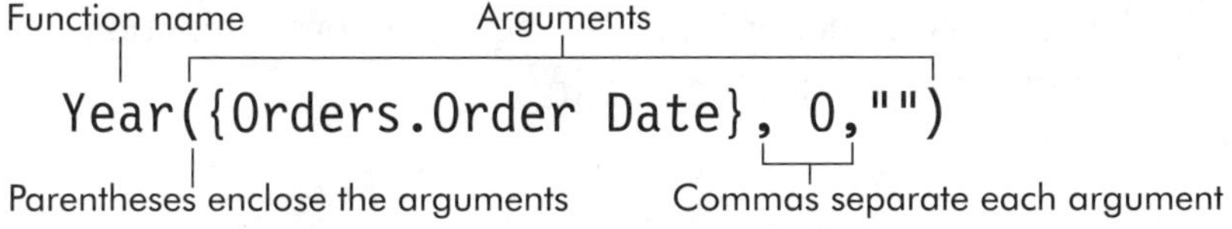

Figure C-1. The structure of a function

Note

In Figure C-1, the curly brackets surrounding the Orders.Order Date field designate a database field. Refer to the following table for a summary of reserved characters and the types of arguments they represent. This information was presented in Chapter10.

Table C-1. Reserved characters of the Crystal Reports and Basic languages

Reserved Character	Name	Description
{ }	Curly brackets	Used to contain the report objects (such as the database or formula fields). For example: {Employee.First Name}
[ ]	Square brackets	Used to create computational formulas. Another common use for them is to return the character of a string field. For example, {Employee.First Name}[1] returns the first character of this string field.
( )	Parentheses	Used with operators to contain the different parts of a formula and define the order the calculations should take place.
.	Period	Separates the table name from the database field. For example: {Employee.Last Name}
" "	Quotation marks	Used to surround text that you wish to display within your formulas. For example, "USA" would display the text USA within your report.
,	Comma	Used to separate multiple parameters within a formula.
@	Formula	Designates formula fields. For example: {@Name_of_Formula}
?	Parameter	Designates parameter fields. For example: {?Name_of_Parameter)
#	Running total	Designates running total field. For example: {#Name of Running Total}
Σ	Summary	Designates a summary field. For example: {ΣName_of_Summary_Field}
%	SQL expression	Designates an SQL Expression field. For example: {%Name_of_SQL_Expression}

The following sections summarize the different functions available within Crystal Reports.

Math

Math functions allow you to perform a variety of calculations, from rounding numbers to finding the percentage of group averages within your report.

Table C-2. Math functions

Function	Description	Arguments
Abs *(x)*	Returns the absolute value of a number. The absolute value of a number is the number without its sign.	*x* is the real number for which you want the absolute value.
Sgn *(number)*	Determines the sign of a number. Returns 1 if the number is positive, 0 if the number is 0, and –1 if the number is negative.	*number* is any real number.
Int *(number)*	Rounds a number down to the nearest integer.	*number* is the real number you want to round down to an integer.
Round *(x, #places)*	Rounds a number to a specified number of digits.	*x* is the number you want to round. *#places* specifies the number of digits to which you want to round *number.* 1. If *#places* is greater than 0, number is rounded to the specified *number* of decimal places. 2. If *#places* is 0, *number* is rounded to the nearest integer. 3. If *#places* is less than 0, *number* is rounded to the left of the decimal point.
Truncate *(x, #places)*	Truncates a number to an integer by removing the fractional part of the number.	*x* is the number you want to truncate. *#places* is a number specifying the precision of the truncation. The default value for *#places* is 0.
Fix *(number, #places)*	Truncates a number to the specified number of decimal places and returns it. If *#places* is omitted, 0 is assumed.	*number* is the Number value to be truncated; it can be positive, 0, or negative. *#places* is an optional Number indicating the number of decimal places to be truncated to. If omitted, 0 is assumed.
Remainder *(num, denom)*	Returns the remainder after the numerator (dividend) has been divided by the denominator (divisor).	*num* is a fractional value (and stands for the numerator). *denom* is a fractional value (and stands for the denominator).

Function	Description	Arguments
Sin *(number)*	Returns the sine of the given angle.	*number* is the angle in radians for which you want the sine. If your argument is in degrees, multiply it by Pi()/180 to convert it to radians.
Cos *(number)*	Returns the cosine of the given angle.	*number* is the angle in radians for which you want the cosine. If the angle is in degrees, multiply it by Pi()/180 to convert it to radians.
Tan *(number)*	Returns the tangent of the given angle.	*number* is the angle in radians for which you want the tangent. If your argument is in degrees, multiply it by Pi()/180 to convert it to radians.
Atn *(number)*	Returns the arctangent of a number. The arctangent is the angle whose tangent is *number*. The returned angle is given in radians in the range –pi/2 to pi/2.	*number* is the tangent of the angle you want.
Pi	Returns the number 3.14159265358979, the mathematical constant pi, accurate to 15 digits.	*(no arguments)*
Sqr *(number)*	Returns a positive square root.	*number* is the number for which you want the square root.
Exp *(number)*	Returns e raised to the power of *number*. The constant e equals 2.71828182845904, the base of the natural logarithm.	*number* is the exponent applied to the base e.
Log *(number)*	Returns the logarithm of a number to the base you specify.	*number* is the positive real number for which you want the logarithm.
Rnd *(seed)*	Returns an evenly distributed random number greater than or equal to 0 and less than 1. A new random number is returned every time the report is refreshed.	*seed* is the optional Number value argument.

Summary

Summary functions summarize field data in a variety of ways. Summary functions can also be designed to perform operations on group data.

Table C-3. Summary functions

Function	Description	Arguments
Sum *(fld)* Sum *(fld, condFld)* Sum *(fld, condFld, cond)* Sum *(x)*	Adds all the numbers that appear within a report.	*fld* is any valid database or formula field that can be evaluated by the function. *condFld* is a field used to group the values in *fld* by. *cond* is a String indicating the type of grouping for *condFld*. You only specify this argument when *condFld* is a Date, Time, DateTime, or Boolean field. *x* is an array of values that can be evaluated by the function being used.
Average *(fld)* Average *(fld, condFld)* Average *(fld, condFld, cond)* Average *(x)*	Enables you to average the values that appear in your report.	*fld* is any valid database or formula field that can be evaluated by the function. *condFld* is a field used to group the values in *fld* by. *cond* is a String indicating the type of grouping for *condFld*. You only specify this argument when *condFld* is a Date, Time, DateTime, or Boolean field. *x* is an array of values that can be evaluated by the function being used.
StdDev *(fld)* StdDev *(fld, condFld)* StdDev *(fld, condFld, cond)* StdDev *(x)*	Enables you to find the standard deviation of a set of values in your report.	*fld* is any valid database or formula field that can be evaluated by the function. *condFld* is a field used to group the values in *fld* by. *cond* is a String indicating the type of grouping for *condFld*. You only specify this argument when *condFld* is a Date, Time, DateTime, or Boolean field. *x* is an array of values that can be evaluated by the function being used.

Function	Description	Arguments
PopulationStdDev *(fld)* PopulationStdDev *(fld, condFld)* PopulationStdDev *(fld, condFld, cond)* PopulationStdDev *(x)*	Enables you to find the population standard deviation of a set of values in your report.	*fld* is any valid database or formula field that can be evaluated by the function. *condFld* is a field used to group the values in *fld* by. *cond* is a String indicating the type of grouping for *condFld*. You only specify this argument when *condFld* is a Date, Time, DateTime, or Boolean field. *x* is an array of values that can be evaluated by the function being used.
Variance *(fld)* Variance *(fld, condFld)* Variance *(fld, condFld, cond)* Variance *(x)*	Enables you to find the variance of a set of values in your report.	*fld* is any valid database or formula field that can be evaluated by the function. *condFld* is a field used to group the values in *fld* by. *cond* is a String indicating the type of grouping for *condFld*. You only specify this argument when *condFld* is a Date, Time, DateTime, or Boolean field. *x* is an array of values that can be evaluated by the function being used.
PopulationVariance *(fld)* PopulationVariance *(fld, condFld)* PopulationVariance *(fld, condFld, cond)* PopulationVariance *(x)*	Enables you to find the population variance of a set of values in your report.	*fld* is any valid database or formula field that can be evaluated by the function. *condFld* is a field used to group the values in *fld* by. *cond* is a String indicating the type of grouping for *condFld*. You only specify this argument when *condFld* is a Date, Time, DateTime, or Boolean field. *x* is an array of values that can be evaluated by the function being used.
Maximum *(fld)* Maximum *(fld, condFld)* Maximum *(fld, condFld, cond)* Maximum *(x)*	Enables you to find the maximum value that appears in a set of values.	*fld* is any valid database or formula field that can be evaluated by the function. *condFld* is a field used to group the values in *fld* by. *cond* is a String indicating the type of grouping for *condFld*. You only specify this argument when *condFld* is a Date, Time, DateTime, or Boolean field. *x* is an array of values that can be evaluated by the function being used.

Function	Description	Arguments
Minimum *(fld)* Minimum *(fld, condFld)* Minimum *(fld, condFld, cond)* Minimum *(x)*	Enables you to find the minimum value that appears in a set of values.	*fld* is any valid database or formula field that can be evaluated by the function. *condFld* is a field used to group the values in *fld* by. *cond* is a String indicating the type of grouping for *condFld*. You only specify this argument when *condFld* is a Date, Time, DateTime, or Boolean field. *x* is an array of values that can be evaluated by the function being used.
Count *(fld)* Count *(fld, condFld)* Count *(fld, condFld, cond)* Count *(x)*	Enables you to count the values that appear in your report (for a specified field).	*fld* is any valid database or formula field that can be evaluated by the function. *condFld* is a field used to group the values in *fld* by. *cond* is a String indicating the type of grouping for *condFld*. You only specify this argument when *condFld* is a Date, Time, DateTime, or Boolean field. *x* is an array of values that can be evaluated by the function being used.
DistinctCount *(fld)* DistinctCount *(fld, condFld)* DistinctCount *(fld, condFld, cond)* DistinctCount *(x)*	Enables you to get a distinct count of the values that appear in your report.	*fld* is any valid database or formula field that can be evaluated by the function. *condFld* is a field used to group the values in *fld* by. *cond* is a String indicating the type of grouping for *condFld*. You only specify this argument when *condFld* is a Date, Time, DateTime, or Boolean field. *x* is an array of values that can be evaluated by the function being used.
Correlation *(fld, fld)* Correlation *(fld, fld, condFld)* Correlation *(fld, fld, condFld, cond)*	Enables you to calculate the correlation of the specified fields (that is, the degree to which the fields vary in the same manner).	*fld* is any numeric field. *condFld* is a field used to group the values in *fld* by. *cond* is a String indicating the type of grouping for *condFld*. You only specify this argument when *condFld* is a Date, Time, DateTime, or Boolean field.

Function	Description	Arguments
Covariance *(fld, fld)* Covariance *(fld, fld, condFld)* Covariance *(fld, fld, condFld, cond)*	Covariance is the measure of the linear relation between paired variables (that is, the tendency of two fields to vary together). Fields are covariant when they vary according to a specific mathematical relationship. The circumference of a circle and the radius of a circle are covariant.	*fld* is any numeric field that can be evaluated by the function. *condFld* is a field used to group the values in *fld* by. *cond* is a String indicating the type of grouping for *condFld*. You only specify this argument when *condFld* is a Date, Time, DateTime, or Boolean field.
WeightedAverage *(fld, fld)* WeightedAverage *(fld, fld, condFld)* WeightedAverage *(fld, fld, condFld, cond)*	Enables you to calculate the weighted average of the specified fields. When you calculate a weighted average, you are actually calculating the average of one field and then using the values in another field to "weigh" the contribution of each value in the first field to the average. In a normal average, all the weights are equal to 1.	*fld* is any valid numeric database or formula field that can be evaluated by the function. *condFld* is a field used to group the values in *fld* by. *cond* is a String indicating the type of grouping for *condFld*. You only specify this argument when *condFld* is a Date, Time, DateTime, or Boolean field.
Median *(fld)* Median *(fld, condFld)* Median *(fld, condFld, cond)*	Calculates the median of the given numeric fields. The median is the middle value in a sequence of numeric values (or the average of the two middle values in an even-numbered sequence of values).	*fld* is any valid database or formula field that can be evaluated by the function. *condFld* is a field used to group the values in *fld* by. *cond* is a String indicating the type of grouping for *condFld*. You only specify this argument when *condFld* is a Date, Time, DateTime, or Boolean field.
PthPercentile *(P, fld)* PthPercentile *(P, fld, condFld)* PthPercentile *(P, fld, condFld, cond)*	Calculates the value for a specified percentile (*P*) in a Number or Currency field.	*P* is any integer from 0 to 100 (inclusive). *fld* is any Number or Currency field that can be evaluated by the function. *condFld* is a field used to group the values in *fld* by.

Function	Description	Arguments
		cond is a String indicating the type of grouping for *condFld*. You only specify this argument when *condFld* is a Date, Time, DateTime, or Boolean field.
NthSmallest *(N, fld)* NthSmallest *(N, fld, condFld)* NthSmallest *(N, fld, condFld, cond)*	Determines the Nth smallest value in a given field, either for the entire report or for each instance of the *condFld* group.	*N* is any integer from 1 to 100 (inclusive). *fld* is any valid database or formula field that can be evaluated by the function. *condFld* is a field used to group the values in *fld* by. *cond* is a String indicating the type of grouping for *condFld*. You only specify this argument when *condFld* is a Date, Time, DateTime, or Boolean field.
Mode *(fld)* Mode *(fld, condFld)* Mode *(fld, condFld, cond)*	Identifies the most frequently occurring value.	*fld* is any valid database or formula field that can be evaluated by the function. *condFld* is a field used to group the values in *fld* by. *cond* is a String indicating the type of grouping for *condFld*. You only specify this argument when *condFld* is a Date, Time, DateTime, or Boolean field.
NthMostFrequent *(N, fld)* NthMostFrequent *(N, fld, condFld)* NthMostFrequent *(N, fld, condFld, cond)*	Determines the Nth most frequent value in a given field, either for the entire report or for each instance of the *condFld* group. If no values in the field appear more than once, the function will return the minimum value, by default.	*N* is any integer from 1 to 100 (inclusive). *fld* is any valid database or formula field that can be evaluated by the function. *condFld* is a field used to group the values in *fld* by. *cond* is a String indicating the type of grouping for *condFld*. You only specify this argument when *condFld* is a Date, Time, DateTime, or Boolean field.

Function	Description	Arguments
PercentOfSum *(fld, condFld)* PercentOfSum *(fld, condFld, cond)* PercentOfSum *(fld, innerCondFld, outerCondFld)* PercentOfSum *(fld, innerCondFld, innerCond, outerCondFld)* PercentOfSum *(fld, innerCondFld, outerCondFld, outerCond)* PercentOfSum *(fld, innerCondFld, innerCond, outerCondFld, outerCond)*	Expresses the sum of the values of the field *fld* for the group determined by *condFld* as a percentage of the grand total sum.	*fld* is a Number or Currency field that can be evaluated by the function. *condFld* is a field used to group the values in *fld* by. *cond* is a String indicating the type of grouping for *condFld*. You only specify this argument when *condFld* is a Date, Time, DateTime, or Boolean field. *innerCondFld* is a field used to group the values in *fld* by. *innerCond* is a String indicating the type of grouping for *innerCondFld*. You only specify this argument when *innerCondFld* is a Date, Time, DateTime, or Boolean field. *outerCondFld* is a field used to group the values in *fld* by. *outerCond* is a String indicating the type of grouping for *outerCondFld*. You only specify this argument when *outerCondFld* is a Date, Time, DateTime, or Boolean field.
PercentOfAverage *(fld, condFld)* PercentOfAverage *(fld, condFld, cond)* PercentOfAverage *(fld, innerCondFld, outerCondFld)* PercentOfAverage *(fld, innerCondFld, innerCond, outerCondFld)* PercentOfAverage *(fld, innerCondFld, outerCondFld, outerCond)* PercentOfAverage *(fld, innerCondFld, innerCond, outerCondFld, outerCond)*	Expresses the average of the values of the field *fld* for the group determined by *condFld* as a percentage of the average of all the values of *fld*.	*fld* is a Number or Currency field that can be evaluated by the function. *condFld* is a field used to group the values in *fld* by. *cond* is a String indicating the type of grouping for *condFld*. You only specify this argument when *condFld* is a Date, Time, DateTime, or Boolean field. *innerCondFld* is a field used to group the values in *fld* by. *innerCond* is a String indicating the type of grouping for *innerCondFld*. You only specify this argument when *innerCondFld* is a Date, Time, DateTime, or Boolean field. *outerCondFld* is a field used to group the values in *fld* by. *outerCond* is a String indicating the type of grouping for *outerCondFld*. You only specify this argument when *outerCondFld* is a Date, Time, DateTime, or Boolean field.

Function	Description	Arguments
PercentOfMaximum *(fld, condFld)* PercentOfMaximum *(fld, condFld, cond)* PercentOfMaximum *(fld, innerCondFld, outerCondFld)* PercentOfMaximum *(fld, innerCondFld, innerCond, outerCondFld)* PercentOfMaximum *(fld, innerCondFld, outerCondFld, outerCond)* PercentOfMaximum *(fld, innerCondFld, innerCond, outerCondFld, outerCond)*	Expresses the maximum of the values of the field *fld* for the group determined by *condFld* as a percentage of the maximum of all the values of *fld*.	*fld* is a Number or Currency field that can be evaluated by the function. *condFld* is a field used to group the values in *fld* by. *cond* is a String indicating the type of grouping for *condFld*. You only specify this argument when *condFld* is a Date, Time, DateTime, or Boolean field. *innerCondFld* is a field used to group the values in *fld* by. *innerCond* is a String indicating the type of grouping for *innerCondFld*. You only specify this argument when *innerCondFld* is a Date, Time, DateTime, or Boolean field. *outerCondFld* is a field used to group the values in fld by. *outerCond* is a String indicating the type of grouping for *outerCondFld*. You only specify this argument when *outerCondFld* is a Date, Time, DateTime, or Boolean field.
PercentOfMinimum *(fld, condFld)* PercentOfMinimum *(fld, condFld, cond)* PercentOfMinimum *(fld, innerCondFld, outerCondFld)* PercentOfMinimum *(fld, innerCondFld, innerCond, outerCondFld)* PercentOfMinimum *(fld, innerCondFld, outerCondFld, outerCond)* PercentOfMinimum *(fld, innerCondFld, innerCond, outerCondFld, outerCond)*	Expresses the minimum of the values of the field *fld* for the group determined by *condFld* as a percentage of the minimum of all the values of *fld*.	*fld* is a Number or Currency field that can be evaluated by the function. *condFld* is a field used to group the values in *fld* by. *cond* is a String indicating the type of grouping for *condFld*. You only specify this argument when *condFld* is a Date, Time, DateTime, or Boolean field. *innerCondFld* is a field used to group the values in *fld* by. *innerCond* is a String indicating the type of grouping for *innerCondFld*. You only specify this argument when *innerCondFld* is a Date, Time, DateTime, or Boolean field. *outerCondFld* is a field used to group the values in *fld* by. *outerCond* is a String indicating the type of grouping for *outerCondFld*. You only specify this argument when *outerCondFld* is a Date, Time, DateTime, or Boolean field.

Function	Description	Arguments
PercentOfCount *(fld, condFld)* PercentOfCount *(fld, condFld, cond)* PercentOfCount *(fld, innerCondFld, outerCondFld)* PercentOfCount *(fld, innerCondFld, innerCond, outerCondFld)* PercentOfCount *(fld, innerCondFld, outerCondFld, outerCond)* PercentOfCount *(fld, innerCondFld, innerCond, outerCondFld, outerCond)*	Expresses the count of the values of the field *fld* for the group determined by *condFld* as a percentage of the count of all the values of *fld*.	*fld* is a Number, Currency, String, Boolean, Date, Time, or DateTime field that can be evaluated by the function. *condFld* is a field used to group the values in *fld* by. *cond* is a String indicating the type of grouping for *condFld*. You only specify this argument when *condFld* is a Date, Time, DateTime, or Boolean field. *innerCondFld* is a field used to group the values in fld by. *innerCond* is a String indicating the type of grouping for *innerCondFld*. You only specify this argument when *innerCondFld* is a Date, Time, DateTime, or Boolean field. *outerCondFld* is a field used to group the values in *fld* by. *outerCond* is a String indicating the type of grouping for *outerCondFld*. You only specify this argument when *outerCondFld* is a Date, Time, DateTime, or Boolean field.
PercentOfDistinct-Count *(fld, condFld)* PercentOfDistinct-Count *(fld, condFld, cond)* PercentOfDistinct-Count *(fld, innerCondFld, outerCondFld)* PercentOfDistinct-Count *(fld, innerCondFld, innerCond, outerCondFld)* PercentOfDistinct-Count *(fld, innerCondFld, outerCondFld, outerCond)*	Expresses the distinct count of the values of the field *fld* for the group determined by *condFld* as a percentage of the distinct count of all the values of *fld*.	*fld* is a Number, Currency, String, Boolean, Date, Time, or DateTime field that can be evaluated by the function. *condFld* is a field used to group the values in *fld* by. *cond* is a String indicating the type of grouping for *condFld*. You only specify this argument when *condFld* is a Date, Time, DateTime, or Boolean field. *innerCondFld* is a field used to group the values in *fld* by. *innerCond* is a String indicating the type of grouping for *innerCondFld*. You only specify this argument when *innerCondFld* is a Date, Time, DateTime, or Boolean field. *outerCondFld* is a field used to group the values in *fld* by.

Function	Description	Arguments
PercentOfDistinct-Count *(fld, innerCondFld, innerCond, outerCondFld, outerCond)*		*outerCond* is a String indicating the type of grouping for *outerCondFld*. You only specify this argument when *outerCondFld* is a Date, Time, DateTime, or Boolean field.

Financial

Financial functions perform common business calculations, such as determining the payment for a loan or the future value or net present value of an investment.

Table C-4. Financial functions

Function	Description	Arguments
ACCRINT *(issueDate, firstInterestDate, settlementDate, rate, parValue, frequency)* ACCRINT *(issueDate, firstInterestDate, settlementDate, rate, parValue, frequency, basis)*	Returns the accrued interest for a security that pays periodic interest.	*issueDate* is the security's issue date. *firstInterestDate* is the security's first interest date. *settlementDate* is the security's settlement date. The security settlement date is the date after the issue date when the security is traded to the buyer. *rate* is the security's annual coupon rate. *parValue* is the security's par value. If you omit *parValue*, ACCRINT uses $1,000. *frequency* is the number of coupon payments per year. For annual payments, *frequency* = 1; for semiannual, *frequency* = 2; for quarterly, *frequency* = 4. *basis* is the type of day count basis to use, for example: 0 - American 30/360 (default) 1 - actual/actual 2 - actual/360 3 - actual/365 4 - European 30/360

Function	Description	Arguments
ACCRINTM *(issueDate, maturityDate, rate, parValue)* ACCRINTM *(issueDate, maturityDate, rate, parValue, basis)*	Returns the accrued interest for a security that pays interest at maturity.	*issueDate* is the security's issue date. *maturityDate* is the security's maturity date. The maturity date is the date when the security expires. *rate* is the security's annual coupon rate. *parValue* is the security's par value. If you omit *parValue*, ACCRINTM uses $1,000. *basis* is the type of day count basis to use. For example: 0 - American 30/360 (default) 1 - actual/actual 2 - actual/360 3 - actual/365 4 - European 30/360
AmorDEGRC *(cost, purchaseDate, firstPeriodEndDate, salvage, period, rate)* AmorDEGRC *(cost, purchaseDate, firstPeriodEndDate, salvage, period, rate, basis)*	Returns the depreciation for each accounting period. This function is provided for the French accounting system. If an asset is purchased in the middle of the accounting period, the prorated depreciation is taken into account. The function is similar to AmorLINC except that a depreciation coefficient is applied in the calculation depending on the life of the assets.	*cost* is the cost of the asset. *purchaseDate* is the date of the purchase of the asset. *firstPeriodEndDate* is the date of the end of the first period. *salvage* is the salvage value at the end of the life of the asset. *period* is the period. *rate* is the rate of depreciation. *basis* is the type of day count basis to use. For example: 0 - American 30/360 (default) 1 - actual/actual 2 - actual/360 3 - actual/365 4 - European 30/360
AmorLINC *(cost, purchaseDate, firstPeriodEndDate, salvage, period, rate)* AmorLINC *(cost, purchaseDate, firstPeriodEndDate, salvage, period, rate, basis)*	Returns the depreciation for each accounting period. This function is provided for the French accounting system. If an asset is purchased in the middle of the accounting period, the prorated depreciation is taken into account.	*cost* is the cost of the asset. *purchaseDate* is the date of the purchase of the asset. *firstPeriodEndDate* is the date of the end of the first period. *salvage* is the salvage value at the end of the life of the asset. *period* is the period. *rate* is the rate of depreciation.

Function	Description	Arguments
		basis is the type of day count basis to use. For example: 0 - American 30/360 (default) 1 - actual/actual 2 - actual/360 3 - actual/365 4 - European 30/360
CoupDayBS (*settlementDate, maturityDate, frequency)* CoupDayBS (*settlementDate, maturityDate, frequency, basis)*	Returns the number of days from the beginning of the coupon period to the settlement date.	*settlementDate* is the security's settlement date. The security settlement date is the date after the issue date when the security is traded to the buyer. *maturityDate* is the security's maturity date. The maturity date is the date when the security expires. *frequency* is the number of coupon payments per year. For annual payments, *frequency* = 1; for semiannual, *frequency* = 2; for quarterly, *frequency* = 4. *basis* is the type of day count basis to use. For example: 0 - American 30/360 (default) 1 - actual/actual 2 - actual/360 3 - actual/365 4 - European 30/360
CoupDays (*settlementDate, maturityDate, frequency)* CoupDays (*settlementDate, maturityDate, frequency, basis)*	Returns the number of days in the coupon period that contains the settlement date.	*settlementDate* is the security's settlement date. The security settlement date is the date after the issue date when the security is traded to the buyer. *maturityDate* is the security's maturity date. The maturity date is the date when the security expires. *frequency* is the number of coupon payments per year. For annual payments, *frequency* = 1; for semiannual, *frequency* = 2; for quarterly, *frequency* = 4. *basis* is the type of day count basis to use. For example: 0 - American 30/360 (default) 1 - actual/actual 2 - actual/360 3 - actual/365 4 - European 30/360

Function	Description	Arguments
CoupDaysNC *(settlementDate, maturityDate, frequency)* CoupDaysNC *(settlementDate, maturityDate, frequency, basis)*	Returns the number of days from the settlement date to the next coupon date.	*settlementDate* is the security's settlement date. The security settlement date is the date after the issue date when the security is traded to the buyer. *maturityDate* is the security's maturity date. The maturity date is the date when the security expires. *frequency* is the number of coupon payments per year. For annual payments, *frequency* = 1; for semiannual, *frequency* = 2; for quarterly, *frequency* = 4. *basis* is the type of day count basis to use. For example: 0 - American 30/360 (default) 1 - actual/actual 2 - actual/360 3 - actual/365 4 - European 30/360
CoupNCD *(settlementDate, maturityDate, frequency)*	Returns a number that represents the next coupon date after the settlement date.	*settlementDate* is the security's settlement date. The security settlement date is the date after the issue date when the security is traded to the buyer. *maturityDate* is the security's maturity date. The maturity date is the date when the security expires. *frequency* is the number of coupon payments per year. For annual payments, *frequency* = 1; for semiannual, *frequency* = 2; for quarterly, *frequency* = 4.
CoupNum *(settlementDate, maturityDate, frequency)*	Returns the number of coupons payable between the settlement date and maturity date, rounded up to the nearest whole coupon.	*settlementDate* is the security's settlement date. The security settlement date is the date after the issue date when the security is traded to the buyer. *maturityDate* is the security's maturity date. The maturity date is the date when the security expires. *frequency* is the number of coupon payments per year. For annual payments, *frequency* = 1; for semiannual, *frequency* = 2; for quarterly, *frequency* = 4.
CoupPCD *(settlementDate, maturityDate, frequency)*	Returns a number that represents the previous coupon date before the settlement date.	*settlementDate* is the security's settlement date. The security settlement date is the date after the issue date when the security is traded to the buyer.

Function	Description	Arguments
		maturityDate is the security's maturity date. The maturity date is the date when the security expires. *frequency* is the number of coupon payments per year. For annual payments, *frequency* = 1; for semiannual, *frequency* = 2; for quarterly, *frequency* = 4.
CumIPMT *(rate, nPeriods, presentValue, startPeriod, endPeriod, type)*	Returns the cumulative interest paid on a loan between *startPeriod* and *endPeriod*.	*rate* is the interest rate. *nPeriods* is the total number of payment periods. *presentValue* is the present value. *startPeriod* is the first period in the calculation. Payment periods are numbered beginning with 1. *endPeriod* is the last period in the calculation. *type* is the timing of the payment. For example: 0 - Payment at the end of the period 1 - Payment at the beginning of the period
CumPrinc *(rate, nPeriods, presentValue, startPeriod, endPeriod, type)*	Returns the cumulative principal paid on a loan between *startPeriod* and *endPeriod*.	*rate* is the interest rate. *nPeriods* is the total number of payment periods. *presentValue* is the present value. *startPeriod* is the first period in the calculation. Payment periods are numbered beginning with 1. *endPeriod* is the last period in the calculation. *type* is the timing of the payment. For example: 0 - Payment at the end of the period 1 - Payment at the beginning of the period
DB *(cost, salvage, life, period)* DB *(cost, salvage, life, period, month)*	Returns the depreciation of an asset for a specified period using the fixed-declining balance method.	*cost* is the initial cost of the asset. *salvage* is the value at the end of the depreciation (sometimes called the salvage value of the asset). *life* is the number of periods over which the asset is being depreciated (sometimes called the useful life of the asset).

Function	Description	Arguments
		period is the period for which you want to calculate the depreciation. *period* must use the same units as *life*. *month* is the number of months in the first year. If *month* is omitted, it is assumed to be 12.
DDB *(cost, salvage, life, period)* DDB *(cost, salvage, life, period, factor)*	Returns the depreciation of an asset for a specified period using the double-declining balance method or some other method you specify.	*cost* is the initial cost of the asset. *salvage* is the value at the end of the depreciation (sometimes called the salvage value of the asset). *life* is the number of periods over which the asset is being depreciated (sometimes called the useful life of the asset). *period* is the period for which you want to calculate the depreciation. *period* must use the same units as life. *factor* is the rate at which the balance declines. If *factor* is omitted, it is assumed to be 2 (the double-declining balance method).
Days360 *(startDate, endDate)* Days360 *(startDate, endDate, method)*	Returns the number of days between two dates using a calendar that has 30 days in a month and 360 days in a year, which is commonly used for financial accounting. If the end date is earlier than the start date, a negative answer is returned.	*startDate* is a Date or DateTime for the start of an interval of time. *endDate* is a Date or DateTime for the end of an interval of time. *method* is an optional Boolean value specifying the type of basis to use. FALSE is the default and implies the American 30/360-day basis, while TRUE implies the European 30/360-day basis.
DISC *(settlementDate, maturityDate, price, redemptionPrice)* DISC *(settlementDate, maturityDate, price, redemptionPrice, basis)*	Returns the discount rate for a security.	*settlementDate* is the security's settlement date. The security settlement date is the date after the issue date when the security is traded to the buyer. *maturityDate* is the security's maturity date. The maturity date is the date when the security expires. *price* is the security's price per $100 face value. *redemptionPrice* is the security's redemption value per $100 face value.

Function	Description	Arguments
		basis is the type of day count basis to use. For example: 0 - American 30/360 (default) 1 - actual/actual 2 - actual/360 3 - actual/365 4 - European 30/360
DollarDE *(fractionNumber, fractionBase)*	Converts a dollar price expressed as a fraction into a dollar price expressed as a decimal number. Use DollarDE to convert fractional dollar numbers, such as securities prices, to decimal numbers.	*fractionNumber* is a number expressed as a fraction. *fractionBase* is the integer to use in the denominator of the fraction.
DollarFR *(decimalNumber, fractionBase)*	Converts a dollar price expressed as a decimal number into a dollar price expressed as a fraction. Use DollarFR to convert decimal numbers to fractional dollar numbers, such as securities prices.	*decimalNumber* is a decimal number. *fractionBase* is the integer to use in the denominator of a fraction.
Duration *(settlementDate, maturityDate, couponRate, yield, frequency)* Duration *(settlementDate, maturityDate, couponRate, yield, frequency, basis)*	Returns the Macauley duration for an assumed par value of $100. Duration is defined as the weighted average of the present value of the cash flows and is used as a measure of a bond price's response to changes in yield.	*settlementDate* is the security's settlement date. The security settlement date is the date after the issue date when the security is traded to the buyer. *maturityDate* is the security's maturity date. The maturity date is the date when the security expires. *couponRate* is the security's annual coupon rate. *yield* is the security's annual yield. *frequency* is the number of coupon payments per year. For annual payments, *frequency* = 1; for semiannual, *frequency* = 2; for quarterly, *frequency* = 4. *basis* is the type of day count basis to use. For example: 0 - American 30/360 (default) 1 - actual/actual 2 - actual/360 3 - actual/365 4 - European 30/360

Function	Description	Arguments
Effect *(rate, nCompoundingPeriods)*	Returns the effective annual interest rate, given the nominal annual interest rate and the number of compounding periods per year.	*rate* is the nominal interest rate. *nCompoundingPeriods* is the number of compounding periods per year.
FV *(rate, nPeriods, payment)* FV *(rate, nPeriods, payment, presentValue)* FV *(rate, nPeriods, payment, presentValue, type)*	Returns the future value of an investment based on periodic, constant payments and a constant interest rate.	*rate* is the interest rate per period. *nPeriods* is the total number of payment periods in an annuity. *payment* is the payment made each period; it cannot change over the life of the annuity. Typically, payment contains principal and interest but no other fees or taxes. If *payment* is omitted, you must include the *paymentValue* argument. *presentValue* is the present value or the lump-sum amount that a series of future payments is worth right now. If *paymentValue* is omitted, it is assumed to be 0, and you must include the *payment* argument. *type* is the timing of the payment. For example: 0 - Payment at the end of the period 1 - Payment at the beginning of the period
FVSchedule *(value, rates)*	Returns the future value of an initial principal after applying a series of compound interest rates. Use FVSchedule to calculate future value of an investment with a variable or adjustable rate.	*value* is the present value. *rates* is an array of interest rates to apply.
IntRate *(settlementDate, maturityDate, price, redemptionValue)* IntRate *(settlementDate, maturityDate, price, redemptionValue, basis)*	Returns the interest rate for a fully invested security.	*settlementDate* is the security's settlement date. The security settlement date is the date after the issue date when the security is traded to the buyer. *maturityDate* is the security's maturity date. The maturity date is the date when the security expires. *price* is the amount invested in the security.

Function	Description	Arguments
		basis is the type of day count basis to use. For example: 0 - American 30/360 (default) 1 - actual/actual 2 - actual/360 3 - actual/365 4 - European 30/360
IPmt *(rate, period, nPeriods, presentValue)* IPmt *(rate, period, nPeriods, presentValue, futureValue)* IPmt *(rate, period, nPeriods, presentValue, futureValue, type)*	Returns the interest payment for a given period for an investment based on periodic, constant payments and a constant interest rate.	*rate* is the interest rate per period. *period* is the period for which you want to find the interest and must be in the range 1 to *nPeropds*. *nPeriods* is the total number of payment periods in an annuity. *presentValue* is the present value, or the lump-sum amount that a series of future payments is worth right now. *futureValue* is the future value, or a cash balance you want to attain after the last payment is made. If *futureValue* is omitted, it is assumed to be 0 (the future value of a loan, for example, is 0). *type* is the timing of the payment. For example: 0 - Payment at the end of the period 1 - Payment at the beginning of the period
IRR *(values)* IRR *(values, guess)*	Returns the internal rate of return for a series of cash flows represented by the numbers in values. These cash flows do not have to be even, as they would be for an annuity. However, the cash flows must occur at regular intervals, such as monthly or annually. The internal rate of return is the interest rate received for an investment consisting of payments (negative values) and income (positive values) that occur at regular periods.	*values* is an array or a reference to cells that contain numbers for which you want to calculate the internal rate of return. *guess* is a number that you guess is close to the result of IRR.

Function	Description	Arguments
ISPMT *(rate, period, nPeriods, presentValue)*	Calculates the interest paid during a specific period of an investment.	*rate* is the interest rate for the investment. *period* is the period for which you want to find the interest and must be between 1 and *nPeriods*. *nPeriods* is the total number of payment periods for the investment. *presentValue* is the present value of the investment. For a loan, *presentValue* is the loan amount.
MDuration *(settlementDate, maturityDate, couponRate, yield, frequency)* MDuration *(settlementDate, maturityDate, couponRate, yield, frequency, basis)*	Returns the modified duration for a security with an assumed par value of $100.	*settlementDate* is the security's settlement date. The security settlement date is the date after the issue date when the security is traded to the buyer. *maturityDate* is the security's maturity date. The maturity date is the date when the security expires. *couponRate* is the security's annual coupon rate. *yield* is the security's annual yield. *frequency* is the number of coupon payments per year. For annual payments, *frequency* = 1; for semiannual, *frequency* = 2; for quarterly, *frequency* = 4. *basis* is the type of day count basis to use. For example: 0 - American 30/360 (default) 1 - actual/actual 2 - actual/360 3 - actual/365 4 - European 30/360
MIRR *(values, financeRate, reinvestRate)*	Returns the modified internal rate of return for a series of periodic cash flows. MIRR considers both the cost of the investment and the interest received on reinvestment of cash.	*values* is an array or a reference to cells that contain numbers. These numbers represent a series of payments (negative values) and income (positive values) occurring at regular periods. *financeRate* is the interest rate you pay on the money used in the cash flows. *reinvestRate* is the interest rate you receive on the cash flows as you reinvest them.
Nominal *(rate, nCompoundingPeriods)*	Returns the nominal annual interest rate, given the effective rate and the number of compounding periods per year.	*rate* is the effective interest rate. *nCompoundingPeriods* is the number of compounding periods per year.

Function	Description	Arguments
NPer *(rate, payment, presentValue)* NPer *(rate, payment, presentValue, futureValue)* NPer *(rate, payment, presentValue, futureValue, type)*	Returns the number of periods for an investment based on periodic, constant payments and a constant interest rate.	*rate* is the interest rate per period. *payment* is the payment made each period; it cannot change over the life of the annuity. Typically, *payment* contains principal and interest but no other fees or taxes. *presentValue* is the present value or the lump-sum amount that a series of future payments is worth right now. *futureValue* is the future value or a cash balance you want to attain after the last payment is made. If *futureValue* is omitted, it is assumed to be 0 (the future value of a loan, for example, is 0). *type* is the timing of the payment. For example: 0 - Payment at the end of the period 1 - Payment at the beginning of the period
NPV *(rate, values)*	Calculates the net present value of an investment by using a discount rate and a series of future payments (negative values) and income (positive values).	*rate* is the rate of discount over the length of one period. *values* are 1 to 29 arguments representing the payments and income.
OddFPrice *(settlementDate, maturityDate, issueDate, firstCouponDate, rate, yield, redemptionValue, frequency)* OddFPrice *(settlementDate, maturityDate, issueDate, firstCouponDate, rate, yield, redemptionValue, frequency, basis)*	Returns the price per $100 face value of a security having an odd (short or long) first period.	*settlementDate* is the security's settlement date. The security settlement date is the date after the issue date when the security is traded to the buyer. *maturityDate* is the security's maturity date. The maturity date is the date when the security expires. *issueDate* is the security's issue date. *firstCouponDate* is the security's first coupon date. *rate* is the security's interest rate. *yield* is a non-negative number specifying the security's yield. *redemptionValue* is the security's redemption value per $100 face value. *frequency* is the number of coupon payments per year. For annual payments, *frequency* = 1; for semiannual, *frequency* = 2; for quarterly, *frequency* = 4.

Function	Description	Arguments
		basis is the type of day count basis to use. For example: 0 - American 30/360 (default) 1 - actual/actual 2 - actual/360 3 - actual/365 4 - European 30/360
OddFYield *(settlementDate, maturityDate, issueDate, firstCouponDate, rate, price, redemptionValue, frequency)* OddFYield *(settlementDate, maturityDate, issueDate, firstCouponDate, rate, price, redemptionValue, frequency, basis)*	Returns the yield of a security that has an odd (short or long) first period.	*settlementDate* is the security's settlement date. The security settlement date is the date after the issue date when the security is traded to the buyer. *maturityDate* is the security's maturity date. The maturity date is the date when the security expires. *issueDate* is the security's issue date. *firstCouponDate* is the security's first coupon date. *rate* is the security's interest rate. *price* is a non-negative number or currency specifying the security's purchase price per $100 of face value. *redemptionValue* is the security's redemption value per $100 face value. *frequency* is the number of coupon payments per year. For annual payments, *frequency* = 1; for semiannual, *frequency* = 2; for quarterly, *frequency* = 4. *basis* is the type of day count basis to use. For example: 0 - American 30/360 (default) 1 - actual/actual 2 - actual/360 3 - actual/365 4 - European 30/360
OddLPrice *(settlementDate, maturityDate, lastInterestDate, rate, yield, redemptionValue, frequency)*	Returns the price per $100 face value of a security having an odd (short or long) last coupon period.	*settlementDate* is the security's settlement date. The security settlement date is the date after the issue date when the security is traded to the buyer. *maturityDate* is the security's maturity date. The maturity date is the date when the security expires. *lastInterestDate* is the security's last coupon date. *rate* is the security's interest rate. *yield* is the security's annual yield.

Function	Description	Arguments
OddLPrice *(settlementDate, maturityDate, lastInterestDate, rate, yield, redemptionValue, frequency, basis)*		*redemptionValue* is the security's redemption value per $100 face value. *frequency* is a number specifying the number of coupons per year. The supported values are 1 (annual payments), 2 (semiannual payments), and 4 (quarterly). *basis* is the type of day count basis to use. For example: 0 - American 30/360 (default) 1 - actual/actual 2 - actual/360 3 - actual/365 4 - European 30/360
OddLYield *(settlementDate, maturityDate, lastInterestDate, rate, price, redemptionValue, frequency)* OddLYield *(settlementDate, maturityDate, lastInterestDate, rate, price, redemptionValue, frequency, basis)*	Returns the yield of a security that has an odd (short or long) last period.	*settlementDate* is the security's settlement date. The security settlement date is the date after the issue date when the security is traded to the buyer. *maturityDate* is the security's maturity date. The maturity date is the date when the security expires. *lastInterestDate* is the security's last coupon date. *rate* is the security's interest rate. *price* is the security's price. *redemptionValue* is the security's redemption value per $100 face value. *frequency* is the number of coupon payments per year. For annual payments, *frequency* = 1; for semiannual, *frequency* = 2; for quarterly, *frequency* = 4. *basis* is the type of day count basis to use. For example: 0 - American 30/360 (default) 1 - actual/actual 2 - actual/360 3 - actual/365 4 - European 30/360
Pmt *(rate, nPeriods, presentValue)* Pmt *(rate, nPeriods, presentValue, futureValue)* Pmt *(rate, nPeriods, presentValue, futureValue, type)*	Calculates the payment for a loan based on constant payments and a constant interest rate.	*rate* is the interest rate for the loan. *nPeriods* is the total number of payments for the loan. *presentValue* is the present value or the total amount that a series of future payments is worth now; also known as the principal.

Function	Description	Arguments
		futureValue is the future value or a cash balance you want to attain after the last payment is made. If *futureValue* is omitted, it is assumed to be 0; that is, the future value of a loan is 0. *type* is the timing of the payment. For example: 0 - Payment at the end of the period 1 - Payment at the beginning of the period
PPmt *(rate, period, nPeriods, presentValue)* PPmt *(rate, period, nPeriods, presentValue, futureValue)* PPmt *(rate, period, nPeriods, presentValue, futureValue, type)*	Calculates the payment for a loan based on constant payments and a constant interest rate.	*rate* is the interest rate for the loan. *period* is a number that specifies the payment period in the range 1 through *nPeriods*. *nPeriods* is the total number of payments for the loan. *presentValue* is the present value, or the total amount that a series of future payments is worth now; also known as the principal. *futureValue* is the future value, or a cash balance you want to attain after the last payment is made. If *futureValue* is omitted, it is assumed to be 0; that is, the future value of a loan is 0. *type* is the timing of the payment. For example: 0 - Payment at the end of the period 1 - Payment at the beginning of the period
Price *(settlementDate, maturityDate, couponRate, yield, redemptionValue, frequency)* Price *(settlementDate, maturityDate, couponRate, yield, redemptionValue, frequency, basis)*	Returns the price per $100 face value of a security that pays periodic interest.	*settlementDate* is the security's settlement date. The security settlement date is the date after the issue date when the security is traded to the buyer. *maturityDate* is the security's maturity date. The maturity date is the date when the security expires. *couponRate* is the security's annual coupon rate. *yield* is the security's annual yield. *redemptionValue* is the security's redemption value per $100 face value. *frequency* is the number of coupon payments per year. For annual payments, *frequency* = 1; for semiannual, *frequency* = 2; for quarterly, *frequency* = 4.

Function	Description	Arguments
		basis is the type of day count basis to use. For example: 0 - American 30/360 (default) 1 - actual/actual 2 - actual/360 3 - actual/365 4 - European 30/360
PriceDisc *(settlementDate, maturityDate, discountRate, redemptionValue)* PriceDisc *(settlementDate, maturityDate, discountRate, redemptionValue, basis)*	Returns the price per $100 face value of a discounted security.	*settlementDate* is the security's settlement date. The security settlement date is the date after the issue date when the security is traded to the buyer. *maturityDate* is the security's maturity date. The maturity date is the date when the security expires. *discountRate* is the security's discount rate. *redemptionValue* is the security's redemption value per $100 face value. *basis* is the type of day count basis to use. For example: 0 - American 30/360 (default) 1 - actual/actual 2 - actual/360 3 - actual/365 4 - European 30/360
PriceMat *(settlementDate, maturityDate, issueDate, interestRate, yield)* PriceMat *(settlementDate, maturityDate, issueDate, interestRate, yield, basis)*	Returns the price per $100 face value of a security that pays interest at maturity.	*settlementDate* is the security's settlement date. The security settlement date is the date after the issue date when the security is traded to the buyer. *maturityDate* is the security's maturity date. The maturity date is the date when the security expires. *issueDate* is the security's issue date, expressed as a serial date number. *interestRate* is the security's interest rate at date of issue. *yield* is the security's annual yield. *basis* is the type of day count basis to use. For example: 0 - American 30/360 (default) 1 - actual/actual 2 - actual/360 3 - actual/365 4 - European 30/360

Function	Description	Arguments
PV *(rate, nPeriods, payment)* PV *(rate, nPeriods, payment, futureValue)* PV *(rate, nPeriods, payment, futureValue, type)*	Returns the present value of an investment. The present value is the total amount that a series of future payments is worth now. For example, when you borrow money, the loan amount is the present value to the lender.	*rate* is the interest rate per period. *nPeriods* is the total number of payment periods in an annuity. *payment* is the payment made each period and cannot change over the life of the annuity. *futureValue* is the future value, or a cash balance you want to attain after the last payment is made. *type* is the timing of the payment. For example: 0 - Payment at the end of the period 1 - Payment at the beginning of the period
Rate *(nPeriods, payment, presentValue)* Rate *(nPeriods, payment, presentValue, futureValue)* Rate *(nPeriods, payment, presentValue, futureValue, type)* Rate *(nPeriods, payment, presentValue, futureValue, type, guess)*	Returns the interest rate per period of an annuity. Rate is calculated by iteration and can have zero or more solutions.	*nPeriods* is the total number of payment periods in an annuity. *payment* is the payment made each period and cannot change over the life of the annuity. *presentValue* is the present value or the total amount that a series of future payments is worth now. *futureValue* is the future value or a cash balance you want to attain after the last payment is made. *type* is the timing of the payment. For example: 0 - Payment at the end of the period 1 - Payment at the beginning of the period *guess* is your guess for what the rate will be.
Received *(settlementDate, maturityDate, investment, discountRate)* Received *(settlementDate, maturityDate, investment, discountRate, basis)*	Returns the amount received at maturity for a fully invested security.	*settlementDate* is the security's settlement date. The security settlement date is the date after the issue date when the security is traded to the buyer. *maturityDate* is the security's maturity date. The maturity date is the date when the security expires. *investment* is the amount invested in the security. *discountRate* is the security's discount rate.

Function	Description	Arguments
		basis is the type of day count basis to use. For example: 0 - American 30/360 (default) 1 - actual/actual 2 - actual/360 3 - actual/365 4 - European 30/360
SLN *(cost, salvage, life)*	Returns the straight-line depreciation of an asset for one period.	*cost* is the initial cost of the asset. *salvage* is the value at the end of the depreciation (sometimes called the salvage value of the asset). *life* is the number of periods over which the asset is being depreciated (sometimes called the useful life of the asset).
SYD *(cost, salvage, life, period)*	Returns the sum-of-years' digits depreciation of an asset for a specified period.	*cost* is the initial cost of the asset. *salvage* is the value at the end of the depreciation (sometimes called the salvage value of the asset). *life* is the number of periods over which the asset is being depreciated (sometimes called the useful life of the asset). *period* is the period and must use the same units as *life*.
TBillEq *(settlementDate, maturityDate, discountRate)*	Returns the bond-equivalent yield for a Treasury bill.	*settlementDate* is the Treasury bill's settlement date. The security settlement date is the date after the issue date when the Treasury bill is traded to the buyer. *maturityDate* is the Treasury bill's maturity date. The maturity date is the date when the Treasury bill expires. *discountRate* is the Treasury bill's discount rate.
TBillPrice *(settlementDate, maturityDate, discountRate)*	Returns the price per $100 face value for a Treasury bill.	*settlementDate* is the Treasury bill's settlement date. The security settlement date is the date after the issue date when the Treasury bill is traded to the buyer. *maturityDate* is the Treasury bill's maturity date. The maturity date is the date when the Treasury bill expires. *discountRate* is the Treasury bill's discount rate.

Function	Description	Arguments
TBillYield *(settlementDate, maturityDate, price)*	Returns the yield for a Treasury bill.	*settlementDate* is the Treasury bill's settlement date. The security settlement date is the date after the issue date when the Treasury bill is traded to the buyer. *maturityDate* is the Treasury bill's maturity date. The maturity date is the date when the Treasury bill expires. *price* is the Treasury bill's price per $100 face value.
VDB *(cost, salvage, lifetime, startPeriod, endPeriod)* VDB *(cost, salvage, lifetime, startPeriod, endPeriod, depreciationFactor)* VDB *(cost, salvage, lifetime, startPeriod, endPeriod, noSwitch)* VDB *(cost, salvage, lifetime, startPeriod, endPeriod, depreciationFactor, noSwitch)*	Returns the depreciation of an asset for any period you specify, including partial periods, using the double-declining balance method or some other method you specify. VDB stands for variable declining balance.	*cost* is the initial cost of the asset. *salvage* is the value at the end of the depreciation (sometimes called the salvage value of the asset). *lifetime* is the number of periods over which the asset is being depreciated (sometimes called the useful life of the asset). *startPeriod* is the starting period for which you want to calculate the depreciation. *startPeriod* must use the same units as *life*. *endPeriod* is the ending period for which you want to calculate the depreciation. *endPeriod* must use the same units as *life*. *depreciationFactor* is the rate at which the balance declines. If factor is omitted, it is assumed to be 2 (the double-declining balance method). *noSwitch* is a logical value specifying whether to switch to straight-line depreciation when depreciation is greater than the declining balance calculation.
XIRR *(values, dates)* XIRR *(values, dates, rateGuess)*	Returns the internal rate of return for a schedule of cash flows that is not necessarily periodic. To calculate the internal rate of return for a series of periodic cash flows, use the IRR function.	*values* is a series of cash flows that corresponds to a schedule of payments in dates. *dates* is a schedule of payment dates that corresponds to the cash flow payments. *rateGuess* is a number that you guess is close to the result of XIRR.

Function	Description	Arguments
XNPV *(rate, values, dates)*	Returns the net present value for a schedule of cash flows that is not necessarily periodic. To calculate the net present value for a series of cash flows that is periodic, use the NPV function.	*rate* is the discount rate to apply to the cash flows. *values* is a series of cash flows that corresponds to a schedule of payments in dates. *dates* is a schedule of payment dates that corresponds to the cash flow payments.
YearFrac *(startDate, endDate)* YearFrac *(startDate, endDate, basis)*	Returns the fraction of a year spanned by the interval of time between the two dates.	*startDate* is the starting period for which you want to calculate the fraction. *endDate* is the ending period for which you want to calculate the fraction. *basis* is the type of day count basis to use. For example: 0 - American 30/360 (default) 1 - actual/actual 2 - actual/360 3 - actual/365 4 - European 30/360
Yield *(settlementDate, maturityDate, couponRate, price, redemptionValue, frequency)* Yield *(settlementDate, maturityDate, couponRate, price, redemptionValue, frequency, basis)*	Returns the yield on a security that pays periodic interest. Use Yield to calculate bond yield.	*settlementDate* is the security's settlement date. The security settlement date is the date after the issue date when the security is traded to the buyer. *maturityDate* is the security's maturity date. The maturity date is the date when the security expires. *couponRate* is the security's annual coupon rate. *price* is the security's price per $100 face value. *redemptionValue* is the security's redemption value per $100 face value. *frequency* is the number of coupon payments per year. For annual payments, *frequency* = 1; for semiannual, *frequency* = 2; for quarterly, *frequency* = 4. *basis* is the type of day count basis to use. For example: 0 - American 30/360 (default) 1 - actual/actual 2 - actual/360 3 - actual/365 4 - European 30/360

Function	Description	Arguments
YieldDisc *(settlementDate, maturityDate, price, redemptionValue)* YieldDisc *(settlementDate, maturityDate, price, redemptionValue, basis)*	Returns the annual yield for a discounted security.	*settlementDate* is the security's settlement date. The security settlement date is the date after the issue date when the security is traded to the buyer. *maturityDate* is the security's maturity date. The maturity date is the date when the security expires. *price* is the security's price per $100 face value. *redemptionValue* is the security's redemption value per $100 face value. *basis* is the type of day count basis to use. For example: 0 - American 30/360 (default) 1 - actual/actual 2 - actual/360 3 - actual/365 4 - European 30/360
YieldMat *(settlementDate, maturityDate, issueDate, interestRate, price)* YieldMat *(settlementDate, maturityDate, issueDate, interestRate, price, basis)*	Returns the annual yield of a security that pays interest at maturity.	*settlementDate* is the security's settlement date. The security settlement date is the date after the issue date when the security is traded to the buyer. *maturityDate* is the security's maturity date. The maturity date is the date when the security expires. *issueDate* is the security's issue date, expressed as a serial date number. *interestRate* is the security's interest rate at date of issue. *price* is a non-negative number or currency specifying the security's purchase price per $100 of face value. *basis* is the type of day count basis to use. For example: 0 - American 30/360 (default) 1 - actual/actual 2 - actual/360 3 - actual/365 4 - European 30/360

Strings

String (or text) functions allow you to control text strings within formulas. For example, these functions allow you to determine the length of a text string or join date information to a text string.

Table C-5. String functions

Function	Description	Arguments
Len *(str)*	Returns the number of characters in a text string. Len and Length are equivalent. However, Len is preferred in Basic syntax, whereas Length is preferred in Crystal syntax.	*str* is the text whose length you want to find. Spaces count as characters.
Length *(str)*	Returns the number of characters in a text string. Len and Length are equivalent. However, Len is preferred in Basic syntax, whereas Length is preferred in Crystal syntax.	*str* is the text whose length you want to find. Spaces count as characters.
Trim *(str)*	Removes all spaces from text except for single spaces between words.	*str* is the text from which you want spaces removed.
LTrim *(str)*	Removes all spaces stored to the left of the given string and returns it. LTrim and TrimLeft are equivalent functions. However, LTrim is preferred in Basic syntax, whereas TrimLeft is preferred in Crystal syntax.	*str* is the text from which you want spaces removed (from the left of the text).
TrimLeft *(str)*	Removes all spaces to the left of a string or data field, which is stored as a right-justified string in a database. LTrim and TrimLeft are equivalent functions. However, LTrim is preferred in Basic syntax, whereas TrimLeft is preferred in Crystal syntax.	*str* is the text from which you want spaces removed (from the left of the text).
RTrim *(str)*	Removes all spaces to the right of the given string and returns it. RTrim and TrimRight are equivalent functions. However, RTrim is preferred in Basic syntax, whereas TrimRight is preferred in Crystal syntax.	*str* is the text from which you want spaces removed (from the right of the text).

Function	Description	Arguments
TrimRight *(str)*	Removes all spaces to the right of the given string and returns it. RTrim and TrimRight are equivalent functions. However, RTrim is preferred in Basic syntax, whereas TrimRight is preferred in Crystal syntax.	*str* is the text from which you want spaces removed (from the right of the text).
UCase *(str)*	Converts text to uppercase. UCase and UpperCase are equivalent functions. However, UCase is preferred in Basic syntax, whereas UpperCase is preferred in Crystal syntax.	*str* is the text you want converted to uppercase. Text can be a reference or text string.
UpperCase *(str)*	Converts text to uppercase. UCase and UpperCase are equivalent functions. However, UCase is preferred in Basic syntax, whereas UpperCase is preferred in Crystal syntax.	*str* is the text you want converted to uppercase. Text can be a reference or text string.
LCase *(str)*	Converts all uppercase letters in a text string to lowercase. LCase and LowerCase are equivalent functions. However, LCase is preferred in Basic syntax, whereas LowerCase is preferred in Crystal syntax.	*str* is the text you want to convert to lowercase. LCase does not change characters in text that are not letters.
LowerCase *(str)*	Converts all uppercase letters in a text string to lowercase. LCase and LowerCase are equivalent functions. However, LCase is preferred in Basic syntax, whereas LowerCase is preferred in Crystal syntax.	*str* is the text you want to convert to lowercase. LowerCase does not change characters in text that are not letters.
ProperCase *(str)*	Capitalizes the first letter in a text string and any other letters in text that follow any character other than a letter. Converts all other letters to lowercase letters.	*str* is text enclosed in quotation marks, a formula that returns text or a reference to a cell containing the text you want to partially capitalize.
StrReverse *(inputString)*	Returns a String in which the character order of *inputString* is reversed. If *inputString* is a zero-length string (""), a zero-length string is returned.	*inputString* is a string whose characters are to be reversed.
IsNumeric *(str)*	Returns True if the String argument can be converted to a Number. Otherwise, the function returns False.	*str* is a string value to be tested.

Function	Description	Arguments
NumericText *(str)*	Tests to see if the content of a text object is a Number.	*str* is a text string being tested for numeric text.
ToNumber *(numeric)* ToNumber *(string)* ToNumber *(Boolean)*	Converts a Number, Currency, text string, or Boolean value to a Number. CDbl and ToNumber are equivalent functions.	*numeric* is a Number or a Currency type value. *string* is a text string that holds numeric text. *Boolean* is a Boolean value that you want to treat as a number.
ToText *(x, y, z, w, q)*	Converts Numbers, Currency, Date, Time, and DateTime values to text strings. CStr and ToText are equivalent functions.	**Boolean Values:** *x* is a Boolean value that is converted to a String, either "True" or "False." **Number and Currency Values:** *x* is a Number or Currency value to be converted into a text string; it can be a whole or fractional value. *y* is a whole number indicating the number of decimal places to carry the value in *x* to. (This argument is optional.) *z* is a single-character text string indicating the character to be used to separate thousands in *x*. The default is the character specified in your International or Regional settings control panel. (This argument is optional.) *w* is a single-character text string indicating the character to be used as a decimal separator in *x*. The default is the character specified in your International or Regional settings control panel. (This argument is optional.) **Number and Currency Values (formatting):** *x* is a Number or Currency value to be converted into a text string; it can be a whole or fractional value. *y* is a text string used to indicate the format for displaying the value in *x*.

Function	Description	Arguments
		z is a whole number indicating the number of decimal places to carry the value in *x* to. (This argument is optional.) *w* is a single-character text string indicating the character to be used to separate thousands in *x*. The default is the character specified in your International or Regional settings control panel. (This argument is optional.) *q* is a single-character text string indicating the character to be used as a decimal separator in *x*. The default is the character specified in your International or Regional settings control panel. (This argument is optional.) Date Values: *x* is a Date value to be converted into a text string. *y* is a text string that defines how the value in *x* is to be formatted. Time Values: *x* is a Time value to be converted into a text string. *y* is a text string that defines how the value in *x* is to be formatted. *z* is a text string to be used as a label for A.M. (morning) hours. (This argument is optional.) *w* is a text string to be used as a label for P.M. (evening) hours. (This argument is optional.) DateTime Values: *x* is a DateTime value to be converted into a text string. *y* is a text string of characters that indicate how the resulting text string will be formatted. *z* is a text string to be used as a label for A.M. (morning) hours. (This argument is optional.) *w* is a text string to be used as a label for P.M. (evening) hours. (This argument is optional.)

Function	Description	Arguments
ToWords *(x)* ToWords *(x, #places)* ToWords *(x, #places, formtype)*	Converts a Number or Currency field value or the result of a numeric calculation to words so it can be used as text. The ability to adjust the number of decimal places can be useful when the number is the result of a calculation that may produce more decimal places than you want.	*x* is a fractional Number to be converted into words. *#places* is a whole number indicating the number of decimal places to be converted. (This argument is optional.) *formtype* specifies what type of form *x* is. This argument is used only for Asian languages—specifically, Japanese, Korean, Simplified Chinese, and Traditional Chinese. It is ignored for English or any other non-Asian language.
ReplicateString *(str, #copies)*	Replicates the string in *str* the number of times specified by *#copies*.	*str* is the text string to be replicated. *#copies* is a whole number indicating the number of times *str* is to be replicated.
Space *(x)*	Returns a specified number of spaces.	*x* is a whole number indicating the number of spaces.
InStr *(str1, str2)* InStr *(start, str1, str2)* InStr *(str1, str2, compare)* InStr *(start, str1, str2, compare)*	Returns the position of the first occurrence of one string within another. This position is a 1-based index of the characters in *str1*. If *str2* is not found in *str1*, the InStr function returns 0. The start argument sets the starting position for the search. If the compare argument is not used, the string comparison will be case-sensitive.	*start* is the character in *str1* where the search is to begin. This is a 1-based index. (This argument is optional.) *str1* is the text string to be searched. *str2* is the text string being sought. *compare* is an optional number value indicating which type of string comparison should be used. 0 indicates case-sensitive comparison, and 1 indicates case-insensitive comparison. If this argument is not used, a case-sensitive comparison is performed.
InStrRev *(inputString, findString)* InStrRev *(inputString, findString, startPosition)*	Indicates the position of the matching string in the string to be matched. The first character of *inputString* (from the beginning) is 1.	*inputString* is a String expression being searched. *findString* is a String expression being searched for. *startPosition* is an optional numeric expression that sets the starting position for each search. If omitted, –1 is used, which means that the search begins at the last character position.

Function	Description	Arguments
InStrRev (inputString, findString, startPosition, compare)		*compare* is an optional numeric value indicating the kind of comparison to use when evaluating substrings: 0 performs a comparison that is case sensitive. 1 performs a comparison that is case insensitive. If omitted, a case-sensitive comparison is performed.
StrCmp *(str1, str2)* StrCmp *(str1, str2, compare)*	Compares two strings.	*str1* is the first text string to be compared. *str2* is the second text string to be compared. *compare* is an optional Number value indicating the kind of string comparison to use: 0 performs a comparison that is case sensitive 1 performs a comparison that is case insensitive If omitted, a case-sensitive comparison is performed.
Mid *(str, start, length)*	Returns a specific number of characters from a text string, starting at the position you specify, based on the number of characters you specify.	*str* is the text string containing the characters you want to extract. *start* is the position of the first character you want to extract in text. The first character in text has *start* 1 and so on. *length* specifies the number of characters you want Mid to return from text.
Left *(str, length)*	Returns the first character or characters in a text string, based on the number of characters you specify.	*str* is the text string that contains the characters you want to extract. *length* specifies the number of characters you want to extract.
Right *(str, length)*	Returns the last character or characters in a text string, based on the number of characters you specify.	*str* is the text string containing the characters you want to extract. *length* specifies the number of characters you want to extract.

Function	Description	Arguments
Val *(str)*	Converts a text string that represents a number to a number.	*str* can be in any of the constant number, date, or time formats recognized by Crystal Reports.
Chr *(x)*	Returns the character specified by a number.	*x* is a number from 1 to 255 specifying which character you want. The character is from the character set used by your computer.
ChrW *(x)*	Returns the single-character text string associated with the Unicode value passed in as *x*.	*x* is a whole number, specifically, any Unicode value. *x* must be from 0 to 65535, or you will get a numeric overflow error.
Asc *(str)*	For Double-byte character set (DBCS) languages, changes half-width (single-byte) English characters to full-width (double-byte) characters.	*str* is the text or a reference to a cell that contains the text you want to change. If the text does not contain any full-width English letters, it is not changed.
AscW *(str)*	Returns the Unicode value of the first character of the string.	*str* is the text or a reference to a cell that contains the text you want to change. If the text does not contain any full-width English letters, it is not changed.
Filter *(inputStrings, searchString)* Filter *(inputStrings, searchString, include)* Filter *(inputStrings, searchString, include, compare)*	Searches an array of strings for a specified string and returns the strings in an array.	*inputStrings* is an array of strings to be searched. *searchString* is a string to search for. *include* is an optional Boolean value indicating whether to return substrings that include or exclude *searchString*. If *include* is True, Filter returns the subset of the array that contains *searchString* as a substring. If *include* is False, Filter returns the subset of the array that does not contain *searchString* as a substring. If omitted, the value True is assumed. *compare* is an optional Number value indicating the kind of string comparison to use: 0 performs a comparison that is case sensitive. 1 performs a comparison that is case insensitive. If omitted, a case-sensitive comparison is performed.

Function	Description	Arguments
Replace *(inputString, findString, replaceString)* Replace *(inputString, findString, replaceString, startPosition)* Replace *(inputString, findString, replaceString, startPosition, count)* Replace *(inputString, findString, replaceString, startPosition, count, compare)*	Replaces part of a text string, based on the number of characters you specify, with a different text string.	*inputString* is text in which you want to replace some characters. *findString* is a substring being searched for. *replaceString* is the text that will replace characters in the old text. *startPosition* is the position of the character in the old text that you want to replace with the new text. *count* is the number of characters in old_text that you want Replace to replace with the new text. *compare* is an optional Number value indicating the kind of string comparison to use: 0 performs a comparison that is case sensitive. 1 performs a comparison that is case insensitive. If omitted, a case-sensitive comparison is performed.
Join *(list)* Join *(list, delimiter)*	Returns a String created by joining a number of substrings contained in an array.	*list* is a String array containing substrings to be joined. *delimiter* is an optional String used to separate the substrings in the returned string. If omitted, the space character (" ") is used. If *delimiter* is a zero-length string (""), all items in the list are concatenated with no delimiters.
Split *(inputString)* Split *(inputString, delimiter)* Split *(inputString, delimiter, count)* Split *(inputString, delimiter, count, compare)*	Takes a String that contains a number of substrings, breaks it up into a specified number of substrings, and returns an array containing the substrings.	*inputString* is a String expression containing substrings and delimiters. *delimiter* is an optional String character used to identify substring limits. If omitted, the space character (" ") is assumed to be the delimiter. If *delimiter* is a zero-length string, a single-element array containing the entire *inputString* string is returned.

Function	Description	Arguments
		count is an optional number value of substrings to be returned. The value –1 indicates that all substrings are returned. If omitted, –1 is assumed. *compare* is an optional Number value indicating the kind of string comparison to use: 0 performs a comparison that is case sensitive. 1 performs a comparison that is case insensitive. If omitted, a case-sensitive comparison is performed.
Roman *(arabicVal, form)*	Converts an Arabic numeral to a Roman numeral, as text.	*(no arguments)*

Date and Time

Date functions allow you to convert numbers to dates. These functions also allow you to convert dates to numbers.

Table C-6. Date and time functions

Function	Description	Arguments
CurrentDate	Returns the current date on a report. The date is taken from your computer's internal clock.	*(no arguments)*
CurrentTime	Returns the current time on a report. The time is taken from your computer's internal clock.	*(no arguments)*
CurrentDateTime	Returns the current date and time on a report. The date and time is taken from your computer's internal clock.	*(no arguments)*
Date *(number)* Date *(string)* Date *(dateTime)* Date *(YYYY, MM, DD)*	Returns a Date value. The CDate, Date, and DateValue functions are equivalent. However, Date can only be used in Crystal syntax since it is a type name in Basic syntax.	*number* is a value representing the number of days starting from December 30, 1899. *string* is a text string representing a date. For example: "September 20, 1999" *dateTime* is a DateTime value.

Function	Description	Arguments
		YYYY is the year argument and can be one to four digits. *MM* is a number representing the month of the year. *DD* is a number representing the day of the month.
Time *(number)* Time *(string)* Time *(dateTime)* Time *(HH, MM, SS)*	Returns a Time value. The CTime, Time, and TimeValue functions are equivalent. However, Time can only be used in Crystal syntax since it is a type name in Basic syntax.	*number* is a Time value given a number in units of 24 hours. *string* is a Time value that represents the time, given a String expression specifying a time from 0:00:00. *dateTime* is a DateTime value. *HH* is a number from 0 to 32767 representing the hour. *MM* is a number from 0 to 32767 representing the minute. *SS* is a number from 0 to 32767 representing the second.
DateTime *(date)* DateTime *(number)* DateTime *(string)* DateTime *(dateTime)* DateTime *(YYYY, MM, DD)* DateTime *(YYYY, MM, DD, HH, MM, SS)*	Returns a DateTime value. The CDateTime, DateTime, and DateTimeValue functions are equivalent. However, DateTime can only be used in Crystal syntax since it is a type name in Basic syntax.	*date* is a Date value. *number* is a Time value given a number in units of 24 hours. *string* is a Time value that represents the time, given a String expression specifying a time from 0:00:00. *dateTime* is a DateTime value. *YYYY* is the year argument and can be one to four digits. *MM* is a number representing the month of the year. *DD* is a number representing the day of the month. *HH* is a number from 0 to 32767 representing the hour. *MM* is a number from 0 to 32767 representing the minute. *SS* is a number from 0 to 32767 representing the second.

Function	Description	Arguments
DateValue *(string)* DateValue *(number)* DateValue *(dateTime)* DateValue *(YYYY, MM, DD)*	Returns a Date value. The CDate, Date, and DateValue functions are equivalent. However, Date can only be used in Crystal syntax since it is a type name in Basic syntax.	*string* is a text value that represents the date. *number* represents the number of days starting from December 30, 1899. *dateTime* is a DateTime value. *YYYY* is the year argument and can be one to four digits. *MM* is a number representing the month of the year. *DD* is a number representing the day of the month.
TimeValue *(number)* TimeValue *(string)* TimeValue *(dateTime)* TimeValue *(HH, MM, SS)*	Returns a Time value. The CTime, Time, and TimeValue functions are equivalent. However, Time can only be used in Crystal syntax since it is a type name in Basic syntax.	*number* is a Time value given a number in units of 24 hours. *string* is a Time value that represents the time, given a String expression specifying a time from 0:00:00. *dateTime* is a DateTime value. *HH* is a number from 0 to 32767 representing the hour. *MM* is a number from 0 to 32767 representing the minute. *SS* is a number from 0 to 32767 representing the second.
DateTimeValue *(date)* DateTimeValue *(dateTime)* DateTimeValue *(number)* DateTimeValue *(string)* DateTimeValue *(YYYY, MM, DD)* DateTimeValue *(YYYY, MM, DD, HH, MM, SS)*	Returns a DateTime value. The CDateTime, DateTime, and DateTimeValue functions are equivalent. However, DateTime can only be used in Crystal syntax since it is a type name in Basic syntax.	*date* is a Date value. *number* is a Time value given a number in units of 24 hours. *string* is a Time value that represents the time, given a String expression specifying a time from 0:00:00. *dateTime* is a DateTime value. *YYYY* is the year argument and can be one to four digits. *MM* is a number representing the month of the year. *DD* is a number representing the day of the month. *HH* is a number from 0 to 32767 representing the hour.

Function	Description	Arguments
		MM is a number from 0 to 32767 representing the minute. *SS* is a number from 0 to 32767 representing the second.
DateSerial *(year, month, day)*	Returns a Date value for the specified year, month, and day. It also handles relative Date expressions.	*year* is a whole Number or numeric expression representing a year, such as 1996. *month* is a whole Number or numeric expression representing a month, such as 12 for December. *day* is a whole Number or numeric expression representing a day of the month, such as 5.
TimeSerial *(hour, minute, second)*	Returns a Time value specifying the time for a specific hour, minute, and second.	*hour* is a Number or numeric expression specifying the hour. *minute* is a Number or numeric expression specifying the number of minutes. *second* is a Number or numeric expression specifying the number of seconds.
IsTime *(string)* IsTime *(number)*	Returns True if the given String or Number value can be converted to a valid Time; returns False otherwise.	*string* is a String value or expression to be tested for being convertible to a Time value. Many forms are accepted. *number* is a Number value or expression to be tested for being convertible to a Time value. It can be positive, negative, or fractional. It is interpreted as units of 24 hours. What this means is that 0 is 12 midnight and 0.5 is 12 noon.
IsDate *(string)* IsDate *(number)*	Returns True if the given String or Number value can be converted to a valid Date and returns False otherwise. A valid Date is any date from January 1, 100, to December 31, 9999.	*string* is a String value or expression to be tested for being convertible to a Date value. Many forms are accepted. *number* is a Number value or expression to be tested for being convertible to a Date value. It can be positive, negative, or fractional. It is interpreted as a number of days since December 30, 1899.

Function	Description	Arguments
IsDateTime *(string)* IsDateTime *(number)*	Returns True if the given String or Number value can be converted to a valid DateTime and returns False otherwise. A valid DateTime is any date-time from January 1, 100, to December 31, 9999.	*string* is a String value or expression to be tested for being convertible to a DateTime value. Many forms are accepted. *number* is a Number value or expression to be tested for being convertible to a DateTime value. It can be positive, negative, or fractional. It is interpreted as a number of days since December 30, 1899.
Year *(x)*	Returns the year corresponding to a date.	*x* is the date of the year you want to find.
Month *(x)*	Returns the month of a date and converts it to a whole number.	*x* is the date of the month you are trying to find.
Day *(x)*	Returns the day of a date and converts it to a whole number.	*x* is the date of the day you are trying to find.
DayOfWeek *(date)* DayOfWeek *(date, firstDayOfWeek)*	Determines the day of the week the given date falls on and converts the day of the week to a Number (1 to 7). Optionally a numeric value for the first day of the week can be specified. If the first day of the week is not specified, Sunday is assumed.	*date* is a Date value or dateTime value. *firstDayOfWeek* is an optional Number indicating the first day of the week.
Hour *(x)*	Returns the hour of a time value.	*x* is the time that contains the hour you want to find.
Minute *(x)*	Returns the minutes of a time value.	*x* is the time that contains the minute you want to find.
Second *(x)*	Returns the seconds of a time value.	*x* is a Time value or DateTime value.
MonthName *(month)* MonthName *(month, abbreviate)*	Returns a string name for the specified month.	*month* is a whole Number representing the month of the year, value between 1 and 12, with 1 being January. *abbreviate* is an optional Boolean value that indicates if the month name is to be abbreviated. If omitted, the default is False.

Function	Description	Arguments
WeekdayName *(weekday)* WeekdayName *(weekday, abbreviate)* WeekdayName *(weekday, abbre-viate, firstDayOfWeek)*	Returns the day of the week corresponding to a date.	*weekday* is a sequential number that represents the date of the day you are trying to find. *abbreviate* is an optional Boolean value that indicates if the weekday name is to be abbreviated. If omit-ted, the default is False. *firstDayOfWeek* is an optional Number indicating the first day of the week.
Timer ( )	Returns the number of sec-onds elapsed since midnight.	(*no arguments*)
DateAdd *(intervalType, nIntervals, startDateTime)*	Returns a DateTime value to which a specified number of time intervals have been added.	*intervalType* is a String expression specifying the interval of time to be added. *nIntervals* is a Number or numeric expression specifying the number of intervals to be added. It can be positive (to get date-times in the future) or negative (to get date-times in the past). *startDateTime* is the DateTime value to which the intervals are to be added.
DateDiff *(intervalType, startDateTime, endDateTime)* DateDiff *(intervalType, startDateTime, endDateTime, firstDayOfWeek)*	Returns a number of time intervals between two speci-fied dates.	*intervalType* is a String expression that is the interval of time you use to calculate the difference between *startDateTime* and *endDateTime*. Possible values can be: *startDateTime* is the first DateTime value used in calculating the difference. *endDateTime* is the second DateTime value used in calculating the difference. *firstDayOfWeek* is an optional con-stant specifying the first day of the week. If not specified, crSunday is assumed.

Function	Description	Arguments
DatePart *(intervalType, inputDateTime)* DatePart *(intervalType, inputDateTime, firstDayOfWeek)* DatePart *(intervalType, inputDateTime, firstDayOfWeek, firstWeekOfYear)*	Returns a Number that specifies a given part of a given date.	*intervalType* is a String expression that specifies the part of a date to be returned. *inputDateTime* is the DateTime value whose part will be extracted. *firstDayOfWeek* is an optional constant used to specify the first day of the week. *firstWeekOfYear* is an optional constant specifying the first week of the year. If not specified, the first week is assumed to be the one in which January 1 occurs (crFirstJan1).

Date Ranges

Date range functions display various date range information that you can utilize within your formulas.

Table C-7. Date range functions

Function	Description	Arguments
WeekToDateFromSun	Specifies a range of Date values that includes all days from last Sunday to today (including today).	*(no arguments)*
MonthToDate	Specifies a range of Date values that includes all dates from the first day of the month to today.	*(no arguments)*
YearToDate	Specifies a range of Date values that includes all days from the first day of the calendar year to today.	*(no arguments)*
Last7Days	Specifies a range of Date values that includes all dates from seven days ago to today (including today).	*(no arguments)*
Last4WeeksToSun	Specifies a range of dates that includes the four weeks previous to last Sunday. A week begins on a Monday and ends on a Sunday.	*(no arguments)*
LastFullWeek	Specifies a range of Date values that includes all dates from Sunday to Saturday of the previous week.	*(no arguments)*
LastFullMonth	Specifies a range of Date values that includes all dates from the first to last day of the previous month.	*(no arguments)*

Function	Description	Arguments
AllDatesToToday	Specifies a range of Date values that includes every day up to and including today.	*(no arguments)*
AllDatesToYesterday	Specifies a range of Date values that includes every day up through the previous day. AllDatesToYesterday includes all dates before today but does not include the present day.	*(no arguments)*
AllDatesFromToday	Specifies a range of Date values that includes any date from the present day to any future Date value that may appear in a field. AllDatesFromToday includes the present day.	*(no arguments)*
AllDatesFromTomorrow	Specifies a range of Date values that fall after the present day. AllDatesFromTomorrow does not include the present day but does include any future date.	*(no arguments)*
Aged0To30Days Aged31To60Days Aged61To90Days	Specifies a range of Date values that fall within a certain time period before the present date. If the current date is 12/30/98, Aged0To30Days specifies the period from 12/1/98 to the present date, Aged31To60Days specifies the period from 11/1/98 to 11/30/98, and Aged61To90Days specifies the period 10/2/98 to 10/31/98.	*(no arguments)*
Over90Days	Specifies a range of Date values that includes all values that are more than 90 days older than the current date.	*(no arguments)*
Next30Days Next31To60Days Next61To90Days Next91To365Days	Specifies a range of Date values that includes all dates in the period specified starting from and including today.	*(no arguments)*
Calendar1stQtr Calendar2ndQtr Calendar3rdQtr Calendar4thQtr	Specifies a range of Date values that falls within the first, second, third, or fourth quarter of the current calendar year. The first quarter of the calendar year includes all dates from January 1 through March 31. The second quarter includes all dates from April 1 through June 30. The third quarter includes all dates from July 1 through September 30. The fourth quarter includes all dates from October 1 through December 31.	*(no arguments)*

Function	Description	Arguments
Calendar1stHalf Calendar2ndHalf	Specifies a range of Date values that includes all dates that fall within the first or second half of the current calendar year, respectively. The first half of the calendar year includes all dates from January 1 through June 30. The second half of the calendar year includes all dates from July 1 through December 31.	*(no arguments)*
LastYearMTD	Specifies a range of Date values in the previous year that matches the current month to date.	*(no arguments)*
LastYearYTD	Specifies a range of Date values that includes all dates in the last year up to the current date last year.	*(no arguments)*

Arrays

Arrays are a list of values separated by commas. The most common arrays are found in fuctions such as Average and Maximum, where you're finding one value stemming from a group of values.

Table C-8. Array functions

Function	Description	Arguments
Array *(x,...)*	Creates an array, initializes it with the given array elements, and returns it.	The given arguments are array elements with which to initialize the array. The number of array elements can be any number from 1 to 1000. All the arguments must be of the same type. Unlike Visual Basic, you may not have zero elements.
MakeArray *(x, ...)*	Creates an array, initializes it with the given array elements, and returns it.	The given arguments are array elements with which to initialize the array. The number of array elements can be any number from 1 to 1000. All the arguments must be of the same type.
UBound *(array)*	Returns a Number containing the largest available subscript for the given array.	*array* is an array value, expression, or variable.
SummaryFunction *(x)*	Summarizes the values in an array of constants, data field values, or formulas (a*b, c/d, and so on) separated by commas.	*x* is an array of values that can be evaluated by the function being used.

Ranges

Range functions allow you to determine the type of range with which you are working. For example, HasUpperBound will return True if the range you're working with contains an upper limit and False if the range does not have an upper limit.

Table C-9. Range functions

Function	Description	Arguments
HasLowerBound *(x)*	Returns True if the range is not of the form "Is<a" or "Is<=a". On any array, HasLowerBound returns True if HasLowerBound evaluates to True on every element of the array.	*x* can be a single range or a range array.
HasUpperBound *(x)*	Returns True if the range is not of the form "Is>a" or "Is>=a". On any array, HasUpperBound returns True if HasUpperBound evaluates to True on every element of the array.	*x* can be a single range or a range array.
IncludesLowerBound *(x)*	Returns True for ranges of the form "a To b", "a To_ b", and "Is>=b". Includes-LowerBound returns True on any array if the range that is the Minimum element of the array IncludesLowerBound.	*x* can be a single range or a range array.
IncludesUpperBound *(x)*	Returns True for ranges of the form "a To b", "a _To b", and "Is<=a". Includes-UpperBound returns True on any array if the range that is the Maximum element of the array IncludesUpperBound.	*x* can be a single range or a range array.

Type Conversion

These functions allow you to convert from one data type to another.

Table C-10. Type conversion functions

Function	Description	Arguments
CBool *(number)*	Changes a number or currency value to a Boolean data type.	*number* is a Number or a Currency type value.
CCur *(number)* CCur *(string)*	Changes a number, currency, or string value to a Currency data type.	*number* is a Number or a Currency type value. *string* is a text string that holds numeric text.

Function	Description	Arguments
CDbl *(number)* CDbl *(string)* CDbl *(Boolean)*	Converts a Number, Currency, text string, or Boolean value to a Number. CDbl and ToNumber are equivalent functions.	*number* is a Number or a Currency type value. *string* is a text string that holds numeric text. *Boolean* is a Boolean value that you want to treat as a number.
CStr *(x, y, z, w, q)*	Converts Numbers, Currency, Date, Time, and DateTime values to text strings.	**Boolean Values:** *x* is a Boolean value that is converted to a String, either "True" or "False." **Number and Currency Values:** *x* is a Number or Currency value to be converted into a text string; it can be a whole or fractional value. *y* is a whole number indicating the number of decimal places to carry the value in *x* to. (This argument is optional.) *z* is a single-character text string indicating the character to be used to separate thousands in *x*. The default is the character specified in your International or Regional settings control panel. (This argument is optional.) *w* is a single-character text string indicating the character to be used as a decimal separator in *x*. The default is the character specified in your International or Regional settings control panel. (This argument is optional.) **Number and Currency Values (formatting):** *x* is a Number or Currency value to be converted into a text string; it can be a whole or fractional value. *y* is a text string used to indicate the format for displaying the value in *x*. *z* is a whole number indicating the number of decimal places to carry the value in *x* to. (This argument is optional.)

Function	Description	Arguments
		w is a single character text string indicating the character to be used to separate thousands in *x*. The default is the character specified in your International or Regional settings control panel. (This argument is optional.) *q* is a single-character text string indicating the character to be used as a decimal separator in *x*. The default is the character specified in your International or Regional settings control panel. (This argument is optional.) **DateTime Values:** *x* is a DateTime value to be converted into a text string. *y* is a text string of characters that indicate how the resulting text string will be formatted. *z* is a text string to be used as a label for A.M. (morning) hours. (This argument is optional.) *w* is a text string to be used as a label for P.M. (evening) hours. (This argument is optional.)
CDate *(string)* CDate *(number)* CDate *(dateTime)* CDate *(YYYY, MM, DD)*	Returns a Date value. The CDate, Date, and DateValue functions are equivalent. However, Date can only be used in Crystal syntax since it is a type name in Basic syntax.	*string* is a text value that represents the date. *number* represents the number of days starting from December 30, 1899. *dateTime* is a DateTime value. *YYYY* is the year argument and can be one to four digits. *MM* is a number representing the month of the year. *DD* is a number representing the day of the month.

Function	Description	Arguments
CTime *(number)* CTime *(string)* CTime *(dateTime)* CTime *(HH, MM, SS)*	Returns a Time value. The CTime, Time, and TimeValue functions are equivalent. However, Time can only be used in Crystal syntax since it is a type name in Basic syntax.	*number* is a Time value given a number in units of 24 hours. *string* is a Time value that represents the time, given a String expression specifying a time from 0:00:00. *dateTime* is a DateTime value. *HH* is a number from 0 to 32767 representing the hour. *MM* is a number from 0 to 32767 representing the minute. *SS* is a number from 0 to 32767 representing the second.
CDateTime *(date)* CDateTime *(number)* CDateTime *(string)* CDateTime *(dateTime)* CDateTime *(YYYY, MM, DD)* CDateTime *(YYYY, MM, DD, HH, MM, SS)*	Returns a DateTime value. The CDateTime, DateTime, and DateTimeValue functions are equivalent. However, DateTime can only be used in Crystal syntax since it is a type name in Basic syntax.	*date* is a Date value. *number* is a Time value given a number in units of 24 hours. *string* is a Time value that represents the time, given a String expression specifying a time from 0:00:00. *dateTime* is a DateTime value. *YYYY* is the year argument and can be one to four digits. *MM* is a number representing the month of the year. *DD* is a number representing the day of the month. *HH* is a number from 0 to 32767 representing the hour. *MM* is a number from 0 to 32767 representing the minute. *SS* is a number from 0 to 32767 representing the second.

Programming Shortcuts

These functions provide additional options to using control structures to achieve the same results.

Table C-11. Programming shortcuts

Function	Description	Arguments
Choose *(index, choice1, choice2, ..., choiceN)*	Returns a value from the list of choices based on the value of *index*. For example, if *index* is 1, it returns *choice1*; if *index* is 2, it returns *choice2*; and so forth.	*index* is a Number or numeric expression that specifies the index of the choice. It should be between 1 and the number of available choices. If it is out of bounds, Choose returns a default value. (The default value returned depends on the type of the choices. For example, if the choices are of Number type, the default value is 0, and if the choices are of String type, the default value is the empty string ("").) *choice* is one of the options to choose from. All choices must be of the same type. A choice can be any simple type (Number, Currency, String, Boolean, Date, Time, or DateTime) or range type (Number Range, Currency Range, String Range, Date Range, Time Range, or DateTime Range), but it may not be an array.
IIF *(expression, truePart, falsePart)*	Returns one of two parts, depending on the evaluation of the expression.	*expression* is a Boolean expression. *truePart* is the value returned if *expression* is True. It can be any simple type (Number, Currency, String, Boolean, Date, Time, or DateTime) or range type (Number Range, Currency Range, String Range, Date Range, Time Range, or DateTime Range), but it may not be an array. *falsePart* is the value returned if *expression* is False. It must be of the same type as *truePart*.

Function	Description	Arguments
Switch *(expr1, value1, expr2, value2, ..., exprN, valueN)*	The argument list for Switch consists of pairs of expressions and values. Switch evaluates the expressions from left to right and returns the value associated with the first expression to evaluate to True.	*expr1, expr2, ..., exprN* are Boolean expressions. *value1, value2, ..., valueN* are the possible values that may be returned. All the values must be of the same type. A value can be any simple type (Number, Currency, String, Boolean, Date, Time, or DateTime) or range type (Number Range, Currency Range, String Range, Date Range, Time Range, or DateTime Range), but it may not be an array.

Evaluation Time

Evaluation time functions control the presentation of data when it is generated.

Table C-12. Evaluation time functions

Function	Description	Arguments
BeforeReadingRecords	Specifies that the formula is to be evaluated before the database records are read.	*(no arguments)*
WhileReadingRecords	Forces the program to evaluate the formula while it is reading database record data.	*(no arguments)*
WhilePrintingRecords	Forces the program to evaluate the formula while it is printing database record data.	*(no arguments)*
EvaluateAfter *(x)*	Used to force one formula to be evaluated after another.	*x* is any valid formula name.

Print State

Print state functions control the state of the report when the data is being previewed.

Table C-13. Print state functions

Function	Description	Arguments
Previous *(fld)*	Returns the value of the specified field in the previous record.	*fld* is any valid database or formula field in the report.
PreviousValue *(fld)*	Returns the value of the previous record of the specified field.	*fld* is the name of a database field.
Next *(fld)*	Returns the value of the specified field for the next record.	*fld* is any valid database field or formula field.
NextValue *(fld)*	Returns the value of the next record of the specified field.	*fld* is the name of a database field.
IsNull *(fld)*	Evaluates the field specified in the current record and returns TRUE if the field contains a NULL value.	*fld* is any valid database, memo, or BLOB field.
PreviousIsNull *(fld)*	Evaluates the field specified in the previous record and returns TRUE if the field contains a NULL value.	*fld* is any numeric, formula, memo, or BLOB field in the report.
NextIsNull *(fld)*	Evaluates the field specified in the next record and returns TRUE if the field contains a NULL value.	*fld* is any valid database, formula, memo or BLOB field in the report.
PageNumber	Inserts the current page number as a field in a formula.	*(no arguments)*
TotalPageCount	Passes the report and returns the total number of pages.	*(no arguments)*
PageNofM	Inserts the "Page [current page number] of [total page count]" as a field in a formula.	*(no arguments)*
RecordNumber	Returns the current record number.	*(no arguments)*
GroupNumber	Returns the current group number.	*(no arguments)*
RecordSelection	Inserts the record selection formula for the report in a formula that you can place on your report.	*(no arguments)*
GroupSelection	Inserts the group selection formula for the report in a formula that you can place on your report.	*(no arguments)*
InRepeatedGroupHeader	Returns TRUE when a Group Header section is repeated on a second, third, and so on, page.	*(no arguments)*

Function	Description	Arguments
OnFirstRecord	Returns TRUE when the current record being evaluated is the first record in the report.	*(no arguments)*
OnLastRecord	Returns TRUE when the current record being evaluated is the last record in the report.	*(no arguments)*
DrillDownGroupLevel	Returns a number that indicates the group level of the current drill-down view, or 0 if it is not a drill-down view.	*(no arguments)*

Document Properties

Document property functions return various document attributes, such as the time or date a report was printed.

Table C-14. Document property functions

Function	Description	Arguments
PrintDate	Inserts the date the report is printed as a field in a formula.	*(no arguments)*
PrintTime	Inserts the time the report is printed as a field in a formula.	*(no arguments)*
ModificationDate	Inserts the date the report was last modified as a field in a formula.	*(no arguments*
ModificationTime	Inserts the time the report was last modified as a field in a formula.	*(no arguments)*
DataDate	Returns the date that the report was last refreshed.	*(no arguments)*
DataTime	Returns the time that the report was last refreshed.	*(no arguments)*
ReportTitle	Inserts the title of the report as a field in a formula.	*(no arguments)*
ReportComments	Inserts the comments included with the report as a field in a formula.	*(no arguments)*
Filename	Inserts (in a formula) the filename and file path that are included with the report as a field.	*(no arguments)*
FileAuthor	Inserts (in a formula) the file author name that is included with the report as a field.	*(no arguments)*
FileCreationDate	Inserts (in a formula) the report creation date that is included with the report as a field.	*(no arguments)*

Alerts

Alert functions allow you to create print time formulas related to Crystal Reports' Report Alerts.

Table C-15. Alert functions

Function	Description	Arguments
IsAlertEnabled *(alertName)*	Returns Boolean value indicating whether or not the alert is enabled.	*alertName* is the name of an alert (in quotation marks) that you've already created. Locate the available alerts in the Alert Names list, which appears in the Formula Workshop's Functions tree once you've created an alert.
IsAlertTriggered *(alertName)*	Returns Boolean value indicating whether or not the alert is "triggered" — that is, whether or not the report data meets the alert condition formula.	*alertName* is the name of an alert (in quotation marks) that you've already created. Locate the available alerts in the Alert Names list, which appears in the Formula Workshop's Functions tree once you've created an alert.
AlertMessage *(alertName)*	Returns the alert message string for records that "trigger" the alert (that is, for records that meet the alert condition formula). Returns an empty string ("") for records that do not meet the alert condition formula.	*alertName* is the name of an alert (in quotation marks) that you've already created. Locate the available alerts in the Alert Names list, which appears in the Formula Workshop's Functions tree once you've created an alert.

Additional Functions

The following are various miscellaneous functions available within Crystal Reports.

Table C-16. Miscellaneous functions

Function	Description	Arguments
DateTo2000 *(Date, Number)*	Returns a date field with a four-digit year.	*Date* accepts only valid date fields with either two-digit or four-digit years. *Number* is a number from 0 to 99 corresponding to the desired windowing year.

Function	Description	Arguments
DTSTo2000 *(DateString, Number)*	Returns a date field with a four-digit year	*Date String* accepts only valid date fields with either two-digit or four-digit years. *Number* is a number from 0 to 99 corresponding to the desired windowing year.
DTSToDate *(DateTimeString)*	Evaluates the string specified and returns only the date.	*DateTimeString* is a string including a Date and a Time value.
DTSToSeconds *(DateTimeString)*	Evaluates the string specified and converts the Time value to the number of seconds from 00:00:00 (12:00 midnight) to the specified time.	*DateTimeString* is a string including a Date and a Time value.
DTSToTimeString *(DateTimeString)*	Evaluates the string specified and returns only the Time value in military format (00:00:00).	*DateTimeString* is a string including a Date and a Time value.
ExchGetId *(address)*	Determines whether the address is in X500 or X400 format. Once this has been solved, the function will then determine the ID. If the field is in X500 format, the function will extract the last instance of the "CN=" code (not case sensitive). If the field is in the X400 format, it will extract the SMTP or MS IDs.	*address* is the address of the sender/recipient (String data type).
ExchGetOrganization *(address)*	Determines whether the address is in X500 or X400 format. Once this has been determined, the function will then decide on the Organization Name. If the field is in X500 format, the function will extract the last instance of the "/O=" code (not case sensitive). If the field is in the X400 format, it will extract the instance of the "P=" code (not case sensitive).	*address* is the Address of the sender/recipient (String data type).

Function	Description	Arguments
ExchGetSite *(address)*	Determines whether the address is in X500 or X400 format. Once this has been solved, the function will then determine the Site Name. If the field is in X500 format, the function will extract the last instance of the "/OU=" code (not case sensitive). If the field is in the X400 format, it will extract the instance of the "O=" code (not case sensitive).	*address* is the address of the sender/recipient (String data type).
ExtractString *(origin, startString, endString)*	Returns the first occurrence (in the origin string) of a string that starts with *startString* and ends with *endString*. If *endString* is not found, the string starting with *startString* until the end of the string is returned.	*origin:* String *startString:* String *endString*: String
EventNumber *(eventNum)*	Returns the appropriate text description of the event logged by Exchange that matches *eventNum*. If there is no appropriate text description for an *eventNum*, the message "Unknown Event" will be returned with *eventNum* in brackets after the message.	*eventNum* is a number value that represents an event logged by Exchange.
ExchGetPath *(Path)*	Returns the container information in an address field. If the address type is X500, the function will return all of the information from the first instance of the "CN=" code until the last instance of the "CN=" code. If there is only one instance of the "CN=" code, the function will return NULL. If the address type is X400, the function will return all "OU*=" codes (residing between the "P=" and "O=" codes). If the address starts with "DDA:", the function will return all information after the "DDA:" code. If the field is blank, "UNKNOWN ADDRESS" will be returned.	*Path* is the address of the sender/receiver (String data type).

Function	Description	Arguments
ByteToText *(numberOfBytes)*	Returns a string description of the number passed in. If the argument is less than 1024, the result will be in bytes. If the argument is between 1024 to 1048576, the result will be in kilobytes. Otherwise, the result will be in megabytes.	*numberOfBytes* is a number that represents an amount of storage in bytes.
FRCurrentRatio *(CurrentAssets, CurrentLiabilities)*	Returns the ratio between *CurrentAssets* and *CurrentLiabilities* (for example, CurrentRatio = *CurrentAssets* / *CurrentLiabilities*).	*CurrentAssets* is a Number or formula. In general, *CurrentAssets* consists of cash, accounts receivable, inventories, prepaid expenses, and short-term marketable investment in a company's balance sheet. *CurrentLiabilities* is a Number or formula. In general, *CurrentLiabilities* consists of bank advances, accounts payable, dividends/income taxes payable, and a portion of long-term loans due within one year in a company's balance sheet.
FRQuickRatio *(CurrentAssets, Inventories, CurrentLiabilities)*	Returns the ratio between *CurrentAssets* (less *Inventories*) and *CurrentLiabilities* (for example, QuickRatio = (*CurrentAssets* – *Inventories*) / *CurrentLiabilities*).	*CurrentAssets* is a Number or formula. In general, *CurrentAssets* consists of cash, accounts receivable, inventories, prepaid expenses, and short-term marketable investments in a company's balance sheet. *Inventories* is a Number or formula. In general, *Inventories* consists of raw materials, work in progress, and finished goods in a company's balance sheet. *CurrentLiabilities* is a Number or formula. In general, *CurrentLiabilities* consists of bank advances, accounts payable, dividends/income taxes payable, and a portion of long-term loans due within one year in a company's balance sheet.

Function	Description	Arguments
FRDebtEquityRatio *(TotalLiabilities, TotalEquity)*	Returns the ratio between *TotalLiabilities* and *TotalEquity* (for example, DebtEquityRatio = *TotalLiabilities / TotalEquity*).	*TotalLiabilities* is a Number or formula. In general, *TotalLiabilities* consists of all the current and long-term liabilities in a company's balance sheet. However, some analysts would only include short- and long-term banks debts in calculating this ratio. *TotalEquity* is a Number or formula. In general, *TotalEquity* consists of common stocks, preferred stocks, capital surplus, and retained earnings in a company's balance sheet.
FREquityVsTotalAssets *(TotalEquity, TotalAssets)*	Returns the ratio between *TotalEquity* and *TotalAssets* (for example, EquityVsTotalAssets = *TotalEquity* / TotalAssets).	*TotalEquity* is a Number or formula. In general, *TotalEquity* consists of common stocks, preferred stocks, capital surplus, and retained earnings in a company's balance sheet. *TotalAssets* is a Number or formula. In general, *TotalAssets* consists of total current assets, net fixed assets, and all other assets in a company's balance sheet.
FRNetProfitMargin *(NetProfit, Sales)*	Returns the ratio between NetProfit and Sales (for example, NetProfitMargin = NetProfit / Sales).	*NetProfit* is a Number or formula. *NetProfit* is the amount a company earns during the year from the sale of its products or services minus all the expense items. It is the bottom-line figure in a company's income statement. Some analysts may want to use the net profit before extraordinary items and/or income taxes for calculating this ratio. *Sales* is a Number or formula. *Sales* is the total sales during the period that appears in a company's income statement.

Function	Description	Arguments
FRGrossProfitMargin *(GrossProfit, Sales)*	Returns the ratio between *GrossProfit* and *Sales* (for example, GrossProfitMargin = *GrossProfit / Sales*).	*GrossProfit* is a Number or formula. In general, *GrossProfit* equals sales minus cost of goods sold in a company's income statement. *Sales* is a Number or formula. *Sales* is the total sales during the period that appears in a company's income statement.
FROperatingProfitMargin *(OperatingProfit, Sales)*	Returns the ratio between *OperatingProfit* and *Sales* (for example, OperatingProfitMargin = *OperatingProfit / Sales*).	*OperatingProfit* is a Number or formula. In general, *OperatingProfit* equals gross profit less all selling, administrative, and general expenses in a company's income statement. *Sales* is a Number or formula. *Sales* is the total sales during the period that appears in a company's income statement.
FRInterestCoverage *(CashFlow, InterestExpenses)*	Returns the ratios between *CashFlow* and *InterestExpenses* (for example, InterestCoverage = *CashFlow / InterestExpenses*).	*CashFlow* is a Number or formula. In general, *CashFlow* equals the net profit of the company plus all the expense items not involving cash (such as depreciation, capital losses, and so on) minus all the profit not involving cash (such as capital gains, and so on). This information can be found in a company's income statement and statement of change in financial position. *InterestExpenses* is a Number or formula. *InterestExpenses* is the total interest expenses that can be found in a company's income statement.

Function	Description	Arguments
FRCashFlowVsTotal-Debt *(CashFlow, TotalDebt)*	Returns the ratio between *Cash-Flow* and *TotalDebt* (for example, CashFlowVsTotalDebt = *CashFlow / TotalDebt*).	*CashFlow* is a Number or formula. In general, *Cash-Flow* equals the net profit of the company plus all the expense items not involving cash (such as depreciation, capital losses, and so on) and minus all the profit not involving cash (such as capital gains, and so on). This information can be found in a company's income statement and statement of change in financial position. *TotalDebt* is a Number or formula. In general, *TotalDebt* is the total short-term and long-term bank borrowings. Some analysts may even include all the short- and long-term liabilities as part of total debt. All this information can be found in a company's income statement.
FRReturnOnEquity *(NetProfit, TotalEquity)*	Returns the ratio between *NetProfit* and *TotalEquity* (for example, ReturnOnEquity = *NetProfit / TotalEquity*).	*NetProfit* is a Number or formula. *NetProfit* is the amount a company earns during the year from the sale of its products or services minus all the expense items. It is the bottom-line figure in a company's income statement. Some analysts may want to use the net profit before extraordinary items and/or income taxes for calculating this ratio. *TotalEquity* is a Number or formula. In general, *TotalEquity* consist of common stocks, preferred stocks, capital surplus, and retained earnings in a company's balance sheet.

Function	Description	Arguments
FRReturnOnNetFixed Assets *(NetProfit, NetFixedAssets)*	Returns the ratio between *NetProfit* and *NetFixedAssets* (for example, ReturnOnNetFixedAssets = *NetProfit* / *NetFixedAssets*).	*NetProfit* is a Number or formula. *NetProfit* is the amount a company earns during the year from the sale of its products or services minus all the expense items. It is the bottom-line figure in a company's income statement. Some analysts may want to use the net profit before extraordinary items and/or income taxes for calculating this ratio. *NetFixedAssets* is a Number or formula. *NetFixedAssets* equals total fixed assets minus accumulated depreciation in a company's balance sheet.
FRReturnOnTotal-Assets *(NetProfit, TotalAssets)*	Returns the ratio between *NetProfit* and *TotalAssets* (for example, ReturnOnTotalAssets = *NetProfit* / *TotalAssets*).	*NetProfit* is a Number or formula. *NetProfit* is the amount a company earns during the year from the sale of its products or services minus all the expense items. It is the bottom-line figure in a company's income statement. Some analysts may want to use the net profit before extraordinary items and/or income taxes for calculating this ratio. *TotalAssets* is a Number or formula. In general, *TotalAssets* consist of total current assets, net fixed assets, and all other assets in a company's balance sheet.

Function	Description	Arguments
FRReturnOnInvested-Capital *(NetProfit, TotalBankDebt, TotalEquity)*	Returns the ratio between *NetProfit* and invested capital, which is *TotalBankDebt* plus *TotalEquity* (for example, ReturnOnInvested Capital = *NetProfit* / (*TotalBankDebt* + *TotalEquity*)).	*NetProfit* is a Number or formula. *NetProfit* is the amount a company earns during the year from the sale of its products or services minus all the expense items. It is the bottom-line figure in a company's income statement. Some analysts may want to use the net profit before extraordinary items and/or income taxes for calculating this ratio. *TotalBankDebt* is a Number or formula. *TotalBankDebt* includes all the short- and long-term bank debts of a company. They can all be found in a company's balance sheet. *TotalEquity* is a Number or formula. In general, *TotalEquity* consists of common stocks, preferred stocks, capital surplus, and retained earnings in a company's balance sheet.
FRReturnOnCommon Equity *(NetProfit, PreferredDividend, CommonEquity)*	Returns the ratio between the net profit distributable to common shareholders (*NetProfit* – *PreferredDividend*) and *CommonEquity* (for example, ReturnOnCommonEquity = (*NetProfit* – *PreferredDividend*) / *CommonEquity*).	*NetProfit* is a Number or formula. *NetProfit* is the amount a company earns during the year from the sale of its products or services minus all the expense items. It is the bottom-line figure in a company's income statement. Some analysts may want to use the net profit before extraordinary items and/or income taxes for calculating this ratio.

Function	Description	Arguments
		PreferredDividend is a Number or formula. *PreferredDividend* is the total dividend paid out to the preferred shareholders during the accounting period being studied. This information can be found in a company's income statement and statement of change in financial position. It can also be derived from a company's balance sheet. *CommonEquity* is a Number or formula. In general, *CommonEquity* is the sum of all common shares, contributed surplus, and retained earnings. All of these can be found in a company's balance sheet.
FREarningsPerCommonShare *(NetProfit, PreferredDividend, NumOfCommonShare)*	Returns the ratio between net profit distributable to common shareholders (*NetProfit* – *PreferredDividend*) and *NumOfCommonShare* (for example, EarningsPerCommonShare = (*NetProfit* – *PreferredDividend*) / *NumOfCommonShare*).	*NetProfit* is a Number or formula. *NetProfit* is the amount a company earns during the year from the sale of its products or services minus all the expense items. It is the bottom-line figure in a company's income statement. Some analysts may want to use the net profit before extraordinary items and/or income taxes for calculating this ratio. *PreferredDividend* is a Number or formula. *PreferredDividend* is the total dividend paid out to the preferred shareholders during the accounting period being studied. This information can be found in a company's income statement and statement of change in financial position. It can also be derived from a company's balance sheet.

Function	Description	Arguments
		NumOfCommonShare is a Number or formula. In general, *NumOfCommonShare* is the number of common shares issued and outstanding. This information can be found in a company's balance sheet.
FRAccRecTurnover *(AccountReceivable, Sales, NumOfDays)*	Returns the average turnover of *AccountReceivable* in days (for example, AccRecTurnover = (*AccountReceivable* / *Sales*) * 360).	*AccountReceivable* is a Number or formula. *AccountReceivable* is the total accounts receivable in a company's balance sheet. *Sales* is a Number or formula. *Sales* is the total sales during the period that appears in a company's income statement. *NumOfDays* is a Number or formula. In general, it is the number of days in a year. Some analysts use 360, and some use 365. The default is 360 for this function.
FRInventoryTurnover *(Inventory, Sales, NumOfDays)*	Returns the average turnover of inventory in days (for example, InventoryTurnover = (*Inventory/Sales*) * 360).	*Inventory* is a Number or formula. Inventory is the total inventories in a company's balance sheet. In general, it includes all raw material, work in progress, and finished goods. *Sales* is a Number or formula. *Sales* is the total sales during the period that appears in a company's income statement. *NumOfDays* is a Number or formula. In general, *NumOfDays* is the number of days in a year. Some analysts use 360, and some use 365. The default is 360 for this function.

Function	Description	Arguments
FRPriceEarningsRatio *(MarketPrice, EarningsPerShare)*	Returns the ratio between *MarketPrice* and *EarningsPerShare* (for example, PriceEarningsRatio = *MarketPrice / EarningsPerShare* (12 months)).	*MarketPrice* is a Number or formula. *MarketPrice* is the current market price of a company's common share. This information is publicly available if the company's shares are traded in a stock exchange. *EarningsPerShare* is a Number or formula. *EarningsPerShare* is the amount of earnings that is attributable to each common share. This information is available in a company's financial reports.
FRDividendYield *(Dividend, MarketPrice)*	Returns the ratio between *Dividend* and *MarketPrice* (for example, DividendYield = *Dividend / MarketPrice*).	*Dividend* is a Number or formula. *Dividend* is the indicated annual dividend per common share. *MarketPrice* is a Number or formula. *MarketPrice* is the current market price of a company's common share. This information is publicly available if a company's shares are traded in a stock exchange.
Now	Prints the current time on a report. The time is taken from your computer's internal clock.	*(no arguments)*
Picture *(string, picture)*	Prints a string or values in a text string in a predetermined format.	*string* is a text string to be formatted according to the picture format. *picture* is a text string representing the way you want the characters in the string to be printed.
LooksLike *(string, mask)*	Enables you to locate field values using a standard DOS wildcard (? = wildcard for single character, * = wildcard for any number of characters). It does this by comparing a string to a mask that contains one or more wildcards. The function returns True if the string matches the mask and False if the string does not match the mask.	*string* is the text string or field containing text string values that are being compared to the mask. *mask* is a text string that provides a mask for comparing the value in the string argument.

Function	Description	Arguments
Soundex *(string)*	Evaluates a text string and returns a four-character value that symbolizes the way string sounds.	*string* is one of two or more strings that sound alike.
DateTimeTo2000 *(dateTime, number)*	**Two-digit years (xx):** If the Year value is greater than the windowing number, 19 is appended before the two-digits (19xx). If the Year value is less than or equal to the windowing number, 20 is appended (20xx). **Four-digit years (19xx):** If the last two digits in the Year value are greater than the windowing number, the Year is preserved as found in the date field (19xx). If the two digits in the Year value are less than or equal to the windowing number, the first two digits are changed to 20 (20xx). If the first two digits in the year field are 20, the Year is preserved as found in the date field (20xx).	*dateTime* accepts only valid date-time fields, with either two-digit or four-digit years. *number* is a number from 0 to 99 corresponding with the desired windowing year.
DTSToDateTime *(DateTimeString)*	Evaluates the string specified and returns a DateTime data type.	*DateTimeString* is a string including a Date and a Time value.
DTSToTimeField *(DateTimeString)*	Evaluates the string specified and returns a Time data type.	*DateTimeString* is a string including a Date and a Time value.
DateTimeToDate *(dateTime)*	Evaluates the DateTime value specified and converts it to a Date value.	*dateTime* is a DateTime value.
DateTimeToTime *(dateTime)*	Evaluates the DateTime value specified and converts it to a Time value.	*dateTime* is a DateTime value.
DateTimeToSeconds *(dateTime)*	Evaluates the DateTime value and returns the number of seconds that have passed between 00:00:00 (12:00 midnight) and the specified time.	*dateTime* is a DateTime value.

Conditional Formatting Functions

A *conditional formatting function* applies specific attributes to a report object or section if certain criteria are met. You learned about conditional formatting in Chapter 10. The conditional formatting functions contain functionality related to conditional formatting.

Table C-17. Conditional formatting functions

Function	Description	Arguments
GridRowColumn-Value *(name)*	Returns the value of a specified level of dimension in an OLAP grid or cross-tab.	*name* is a String value that is an Alias for Formulas. The Alias for Formulas is a name you have specified for a level of dimension in an OLAP grid or a cross-tab.
CurrentFieldValue	Returns the current value of the field that is about to be printed.	*(no arguments)*
DefaultAttribute	The value returned by DefaultAttribute depends upon the value selected for the attribute being formatted in the attribute value interface.	*(no arguments)*
RGB *(red, green, blue)*	Returns the color attribute as specified by the red, green, and blue components.	*red* is a Number value representing the red component of the resultant color; value can be from 0 to 255. *green* is a Number value representing the green component of the resultant color; value can be from 0 to 255. *blue* is a Number value representing the blue component of the resultant color; value can be from 0 to 255.

Conditional Formatting Functions

Appendix D

Crystal Reports Resources

Hopefully, you've been successful in getting your reports up and running. However, report development can get tricky, and you might encounter some pitfalls along the way. This appendix contains some further areas of reference that might provide you with additional information in regard to your development endeavors.

Online Links

- **Crystal Decisions Home Page:** www.crystaldecisions.com. This is the company site for Crystal products and provides excellent developer information, forums, training classes, and product ordering information. This site also provides great "self-service support," as well as contact information via e-mail or telephone.
- **Crystal Decisions User Group of North America (CDUGNA):** www.cdugna.org. This is the largest Crystal Decisions user group in North America. The CDUGNA holds a conference once a year, which includes informative, interactive sessions regarding Crystal Decisions product futures, customer presentations, technical track information, vendor pavilions, hands-on training, and more. To register with CDUGNA, check out the group's web site.
- **Independent North American Crystal Decisions User Groups:** The following list contains other North American regional user groups that typically meet once a quarter to share

information and experiences regarding Crystal Decisions products. This list contains only some of the user groups with web sites. To view a larger listing, check out www.crystaldecisions.com/about/user_group.

- **Austin/Central Texas:** www.ctcug.org
- **Central Virginia:** http://groups.yahoo.com/group/CentralVaCrystal/
- **Dallas/Fort Worth:** www.dfwcug.com
- **DC Area:** http://dcacug.iracorp.com
- **Midwest Area:** www.mwcug.org
- **New England:** www.necrug.com
- **Ohio:** www.resultdata.com/crystalUsersGroup
- **Omaha:** http://groups.msn.com/seagatesoftwareusersgroup
- **Pacific Northwest:** www.cugpnw.org
- **British Columbia:** www.cdugbc.org
- **Kansas City SIG:** www.crystalsig.org

Business Reporting Resources

The following books provide detailed information on financial, statistical, and engineering methods.

- *Handbook of Mathematical Functions with Formulas, Graphs, and Mathematical Tables*, by Milton Abramowitz and Irene A. Stegun.
- *Probability and Statistics for Engineering and the Sciences*, by Jay L. Devore.
- *The Handbook of Fixed-Income Securities*, by Frank J. Fabozzi.
- *Standard Securities Calculation Methods, Fixed Income Securities Formulas*, by John J. Lynch Jr. and Jan H. Mayle.
- *Fundamental Statistics for the Behavioral Sciences*, by Robert B. McCall.
- *Operations Management: Theory and Problems*, by Joseph G. Monks.

- *Money Market Calculations: Yields, Break-Evens, & Arbitrage*, by Marcia Stigum and John Mann.

Downloadable Exercises

All report files and exercises presented in this book are available at www.wordware.com/files/crystal.

Third-Party Software

In addition to the useful products available from Crystal Decisions (www.crystaldecisions.com), you can also find third-party software products that will enhance your report development and delivery capabilities.

The following products are some of the better products available today. All are available from their vendor's web sites, both in trial and full versions.

The Fiscal Calendar UFL

Fiscal Calendar UFL is a Visual Basic-developed User Function Library that contains functions for determining the fiscal year, quarter, month, and week that a date falls into. It can be used with Visual Basic, MS Access, ASP, MS Excel, and MS Word, just like any other COM object. Fiscal Calendar UFL is provided by Tatum Consulting (www.tatumconsulting.com).

CRW Reporting

Another excellent product provided by Tatum Consulting is CRW Reporting. This software is a Visual Basic program that provides a run-time interface to run Crystal Reports on any computer in your organization

Crystal Dashboard

Crystal Dashboard, another useful reporting window, is provided by Solutional (www.solutional.co.za). Crystal Dashboard allows you to embed an unlimited number of Crystal Reports into its customizable tabbed display. The reports are then automatically refreshed as often as you wish.

CustomInvoicing

CustomInvoicing is a superb product provided by Synergration (www.synergration.com). This software enables you to print and e-mail custom invoice and sales receipts directly from data stored in your QuickBooks file. Personalize invoices and sales receipts using Crystal Reports with your company logo, hyperlink, etc. CustomInvoicing then allows you to export data in PDF, HTM, and RTF formats.

ReCrystallize Pro

ReCrystallize Pro is a great product, provided by Recrystallize Software (www.recrystallize.com). ReCrystallize Pro allows you to quickly make your Crystal Reports reports available on your intranet or extranet, providing user-specific information to your managers, customers, sales force, and employees.

Financial Calculators

Financial Calculators is an invaluable tool for the report writer. Provided by RWENT, Inc. (www.rwent.com), Financial Calculator software allows you to create, save, and update a variety of different financial calucations, which you can then easily utilize in Crystal Reports for extensive printing options.

Crystal Reports Distributor

The Crystal Reports Distributor, provided by ChristianSteven Software Ltd. (www.christiansteven.com), is a powerful automation tool for Crystal Reports, allowing you to control the output of your reports in numerous ways. Check out Chapter 14 for more information on the Crystal Reports Distributor.

Appendix E

Accounting Reference

This appendix contains basic accounting principles discussed in most first- and second-semester accounting classes. These concepts are aimed at report developers whose primary disciplines are not accounting.

Basic Accounting Principles

The following are general accounting principles utilized by most companies:

- The accounting period is usually defined as one year, ending on December 31. The fiscal year may end on any date of the year.
- Revenue is earned when the business has completed rendering services to the customer. The amount to record is equal to the cash value of the services or goods.
- Expenses are matched against the revenues in the same accounting period.
- Financial information is reported at regular intervals.
- Most accounts list information as debits or credits. A *debit* is an item of debt as recorded in an account. A *credit* is the deduction of a payment made by a debtor from an amount due.
- Debits are entered on the left side of an account. Credits are entered on the right side of an account (see the section titled "Recording Transactions" later in this appendix for more information).

- The basic accounting equation is: *assets = liabilities + owners' equity*. Figure E-1 summarizes this equation in a graphical representation:

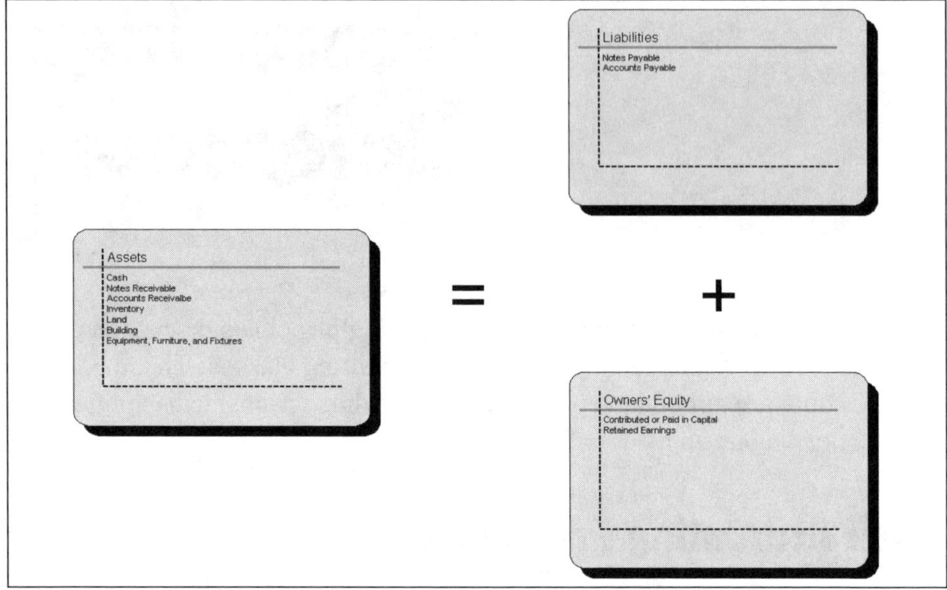

Figure E-1. The accounting equation

The accounts of the accounting equation are defined in the following sections.

Asset Accounts

Assets are the economic resources expected to benefit a company in the future. Assets are usually divided into the following seven accounts:

- **Cash:** Money, certificates of deposit, and checks
- **Notes Receivable:** Promissory notes
- **Accounts Receivable:** A promise (either oral or implied). These usually come from sales made to customers where no promissory note exists.
- **Inventory:** Merchandise that a company holds or manufactures to sell.
- **Land:** The property the company owns and uses to operate.

- **Building:** The cost of offices, warehouses, garages, etc.
- **Equipment, furniture, and fixtures:** The cost of all office equipment of a company.

Liabilities

Liabilities are the economic obligations, or debts, of a company. Liabilities are usually divided into the following two accounts:

- **Notes Payable:** The amounts a company must pay as a result of signing a promissory note for goods or services.
- **Accounts Payable:** The promise (either oral or implied) to pay debts from credit purchases.

Owners' Equity

Owners' Equity includes all claims held by the company's owners. Owners' equity is usually divided into the following two accounts:

- **Contributed or Paid in Capital:** The amounts invested in the company by the owners.
- **Retained Earnings:** The incomes earned from the company operations. Often, you'll find this area divided into three subareas.
  1. **Expenses:** The decreases in retained earnings resulting from company operations.
  2. **Revenues:** The increases in retained earnings resulting from company operations.
  3. **Dividends:** The distributions of assets to shareholders (which result in a decrease in retained earnings).

Recording Transactions

Transactions occur in the normal course of business and are recorded. Transactions affect both sides of the accounting equation.

Transactions are recorded into accounts known as "T Accounts." This is because the increases and decreases in the account amounts are listed in a T structure. In a T structure, the left side is considered the debit side, and the right side is considered the credit side. Figure E-2 summarizes the T structure of Asset, Liability, and Owners' Equity accounts.

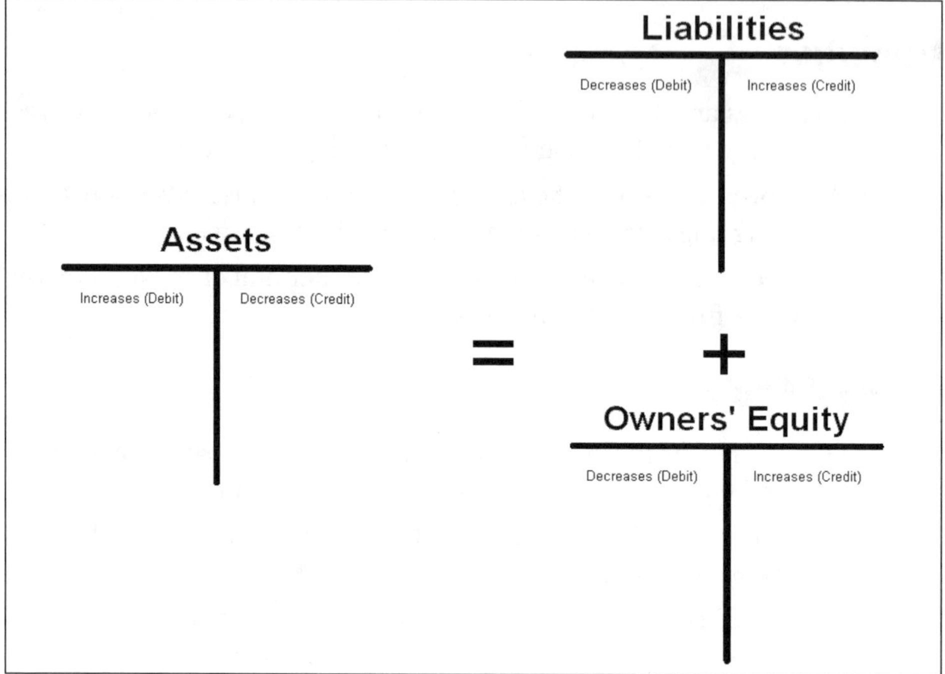

Figure E-2. T Accounts

The Accounting Cycle

The following steps summarize the general accounting cycle:

1. Transactions are first recorded in journals. The process of recording transactions into journals is called *journalizing*. Each transaction is recorded as a *journal entry*.
2. Journal entries are posted to the general ledger. This process is called *posting*.
3. Adjusting entries are made (journalized) and posted to the general ledger.
4. A trial balance can now be created, which shows all accounts and their up-to-date balances. A *balance* is the

monetary amount of the transaction, along with the information of whether this transaction is a debit or credit.

A trial balance is not the same as a *balance sheet*, which is a formalized financial statement.

5. Formalized financial statements are written.
6. Closing journal entries are made (journalized) and posted to the ledger. Often, another trial balance, called the "after-closing" or "post-closing" trial balance, is prepared with closing journal entries.

The Formalized Reports of the Accounting Cycle

The goal of the accounting cycle is to reflect the true financial condition and transactions of a company. These goals are met through the creation of the following formalized reports:

- **Balance Sheet:** Displays the assets of a company, balanced with the sum of liabilities and owners' equity. The Balance Sheet displays information as of a specific date.

  This report is sometimes known as a *Statement of Financial Position.*

- **Income Statement:** Displays a summary of revenue and expenses of a company for a defined period of time. This statement does not report net income or net loss for the defined period.

  This report is sometimes known as a *Statement of Earnings* or *Statement of Operations.*

- **Statement of Changes in Owners' Equity:** Displays the capital invested in the business by the owners and the profit earned by and retained in the business.
- **Statement of Cash Flows:** Displays the cash flows obtained from operating, investing, and financing activities.

Index

G

T

Looking for more?

Check out these and other titles from Wordware's complete list

Don't miss our titles on these popular applications

Learn Arts & Letters EXPRESS 7: The Official Guide

1-55622-969-0 • $39.95
6 x 9 • 544 pp.

Learn to Diagram with Microsoft Visio 2002

1-55622-866-X • $29.95
7½ x 9¼ • 256 pp.

Learn Peachtree Accounting

1-55622-710-8 • $39.95
7½ x 9¼ • 464 pp.

Learn FileMaker Pro 6

1-55622-974-7 • $39.95
6 x 9 • 504 pp.

Our Developer Guides for professionals

Advanced FileMaker Pro 6 Web Development

1-55622-860-0 • $59.95
6 x 9 • 464 pp.

Essential LightWave 3D 7.5

1-55622-226-2 • $44.95
6 x 9 • 424 pp.

Photoshop 7.0 for Screen Printers

1-55622-031-6 • $59.95
6 x 9 • 584 pp.

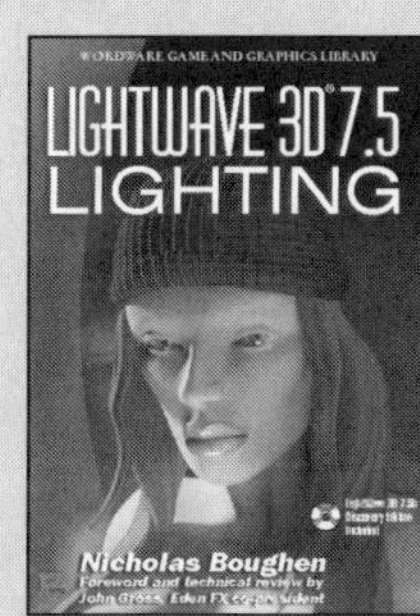

LightWave 3D 7.5 Lighting

1-55622-354-4 • $69.95
6 x 9 • 496 pp.

Visit us online at **www.wordware.com** for more information. Use the following coupon code for online specials:

cr-2939

ReCrystallize Pro Software Rebate

Get $50 U.S. Cash Back

on any ReCrystallize Pro software purchase made from www.recrystallize.com.

General Terms and Conditions:

- Offer good on purchases of ReCrystallize Pro software at www.recrystallize.com between August 1, 2003 and December 31, 2004.
- Offer valid only for purchases of the ReCrystallize Pro software product. Other software products are not eligible.
- Requests must be postmarked within 45 days of software purchase date. Purchase date is determined by invoice, receipt, or ship date.
- This offer may not be combined with any other offers or discounts. Offer not valid on electronic auction purchases or demo products.
- Offer is limited to products purchased directly from www.recrystallize.com.
- Offer not valid if product is returned for credit or refund.
- Rebate checks are void if not cashed within 90 days of issuance and cannot be reissued.
- Not responsible for lost or misdirected mail or illegible requests.
- Noncompliant materials will not be honored or returned. Other limitations may apply.

Mail-in Offer Checklist:

To qualify for this offer, you must include this original rebate coupon along with the ReCrystallize Pro receipt or invoice to:

ReCrystallize Pro / Mastering Crystal Reports 9 Rebate
9160 Hwy 64, Suite 12
Box 116
Lakeland, TN 38002

Copies of the rebate coupon will not be accepted.
Allow 4 – 6 weeks for delivery of rebate check.